THE FATHERS
OF THE CHURCH

MEDIAEVAL CONTINUATION

VOLUME 3

THE FATHERS OF THE CHURCH

MEDIAEVAL CONTINUATION

EDITORIAL BOARD

Thomas P. Halton
The Catholic University of America
Editorial Director

M. Josephine Brennan, I.H.M.
Marywood College

Kathleen McVey
Princeton Theological Seminary

Elizabeth Clark
Duke University

Robert D. Sider
Dickinson College

Robert B. Eno, S.S.
The Catholic University of America

Michael Slusser
Duquesne University

Frank A. C. Mantello
The Catholic University of America

David J. McGonagle
Director
The Catholic University of America Press

FORMER EDITORIAL DIRECTORS

Ludwig Schopp, Roy J. Deferrari, Bernard M. Peebles,
Hermigild Dressler, O.F.M.

Cynthia Kahn
Michael C. Santistevan
Staff Editors

PETER DAMIAN
LETTERS
61–90

Translated by
OWEN J. BLUM, O.F.M.
Quincy College
Quincy, Illinois

THE CATHOLIC UNIVERSITY OF AMERICA PRESS
Washington, D.C.

Copyright © 1992
The Catholic University of America Press, Inc.
All rights reserved
Printed in the United States of America

The paper used in this publication meets the minimum requirements of American National Standards for Information Sciences—Permanence of Paper for Printed Library Materials. ANSI Z39-48-1984.
∞

LIBRARY OF CONGRESS CATALOGING-IN-PUBLICATION DATA
(Revised for volume 3)
Peter Damian, Saint, 1007–1072.
   [The letters of Peter Damian.
   (The Fathers of the church, mediaeval continuation ; vv. 1–)
   Translation of the Latin letters of Peter Damian.
   Vol. 2– has title: Letters / Peter Damian.
   Includes bibliographical references and indexes.
   Contents: [1] 1–30 — [2] 31–60 — [3] 61–90.
   1. Peter Damian, Saint, 1007–1072—Correspondence. 2. Christian saints—Italy—Correspondence.   I. Blum, Owen J., 1912–   .   II. Series: Fathers of the Church, mediaeval continuation ; v. 1, etc.
BX4700.P77A4   1989   270.3   88-25802
ISBN 0-8132-0702-9 (v. 1)
ISBN 0-8132-0707-X (v. 2)
ISBN 0-8132-0750-9 (v. 3)
ISBN 978-0-8132-2638-5 (v. 3 pbk.)

CONTENTS

Preface	vii
Abbreviations	ix
Select Bibliography	xiii
Concordance	xxi
Letter 61	3
Letter 62	14
Letter 63	16
Letter 64	21
Letter 65	24
Letter 66	40
Letter 67	70
Letter 68	79
Letter 69	88
Letter 70	102
Letter 71	113
Letter 72	116
Letter 73	147
Letter 74	151
Letter 75	157
Letter 76	159
Letter 77	167
Letter 78	169
Letter 79	182
Letter 80	185
Letter 81	202

CONTENTS

Letter 82	233
Letter 83	241
Letter 84	247
Letter 85	250
Letter 86	255
Letter 87	299
Letter 88	309
Letter 89	326
Letter 90	370

Indices
  Index of Proper Names   381
  Index of Sacred Scripture   391

PREFACE

This third volume of the English translation of the *Letters of Peter Damian* contains *Letter* 61–*Letter* 90, written during the years 1059–1062. Once again this volume is enhanced by its own bibliography of appropriate sources and literature, given in full form, from which short forms in the footnotes will be easily understood. A somewhat enhanced list of abbreviations is repeated from the first two volumes, and the concordance of the new letter numbering is included. Also following earlier usage, Volume 3 will present its own index of proper names and places, and a listing of Damian's citations from sacred Scripture. With the completion of *Letter* 90 the project has now reached the halfway mark.

Ill health has continued to hinder the progress of the edition. But for the enthusiastic support of my confreres, especially of Professor James W. Kelly, O.F.M., my Father Guardian, and of Professor Dr. Kurt Reindel, the editor of the Latin letters in Regensburg, the work would have lingered in limbo longer than it has.

An important point can be made at this time. In the three volumes of Damian's *Letters* now in print, we have accounted for most of the larger works that emerged from his pen. There are still two to be published in the following volumes: *Letter* 119 "On Divine Omnipotence" and *Letter* 165 "On Contempt of the World," both of which are major pieces.

Quincy College, October 1991   Owen J. Blum, O.F.M.

ABBREVIATIONS

AA SS	*Acta Sanctorum.* 70 vols. Paris, 1863–1940.
Abh B	*Abhandlungen der Preussischen Akademie der Wissenschaften*
AUF	*Archiv für Urkundenforschung*
Beuron	*Vetus Latina. Die Reste der altlateinischen Bibel.* Ed. Archabbey of Beuron, 1949– .
BHL	*Bibliotheca Hagiographica Latina*
Biblia sacra	*Biblia sacra iuxta Latinam vulgatam versionem iussu Pii Papae XI . . . edita,* 1926– .
CC	*Corpus Christianorum, Series Latina.* Brepols, 1954– .
CCCM	*Corpus Christianorum, Continuatio Mediaevalis.* Brepols, 1971–.
CSEL	*Corpus Scriptorum Ecclesiasticorum Latinorum.* Vienna.
DA	*Deutsches Archiv für Erforschung des Mittelalters*
DACL	*Dictionnaire d'archéologie chrétienne et de liturgie.* Ed. Fernand Cabrol et Henri Leclercq. 15 vols. Paris, 1907–1953.
DHGE	*Dictionnaire d'histoire et de géographie ecclésiastiques.* Ed. Alfred Card. Baudrillart. Paris, 1912– .
DTC	*Dictionnaire de théologie catholique.* 15 vols. Paris, 1903–1950.
DuCange	*Glossarium mediae et infimae Latinitatis.* Ed. Charles de Fresne DuCange. 10 vols. Paris, 1883–1887.
FOTC	The Fathers of the Church. New York and Washington, D.C., 1947– .
Gaetani	*S. Petri Damiani . . . Opera omnia.* 4 vols. 1606–1640. Later editions will be cited by year of publication.
GCS	*Die griechischen christlichen Schriftsteller der ersten drei Jahrhunderte.* Leipzig, 1897– .
HJb	*Historisches Jahrbuch*
HV	*Historische Vierteljahrschrift*
HZ	*Historische Zeitschrift*
Itala	*Itala: Das Neue Testament in altlateinischer Überlieferung.* Ed. A. Jülicher. 4 vols. 1963–1976.
ItPont	*Italia Pontificia.* Ed. P. F. Kehr. Berlin, 1906–1935.

JE	Jaffé-Ewald ⎫
JK	Jaffé-Kaltenbrunner ⎬ Regesta Pontificum Romanorum
JL	Jaffé-Löwenfeld ⎭
LThK	*Lexikon für Theologie und Kirche*
MA, ma.	Mittelalter, mittelalterlich
Mansi	*Sacrorum conciliorum nova et amplissima collectio.* Ed. Joannes Dominicus Mansi. 53 vols. Paris, 1900–1927.
MGH	Monumenta Germaniae Historica
Auct.ant.	Auctores antiquissimi
Capit.	Capitularia regum Francorum
Conc.	Concilia
Const.	Constitutiones et acta publica imperatorum
D—DD	Diploma—Diplomata
Epp.	Epistolae (in Quarto)
Ldl	Libelli de lite
LL	Leges (in folio)
Necr.	Necrologia Germaniae
Poetae	Poetae Latini medii aevi
SS	Scriptores (in folio)
SS rer. Germ.	Scriptores rerum Germanicarum in usum scholarum
SS rer. Lang.	Scriptores rerum Langobardorum
SS rer. Merov.	Scriptores rerum Merovingicarum
MIÖG	*Mitteilungen des Instituts für Österreichische Geschichtsforschung.* 1923–1942.
Muratori	*Rerum Italicarum Scriptores.* Ed. Muratori. 2d ed. 1900ff.
NA	*Neues Archiv der Gesellschaft für ältere deutsche Geschichtskunde*
NCE	*New Catholic Encyclopedia*
NDB	*Neue deutsche Biographie*
Nom.hebr.	*Liber interpretationis hebraicorum nominum*
PL	*Patrologia Latina.* Ed. J.-P. Migne. Paris, 1844–1855.
RAC	*Reallexikon für Antike und Christentum*
RE	*Real-Encyclopädie der Classischen Altertumswissenschaft.* Ed. Pauly-Wissowa.
RHE	*Revue d'Histoire Ecclésiastique*
Sabatier	*Bibliorum sacrorum Latinae versiones antiquae.* Ed. P. Sabatier. 3 vols. Paris, 1743.
SBA	*Sitzungsberichte der Bayerischen Akademie der Wissenschaften*
SC	*Sources chrétiennes.* Paris, 1942– .
StMGBO	*Studien und Mitteilungen zur Geschichte des Benediktiner-Ordens und seiner Zweige*

ABBREVIATIONS

TU	Texte und Untersuchungen zur Geschichte der Altchristlichen Literatur. Berlin, 1882– .
Vulg	*Biblia sacra iuxta vulgatam versionem.* Ed. Robert Weber. 2 vols. 2d ed., 1975.
ZKG	*Zeitschrift für Kirchengeschichte*
ZRG	*Zeitschrift der Savigny-Stiftung für Rechtsgeschichte, Kanonistische Abteilung*

SELECT BIBLIOGRAPHY

Sources

Actus Nazarii et Celsi. AA SS 28, Jul. VI (1868) 530D–533D.
Ambrose. *De sacramentis.* Ed. O. Faller, CSEL 73 (1955) 13–85.
———. *Epistolae.* PL 16.875–1286.
———. *Exameron.* Ed. C. Schenkl, CSEL 32.1 (1897) 1–261.
———. *Hymnus* 3. Ed. A. S. Walpole. *Early Latin Hymns.* Cambridge, 1922.
Anastasius Bibliothecarius. *Interpretatio Synodi VIII Generalis.* Concilium CPL IV. 869. Actio I, *Libellus fidei.* PL 129.27f.
Annales Parmenses. Ed. P. Jaffé. MGH SS 18 (1863) 662.
Anselm of Lucca. *Collectio canonum* 1. Ed. F. Thaner. Aalen, 1906.
Atto of Vercelli. *Libellus de pressuris ecclesiasticis.* Ed. J. Bauer (1975).
Augustine. *Confessionum libri tredecim.* Ed. P. Knöll, CSEL 33 (1896).
———. *Contra Faustum Manichaeum libri XXXIII.* Ed. J. Zycha, CSEL 25.1 (1891) 249–797.
———. *De civitate Dei.* Ed. B. Dombart and A. Kalb, CC 47–48 (1955).
———. *De trinitate* 15.17. Ed. W. J. Moutain and F. Glorie, CC 50 (1968) 503.
———. *Enarrationes in psalmos.* 3 vols. Ed. E. Dekkers and J. Fraipont, CC 38–40 (1956).
———. *Epistulae.* 4 vols. Ed. A. Goldbacher, CSEL 34, 44, 57, 58 (1895–1923).
———. *Quaestiones in Heptateuchum libri VII.* Ed. J. Fraipont, CC 33 (1958) 1.372.
Bede. *De temporum ratione.* Ed. C. W. Jones, CC 123 B (1977).
Benedicti Regula. Ed. R. Hanslik, CSEL 75 (1977).
Burchard of Worms. *Decretorum libri XX.* PL 140.537–1058.
Cassiodorus. *Historia ecclesiastica tripartita.* Ed. W. Jacob and R. Hanslik, CSEL 71 (1952).
———. *Institutiones* 1.29.3. Ed. R. A. B. Mynors, *Cassiodori senatoris institutiones.* Oxford, 1937.
Chronica monasterii Casinensis. 2.80. Ed. H. Hoffmann, MGH SS 34 (1980).
Collectio Dionysio-Hadriana. PL 67.39–346.
Collectio Hadriana aucta 89, 133. In *Decretum Gelasianum* 3.2.30ff. Ed. E. von Dolschütz, TU 38.4 (1912).
Constitutum Constantini. Ed. H. Fuhrmann, MGH Fontes iuris 19 (1968).
De bestiis et aliis rebus libri quatuor. PL 177.9–164.
Decretum Gelasianum. Ed. E. von Dobschütz, *Das Decretum Gelasianum de libris recipiendis et non recipiendis.* TU 38.4 (1912).
Desiderius of Monte Cassino. *Dialogi de miraculis sancti Benedicti.* Ed. G. Schwartz and A. Hofmeister, MGH SS 30.2.3.9 (1934).
Epistola Paladii episcopi Cappadociae 51. PL 74.334C–335C.

Eutropius. *Breviarium ab urbe condita*. Ed. H. Droysen, MGH Auct.ant. 2 (1879).
Florence of Worchester. *Chronicon* 1. Ed. B. Thorpe (1848, reprint 1964).
Gelasius I. *Tractatus*. Ed. A. Thiel, *Epistolae Romanorum pontificum genuinae* 1 (1867–1868) 510–607.
Gratian. *Decretum*. Ed. E. Friedberg, *Corpus iuris canonici* 1 (1879).
Gregory I. *Dialogi*. 3 vols. Ed. A. de Vogüe, SC 251, 260, 265 (1978–1980).
———. *Expositiones in librum primum Regum*. Ed. P. Verbraken, CC 144 (1963) 47–614.
———. *Homiliae in Hiezechihelem prophetam*. Ed. M. Adriaen, CC 142 (1971).
———. *Moralia in Iob*. 3 vols. Ed. M. Adriaen, CC 143 (1979–1985).
———. *Registrum epistolarum*. Ed. D. Norberg, CC 140 (1982).
Hugh of Fleury. *Liber qui modernorum Francorum continet actus* 1.10. Ed. G. Waitz, MGH SS 9 (1951).
Isidore of Seville. *De fide catholica*. PL 83.450–538.
———. *Etymologiarum sive originum libri XX*. Ed. W. M. Lindsay. Oxford, 1911.
Jerome. *Adversus Iovinianum libri duo*. PL 23.221–352.
———. *Commentariorum in Esaiam libri duodeviginti*. Ed. M. Adriaen, CC 73 (1963) 1–799.
———. *De viris illustribus*. Ed. E. C. Richardson, TU 14.1 (1896).
———. *Epistulae*. 3 vols. Ed. I. Hilberg, CSEL 54–56 (1910–1918).
———. *Liber interpretationis hebraicorum nominum*. Ed. P. de Lagarde, CC 72 (1959).
John of Lodi. *Vita beati Petri Damiani*. PL 144.113–146.
John the Deacon. *Sancti Gregorii magni vita*. PL 75.59–242.
Jordanes. *Romana et Getica* 30. MGH Auct.ant. 5.1 (1882) 99.
Leo I. *Epistolae*. PL 54.551–1218. Tr. E. Hunt, FOTC 34 (1957).
———. *Sermo* 5.2. PL 54.153D.
Liber pontificalis. 3 vols. Ed. L. Duchesne. Paris, 1886–1957.
Martyrologium Romanum . . . Ed. J. B. O'Connell. Westminster, MD, 1962.
Origen. *In Numeros homiliae XXVIII. Homilien zur Hexateuch in Rufins Übersetzung* 2. Ed. W. A. Baehrens, GCS 30 (1921).
Orosius. *Historiarum adversus paganos libri septem*. Ed. A. Lippold, *Orosio, Le storie contro i pagani*. 2 vols. Milan, 1976. For an English translation see R. Deferrari, *Paulus Orosius: The Seven Books of History against the Pagans*, FOTC 50 (1964).
Papias. *Vocabularium latinum* (1491, reprint 1966).
Passio sancti Apollinaris, AA SS July 5.744.
Paul the Deacon. *Historia Langobardorum* 3.12. MGH SS rer. Lang. (1878).
———. *Historia Romana* 11.10–11. In Eutropius, *Breviarium ab urbe condita*. Ed. H. Droysen, MGH Auct.ant. 2 (1879).
———. *Liber de episcopis Mettensibus*. Ed. G. H. Pertz, MGH SS 2 (1829).
Physiologus latinus versio B (= *Physiol. lat. B*). Ed. F. J. Carmody (1939).
Physiologus latinus versio C (= *Physiol. lat. C*) = *Physiologus Bernensis*. Commentary by C. von Steiger and O. Homburger (1964).
Physiologus latinus versio Y (= *Physiol. lat. Y*). Ed. F. J. Carmody. *University of California Publications in Classical Philology* 12 (1941) 95–134.
Prudentius. *Liber Cathemerinon*. Ed. M. P. Cunningham, CC 126 (1966) 3–72.
Pseudo-Ambrose. *Epistola segregata* 2.4. PL 17.821f.
Pseudo-Augustine. *Sermo* 245. PL 39.2196.

SELECT BIBLIOGRAPHY

Pseudo-Jerome. *Quaestiones hebraicae in librum I Paralipomenon.* PL 25.1444A.
Richer. *Gesta Senoniensis ecclesiae.* Ed. G. Waitz, MGH SS 25 (1880).
Rodulfus Glaber. *Historiarum libri quinque* I.4. Ed. M. Prou, *Raoul Glaber, Les cinq livres de ses histoires.* Collection des textes (1886) 1.4.12.
Rufinus. *Historia ecclesiastica.* Ed. Th. Mommsen in Eusebius, *Werke* 2. Ed. E. Schwartz, GCS 9 (1903–1909).
Smaragdus. *Libellus de processione sancti Spiritus.* Ed. A. Werminghoff, MGH Conc. 2.1 (1906) 238.
Sulpicius Severus. *Vita sancti Martini.* Ed. J. Fontaine, SC 133 (1967).
Theodomar of Monte Cassino. *Epistola ad Theodoricum* 32. Ed. K. Hallinger, *Corpus consuetudinum monasticarum* 1 (1963) 135.
Victor of Vita. *Historia persecutionis africanae provinciae* 1.15. Ed. M. Petschenig, CSEL 7 (1881) 8.
Vita Iohannis Gualberti auctore Andrea abbate Strumensi. Ed. F. Baethgen, MGH SS 30/2 (1934) 1076–1104.
Vita sancti Arnulfi. Ed. B. Krusch, MGH SS rer. Merov. 2 (1888).

Literature

Adler, N. "Simon der Magier." LThK 9 (1964) 768–769.
Aubert, R. "Gaudiosus." DHGE 20 (1982) 47.
Audollent, A. "Abitinae." DHGE 1 (1912) 129–131.
Baix, F. "Cadalus." DHGE 11 (1949) 53–99.
Balboni, De. "San Pier Damiano, maestro e discepolo in Pomposa." *Benedictina* 22 (1975) 73–89.
Baronius, Caesar. *Annales ecclesiastici* 11 (1608).
Barroux, M. "Anne de Russie." *Dictionnaire de biographie française* 2 (1936).
Bentivegna, J. "Apollinaris of Laodicea." NCE 1 (1967) 667f.
Bertoni, G. "Lingua e stile di S. Pier Damiani in S. Pier Damiani." *Atti del Convegno di Studi nel IX centenario della morte.* Faenza, 1973. Pp. 61–68.
Bloch, Herbert. *Monte Cassino in the Middle Ages* 1. Cambridge, MA, 1986. Pp. 40–110.
Blum, Owen J. *St. Peter Damian: His Teaching on the Spiritual Life.* Studies in Mediaeval History n.s. 10. Washington, DC, 1947.
Borino, Giovanni Battista. "L'archidiaconato di Gregorio VII." *Studi Gregoriani* 3 (1948) 463–516.
Botti, Ferruccio. *San Pier Damiani e Parma* (1959).
Boyd, Catherine. *Tithes and Parishes in Medieval Italy.* Ithaca, 1952.
Browe, Peter. *Die Judenmission in Mittelalter und die Päpste.* Miscellanea historiae pontificiae 7 (1942) 116f.
Bulst-Thiele, Marie Luise. "Kaiserin Agnes." *Beiträge zur Kulturgeschichte des MA und der Renaissance* 52 (1933).
Camelot, P. T. "Eutyches." NCE 5 (1967) 642.
———. "Nestorius." NCE 10 (1967) 348.
Cantin, André. "Saint Pierre Damien e la cultura de son temps." *Studi Gregoriani* 10 (1975) 245–285.
Capitani, Ovidio. "Benedetto IX." *Dizionario biographico degli Italiani* 8 (1966) 354–366.
———. "Problematica della *Disceptatio synodalis.*" *Studi Gregoriani* 10 (1975) 141–174.

Chasteigner, J. De. "Le célébat sacerdotal dans les écrits de saint Pierre Damien." *Doctor communis* 24 (1971).
Chiovaro, F. "Apollinarianism." NCE 1 (1967) 665–666.
Cottineau, L. H. *Répertoire topo-bibliographique des abbeys et prierés* 2.1 (1937) 1851.
Coudrey, Herbert E. J. *The Age of Abbot Desiderius, Montecassino, the Papacy and the Normans in the Eleventh and Early Twelfth Centuries.* Oxford, 1983.
Cummings, J. T. "Gregory of Nazianzus, St." NCE 6 (1967) 791–794.
Davidsohn, Robert. *Forschungen zur älteren Geschichte von Florenz.* Berlin, 1896.
———. *Geschichte von Florenz* 1. Osnabruck, 1896.
DeClercq, V. C. "Arianism." NCE 1 (1967) 791–794.
Delagu, Paolo. "Benedetto VII." *Dizionario biographico degli Italiani* 8 (1966) 346–350.
Detschew, D. "Apollon." RAC 1 (1950) 524–529.
Dressler, Fridolin. *Petrus Damiani. Leben und Werk.* Studia Anselmiana 34 (1954).
Duchesne, Louis. *Mélanges d'archéologie et d'historie* 10 (1890) 225–250.
Dvornick, Francis. *The Photian Schism: History and Legend.* Cambridge, 1948.
Einhorn, Jürgen W. *Spiritalis unicornia....* Münstersche Mittelalter-Schriften 13 (1967) 53ff.
Eisenhut, W. "Vertumnus." RE 2.8 (1958) 1669–1687.
Falce, Antonio. *Il marchese Ugo di Tuscia.* Pubblicazioni del R. Istituto di studi superiori pratici e di perfezionamento in Firenze: Sezione di filologia e filosofia, n.s. 2 (1921).
Filas, F. L. "Joseph St., Devotion to." NCE 7 (1967) 1108–1113.
Fischer, Balthasar. *Kyriakon: Festschrift für Johannes Quasten.* 2 vols. Ed. P. Granfield and J. A. Jungmann. Münster, 1970. 2.527–531.
Frugoni, Chiara. "Letteratura didattica...." *Rivista di storia della chiesa in Italia* 34 (1980) 7–59.
Furhmann, Horst. *Einfluss und Verbreitung der pseudo-isidorischen Fälschungen. Von ihrem Auftauchen bis in die neuere Zeit.* Schriften der MGH 24 (1972–1974) (= Fuhrmann, *Fälschungen*).
———. "'Quod catholicus non habeatur, qui non concordat Romanae ecclesiae.'" "Randnotizen zum Dictatus Papae." In *Festschrift für Helmut Beumann.* Ed. K. U. Jäschke and R. Wenskus. Sigmaringen, 1977. Pp. 263–287. (= Fuhrmann, "Randnotizen").
———. "Studien zur Geschichte ma. Patriarchate." ZRG 39 (1953) 112–176; 40 (1954) 1–84; 41 (1955) 95–183. (= Fuhrmann, "Patriarchate").
Gams, Pius Bonifacius. *Series episcoporum ecclesiae catholicae* 1. Ratisbonae, 1873.
Gaudenzi, Augusto. "Il codice vaticano del monastero di Acerata." *Studi medievali* 3 (1908–1911) 301–312.
Gellhaus, Victor. "Benedict IX." NCE 2 (1967) 274–275.
Gilchrist, John. *Diversorum patrum sententie sive Collectio in LXXIV titulos digesta.* In *Monumenta iuris canonici* 1 (1973) xxiff.
Gill, J. "Filioque." NCE 5 (1967) 913–914.
Gougaud, Louis. *Dévotions et pratiques ascétiques du moyen âge.* Collection Pax 21 (1925).
Haller, Johannes. *Das Papsttum. Idee und Wirchlichkeit.* 5 vols. Berlin, 1957.
Hamilton, Bernard. "The Monastic Period in Tenth-Century Rome." *Studia monastica* 4 (1962) 35–68.

SELECT BIBLIOGRAPHY xvii

Hefele, Carl Joseph and Leclercq, Henri. *Histoire des conciles.* 11 vols. Paris, 1907–1952.
Herrmann, Klaus-Jürgen. "Das Tuskulanerpapsttum (1012–1046). Benedict VIII, Johannes XIX, Benedict IX." *Päpste und Papsttum* 4. Stuttgart, 1973.
Hüls, Rudolf. *Kardinäle, Klerus und Kirchen Roms 1049–1130.* Bibliothek des deutschen historischen Instituts in Rom 48. Göttingen, 1977.
Jadin, L. "Barbatus." DHGE 6 (1932) 622f.
Jasper, Detlev. *Das Papstwahldekret von 1059. Überlieferung und Textgestalt.* Beiträge zur Geschichte und Quellenkunde des MA 12 (1986).
Krappe, A. H. "An Italian Legend in Pierre Damian." *The Romanic Review* 15 (1924).
Krause, Hans-Georg. "Das Papstwahldekret von 1059 und seine Rolle im Investiturstreit." *Studi Gregoriani* 7 (1960).
———. "Über den Verfasser der Vita Leonis IX papae." DA 32 (1976) 49–85.
Kretschmayr, H. *Geschichte von Venedig* 1. Stuttgart, 1905.
Kurtscheid, B. *Historia iuris canonici.* Rome, 1951.
Landau, P. "Ursprünge und Entwicklung des Verbotes doppelter Strafverfolgung wegen desselben Verbrechens." ZRG 56 (1970) 124–156.
Lapide, Cornelius a. *Commentaria in scripturam sacram.* 24 vols. Paris, 1874–1877.
Laqua, Hans Peter. *Traditionen und Leitbilder bei dem Ravennater Reformer Petrus Damiani (1042–1052).* Münstersche Mittelalter-Schriften 30(1976).
Lebeau, P. "Patripassianism." NCE 10 (1967) 1102.
———. "Sabellianism." NCE 12 (1967) 783.
Leclercq, Jean. "L'idée de la royauté du Christ au moyen âge." *Unam sanctam* 32 (1959).
———. "Saint Pierre Damien: ermite et homme d'Église." *Uomini e dottrine* 8 (1960).
Lesne, E. *Histoire de la propriété ecclésiastique en France* 1. Paris, 1910.
Lippold, Adolph. *Theodosius der Grosse und seiner Zeit.* Stuttgart, 1980.
Lohmer, Christian. "Ausgewählte Aspekte der mittelalterlichen Ernährung für Mönche, untersucht an Beispiel der monastischen Bestimmungen des Petrus Damiani." *Aktuelle Ernährungsmedizin* 13 (1988) 179–182.
Lokrantz, Margareta. *L'opera poetica di S. Pier Damiani.* Studia Latina Stockholmiensia 12. Stockholm, 1964.
Lucchesi, Giovanni. *Clavis S. Petri Damiani.* Faenza, 1970.
———. "Giovanni da Lodi, il discepolo." In *San Pier Damiano nel IX centenario della morte* 4 (1978) 7–66.
———. "Per una vita di San Pier Damiani. Componenti cronologiche et topografiche." In *San Pier Damiano nel IX centenario della morte (1072–1972)* 1 (1972) 13–179 (Nos. 1–153) and 2 (1972) 13–160 (Nos. 154–231) (= Lucchesi, *Vita*).
Maassen, Friedrich. *Geschichte der Quellen und Literatur des canonischen Rechts im Abendlande* 1. Gratz, 1870.
Maccarrone, Michele. "La theologia del primato romano del secolo XI." In *Le istituzioni ecclesiastiche della "societas christiana" dei secoli XI–XII, Papato, cardinalato ed episcopato.* Miscellanea del centro di studi mediaevali 7 (1874) 21–122.
———. "Vicarius Christi. Storia del titolo papale." *Lateranum*, n.s. 18 (1952).
McGuire, Martin R. P. "Ambrose, St." NCE 1 (1967) 372–375.

McKenna, S. J. "Adoptionism." NCE 1 (1967) 140–141.
Melville, G. "De gestis sive statutis Romanorum pontificum, Rechtssätze in Papstgeschichtswerken." *Archivum historiae pontificiae* 9 (1971) 377–400.
Meyer, Heinz. *Die Zahlenallegorese im MA*. Münstersche Mittelalter-Schriften 25 (1975).
Miccoli, Giovanni. *Chiesa Gregoriana. Ricerche sulla riforma del secolo XI. Storici antichi et moderni*, n.s. 17 (1966).
Michel, Anton. "Die Anfänge des Kardinals Humbert bei Bischof Bruno von Toul (Leo IX)." *Studi Gregoriani* 3 (1948) 299–319.
——. *Die Sentenzen des Kardinals Humbert, das erste Rechtsbuch der päpstlichen Reform*. Schriften der MGH 7 (1943).
——. *Papstwahl und Königsrecht oder das Papstwahl-Konkordat von 1059*. Leipzig, 1936.
Mittarelli, Johannes-Benedictus and Costadoni, Anselmus. *Annales Camaldulenses ordinis sancti Benedicti*. 9 vols. Venice, 1755–1773.
Murphy, F. X. "Creed." NCE 4 (1967) 432–438.
——. "Dioscorus." NCE 4 (1967) 879.
Neukirch, Franz. *Das Leben des Petrus Damiani* (1875).
Palazzini, Pietro, ed. *Dizionario dei concili*. 6 vols. Rome, 1963–1967.
——. "Le missione milanese di San Pier Damiani e il 'Privilegium S.R. Ecclesiae.'" In *Atti e memorie della deputazione di storia patria per le Marche*. Serie 8, vol. 7 (1971–1973; published 1974) 171–195.
——. "San Pier Damiani al centro della riforma della Chiesa Marchigiana nel secolo XI." In *San Pier Damiano nel IX centenario della morte (1072–1972)* 2 (1972) 161–232 (= Palazzini, "Chiesa Marchigiana").
Penco, Gregorio. "Il simbolismo animalesco nella letteratura monastica." *Studia monastica* 6 (1964) 7–38.
Pierucci, Celestino. "San Pier Damiano e i beni temporali." In *San Pier Damiano nel IX centenario della morte (1072–1972)* 2 (1972) 291–305.
Prete, Serafino. "Fermo." DHGE 16 (1967) 1084–1091.
——. "S. Pier Damiani: le chiese Marchigiane, la riforma nel secolo XI." *Studia Picena* 19 (1949) 119–128.
Redle, M. J. "Plagues of Egypt." NCE 11 (1967) 422–424.
Reindel, Kurt. *Die Briefe des Petrus Damiani*. 3 vols. In MGH, *Die Briefe des deutschen Kaiserzeit* (1983–1989).
——. "Gottfried II., der Bärtige, Herzog von Oberund Niederlothringen." NDB 6 (1964) 662.
——. "Neue Literatur zu Petrus Damiani." DA (1976) 405–444.
——. "Studien zur Überlieferung der Werke des Petrus Damiani I–III." DA 15 (1959) 23–102; 16 (1960) 73–154; 18 (1962) 317–412.
Riché, P. "Recherches sur l'instruction des laics du IXe–XIIe siècle." *Cahiers de civilization médiévale* 5 (1962) 115–182.
Ries, J. "Manichaeism." NCE 9 (1967) 153–160.
Robinson, Ian S. *Authority and Resistance in the Investiture Contest*. Manchester, 1978.
Roschini, G. M. "La Mariologia di S. Pier Damiano." In *San Pier Damiano nel IX centenario della morte (1072–1972)* 1 (1972) 195–237.
Ryan, J. Joseph. *Saint Peter Damian and His Canonical Sources. A Preliminary Study in the Antecedents of the Gregorian Reform*. Pontifical Institute of Mediaeval Studies and Texts 2 (1956) (= Ryan, *Sources*).
Scheffer-Boichorst, Paul. *Kleinere Forschungen zur Geschichte des MA* 17.

SELECT BIBLIOGRAPHY xix

Exkurs: *Textkritische Bemerkungen zu des Petrus Damiani* Disceptatio synodalis. MIÖG 13 (1892) 129–137.
Schmale, F. J. "Die Absetzung Gregors VI. in Sutri und die synodale Tradition." *Annuarium historiae conciliorum* 11 (1979) 55–103.
Schmidt, Tilmann. "Alexander II (1061–1073) und die Römische Reformgruppe seiner Zeit." *Päpste und Papsttum* 11 (1972).
Schwartz, Gerhard. *Die Besetzung der Bistümer Reichsitaliens unter den sächsischen und salischen Kaisern mit den Listen der Bischöfe 951–1122.* Leipzig, 1913. (= Schwartz, *Bistümer*).
Siegman, E. F. "Nicolaites." NCE 10 (1967) 459.
Somigli, Constanzo. "San Pier Damiano e la Pataria." In *San Pier Damiano nel IX centenario della morte (1072–1972)* 2 (1973) 193–206.
Steindorff, Ernst. *Jahrbücher des deutschen Reichs unter Heinrich III.* 2 vols. Jahrbücher der deutschen Geschichte. Leipzig, 1874–1881. (= Steindorff, *Heinrich III*).
Tamassia, Nino. "Le opere di Pier Damiano. Note per la storia giuridica del secolo undecimo." *Atti del Reale Istituto Veneto di scienze, lettere ed arti* 62 (1902–1903) 881–908.
Tellenbach, Gerd. "Benedetto VIII." *Dizionario biographico degli Italiani* 8 (1966) 350–354.
Uhlirz, Karl and Mathilde. *Jahrbücher des deutschen Reiches unter Otto II. und Otto III.* 2 vols. Jahrbücher der deutschen Geschichte. Vol. 1—Leipzig, 1902. Vol. 2—Berlin, 1954.
Ullmann, Walter. *The Growth of Papal Government in the Middle Ages*, 2d ed. New York, 1962.
Wemple, Suzanne Fonay. "Atto of Vercelli. Church, State, and Christian Society in Tenth-Century Italy." *Temi e testi* 27 (1979).
Williams, M. E. "Anathemas of Cyril." NCE 1 (1967) 481–482.
Wilmart, André. "Une lettre de S. Pierre Damien à l'impératrice Agnes." *Revue Bénédictine* 44 (1932) 125–146.
Woody, Kennerly Merritt. *Damiani and the Radicals.* Ph.D. diss., Columbia University (1966).
———. "Sagena piscatoris." *Viator* 1 (1970) 33–54.
Zafarana, Zelina. "Bonifazio," *Dizionario biografica degli italiani* 12 (1970).
Ziegler, Aloysius K. "Pope Gelasius I and His Teaching on the Relation of Church and State." *Catholic Historical Review* 27 (1942) 412–437.
Zimmermann, Gerd. *Ordensleben und Lebensstandard. Die cura corporis in den Ordensvorschriften des abendländischen Hochmittelalters.* Beiträge zur Geschichte des alten Mönchtums und des Benedictinerordens 32 (1973).

CONCORDANCE

Since the new edition of Damian's letters in Kurt Reindel, *Die Briefe des Petrus Damiani*, MGH Die Briefe der deutschen Kaiserzeit (München, 1983) has assigned new numbers in chronological order, the old system of numbering for *epistolae* and *opuscula* is now outmoded. To correlate the new with the old, the following concordance is herewith provided. There is no longer a distinction between "letters" and "works," and Letters 171–180 are placed at the end of the series because they are undatable.

MGH (Chronological) Numeration in Earlier Editions

Reindel	Migne Number	Reindel	Migne Number
1	opusc. 2 and 3	23	epist. 8, 9 = opusc. 58
2	epist. 7, 15	24	epist. 6, 14 = opusc. 29
3	epist. 3, 2	25	epist. 8, 7 = opusc. 42/2
4	epist. 3, 3	26	epist. 1, 3
5	epist. 4, 2	27	epist. 6, 24 = opusc. 48
6	epist. 6, 6	28	opusc. 11
7	epist. 3, 5	29	epist. 6, 15
8	epist. 5, 12	30	epist. 4, 4
9	epist. 6, 28	31	opusc. 7
10	epist. 6, 23	32	epist. 4, 13
11	epist. 2, 19	33	epist. 1, 4
12	epist. 4, 6	34	epist. 4, 10
13	epist. 1, 1	35	epist. 5, 6
14	epist. 4, 7	36	epist. 5, 17 = opusc. 8/2
15	epist. 8, 4	37	epist. 6, 7
16	epist. 1, 2	38	opusc. 16
17	opusc. 10	39	epist. 5, 9 = opusc. 27
18	opusc. 14	40	opusc. 6
19	opusc. 8/1	41	Ad Heinricum
20	epist. 7, 2	42	Ad Odalricum
21	epist. 8, 8	43	epist. 7, 1
22	epist. 4, 5	44	epist. 6, 30 = opusc. 51

Reindel	Migne Number	Reindel	Migne Number
45	epist. 5, 8	88	epist. 1, 20
46	epist. 1, 5	89	epist. 1, 21 and opusc. 4
47	epist. 4, 14 = opusc. 26	90	epist. 2, 13
48	epist. 2, 1	91	epist. 3, 1 = opusc. 38
49	epist. 2, 5	92	epist. 6, 16 = opusc. 59
50	opusc. 15	93	epist. 8, 13
51	epist. 7, 14	94	epist. 8, 14
52	epist. 2, 4	95	epist. 2, 11
53	Ad Iohannem	96	epist. 1, 15
54	epist. 6, 18 = opusc. 46	97	epist. 2, 2 = opusc. 31
55	epist. 6, 19	98	epist. 1, 18 = opusc. 24
56	epist. 6, 27	99	epist. 3, 6
57	epist. 1, 10 = opusc. 20	100	epist. 6, 5
58	epist. 3, 4	101	epist. 3, 7
59	epist. 3, 9 = opusc. 25	102	epist. 2, 15 = opusc. 34/1
60	epist. 1, 7	103	epist. 6, 2
61	epist. 1, 6 = opusc. 17	104	epist. 7, 5 = opusc. 56
62	epist. 4, 11	105	epist. 6, 8 = opusc. 21
63	epist. 2, 9	106	epist. 2, 14 = opusc. 33
64	epist. 7, 9	107	epist. 1, 16
65	opusc. 5	108	epist. 1, 17 = opusc. 23
66	epist. 7, 19 = opusc. 50	109	epist. 1, 19 = Vita Rodulphi et Dominici
67	epist. 7, 11 = opusc. 57/1	110	opusc. 9
68	epist. 7, 12 = opusc. 57/2	111	epist. 3, 8 = opusc. 39
69	epist. 2, 3 = opusc. 22	112	epist. 4, 3 = opusc. 18/2
70	epist. 5, 16 = opusc. 42/1	113	epist. 6, 4
71	epist. 7, 4	114	epist. 7, 16 = opusc. 18/3
72	epist. 1, 9 = opusc. 19	115	epist. 4, 16
73	epist. 4, 1	116	epist. 6, 10
74	epist. 4, 12	117	epist. 6, 17 = opusc. 45
75	epist. 2, 8	118	epist. 6, 35 = opusc. 55
76	epist. 6, 31 = opusc. 53	119	epist. 2, 17 = opusc. 36
77	epist. 5, 5	120	epist. 7, 3
78	epist. 6, 11 = opusc. 44	121	epist. 5, 1
79	epist. 1, 8	122	epist. 1, 11
80	epist. 4, 17 = opusc. 40	123	epist. 6, 21 = opusc. 47
81	opusc. 1	124	epist. 7, 6
82	epist. 2, 12	125	epist. 6, 3
83	epist. 8, 5	126	epist. 2, 20 = opusc. 37/1
84	epist. 5, 7	127	epist. 2, 21 = opusc. 37/2
85	epist. 8, 3	128	Ad Ambrosium et Liupardum
86	epist. 2, 18 = opusc. 52	129	epist. 5, 14 and 5, 15
87	epist. 4, 9		

CONCORDANCE

Reindel	Migne Number
130	epist. 7, 7
131	epist. 6, 13
132	epist. 6, 26 = opusc. 49
133	epist. 6, 34
134	epist. 6, 36
135	Ad Cinthium
136	epist. 8, 12
137	epist. 6, 33 = opusc. 54
138	epist. 5, 2
139	Ad Tebaldum
140	epist. 1, 13
141	epist. 5, 13
142	epist. 6, 32
143	epist. 7, 18
144	epist. 7, 8
145	epist. 8, 1
146	epist. 8, 11 = opusc. 30
147	epist. 5, 10
148	epist. 7, 13
149	Ad Agnetem
150	epist. 6, 20
151	epist. 7, 17
152	epist. 6, 12
153	opusc. 13
154	epist. 7, 10
155	epist. 8, 2

Reindel	Migne Number
156	epist. 2, 6
157	epist. 4, 8
158	epist. 6, 22
159	epist. 2, 16 = opusc. 35
160	epist. 2, 7 = opusc. 32
161	epist. 6, 1 = opusc. 43
162	epist. 2, 10 = opusc. 18/1 and epist. 5, 4
163	epist. 5, 3
164	epist. 1, 12
165	opusc. 12
166	epist. 6, 29
167	epist. 1, 14
168	epist. 3, 10 = opusc. 34/2
169	epist. 6, 25
170	epist. 8, 10
171	epist. 8, 15
172	epist. 5, 11 = opusc. 41
173	Ad Bucconem
174	epist. 4, 15
175	Ad Honestum
176	epist. 6, 9
177	epist. 5, 18
178	Ad abbatem A.
179	epist. 8, 6
180	Ad episcopum W.

Numeration of Earlier Editions in MGH

Migne Number	Reindel
epist. 1, 1	13
epist. 1, 2	16
epist. 1, 3	26
epist. 1, 4	33
epist. 1, 5	46
epist. 1, 6 = opusc. 17	61
epist. 1, 7	60
epist. 1, 8	79
epist. 1, 9 = opusc. 19	72
epist. 1, 10 = opusc. 20	57
epist. 1, 11	122
epist. 1, 12	164
epist. 1, 13	140
epist. 1, 14	167

Migne Number	Reindel
epist. 1, 15	96
epist. 1, 16	107
epist. 1, 17 = opusc. 23	108
epist. 1, 18 = opusc. 24	98
epist. 1 19 = Vita Rodulphi et Dominici	109
epist. 1, 20	88
epist. 1, 21	89
epist. 2, 1	48
epist. 2, 2 = opusc. 31	97
epist. 2, 3 = opusc. 22	69
epist. 2, 4	52
epist. 2, 5	49
epist. 2, 6	156

Migne Number	Reindel	Migne Number	Reindel
epist. 2, 7 = opusc. 32	160	epist. 5, 3	163
epist. 2, 8	75	epist. 5, 4 = part of opusc. 18/1	162
epist. 2, 9	63		
epist. 2, 10 = opusc. 18/1	162	epist. 5, 5	77
epist. 2, 11	95	epist. 5, 6	35
epist. 2, 12	82	epist. 5, 7	84
epist. 2, 13	90	epist. 5, 8	45
epist. 2, 14 = opusc. 33	106	epist. 5, 9 = opusc. 27	39
epist. 2, 15 = opusc. 34/1	102	epist. 5, 10	147
epist. 2, 16 = opusc. 35	159	epist. 5, 11 = opusc. 41	172
epist. 2, 17 = opusc. 36	119	epist. 5, 12	8
epist. 2, 18 = opusc. 52	86	epist. 5, 13	141
epist. 2, 19	11	epist. 5, 14	129
epist. 2, 20 = opusc. 37/1	126	epist. 5, 15	129
epist. 2, 21 = opusc. 37/2	127	epist. 5, 16 = opusc. 42/1	70
epist. 3, 1 = opusc. 38	91	epist. 5, 17 = opusc. 8/2	36
epist. 3, 2	3	epist. 5, 18	177
epist. 3, 3	4	epist. 5, 19 = opusc. 28	spuria
epist. 3, 4	58	epist. 6, 1 = opusc. 43	161
epist. 3, 5	7	epist. 6, 2	103
epist. 3, 6	99	epist. 6, 3	125
epist. 3, 7	101	epist. 6, 4	113
epist. 3, 8 = opusc. 39	111	epist. 6, 5	100
epist. 3, 9 = opusc. 25	59	epist. 6, 6	6
epist. 3, 10 = opusc. 34/2	168	epist. 6, 7	37
epist. 4, 1	73	epist. 6, 8 = opusc. 21	105
epist. 4, 2	5	epist. 6, 9	176
epist. 4, 3 = opusc. 18/2	112	epist. 6, 10	116
epist. 4, 4	30	epist. 6, 11 = opusc. 44	78
epist. 4, 5	22	epist. 6, 12	152
epist. 4, 6	12	epist. 6, 13	131
epist. 4, 7	14	epist. 6, 14 = opusc. 29	24
epist. 4, 8	157	epist. 6, 15	29
epist. 4, 9	87	epist. 6, 16 = opusc. 59	92
epist. 4, 10	34	epist. 6, 17 = opusc. 45	117
epist. 4, 11	62	epist. 6, 18 = opusc. 46	54
epist. 4, 12	74	epist. 6, 19	55
epist. 4, 13	32	epist. 6, 20	150
epist. 4, 14 = opusc. 26	47	epist. 6, 21 = opusc. 47	123
epist. 4, 15	174	epist. 6, 22	158
epist. 4, 16	115	epist. 6, 23	10
epist. 4, 17 = opusc. 40	80	epist. 6, 24 = opusc. 48	27
epist. 5, 1	121	epist. 6, 25	169
epist. 5, 2	138	epist. 6, 26 = opusc. 49	132

CONCORDANCE

Migne Number	Reindel	Migne Number	Reindel
epist. 6, 27	56	opusc. 1	81
epist. 6, 28	9	opusc. 2	1
epist. 6, 29	166	opusc. 3	1
epist. 6, 30 = opusc. 51	44	opusc. 4	89
epist. 6, 31 = opusc. 53	76	opusc. 5	65
epist. 6, 32	142	opusc. 6	40
epist. 6, 33 = opusc. 54	137	opusc. 7	31
epist. 6, 34	133	epist. 8/1	19
epist. 6, 35 = opusc. 55	118	opusc. 8/2 = epist. 5, 17	36
epist. 6, 36	134	opusc. 9	110
epist. 7, 1	43	opusc. 10	17
epist. 7, 2	20	opusc. 11	28
epist. 7, 3	120	opusc. 12	165
epist. 7, 4	71	opusc. 13	153
epist. 7, 5 = opusc. 56	104	opusc. 14	18
epist. 7, 6	124	opusc. 15	50
epist. 7, 7	130	opusc. 16	38
epist. 7, 8	144	opusc. 17 = epist. 1, 6	61
epist. 7, 9	64	opusc. 18/1 = epist. 2, 10	162
epist. 7, 10	154	opusc. 18/2 = epist. 4, 3	112
epist. 7, 11 = opusc. 57/1	67	opusc. 18/3 = epist. 7, 16	114
epist. 7, 12 = opusc. 57/2	68	opusc. 19 = epist. 1, 9	72
epist. 7, 13	148	opusc. 20 = epist. 1, 10	57
epist. 7, 14	51	opusc. 21 = epist. 6, 8	105
epist. 7, 15	2	opusc. 22 = epist. 2, 3	69
epist. 7, 16 = opusc. 18/3	114	opusc. 23 = epist. 1, 17	108
epist. 7, 17	151	opusc. 24 = epist. 1, 18	98
epist. 7, 18	143	opusc. 25 = epist. 3, 9	59
epist. 7, 19 = opusc. 50	66	opusc. 26 = epist. 4, 14	47
epist. 8, 1	145	opusc. 27 = epist. 5, 9	39
epist. 8, 2	155	opusc. 28 = epist. 5, 19	spurium
epist. 8, 3	85	opusc. 29 = epist. 6, 14	24
epist. 8, 4	15	opusc. 30 = epist. 8, 11	146
epist. 8, 5	83	opusc. 31 = epist. 2, 2	97
epist. 8, 6	179	opusc. 32 = epist. 2, 7	160
epist. 8, 7 = opusc. 42/2	25	opusc. 33 = epist. 2, 14	106
epist. 8, 8	21	opusc. 34/1 = epist. 2, 15	102
epist. 8, 9 = opusc. 58	23	opusc. 34/2 = epist. 3, 10	168
epist. 8, 10	170	opusc. 35 = epist. 2, 16	159
epist. 8, 11 = opusc. 30	146	opusc. 36 = epist. 2, 17	119
epist. 8, 12	136	opusc. 37/1 = epist. 2, 20	126
epist. 8, 13	93	opusc. 37/2 = epist. 2, 21	127
epist. 8, 14	94	opusc. 38 = epist. 3, 1	91
epist. 8, 15	171	opusc. 39 = epist. 3, 8	111

Migne Number	Reindel	Migne Number	Reindel
opusc. 40 = epist. 4, 17	80	opusc. 50 = epist. 7, 19	66
opusc. 41 = epist. 5, 1	172	opusc. 51 = epist. 6, 30	44
opusc. 42/1 = epist. 5, 16	70	opusc. 52 = epist. 2, 18	86
opusc. 42/2 = epist. 8, 7	25	opusc. 53 = epist. 6, 31	76
opusc. 43 = epist. 6, 1	161	opusc. 54 = epist. 6, 33	137
opusc. 44 = epist. 6, 11	78	opusc. 55 = epist. 6, 35	118
opusc. 45 = epist. 6, 17	117	opusc. 56 = epist. 7, 5	104
opusc. 46 = epist. 6, 18	54	opusc. 57/1 = epist. 7, 11	67
opusc. 47 = epist. 6, 21	123	opusc. 57/2 = epist. 7, 12	68
opusc. 48 = epist. 6, 24	27	opusc. 58 = epist. 8, 9	23
opusc. 49 = epist. 6, 26	132	opusc. 59 = epist. 6, 16	92

Letters That Are Not Found in Migne

To Abbot A.	178	To Henry	41
To Agnes	149	To Honestus	175
To Ambrose and Liupardus	128	To John	53
To Bucco	173	To Odalricus	42
To Cinthius	135	To Tebaldus	139
		To Bishop W.	180

LETTERS
61–90

LETTER 61

Peter Damian to Pope Nicholas II. He deplores the situation in which bishops live in public concubinage to the scandal of some, and to the delight of others who ridicule the leadership of the Church on this account. After exhorting the pope to emulate the example of Phinehas in opposing blatant immorality, he warns him against imitating Heli who fell from office because he indulged evil. An impassioned address to the offending bishops themselves recalls their dignity and the sacred functions that they perform, so contradictory to the lives they are leading. He advises the pope to depose those who refuse reform, as a deterrent to others and as a means of escaping blame for tolerating such open violation of the Church's law.

(January–July 1059)[1]

O THE SUPREME pontiff, the Lord Nicholas, the monk Peter the sinner sends the obedience of dutiful subservience.[2]

(2) Recently, as I conversed with several bishops by authority of your majesty,[3] I sought to bar the door of their loins and tried, as it were, to apply safeguards of chastity to their priestly genitals. But since this is a sect for which no one has a good thing to say,[4] I confidently took an altogether different approach, with the hope of carrying out the command of your decree.

(3) Only with difficulty was I able to extort from their trembling lips the bare promise to observe this provision: in the first

---

1. The several attempts to date this letter, undertaken by Blum, Dressler, Lucchesi, Neukirch, and Woody, explain the lack of precision adopted here.
2. For a selection from the rich literature on this theme, see Reindel, *Briefe* 2 (1988) 206 n. 1. On Damian's role in the discussion, see J. de Chasteigner, "Le célibat sacerdotal dans les écrits de Saint Pierre Damien," *Doctor Communis* 24 (1971) 169–83, 261–76.
3. Lucchesi, *Vita* no. 137 places this confrontation at the Easter Synod at Rome in 1059.
4. Cf. Acts 28.22.

place, because they despaired of ever being able to reach the heights of chastity; and then because they had no fear of being punished by a synodal decree for practicing the vice of impurity.[5] Indeed, in our day the genuine custom of the Roman Church seems to be observed in this way, that regarding other practices of ecclesiastical discipline, a proper investigation is held; but a prudent silence is maintained concerning clerical sexuality for fear of insults from laymen. But this is something that badly needs correction, so that precisely what all the people are complaining about should not be hushed up in council by the leaders of the Church. For, indeed, if this evil were secret, silence could perhaps somehow be condoned.[6] But what a criminal situation! Shamelessly, this epidemic has been so audaciously revealed that everyone knows the houses of prostitution, the names of the mistresses, the fathers-in-law and mothers-in-law, brothers, and other close relatives; and lest anything be lacking in these assertions, they give evidence of messengers running to and fro, of the sending of presents, of the jokes they laughed at, and of their private conversation. And lastly, to remove all doubt, you have the obvious pregnancies and the squalling babies. Therefore, because of the ignominy involved, I do not see how something that is everywhere publicly discussed can be suppressed at the synod, so that not only the offenders be properly branded with infamy, but also that those whose duty it is to punish them be found guilty.

(4) This kind of shame was not evident in the face of the priest Phinehas who, in the presence of all the people, took up a spear against the Israelite and the Midianite woman with whom he was having intercourse, and transfixed them both through the genitals.[7] Contrary to God's command, however, we are not impartial.[8] For we indeed punish acts of impurity performed by priests in the lower ranks, but with bishops, we pay our reverence with silent tolerance, which is totally absurd.

---

5. Damian's reference to a synodal decree is uncertain. But in *Letter* 112 he cites a synodal decree of Pope Leo IX, condemning mistresses of priests living within the walls of Rome to becoming "slaves of the Lateran palace."
6. See Dressler, *Petrus Damiani* 127.
7. Cf. Num 25.6–8.   8. Cf. Deut 1.17.

But notice that Phinehas, roused by the zeal of the Holy Spirit, after almost all the Israelites had had intercourse with Moabite women and had joined in the worship of the Baal of Peor, as the defender of God's Law did not attack those who were unknown or of lower estate, but chose to kill outstanding and famous people to cause terror among the rest, as Scripture asserts when it says, "The name of the Israelite struck down with the Midianite woman was Zimri, son of Salu, a chief in a Simeonite family."[9] And if one should also inquire about the noble status of the woman, one will find this in the following statement: "And the Midianite woman, who was also killed, was named Cozbi, daughter of Zur, a noble prince in Midian."[10] Now after relating the history of this fornication and how it was properly punished, why was it necessary for Moses to construct genealogies for both sinners, stating that one was a chief, and the other the daughter of a noble prince, except to teach us that the carnal sins of highly placed persons should be prosecuted with greater vigor? This is why the Lord himself, while the whole Israelite people was no less guilty of this crime, was silent regarding commoners, but vented his fury in condign punishment only on their leaders. "And the Lord was angry and said to Moses, 'Take all the leaders of the people and hang them on gallows in the full light of day, that the fury of my anger may turn away from Israel.'"[11] And then Moses said to none other but the judges of Israel, "Put to death, each one of you, those of his tribe who have joined in the worship of the Baal of Peor."[12]

(5) And so, while Phinehas was quick to punish especially those who were the leaders, to avenge the general acts of fornication of the whole people; and, as divine judgment, in like manner ordered the leaders of the people to be hanged on gallows; so Moses also commanded not just some weaklings, but the judges of Israel to kill their neighbors to avenge the sins of fornication. What are we to understand in all this, if not the fact that the crime of adultery committed by eminent people

9. Num 25.14.
11. Num 25.4.
10. Num 25.15.
12. Num 25.5.

must be more harshly punished? And he who is aroused to punish such men doubtless wins peace from the heavenly judge, and grace, not only for himself, but also for the people. Hence the voice of God spoke: "Phinehas has turned my wrath away from the Israelites, for he displayed among them the same jealous anger that moved me, and therefore in my anger I did not exterminate them."[13]

(6) And now we have heard how the Lord's anger with the Israelites was placated because of the anger of Phinehas; let us also note how by his agitation he established an everlasting peace with the Lord. "Tell him that I hereby grant him my covenant of peace. He and his descendants after him shall enjoy the priesthood under a covenant for all time, because he showed his zeal for his God and made expiation for the Israelites."[14] Surely the Lord gave him his covenant of peace, because after quieting all vexations of the flesh, he arranged for him to live in the joys of paradise until the end of the world. Unless I am mistaken, he is surely the prophet Elijah who was carried up to heaven by fiery horses and chariot while Elisha looked on.[15] Should anyone think I am lying, let him rather censure Jerome, the interpreter of God's Law, who states this in his book on Hebrew problems.[16] In the time of King David, moreover, the same Phinehas is clearly found still alive and functioning in the priestly office, as Scripture asserts: "These are members of the Korahite family, responsible for service as guards of the thresholds of the Tabernacle, and their families took turns guarding the entrances to the camp of the Lord. And Phinehas son of Eleazar was their overseer before the Lord."[17] The name Phinehas was given him by his parents, but the surname Elijah was imposed on him by accident. Elijah can be interpreted 'the Lord God,'[18] a name, I think, given him on

13. Num 25.11. Damian here departs from the Vulgate.
14. Num 25.12–13.   15. Cf. 2 Kgs 2.11–12.
16. This unique interpretation was known to Cornelius a Lapide (1567–1637), *Commentaria* 2 (Paris, 1877) 342, where Damian's opinion is reported and rejected. Damian perhaps used Pseudo-Jerome, *Quaestiones hebraicae in librum I Paralipomenon* (PL 25.1444A).
17. 1 Chr 9.19–20.
18. Jerome, *Nom.hebr.* 74.8 (CC 72.152).

the occasion of his appointment as ambassador, sent by the Israelite people to the two half-tribes, namely Reuben and Gad, and to the half-tribe of Manassah, who had built a great altar, and received this explanation from them: "The Lord God most powerful," they said, "the Lord God most powerful, he knows whether we built this altar as an act of defiance."[19] From these words of explanation he is said to have been called Elijah, while up to then his name had been Phinehas, taking his name, as it were, from their reply.

(7) It should be noted that the learned Bede stated in his Chronicle[20] that we can reckon 620 years from the exodus of the people of Israel from Egypt until the ascent of Elijah into heaven. It was therefore proper that he who caused the sudden death of the adulterers should have been granted a long life, and that he who on earth had been inflamed with the anger of God should most aptly be taken into heaven by fiery horses.

(8) But, quite the contrary, because Eli was aware of his sons' sins, yet did not correct them with the sharpness that they deserved, he fell backwards from his seat, broke his neck, and died,[21] when these sons were killed in battle by the Philistines. Then the ark of the Lord was captured by the enemy, and 4,000 fell in the first encounter while, afterwards, 30,000 more were killed by the Philistines. Indeed, Eli reprimanded his sons and corrected them, but with the mild leniency of a father and not with the severity and authority of a high priest: "Why," he said, "Do you do these things? I hear from all the people how wickedly you behave. Have done with it, my sons; for it is no good report that I hear."[22] For as Scripture relates, he had heard "how they had slept with women who were serving at the entrance of the Tabernacle."[23] Moreover, those whom he saw as enemies of God, in his death he recognized to be his sons; and those he should have violently attacked with the sword, he

---

19. Josh 22.22.
20. Cf. Bede, *De temporum ratione*, c. 66 (CC 123.477). After dating both events, Bede does not relate Elijah's ascent to the book of Exodus. It is likely that Damian made his own computation to arrive at his 620 years.
21. Cf. 1 Sam 4.17–18. 22. 1 Sam 2.23–24.
23. 1 Sam 2.22.

lightly patted on the head like a flattering father. It was not so with Moses, that faithful servant in the household of the Lord, and the teacher of the noble Phinehas. Taking his place at the gate of the camp, he said, "Who is on the Lord's side? Come here to me." And the Levites all rallied to him. He said to them, "These are the words of the God of Israel: 'Arm yourselves, each of you, with the sword. Go through the camp from gate to gate and back again. Each of you kill his brother, his neighbor, and his friend.'"[24] After 23,000 men had been slain, Moses said, "Today you have consecrated yourselves to the Lord, because you have turned each against his own son and his own brother and so brought a blessing upon yourselves."[25]

(9) Obviously, just as they who corrected sins were worthy of receiving a blessing, so too those who dealt lightly with sinners were likely to be cursed, as the prophet said, "A curse on him who withholds his sword from bloodshed."[26] One surely withholds his sword from bloodshed if he refrains from inflicting condign punishment on the wicked. "He who fails to correct, when it is possible for him to do so, makes himself guilty of the other's fault."[27] And so a man of God, who was thought to have been Phinehas, said to Eli whom I mentioned above, "This is the word of the Lord: 'Why do you show disrespect for my sacrifices and for my temple-offerings that I have ordained, and honor your sons more than me?'"[28] Therefore, if Eli perished with his sons, together with such a vast number of others, only because he did not correct his two sons as harshly as they deserved, what sort of sentence, do we think, will be given those who preside at the bench of justice in an ecclesiastical court and remain silent when confronted with the recognized crimes of evil men? While fearing publicly to disgrace men, they cause the commands of God's Law to be in disarray and dishonor the heavenly judge. And while they keep profligate men from los-

---

24. Exod 32.26–27. 25. Exod 32.28–29.
26. Jer 48.10. Cf. Robinson, *Authority* 25 on the use of this Jeremiah text to justify violent action against evildoers.
27. Ryan, *Sources* 58f. no. 104, cites John the Deacon, *Sancti Gregorii magni vita* 3.2 (PL 75.128C) and Gregory I, *Reg.* 9.215 (MG Epist. 2.202 [JE 1744]).
28. 1 Sam 2.27, 29.

ing the honors of their office, they harshly bring the very author of ecclesiastical dignity into disrepute. Thus was the word of God spoken to the same Eli who despised God in honoring his sons: "I will honor those who honor me, and those who despise me shall meet with contempt." And then the following words were added: "The time is coming when I will lop off every limb of your own and of your father's family."[29] With these words, he said, as it were, Since by granting you the dignity of the pastoral office I strengthened your arm against my enemies, although you refused to use force in punishing them, I will now cut off your arm, that is, I will take away from you the power of the priestly office, so that as you were lacking an arm in fighting for me, you will now be without a hand to defend yourself.

(10) Now let us say that Hophni and Phinehas are bishops and that Eli holds the office of metropolitan. Is there anything worse that one can do than to exonerate lustful bishops when one is in a position to reform them? This is especially so since the Lord said to Eli, "I foretold to him that my judgment on his house will stand forever because of his evil deed, since he knew that his sons were wicked, and he did not rebuke them. Therefore I have sworn to the family of Eli that the wickedness of his house will never be expiated by sacrifices and offerings."[30] Therefore, if every crime is washed away by sacrifices and offerings, and only mistaken compassion for bishops is undeserving of forgiveness, let him who neglects to pass judgment on their evil deeds be aware that he is making himself liable to harsh punishment at the hands of a severe judge. But since I do not dare revile the highest bishop in the universal Church, I will briefly address myself to the one who has sinned.

(11) O bishop, you whose name means to make sacred, that is, that you should offer sacrifice to God, why are you not terrified to offer yourself in sacrifice to the evil spirit? By committing fornication you cut yourself off from the members of Christ, and make yourself physically one with a harlot, as the Apostle attests when he says, "Anyone who links himself with

---

29. 1 Sam 2.30–31.   30. 1 Sam 3.13–14.

a harlot becomes physically one with her."³¹ And again, "Shall I then take from Christ his bodily parts and make them over to a harlot? Never!"³² What business have you to handle the body of Christ, when by wallowing in the allurements of the flesh you have become a member of antichrist? "Can light consort with darkness, or can Christ associate with Belial?"³³ Are you unaware that the Son of God was so dedicated to the purity of the flesh that he was not born of conjugal chastity, but rather from the womb of a virgin? And if that were not enough, that only a virgin should be his mother, it is the belief of the Church that his foster father also was a virgin.³⁴ Therefore, if our redeemer so loved the integrity of flowering chastity that not only was he born of the womb of a virgin, but that he was cared for by a guardian who was also a virgin, and that, when he was still a baby crying in his crib, by whom, I ask, does he now wish his body to be handled as he reigns supremely in heaven? If he wished to be fondled by hands that were unsullied as he lay in the crib, with what purity does he now wish to surround his body as he reigns on high in the glory of the Father's majesty? Clearly, if a father incestuously seduces his daughter, he will be promptly excommunicated, forbidden communion, and either sent to prison or exiled.³⁵ How much worse, therefore, should be your degradation, since you had no fear of perishing with your daughter, not indeed in the flesh, which would be bad enough, but rather with your spiritual daughter? All the children of the Church are undoubtedly your children. And it is also quite obvious that spiritual generation is something greater than carnal parenthood. Moreover, since you are the husband, the spouse of your church, symbolized by the ring of your betrothal and the staff of your mandate,³⁶ all who are reborn in her by the sacrament of baptism must be ascribed to you as your children. Therefore, if you commit incest with your

---

31. 1 Cor 6.16.   32. 1 Cor 6.15.
33. 2 Cor 6.14–15.
34. Damian also refers to St. Joseph in *Letter* 172. See also F. L. Filas, "Joseph, St., Devotion to," NCE 7 (1967) 1108–13.
35. No precedent for these punishments could be located.
36. On the ring and staff as symbols of episcopal rank, see *infra*, *Letter* 72 n. 6.

spiritual daughter, how in good conscience do you dare perform the mystery of the Lord's body?

(12) But perhaps you might argue that she was born long before you acquired the lofty office of bishop, or that she was not baptized in your cathedral, but in some parish church, as if you were the father only of those who were born later, and as if all the parishes of your diocese were not your churches. But since the Lord says, "Do not give dogs what is holy,"[37] how will you be judged since you give over your body, sanctified when you were consecrated, not to dogs but to houses of ill repute? And since all ecclesiastical orders are accumulated in one awesome structure in you alone, you surely defile all of them as you pollute yourself by associating with prostitutes. And thus you contaminate by your actions the doorkeeper, the lector, the exorcist, and in turn all the sacred orders, for all of which you must give an account before the severe judgment seat of God. As you lay your hand on someone, the Holy Spirit descends upon him; and you use your hand to touch the private parts of harlots. God accommodates himself to your word, and do you not fear to obey the devil? Moreover, you who appear to be outstanding because of your ecclesiastical authority, are you not ashamed to visit the brothels of panderers? And you, who are appointed to be the preacher of chastity, have you no shame at being the slave of impurity?

(13) The day will come, and that certainly, or rather the night, when this impurity of yours will be turned into pitch on which the everlasting fire will feed, never to be extinguished in your very being; and with never-ending flames this fire will devour you, flesh and bones. Since you burn with this passionate desire, how can you be so bold, how can you dare approach the sacred altar? Do you not know that Nadab and Abihu, sons of Aaron, were destroyed by fire from heaven because they dared to present illicit fire before the Lord?[38] The altars of the Lord will not accept illicit fire, but only that of divine love. Therefore, if one should be inflamed with the fire of carnal passion and does not fear to participate in the sacred mysteries,

---

37. Matt 7.6.   38. Cf. Lev 10.1–2; Num 3.4.

he will surely be devoured even now by the fire of God's vengeance, of which Scripture says, "And now fire consumes his enemies."[39] And as even now he is wasted by the flames of burning passion, so later he must broil in the dreadful and neverending fires of hell. What is more, O unhappy bishop, have you no fear that as you wallow in the mire of impurity, you have become guilty of the heresy of the Nicolaitans?[40] It was Nicolas, one of those whom the Apostle Peter had ordained deacons, who boldly taught that clerics of every rank should be married. And so, what he taught in words, you, as you take your seat among the scornful,[41] much more wickedly invite others to do by your example. The voice of God spoke of this crime through the angel of the Church at Ephesus: "You hate the practices of the Nicolaitans, as I do."[42] And since the Apostle says, "No one given to fornication has any share in the kingdom of Christ and of God,"[43] you who have no share in the kingdom of God, that is, in heaven, how can you maintain yourself within the honor of the episcopate in the Church, which is surely the kingdom of God?

(14) But you, my lord and venerable pope, you who take the place of Christ[44] and are the successor to the supreme shepherd in apostolic dignity, do not through sloth allow this pestilence to grow, do not by conniving and dissimulation loosen the reins on this raging impurity! This disease is spreading like a cancer, and its poisonous breed will reach out endlessly unless its evil growth is cut off by the scythe of the gospel. God forbid that Eli's sluggish inactivity should soften your holy resolve; rather may the zeal of the noble Phinehas enkindle it to punish this crime. Let those who have no fear of soiling the purity of ecclesiastical chastity be deposed, and may those so expelled deter others whom, by their evil example, they incited to this insulting and shameful sensuality. Therefore, let the force of

---

39. Heb 10.27.
40. On the Nicolaitans, see E. F. Siegman, "Nicolaites," NCE 10 (1967) 459.
41. Cf. Ps 1.1.   42. Rev 2.6.
43. Eph 5.5.
44. Damian uses this title also in writing to Pope Clement II and to Pope Victor II; see Maccarrone, "Vicarius" 21–58.

the canons reach out to punish and suppress the evils of impudent clerics,[45] so that (God forbid) the blemish of infamy may not take your holiness by surprise, and so that the accustomed splendor of ecclesiastical discipline may be in evidence. Your Grace will not be unaware that when Ahab, the king of Israel, spared Benhadad, the king of the Assyrians, with excessive compassion, he provoked the wrath of God to pass sentence on him. For the man of God said to him, "This is the word of the Lord: 'Because you let that man go when he was guilty of death, your life shall be forfeit for his life, your people for his people.'"[46] When the same man of God said to his companion, "It is God's command that you strike me," and when the man refused, he said, "Because you have not obeyed the Lord, when you leave me, a lion will attack you."[47] Just as the man had left him, as Scripture attests, a lion met and attacked him.

(15) What else does Scripture mean to say by all this, but that improper compassion is undoubtedly deserving of wrath, since the guilty were not punished according to the strict letter of the Law? He who failed to discipline his subjects must rightly suffer punishment from the supreme judge, and will deservedly be exposed to the lion "that prowls around looking for someone to devour,"[48] since by his sloth and inertia he failed to impose salutary penance. May your noble spirit, therefore, eagerly prepare to remove this reproach to chastity; may it vigorously and manfully be aroused to punish the heresy of the Nicolaitans, that, according to the promise made to Phinehas, almighty God may grant you his covenant of peace.[49] In addition, like Elijah after he figuratively slaughtered the 450 priests,[50] may the Lord take you to heaven, not with fiery horses, but in the company of the angels.

---

45. Cf. Ryan, *Sources* 59 no. 105.
46. 1 Kgs 20.42.
47. 1 Kgs 20.35–36.
48. 1 Pet 5.8.
49. Cf. Josh 22.30–31.
50. Cf. 1 Kgs 18.40.

LETTER 62

Peter Damian to Theodosius, bishop of Senigallia, and Rodulfus, bishop of Gubbio, requesting them to act as censors of his writings. He inserts an autobiographical note on his addiction to writing: not knowing how to engage in manual labor, he turned to dictating his ideas to avoid inactivity and melancholy, and to repel idle and lascivious thoughts.

(After April 1059)[1]

 O THE MOST reverend Bishop Theodosius of Senigallia[2] and Bishop Rodulfus of Gubbio,[3] the monk Peter the sinner sends his personal devotion.

(2) Your holiness must be aware, my beloved fathers and lords, that I have undertaken to write several small works, not, indeed, that I might place them on the pulpits in the churches (which would be presumptuous) but especially because without some sort of occupation I could not bear the idle leisure and the tedium of a remote cell. As one who does not know how to engage in useful manual labor, I write that I might restrain my wandering and lascivious mind with a leash, so to speak, of careful thought, the more easily to repulse the confusion of attacking thoughts and the importuning of creeping melancholy.

(3) But since I am even now approaching the investigating court where I must certainly give an account, not only of my words and writing, but even of my slightest thoughts, I beg your excellencies with all my being that in your good judgment, if you have the time, while I am still alive or after I am dead, you carefully read through whatever you can find of my writ-

---

1. The dating follows Lucchesi, *Vita* no. 44.
2. On Theodosius, Bishop of Senigallia, see Schwartz, *Bistümer* 253; Palazzini, "Chiesa Marchigiana" 195. I have here normalized the MS reading, "Theodisius."
3. On Rodulfus of Gubbio, see *Letter* 109.

ings.⁴ And if anything is there contained that is contrary to the Catholic faith, or that is opposed to the authority of sacred Scripture, delete it, if you see fit, or by correcting my opinion, bring it into line with sound doctrine. By so doing, whatever has been perverted by my stolid ignorance may, through the effort of your holiness, be made to agree with the provisions of the true faith, and that because of you, the love that builds may preserve from error that which was at fault because of my knowledge that perhaps bred conceit.⁵

(4) Why should one wonder that I, an unskilled and carnal man, should employ holy men to judge my meager dictation, when indeed Luke and Mark, in writing the Gospels, which were dictated by the Holy Spirit, had the apostles Peter and Paul as their censors? And furthermore, since I do not consider myself to have a purer faith and a more abundant love than those who are trained in the study of the Scriptures, I therefore place this burden on your shoulders.⁶

(5) And so, my dear friends, even after my death, be faithful to this loving task. So carry out the last rites of our old friendship, that my offensive errors, should they be found, may no longer have power over me, and that in performing this labor of love, you may enjoy a greater reward in heaven.

4. For further discussion of Damian's use of censors, see Reindel, "Studien" 1.63.
5. Cf. 1 Cor 8.1.
6. In or about 1064, because perhaps these two bishops were already dead, Damian commissioned the abbots, Gebizo and Tebaldus, and his fellow hermit, John of Lodi, to be his censors; see *Letter* 116.

LETTER 63

Peter Damian to the archdeacon Hildebrand. Here Damian defends himself against the calumny of the court of Count Guido, in which it was claimed that in 1055 he had built his hermitage of St. John the Baptist in the valley of Acereta on property belonging to the count. Damian claims that the land had been willed to Fonte Avellana by the count's uncle, Tehtgrimus, and he chides Hildebrand for listening favorably to these detractors.

(Fall 1059)[1]

O SIR HILDEBRAND, the archdeacon and immobile pillar of the Apostolic See, the monk Peter the sinner sends greetings.

(2) I am most grateful, esteemed brother, that while you were striving to reach the heights at the royal court,[2] I perceived the warmth of your affection for me, streaming forth from the depths of your heart. Nor is this any wonder, since God is said to be a consuming fire,[3] that the dwelling place of the Holy Spirit appears to be set afire by the flames that emerge from it. For wherever on your trips my name happened to be mentioned, as far as you were concerned, I was always favorably remembered. This good deed gave heart to my friends and closed the lips of detractors by opposing them with proper answers. Yet in Florence,[4] your judgment, which is normally on its guard and is unyielding when confronted by braggarts and

---

1. The dating follows Borino, "L'arcidiaconato" 514 and Dressler, *Petrus Damiani* 145. For further discussion of this date, see Reindel, *Briefe* 2 (1988) 221.
2. Hildebrand's journey to the imperial court must have occurred between October 1057 and May 1058 (cf. *Letter* 58 n. 9); see Schmidt, "Alexander II" 62f.
3. Cf. Deut 4.24; Heb 12.29.
4. On Hildebrand's visit to Florence after Easter, 1058, see Lucchesi, *Vita* no. 122ff.

liars, was made more flexible by the soothing persuasion of certain detractors.

(3) In truth the courtiers of Count Guido,[5] along with their servile dependents, have been slandering me by saying that I had constructed a monastery on the very land that, as a result of their lord's liberality, they had formerly given to their serfs. Why, I ask, did you not then recall the statement of the person who said, "Fodder, the stick, and burdens are for the donkey; bread and discipline and work for the servant"?[6] And then he adds, "Relax your restraint on him, and he will be looking for his liberty."[7] And why did this verse escape your memory: "Yoke and harness will bend the stubborn neck, and constant work will tame the servant"?[8] Why did you not also remember this saying: "Torture and shackles for the bad servant; put him to work to keep him from being idle"?[9] But why should I wonder that you, even though you are a prudent and holy man, should be deceived by sly and cunning servants, when Saul's servant, Ziba, compelled David by artful lies to depart from the path of justice, even though he possessed the spirit of prophecy? "You and Ziba," he said, "are to share the estate."[10] Just as Ziba had lied about Mephibosheth, saying that he opposed the king's majesty, so these too state that I had confiscated property belonging to the serfs.

(4) But I ask you, brother, was it not allowed Tehtgrimus,[11] Guido's uncle who died childless, to bequeath some small part of his many lands and villas that bordered on the monastery?[12] Could one say that there was any one of his numerous servants who was still in want, when upon his death the prince had no posterity to succeed him? Was it not permissible for him, while

---

5. For bibliography on the family of the Counts Guido, see *Letter* 14 n. 17, and Davidsohn, *Geschichte* 155. On the problem of identifying the monastery here under discussion, see Reindel, *Briefe* 2 (1988) 222 n. 5, and the literature there cited.
6. Sir 33.25.   7. Sir 33.26.
8. Sir 33.27.   9. Sir 33.28.
10. 2 Sam 19.29.
11. On Tehtgrimus, see Lucchesi, *Vita* no. 23.
12. On Damian's vague language, used to describe the lands in question, see Woody, *Damiani* 53.

he was still alive, to grant something of his land to God, because his vassals possessed everything? Do you think that those who were assigned the task of turning the spits over the fire, or of washing the kettles, possessed so much of the lord's property, that as he left this world he was unable to bequeath anything of his wealth to the holy churches? Do you consider it proper that our dependents should be the picture of health, that they clothe themselves in precious attire, and we be made to endure the fiery pains of the netherworld?[13] What a shameful thing it would be if they should prosper, and we be forced to beg! That they should still be able to taste yesterday's banquet, and we should search for crumbs in hell! He who makes his serf his heir deserves to see his inheritance destroyed.[14] He is rightly excluded from the list of sons if, while despising his own welfare, he makes his serf his substitute. Let the voice that speaks evil be silenced and, in the words of the prophet, let your ears be hedged with thorns against the lies of cunning detractors,[15] who, to your face, indeed, offer flattering words, but cover up the malicious poison within them. Like bees they bear honey in their mouths, but prick you with their stings. Why should it surprise us if, as we strive to reach the land flowing with honey, we are stung by bees that fly around us? He, to be sure, was hurrying to that land, who said, "They surrounded me like bees; they attacked me, as fire attacks brushwood."[16]

(5) To this I might add that as we hurry to reach this honey in the land of the living, and also drink of the sweetness of God's word, we likewise have pieces of honeycomb in our mouth. For it is written, "Honey comes forth from the mouth of the prudent man."[17] And the beloved said this to his bride: "Your lips drop sweetness like the honeycomb, my bride, honey and milk are under your tongue."[18] And then she said this of the bridegroom: "His throat is sweetness itself and wholly de-

---

13. On this reference to Lake Avernus, see also Isidore, *Etymologies* 13.19.8.
14. On the possibility of serfs inheriting from their lords, see Reindel, *Briefe* 2 (1988) 223 n. 9.
15. Cf. Ps 62.12; Prov 14.25; Sir 28.28.
16. Ps 117.12.   17. Cf. Prov 16.23–24.
18. Cant 4.11.

sirable."[19] Why, therefore, should we marvel that as we hurry toward the honey, and as we carry honey in our mouths, a swarm of bees should buzz around us to goad us with the stings of detraction?

(6) Thus it was that the people of Israel, as they hurried along through the wilderness to reach the promised land, first made camp in Gai, as the ancient version has it, and then came to Dibon-gad.[20] Now Gai is interpreted to mean 'chaos.'[21] And what do we mean by chaos, if not the heart of evil men that is dark, deep, and obscure? "The heart of man is evil and inscrutable," as Scripture says, "and who among men can fathom it?"[22] But Dibon-gad has the meaning of 'beehive of temptations.'[23] So, after being in chaos, we come to the beehive. For after the gloom of malice and deceit, like chaos, darkens the heart that is obscure, cunning, and deep, by increasing its wickedness it at length reaches the stage where, like bees, it sooths its neighbors who are present with the honey of flattery, and goads the absent with the sting of detraction. And so we go from Gai to Dibon-gad, from chaos to the beehive, because every wicked man, whose heart is darkened by malicious deceit, goes on to afflict others with the arrows of detraction.

(7) But now, what shall I say of you, who, although at first observing the amenities of close friendship for me, at times neglected to muzzle the jaws of these barking dogs, and did not shudder at believing these detractors? "A herd of bullocks surrounds me, great bulls beset me,"[24] and you patiently listened to them. And so I will say of the archdeacon of the greatest see what formerly was said of the Apostle James: "Look, the just man also has erred."[25] But since one must pray alike for friends

---

19. Cant 5.16. For Damian's variation from the Vulgate, cf. Sabatier 2.384.
20. Cf. Num 33.45. The *Gai*, cited here from the *versio antiqua*, is taken from Origen, *In Numeros homilia* 27.12.277, courtesy of Dr. Walter Thiele of the Vetus-Latina-Institut in Beuron.
21. Cf. Jerome, *Nom.hebr.* 22.23 (CC 72.80).
22. Jer 17.9.
23. Cf. Origen, *In Numeros homilia* 27.12.278.
24. Ps 21.13.
25. Cf. Rufinus, *Historia ecclesiastica* 2.23, ed. Th. Mommsen in Eusebius, *Werke* 2, ed. E. Schwartz, GCS 9 (1903–1909) 171.

and for those who do you harm, I will conclude my complaint against this calumny with a prayer. May almighty God, venerable brother, reward you in great measure for all the love you have shown, and in his mercy may he forgive you for having agreed with my detractors.

LETTER 64

Peter Damian, writing in the name of Pope Nicholas II, to Anne, queen of France. Acting as papal ghostwriter, as he did on several other occasions, Damian praises the queen for her generosity to the poor and underprivileged, exhorts her to influence her husband, King Henry I, to practice justice and equity in government, and to protect and promote the rights of the Church—all in the interest of the soul of the man she loves. She should, moreover, instruct the children, with whom she has been blessed, in the love of their creator. So doing, she will merit God's generosity in this life and in the life to come.

(October 1059)[1]

ISHOP NICHOLAS,[2] servant of the servants of God, to the glorious queen[3] sends his greetings and apostolic blessing.

(2) We give proper thanks to almighty God, the author of all good will, since we hear that virtue of manlike proportions lives in the heart of a woman. It has come to our attention, most excellent daughter, that your highness abounds in munificent and kindly generosity to the poor, that you are constant in dedicating yourself to prayer, exact strict penalties of those who use violence against others, and by other good works fulfill the office of royal authority insofar as it lies within your competence. We therefore exhort you to hold to the path that God inspired you to follow, and that you influence your indomitable

---

1. The dating follows Lucchesi, *Vita* no. 139.
2. This letter, written in the name of Pope Nicholas II (1058–1061), is confirmed as the work of Peter Damian, not only by its style, but also by its preservation among the MSS of Damian. Both Monte Cassino Cod. 358 and Vat. lat. 6749 testify to his authorship.
3. Despite the identification of the queen as Agnes by MS Chigi A. VII 218, we are, in fact, dealing with a letter to Anne of Kiev, the second wife (1051) of Henry I of France. For further literature, see M. Barroux, "Anne de Russie," *Dictionnaire de biographie française* 2 (1936) 1337f; Reindel, *Briefe* 2 (1988) 226 n. 2.

husband, our son, the king, to govern with equity and compassion, and to protect the interests of the Church. For if the eloquence of Abigail protected the good-for-nothing Nabal from the sword of the angry David,[4] how much more will your blessed love render your prudent husband pleasing in the eyes of God?

(3) You will truly love him if, by your tender advice, you cause him to protect the things that are God's. Otherwise, how are we to believe that wives truly love their husbands, if they cherish, so to speak, the purse that is their body, but pay no heed to the gold of their soul therein contained? For according to the Apostle, "We are no better than pots of earthenware that contain this treasure."[5] Such wives embrace only that which worms devour in the tomb, and foolishly have no regard for that which is destined for unfading glory in heaven. She, indeed, who ironically insulted David who had little regard for himself, had set her heart to love his body when she said, "What a glorious day for the king of Israel, when he exposed his person in the sight of his servants and went naked like any empty-headed fool!"[6] Because she was interested only in his body, she was rightly punished by being deprived of bodily offspring. And so, a little further on, Scripture added, "Michal, Saul's daughter, had no child to her dying day."[7]

(4) But you, glorious daughter, because you merited to receive from God the gift of children, rear your noble offspring[8] so that, from the very day you nursed them as babies, they may be fostered to love their creator. From you, let them learn to whom especially they belong, that they were nobly born to the throne in the royal house, but that still more nobly they were reborn in the bosom of the Church by the grace of the Holy Spirit. Do not ever prefer money to justice, but eagerly search for the treasure of true wisdom. The Queen of Sheba did not come to view the riches of Solomon, but to listen to his wisdom,[9]

---

4. Cf. 1 Sam 25.
6. 2 Sam 6.20.
5. 2 Cor 4.7.
7. 2 Sam 6.23.
8. See Hugh of Fleury, *Liber qui modernorum Francorum continet actus* 1.10.388f.: ". . . she bore him three sons, viz., Philip, Hugh, and Robert."
9. Cf. 1 Kgs 10.1–7.

and that which she had not sought she took back with her in abundance. And you also, my daughter, by obeying God's commands, come to possess wisdom, so that for the welfare of your soul you may deserve an abundance of the things of this world, and pass from the heights of a kingdom that will fade away to that which is in heaven.

LETTER 65

Peter Damian to the archdeacon Hildebrand. Entitled in the manuscripts, "On the privilege of the Roman Church," this letter is a glowing report on Damian's legation to Milan, undertaken at the command of Pope Nicholas II. While the main issue at stake in this mission was the subsidiary position of Milan relative to the Roman Church, as Damian saw it, other problems were also urgent. Damian had to deal with a weak archbishop, with the Patarins, and with a married and simonist clergy. His sermon, included in this report, was addressed to the first problem; the oaths elicited, and the penances ordained, refer to the last.

(December 1059)[1]

O[2] THE VENERABLE archdeacon,[3] Sir Hildebrand, the monk Peter the sinner sends his love and sincere devotion.

(2) The privilege of the Roman Church[4] should possess such power to preserve the law of canonical equity and justice, and have at its disposal such vigor to exercise discipline in the ecclesiastical domain, that it alone will clearly understand how it might customarily handle ecclesiastical affairs.[5] One who is unacquainted with it will belittle this privilege; but he who is learned in these matters will accept it. For just as someone who is unfamiliar with combat has no regard for arms, so, on the other hand, a man will eagerly buckle on his sword if he is in-

---

1. The dating follows Lucchesi, *Vita* no. 147.
2. The major MSS of this letter bear the superscription: "On the privilege of the Roman Church." But John of Lodi, *Vita s. Petri Damiani*, c. 16 (PL 144.133D) entitles it "Actus Mediolani."
3. See Jasper, *Papstwahldekret* 34ff., who attempts to prove that Hildebrand was given this title in 1058.
4. For a general interpretation of this work, see Maccarrone, "La teologia" 63ff.; Palazzini, "Le missione" 171–95.
5. See W. Ullmann, *The Growth of Papal Government in the Middle Ages*, 2d ed. (New York, 1962) 401, where he cites Rom 1.17 and Heb 10.38 as the groundwork of these ideas.

spired by habitually coming back victorious from battle. It may not be improper for me to compare the privilege of the Roman Church to weapons,[6] since she alone was established as the head of the whole Christian Church as a result of the chair of blessed Peter, and she presides over all the churches of the world, like a general at the forefront of his army. Supported by the forces of all the faithful, and armed with the authority of her special prerogative, she lops off the heads of those who resist the truth, by using the sword of the gospel, and unites the entire army of Christ in one alliance of love and faith, to fight together until victory. Minutely considering this matter, as was your custom on many other occasions, you frequently asked me, with the charity that overcomes all things, that as I read through the decrees and statutes[7] of the Roman pontiffs, I should from here and there thoughtfully excerpt whatever specifically was seen to belong to the authority of the Apostolic See, and put it all together in some small volume as a new collection.[8] As I neglected this urgent request, thinking it to be of little importance, and considering it superfluous rather than necessary, it happened providentially, I think, that I was commissioned to travel to Milan as the legate of blessed Pope Nicholas.[9]

(3) Because of the two heresies, namely, simony and that of the Nicolaitans, rather violent fighting broke out, involving the clergy and the people.[10] Now clerics are called Nicolaitans when they live with women in violation of the rule of ecclesiastical chastity. These at first become fornicators as they enter this kind of sordid union, but then are rightly called Nicolaitans when they defend this deadly disease with arguments they think bear authority. A vice, indeed, turns into heresy when it is defended by arguments dependent on false doctrine. What

---

6. Cf. Michel, *Sentenzen* 132 n. 2.
7. See Fuhrmann, "Randnotizen" 270 n. 17; G. Melville, "De gestis."
8. An extensive literature has developed on the meaning of this statement; see Ryan, *Sources* 166 n. 34; Gilchrist, *Diversorum patrum sententie sive Collectio in LXXIV titulos digesta* xxiff.
9. But see *infra*, n. 29, where Damian has second thoughts in the matter. The exact date of this mission is hotly debated, ranging from 24 January 1059 to 1060/1061; see Reindel, *Briefe* 2 (1988) 230 n. 10.
10. See Dressler, *Petrus Damiani* 130ff.

more shall I say? I was received with due regard for the Apostolic See. Three days after I had announced the purpose that had brought me there, a rebellious cry sponsored by the clerical faction arose among the people. They claimed that the Church of St. Ambrose should not be subjected to Roman laws, and that the Roman pontiff had no right to judge or act in matters pertaining to that see. "It is most improper," they said, "that our diocese, which in the days of our ancestors was always free, should now to our shame and disgrace, God forbid, be subjected to another church." And finally, the shouting of the rioters grew worse. They gathered from various districts of the city before the episcopal palace, rang the bells, and the whole city was aroused by the blaring of a mighty brass trumpet that was on the scene. Everything, I might say, seemed to point to my death and, as my friends frequently advised me, some of these people were thirsting for my blood. This mighty conflagration increased as all the clergy of the Ambrosian Church gathered as if they were attending a synod, with me sitting or rather presiding in their midst. I was accused of placing the most reverend archbishop of Milan[11] to my left, and Anselm, the bishop of Lucca, a man known for his holiness and sanctity, at my right.[12]

(4) But it is not necessary to produce here in writing everything that was said by the furious crowd, which, of course, one could well understand, given the circumstances. And, to be sure, the lord archbishop himself, as soon as he was aware that I had sat down, quickly offered willingly that, if I should so order, he would, without any argument take his place on the footstool on which I had placed my feet. Let those who are of such a mind say that he acted out of ulterior motives, but on my part I do not ascribe his action, as reported, to irritation at the angry mob, but to his reverence for the Apostolic See. But, to sum up what happened, I went up to the pulpit, and after

---

11. On Archbishop Guido, see Schwartz, *Bistümer* 79f.
12. Anselm was from Baggio in the vicinity of Milan, and thus a good diplomatic choice to accompany Damian on this mission. Appointed bishop of Lucca in 1057, he was elected Pope Alexander II on 1 October 1061. See Schmidt, "Alexander II" 64f.

the crowd was quieted with difficulty, I began to speak in approximately these words:[13]

(5) My dear friends, in your charity you should know that I did not come here to promote the honor of the Roman Church but to seek your glory and, if you will allow, to provide for you, with his help, salvation, and the grace that is in Christ. Why should it need honor from an insignificant man like me, when it received praise and honor from the very lips of the savior himself? Is there a province throughout all the kingdoms of the earth that is found exempt from its authority, at whose will heaven itself is bound and loosed?[14] Some king or emperor, or a mere man of whatever station, as he saw fit or found it in his power, prescribed the rights of the special privileges of all the honors[15] of a patriarch, a metropolitan primacy, the episcopal sees, and the dignity of the churches of every rank. But only he who granted to the blessed custodian of the keys to eternal life the powers of earthly and heavenly dominion founded the Roman Church and built it on the rock[16] of faith that would soon emerge.[17] It was no ordinary earthly utterance, but the Word by whom heaven and earth were made, and through whom finally the elements of all things were structured, who founded the Roman Church. Clearly, it enjoys his privilege and is supported by his authority.[18] And so, without doubt, whoever deprives any church of its rights commits an injustice; but if one attempts to deny the Roman Church the privilege granted it by the head of all the churches himself, he doubtless falls into heresy; and while the former may be called an unjust man, the latter must be labeled a heretic. He who acts contrary to her who is the mother of faith certainly does violence to the faith and obstinately opposes him who is known to have preferred her to all other churches.[19]

13. The superscription in the MSS at this point calls Damian's address *Sermo*. Only one MS (G1, Graz 1404) has *Sermo ad clerum*, while none has *Sermo ad populum*, often found in the literature. See Ryan, *Sources* 59ff. for the background documents used by Damian.
14. Ryan, *Sources* 60 no. 106 cites the *Collectio Hadriana aucta* 89 and 133; *Decretum Gelasianum* 3.1.29ff.
15. The rest of this paragraph, beginning "All the honors," is repeated verbatim in *Letter* 89.
16. Cf. Matt 16.18.
17. Ryan, *Sources* no. 60, notes that Damian's text, cited in n. 15, found its way into Anselm of Lucca, *Collectio canonum* 1.63.31f. and into Gratian, *Decretum* 22, c. 1.73.
18. Nicholas II (JL 4424) in *Deusdedit*, ed. W. von Glanvell 1.167; cf. Fuhrmann, "Patriarchate," ZRG Kan 41 (1955) 127 n. 106.
19. Cf. Ryan, *Sources* 63 no. 107, who cites Anastasius Bibliothecarius, *In-*

(6) But let us pass over other matters and return to that which at the moment engages our attention. Your gracious loyalty should not be unaware that the blessed princes of the apostles, Peter and Paul, had consecrated the Roman Church by their blood.[20] So also, at the very beginning of the newborn faith, they won for Christ this Church of Milan through their disciples.[21] The celebrated martyr Nazarius, as the sources attest, received the baptism of Peter from his successor Linus and, with blessed Celsus, was later crowned with martyrdom in this holy city;[22] also the holy martyrs Protase and Gervase are known to have had the blessed Apostle Paul as their master and teacher, as blessed Ambrose himself confirmed: "These were the men," he said, "who in taking my advice turned their back on lands and riches and followed in the footsteps of our Lord."[23] Just as our savior sent the disciples two by two to precede him,[24] so also both blessed apostles dispatched to this city twin preachers of the holy faith whom they had taught.

(7) Therefore, since the agents of your salvation came from the discipline of the Roman Church,[25] it follows in the order of equity that the Roman Church is the mother, and the Ambrosian Church is the daughter. This relationship between the two, namely, the Ambrosian Church and the Apostolic See, is not of recent origin but is undoubtedly very ancient: When St. Ambrose was saddened by the Nicolaitan[26] blight that had spread to the ruin of many in this city, and was unable to control it alone, he at once sought assistance from the Apostolic See. Pope Siricius, who then presided over that see, sent three people—a priest, a deacon, and a subdeacon—to correct and punish this crime. As this holy bishop, together with these men, was unable to reform these offenders, he threw them from the ship of this city, like bilge-water swarming with worms.[27] Thus, St. Ambrose himself

---

terpretatio synodi VII generalis, actio II (Mansi 12.1074); for further literature see Reindel, *Briefe* 2 (1988) 233 n. 24. But in view of n. 50 *infra*, did Damian know the work of Anastasius?

20. Cf. *Collectio Hadriana aucta* 89 and 133; *Decretum Gelasianum* 3.2.30f.

21. The *Collectio Dionysio-Hadriana* (PL 67.237f.) contains the *Decretum Innocentii I* to Decentius (JK 311); see Damian, *Letter* 11 n. 10.

22. See *Actus Nazarii et Celsi*, AA SS 28, July 6 (1868) 530D, 533D.

23. Cf. Pseudo-Ambrosius, *Epistola segregata* 2.4 (PL 17.821f.); see also AA SS 19, June 4 (1867) 683f.; cf. Ryan, *Sources* 66 no. 111.

24. Cf. Luke 19.29.

25. See Ryan, *Sources* 66f. no. 112, citing the *Collectio Hadriana aucta* 90: *Epistola papae Siricii* (PL 56.565B); Maassen, *Geschichte* 1.457; JK 260.

26. On which see Reindel, *Briefe* 2 (1988) 235 n. 31.

27. See Ryan, *Sources* 67f. no. 113. The text is in Ambrose, *Epistola* 1.42 (PL 16.1177A).

claimed that in all things he followed his teacher, the holy Roman Church.[28] Therefore, search your written records, use whom you will to investigate the matter and, if you are unable to find what I say in your own sources, you may charge me with lying; but if you are successful, do not oppose the truth. Do not bitterly attack your mother, but always rejoice that you are nourished with the solid food of heavenly doctrine, just as you were fed at her breast with the milk of apostolic faith.

(8) After I had finished my presentation on the privileges and primacy of the Apostolic See, the people became thoroughly well-disposed, and with one voice promised to carry out anything that I should enjoin. Then, indeed, I clearly understood how helpful it is in ecclesiastical affairs to be aware of the prerogatives of the Roman Church, a thing that in your holy prudence you had sought not idly from me. To be sure, with God's help I will study the matter once I have brought this undertaking to a successful conclusion.[29]

(9) But to get on. There was this large gathering of clerics, and after thoroughly investigating them as a group, and each one singly, hardly anyone in the whole assembly was found to have been promoted to orders without payment. It was the authentic and clearly irregular practice, and the inescapable rule of this church, that anyone who approached ordination to any rank, even to be consecrated bishop, must without any discussion first pay the prescribed tax. Obviously, an eloquent man could hardly explain how much I was worried over this matter, how wearied I was by tormenting thoughts, how deep was the fatigue I experienced. It seemed to be the total overthrow of the Christian religion to see how these men had desecrated the sacred mysteries in all the churches of this wide-spread diocese and of this noble city. But for me to exempt a few would have caused a dispute, since almost all of them were guilty; nor did it seem permissible to impose varying sentences on them, since the inducement was the same for all. This also added to my

---

28. Cf. Ambrose, *De sacramentis* 3.1.5.40.
29. Damian here changed his mind on the matter of preparing a collection on the privileges of the Roman Church at Hildebrand's request, which previously he had so cavalierly cast aside.

worry that, unless this case were concluded with some measured decision, the furious mob would not be quieted without a great number of men being massacred.

(10) Then, in the midst of much discussion, this opinion of Pope Innocent, already known to ancient writers, came to the fore, that "where many have sinned, the crime cannot be punished."[30] I was also reminded of the discretion used by holy pontiffs and the original authors of the canons in dealing with the Donatists, Novatians, and others who were ordained in various heresies.[31] It had likewise not escaped my memory that Pope Leo IX had reordained, as it were, many simonists and others who had been improperly promoted to orders.[32] Thinking over these and many other ideas, and after conferring with others, the opinion that the celebrated Pope Leo IV[33] had written to Bishop Januarius came to our attention: "After reading your fraternity's letter," he said, "I understood the strength of your faith, of which I had known before. I congratulate you on the care and pastoral solicitude you employ in guarding the flock of Christ, so that wolves,[34] which not only fail to profit from correction, but corrupt all that is sound, do not enter the flock under the guise of sheep, and savagely tear to pieces the artless ones. And that the serpent's deceit may not prevail, I have decided to remind you of this, my friend: It clearly constitutes a danger to souls if anyone of those who abandon union with us and lapse into heretical and schismatic sects should repent after defiling himself in any way by the infection of joining a heretical group—especially if he is taken back to Catholic unity without making due satisfaction. For it is most profitable and something most useful as a spiritual remedy that priests, deacons, or subdeacons—or clerics of whatever rank—who

---

30. See *Collectio Dionysio-Hadriana*: Innocent I, *Epistolae et decreta* 17, c. 6 (PL 67.261D); JK 303; Ryan, *Sources* 68 no. 115.

31. Cf. Ryan, *Sources* 68 no. 116.

32. On the reordination of simonists by Leo IX, see Laqua, *Traditionen* 300 n. 108.

33. All MSS at this point have Leo IV, but it is obvious that Damian was citing from Leo I, *Epistola* 18 (PL 54.706f.); JK 416. He uses the same text in his *Letter* 40 n. 267.

34. Cf. Matt 7.15.

wish to be accepted as reformed and who seek to return to the Catholic faith that they had previously deserted, must without equivocation first admit their own errors and the condemned authors of error. This should be done so that there be no occasion to despise their previous intentions, once they had been rejected. In this way no member may be harmed by associating with such as these, since in all that they do their own declaration would begin to oppose them. Regarding these people, I also ordain that this constitution of the canons, by which they will be greatly benefited, be observed: After removing every hope of their promotion they should be forced to remain at the rank in which they now stand, so long as they were not defiled by re-baptism. Nor is it only a slight offense against God for one to allow such men to be promoted to sacred orders. For if promotion should be granted to those who are blameless only after a full examination, how much more must it not be allowed to those who are suspect?"[35]

(11) The same Leo, in the matter of reconciling heretics, gave the following order to Anatholius, the bishop of Constantinople: "Those who condemn their erroneous deeds, making full satisfaction, and who choose to accuse rather than defend themselves, may rejoice in being united with us in peace and fellowship. But this is only to be if they previously condemn by a suitable anathema the doctrines that they accepted contrary to the Catholic faith. If the true high priest does not atone for us, using the nature proper to us, and the true blood of the spotless lamb does not cleanse us, then a true priesthood and true sacrifices do not exist in any other way in the Church of God, which is the body of Christ. The favor of being associated with us is not to be harshly denied, nor should it be bestowed at random."[36] And the same Leo, writing to the bishop of Aquileia said, "In their frank professions let them condemn the authors of this arrogant heresy, and let them repudiate

---

35. *Collectio Dionysio-Hadriana: Decretum Leonis*, c. 14 (PL 67.286A–C); Ryan, *Sources* 68 no. 117.

36. Cf. Ryan, *Sources* 69 no. 118, citing the *Collectio Hadriana aucta* 118; JK 460. Damian's text is from Leo I, *Epistola* 80, c. 2 (PL 54.914A), tr. E. Hunt, FOTC 34 (1957) 148–49.

whatever the universal Church has disapproved of in their teaching. And, embracing all those synodal decrees that the authority of the Apostolic See has ratified for stamping out the heresy of simony, let them announce in complete and frank statements, signed by their own hands, that they also completely agree with those decrees."[37]

(12) This, too, has not escaped my attention, that Fulbert, the bishop of Chartres, on the authority of the Council of Toledo, was seen giving advice to his primate[38] in the case of a priest who was ordained after payment for his office. After discussing other matters, he spoke as follows: "Wherefore, you should not reordain him who was deposed, but should return his orders to him by handing him the instruments and vestments pertaining to those orders,[39] with these words: I grant you the order of doorkeeper and restore you to this rank, and so forth, in the name of God the Father, and of the Son, and of the Holy Spirit. Finally you shall cheer him with this blessing by concluding in this fashion: May the blessing of God the Father, and of the Son, and of the Holy Spirit descend upon you, that you may be restored to priestly orders, that you may offer to almighty God pleasing sacrifices of praise for your sins and for the transgressions of the people. To him be honor and glory for ever and ever."[40] I have also not forgotten that the blessed Pope Gregory, by way of dispensation, for a time allowed the neophyte Angles to marry contrary to the prescription of the canons.[41] I have likewise called to mind the decision of the apostles, in which they imposed no other burden on the gentiles recently converted to the faith except to abstain from meat that had been offered to idols, from blood, from anything that

---

37. Cf. Ryan, *Sources* 69 no. 119, citing the *Collectio Hadriana aucta* 107; JK 398; Leo I, *Epistola* 1, c. 2 (PL 54.594B), tr. E. Hunt, FOTC 34 (1957) 20.
38. The dean of bishops in a county.
39. Following the *Pontificale Romanum* where, along with the *traditio instrumentorum et vestimentorum*, the essential element of ordination, the *impositio manuum*, are prescribed. It is noteworthy that in Damian's text the *impositio manuum* is not repeated.
40. Cf. Ryan, *Sources* 70 no. 120.
41. Cf. Ryan, *Sources* 70 no. 121, citing Burchard, *Decretum* 7.19 (PL 140.782D–783A).

had been strangled, and from fornication.⁴² Finding myself in a difficult position because I was unable to correct the malpractices of the Church on the mere authority of the canons,⁴³ I strove at least to put an end to its evil customs, and to make promotion to orders free in the future. I therefore required a solemn and irrevocable promise of free ordinations for now and hereafter, first in written documents, then by giving their hand, and lastly by swearing an oath on the Gospels. This solemn promise put in writing is a straightforward copy of what I have here before me.

The Promise of Guido, the Archbishop of Milan

(13) Guido,⁴⁴ by the grace of God, archbishop of the church of Milan, to all the faithful sons of the Church in Christ, to the clergy and people, eternal salvation in the Lord.

(14) Your holy devotedness,⁴⁵ dearly beloved brothers and sons, is not unaware of the detestable custom that grew up from of old in this holy Church, which with God's assent I serve; of how hateful to God it is, how shameful and perverse and condemned by the authority of all the holy canons, and of how it spread to the souls of innocent people by contaminating them with its deadly and pestilential leprosy. This damnable graft, forever worthy of condemnation, that flowed from the heresy of simony, and all pernicious trafficking of this kind, was customarily practiced in the holy Church, so that anyone who came forward to be promoted to clerical orders would give, as by a previously ordained condition, twelve pennies for the subdiaconate, eighteen for the diaconate, and lastly, twenty-four for receiving the priesthood. In this way, alas, Simon Magus converted the holy church of St. Ambrose into his perverted workshop. This forger⁴⁶ and evil master of the mint was

---

42. Cf. Acts 15.23–29.
43. See John of Lodi, *Vita*, c. 16 (PL 144.135C).
44. On Guido, see *supra*, n. 11.
45. For the possible sources of this speech, see Reindel, *Briefe* 2 (1988) 240 n. 46.
46. On the use of *trapezita* in the pejorative sense of 'forger,' see *Letter* 18 n. 35.

equipped with bellows, hammers, and anvil, and forged nothing more than universal peril for the souls of all men.

(15) In our own day, our good and merciful savior had compassion for his people whom, perishing under the atrocity of this deadly disease, he had redeemed by his sacred blood, by infusing the grace of the Holy Spirit, he lovingly inspired your hearts to withstand and manfully oppose this greedy and poisonous dragon. Thus, after some of our people had gone to the Apostolic See, the holy Pope Nicholas,[47] worthy of God, came to recognize how great was the danger to this area and he commissioned Peter, the lord bishop of Ostia, to repress and thoroughly eradicate this outrageous crime.

(16) Wherefore, beloved brothers, in the sight of almighty God and of his son Jesus Christ, who will judge the living and the dead, and of the Holy Spirit who especially condemns and wills the destruction of this pestilence, with all the holy angels and saints of God as my witnesses, in the presence of the aforementioned lord Bishop Peter and also of the honorable lord Bishop Anselm of Lucca, and of all of you, I condemn, detest, and judge worthy of reprobation, this depraved custom (and every kind of simoniacal heresy), which has flourished up to now in the Church. Moreover, I oblige not only myself, but also all my clerics who are now in orders, and all my successors, and bind them with the inviolable knot of this most powerful promise: that neither I, nor any successor of mine, nor any magistrate nor notary, nor any such officer may exact any payment from those who are being promoted to orders. But if, at the prompting of the devil, anyone of my curia, while I am in office, or anyone of my successors who shall come after me, should violate this most salutary promise and should presume by some pernicious deal to accept anything for having granted ordination, both the giver and the receiver shall be placed under the ban of perpetual anathema. Along with Simon, the originator of this heresy, he shall be removed from fellowship with almighty God and all the saints, and condemned with Judas and Caiaphas, and with Dathan and Abiram, to suffer the

---

47. Pope Nicholas II (6.[?] 12.1058–19.27.7.1061).

tortures of eternal damnation. I also denounce the heresy of the Nicolaitans and promise, insofar as it will be possible for me, that not only priests, but also deacons and subdeacons, shall be bound by the same attestation mentioned above: to abandon their abominable union with wives or concubines.

(17) But, that this might be more readily believed, my clergy and I confirm this promise by subscribing in our own hand, and I ordain that this document shall bear the stamp of my own seal. I also add and inviolably promise under restraint of this same pledge that neither any member of my curia nor I will ever accept anything for installing an abbot, for investing, ordaining, or granting anyone a chapel or any church, for preferring a bishop, or for blessing sacred chrism, or for consecrating a church. May the Holy Spirit, who is the author of all good gifts, loose me and my successors from the bonds of the aforementioned curse, and thus grant that we persevere in fulfilling this most salutary regulation, he who lives and reigns with the Father and the Son for ever and ever. Amen.

(18) I, Guido, by the grace of God archbishop of the Church of Milan, have confirmed, certified, and subscribed to this pledge which I have drawn up. I, Odalaericus, archepiscopal vicar and priest, have subscribed. I, Eribertus the priest, have subscribed. I, Arderatus the priest, have subscribed. I, Atto the priest, have subscribed. I, Ariprandus[48] the unworthy deacon, have subscribed. I, Ardericus the deacon, have subscribed. I, Ambrose the deacon, have subscribed. I, Atto the deacon, have subscribed. I, Adam the subdeacon, have subscribed. I, Arnulfus the subdeacon, have subscribed. I, Liprandus the subdeacon, have subscribed. I, Landulfus the subdeacon, have subscribed. I, Atto the subdeacon, have subscribed.

(19) After this the same archbishop, proceeding to the holy altar, in the presence of the bishop of Lucca, swore by placing his hands in mine, saying, "If I do not faithfully undertake to eradicate and totally destroy the heresies of simony and Nicolaitism, may I be excommunicated and cursed by almighty God and all the saints, and find myself excluded from the com-

---

48. On Ariprandus, see Reindel, *Briefe* 2 (1988) 242 n. 52.

pany of all Christians." Similarly, both his vicar and his chancellor, and all other clerics who were present, placed their hands in mine and repeated the same words of curse and excommunication. Then Arnulfus, the nephew of the archbishop, a decent and prudent cleric, came forward, and while the archbishop held him by one hand, he placed his other on the holy Gospels and took the following oath: "My Lord, Guido the archbishop, here present, from this day and henceforth will faithfully observe what he promised concerning the celibacy of clerics. He will, moreover, never ordain a cleric of any rank in his diocese, with the exception of monks, whom he has not compelled to take the oath contained in this document. So help me God and these holy Gospels."

The Formula of an Oath for Those to Be Ordained

(20) For receiving ecclesiastical orders, either by me or by my deputy, or by any other means, I have not given or promised anything, nor will I promise to give anything in the future. So help me God and these holy Gospels.

(21) After this was completed, the lord archbishop in all humility then prostrated himself on the floor, and asked that a penance be imposed on him in keeping with this abominable trafficking and venality; that although he was not the originator of this crime in his diocese, he had not, as was his duty, rooted it out. And so I enjoined on him a penance of one hundred years, prescribing that it could be redeemed by the annual payment of a specific amount of money.

(22) Next, after we had entered the cathedral[49] together, I went up to the pulpit. Then in the presence of a great gathering of the people and the clergy, he had his chaplain swear by touching the holy Gospels: that the archbishop, so long as he lived, and so far as he was able, not including the expenditure of his own goods, if he were unwilling, would strive sincerely and faithfully and with all his powers to root out these two heresies, namely, that of the Nicolaitans and that of si-

---

49. The text calls it the *ecclesia maior* (= *Sancta Maria hyemalis*); see Borino, "L'arcidiaconato" 479.

mony; he will not allow a priest, a deacon, or a subdeacon to have a woman and at the same time be in orders; also that he will totally forbid all trafficking in the administration of the sacraments of the Church. Then the greater part of the people, not only from the city but also from the suburbs—more than a thousand, it was reported—took the same oath against simonists and Nicolaitans. When these events were completed, after considering the opinions of the holy Fathers I had referred to above, and of others which, for the sake of brevity, I will here omit, I decided that all these clerics should receive their penance and be reconciled during the Mass; they should receive the symbols of their rank from the hands of the bishop, as Fulbert the bishop had advised, and to which I referred above, taking first before the holy altar the oath that follows:

(23) I, Arialdus, known as the deacon of the chapel of the archbishop of Milan, by this document, which I have written with my own hand, profess that faith which the seven holy councils established on the authority of the Gospels and the apostles,[50] and which the holy Roman pontiffs have set forth on various occasions as they clearly preached the truth. I also condemn in general all heresies that have arisen against the holy, catholic, and apostolic Church. Specifically, however, and by name, I condemn the simonist heresy, which attempts to bring into the Church this damnable trafficking in holy orders or offices, and the equally abominable heresy of the Nicolaitans, which shamelessly demands that the ministers of the holy altar should or can licitly have wives, as if they were laymen. And since in our day these two heresies, namely, of the simonists and of the Nicolaitans, seriously disturb and attack the Church of God, I hereby proclaim that all simonists and Nicolaitans, along with their teachings, their promoters, and their

---

50. See F. Dvornick, *The Photian Schism* (1948) 317; Ryan, *Sources* 70–71 nos. 123, 164. The argument that Damian also spoke of eight councils in *Opusc.* 28 (PL 145.515C) misses the mark, since *Opusc.* 28 is spurious. Cf. Lucchesi, *Vita* 2.159; *Clavis* (1961) 313–14. It follows, then, that Damian was not acquainted with Anastasius Bibliothecarius, *Interpretationes synod. VII–VIII*. On Arialdus, mentioned as the author of the document cited by Damian, see Reindel, *Briefe* 2 (1988) 244 n. 58.

followers, are worthy of eternal condemnation, as I take my oath by the holy consubstantial Trinity.

(24) The penance imposed on the clergy is the following: Those who simply paid their fee according to the norm established by the devil, in such a manner that many of them were hardly aware that it was a sin, shall receive five years of penance. It shall be carried out in this way: Throughout this period, in summer and in winter, they shall fast on bread and water two days each week, but during the two Lents that precede Christmas and Easter, for three days each week. For those who have paid more, the penance shall last for seven years, carried out with the same amount of fasting and, after seven years, they shall fast on Friday as long as they live. But those who find it difficult to fast have permission to commute one day of fasting per week, either by meditatively reciting one psalter, by saying half of a psalter with fifty prostrations, or by feeding a poor person and, after washing his feet, giving him a denarius. In addition, the lord archbishop promised to send all of them on a prayerful pilgrimage, either to Rome or to Tours; but the archbishop proposed that he would travel to the sacred tomb of St. James, which is in Spain.[51]

(25) After all had been reconciled in this fashion, it was decreed that all would not then indiscriminately be returned to office, but only those who were well educated, chaste, and were considered to be upright and serious in their behavior. For the others, however, it would suffice that by the grace of God they be again brought into the Church from which, by the pruning knife of divine punishment, they had previously been cut off. Both the former and the latter, to whom permission to function was returned, recovered their lost position, not from the former ordination they had so evilly purchased, but rather from that most efficacious authority of the blessed prince of the apostles with which he suddenly addressed the blessed Apollinaris, when he said, "Arise and receive the Holy Spirit, together with the office of bishop."[52]

51. On pilgrimages in general, and on those specifically to Rome and Compostela, see Reindel, *Briefe* 2 (1988) 246 nn. 61, 62.
52. Cf. *Passio sancti Apollinaris*, AA SS July 5.744. On this source and its authenticity, see Reindel, *Briefe* 2 (1988) 246 n. 64.

(26) Here, then, I have briefly explained the procedure used with all discretion at the city of Milan, but at this point I am not aware whether it is acceptable in the judgment of the Apostolic See. But if I have erred in anything, I gladly come before the teaching authority of Peter[53] to be corrected, and do not fear the stigma of retraction. If I might put it so, here we have the workshop in which he, who was called the workman's son, presides.[54] All coinage must rightly agree with his die, and anything that had anywhere been perverted should be reformed according to his norms of rectitude. Whether I have erred in reconciling these men, I do not know. But one thing I hope for through the goodness of almighty God: that, after all these varied oaths by which the archbishop confirmed his promises, after the sacred pledges of so many people given on the Gospels, after the sworn commitment of all the clergy made in writing and by word of mouth before the holy altar, these two heresies have in this diocese been so impaired by prudent coercion, that with the help of God they will not in our time recover to fight again. But let the Apostolic See examine these matters by requiring them to be re-appraised by its own counsel, and determine according to the judgment of its own authority whether they are worthy of approval or revision.

53. Here we have a rare, but clear recognition of papal magisterial primacy.
54. Damian, apparently, thought of Joseph, the workman (*faber*), not as a carpenter, but as a metal worker.

LETTER 66

Peter Damian to the former Countess Blanche, now a nun in Milan. In a fine example of his mystical writing, Damian praises Blanche for having deserted the world in exchange for the spiritual nuptials in which she is espoused to Christ. Her conversion should be fostered by meditation on the vanity of earthly things and on the spiritual combat in which the soul must engage if it wishes to progress in the love of God. He advises her to contemplate the transitory character of earthly glory, sharpened by the thought of death, of judgment, of the pains of hell and the everlasting joys of heaven. This letter is the prose counterpart of his poetic tetralogy on the eschata.

(the end of 1059–October 1060)[1]

O THE FORMER Countess Blanche,[2] now united to the heavenly bridegroom, the monk Peter the sinner expresses the great joy of his heart in the Holy Spirit.
(2) I come to feast at the royal nuptials and wish to see the bridechamber adorned with gold and glittering gems. With great longing I desire to be nourished at the nuptial banquet. Let mystical gifts be brought from everywhere, nor should prophetic and apostolic adornment be wanting at this most excellent wedding. Therefore, our evangelical Isaiah may now step forward and munificently display what he has prepared: ankle ornaments, tiaras, pendants and bracelets, veils and headbands, footchains and belts, scent bottles and amulets, earrings

---

1. The dating follows Lucchesi, *Vita* 2.156, who places this letter after the mission to Milan (late 1059) and before the death of Dominic Loricatus (October 1060). But see also Woody, *Damiani* 215f.
2. A Milanese Countess Blanche appears in no other contemporary source, leading to the conjecture that she may be fictitious. Damian refers to her again in *Letter* 92, *Letter* 93, and *Letter* 109. Is this, perhaps, another letter to the Empress Agnes, now a widow since the death of her husband, the emperor Henry III (d. 1056)? Agnes also had an only son, Henry IV, six years of age at his father's death, kidnapped by the archbishop Anno of Cologne. Six authentic letters to Agnes are found in Damian's letter collection.

and signet rings and jewels that hang on the forehead, expensive dresses and mantles and cloaks, pins and mirrors and linen garments, turbans and mantillas.[3] All of these should be given at a spiritual wedding and carefully fitted for the new bride so that they might please the eye of the true bridegroom. These lovely adornments, rich in their variety, were a part of the attire of that queen, of whom the psalmist spoke when he saw her, "The queen stood at your right in a dress made of gold, surrounded by variety."[4]

(3) There was a wedding at Cana in Galilee and, as the evangelist reports, Jesus with his disciples had been invited.[5] He went as a groomsman, not as the bridegroom; as one taking part in the feast, and not to be married. But this wedding so far surpasses all others in dignity in that here, Jesus is not considered a friend of the groom, but the bridegroom himself. And "since anyone who is joined to the Lord is one spirit with him,"[6] this bridegroom is not only joined to his bride but united with her. This union does not beget corruption, but rather restores the integrity of virginity. In that former wedding, Jesus changed water into wine; but here the same Jesus makes of himself wine and food. He becomes food, because he is the living bread that came down from heaven;[7] he is the wine that cheers the heart of man.[8] It is of his spirit that it is said again, "Your cup makes one drunk, how goodly it is!"[9] The spirit of God, indeed, inebriates the hearts of men so that, like strangers to themselves, they might disdain the riches of this world—honor and glory—that they might burn with ardent desire to undergo all that is harsh and burdensome for the sake of God. Those men were drunk with this new wine; the Jews, thinking them to be out of their minds and in a frenzy said, "They have been drinking too much new wine."[10] The man who belonged to the prophetic brotherhood, whom Elisha sent to anoit Jehu king, had also drunk of this new wine, and they who thought him crazy said to him, "Why did this madman come to you?"[11]

---

3. Cf. Isa 3.18–23.
4. Ps 44.10.
5. Cf. John 2.2.
6. 1 Cor 6.17.
7. Cf. John 6.33–35.
8. Cf. Ps 103.15.
9. Ps 22.5.
10. Acts 2.13.
11. 2 Kgs 9.11.

Why, then, should we wonder that men who are pure of heart and are filled with the Spirit of God should be judged insane by the wise of this world, who, therefore, fail to understand? They also said that the Lord of the angels himself was possessed by a devil[12] and, what is more, as Mark the evangelist testifies, thought him to be a madman. "He went home again," he said, "and once more such a crowd collected that they could not even have a meal. When his relatives heard of this, they set out to take charge of him, convinced that he was out of his mind."[13]

(4) This inebriation of the Holy Spirit you, too, venerable lady, experienced with full control of your senses when you decided to leave the world: and spreading your wings like a simple dove, you flew to the nest of the innocent and guileless. You could then say, "Oh for the wings of a dove to fly away and find rest."[14] And now indeed you sing assuredly: "How far I have gone in my flight and made a new home in the desert, awaiting him who saves me from timidity of spirit and from the storm."[15] This inebriation, too, has compelled you to despise your spacious and fertile land, so rich in produce; to turn away from the fortified towers and defenses of your castles; to give up the intimacy of dear relations and the affection of your servants; and, what is more important than all of these, to leave your only son,[16] still in his youth and not of age, without the comfort of family ties. And you, who were once accustomed to move about in the company of a host of attendants, have now learned to reside humbly in the narrow confines of the monastery with holy women who are poor in spirit. This sober inebriation,[17] if I may put it so, has taught you to exchange garments of fine linen for those of wool, purple and brilliant attire for an unattractive gown of dark gray. This inebriation has persuaded you to give up fine wheat flour and dishes filled with delicious food, and to restrict yourself to the amount of

12. Cf. John 8.48–52.
13. Mark 3.20–21.
14. Ps 54.7.
15. Ps 54.8–9.
16. See *supra*, n. 2.
17. For this "sober inebriation," see Ambrose, *Hymnus* 3, ed. A. S. Walpole, *Early Latin Hymns* (Cambridge, 1922) 38.

bread made from coarse grain as prescribed by the *Rule*.[18] This expert and sober inebriation also prompted you, left alone at the death of your husband when still in the flower of youth, to pay no attention to important and magnificent suitors; you did not marry again as everyone seemed to advise, but appeared as if dead to the world, so that you might overcome through Christ alone. As an experienced woman of affairs, intent on sales in the marketplace, you rejected the world that you might acquire heaven; you forestalled death that you might avoid the sentence of death; you chose poverty that you might possess an abundance of imperishable riches.

That at Times the Just Are Permitted to Be Afflicted by the Wicked, So That They May Be Satisfied, Even Perforce, to Be Converted to God

(5) And, that your conversion might appear that much more admirable, the world did not expel you, but the ardor of God's Spirit alone attracted you. On the other hand, as divine providence prepared to deliver the people of Israel from Egypt,[19] Moses was sent at the time that Pharaoh was disposed to oppress them with hard labor. So while the hearts of the Israelites were disgracefully attached to Egypt, when the one called, he attracted them; when the other savaged them, he, as it were, urged them to go; and thus while the people were shamefully bound in servitude, they were moved either under the impulse of oppression or under the provocation of good. This also frequently happens to the people of God: After hearing about heavenly rewards, the elect are permitted by God to be oppressed by the wicked so that if, after being called to the promised land we should refuse to go, we are then forced to do so under pressure of attack. And this Egypt, namely the present life, while oppressing us with its favors, may assist us with its burdens. As it shows favor, it abuses us under the yoke of slavery; as it afflicts us, it shows us the way to freedom. This, therefore, is the reason that the just are permitted to suffer at the hands of the wicked: that as they hear of the future good things that they love, they may also endure the present ills at which

18. Cf. *Benedicti Regula*, c. 39.   19. Cf. Exod 3.

they shudder; and as the impulse of love makes their farewell the easier, misfortune compels them to depart. When this life with all its prosperity was shining on you, it was not the flattering world that drew you, but Christ, "of all men the most handsome,"[20] who beckoned you by the inspiration of the Holy Spirit to embrace him in marriage. "Arise, then, my love," he said, "my bride, come. My dove, hiding in the clefts of the rocks, in the coverts of the wall, show me your face, let me hear your voice; for your voice is sweet and your face is beautiful."[21] Surely the holy soul is rightly called the loved one and the bride of Christ because it is joined to him by faith and love. But this bride seems still to be reclining as if involved in worldly affairs; but then she rises as she is encouraged to enter God's service, as if he were saying, "You who lie in the soft embrace of secular life, now get up and bestir yourself to join in the intimate circle of those who contemplate me." "My dove, in the clefts of the rocks."[22] If, according to the Apostle, Christ is the rock,[23] the clefts in the rock are the wounds of our redeemer, which, indeed, are five, namely, the wounds caused by the lance and the nails.[24] But because we had been impaired by the five wounds of our senses, by these five wounds we were restored to perpetual health. These, indeed, were the gates through which the prophet forbade one to enter on the Sabbath, bearing heavy burdens.[25] In these clefts the dove of God found shelter, because every holy soul places the entire hope for its salvation in the passion of the redeemer.[26] There, as it were, it is safe from the hawk's attack, because it is shielded from all the wiles of evil spirits. There, too, it builds its nest and gathers its offspring of good works. The psalmist says of this rock, "The high mountains are for the deer, while the rocks provide shelter for

20. Ps 44.3.
21. Cant 2.13–14. For the variant from the Vulgate, cf. Sabatier 2.378.
22. Cant 2.14.   23. Cf. 1 Cor 10.4.
24. For this comparison of the five wounds of the savior with the five wounds of the senses, see Gougaud, *Dévotions* 78; Dressler, *Petrus Damiani* 210, who found the same idea in *Letter* 161, and recognized here the earliest hint of the veneration of Christ's five wounds.
25. Cf. Jer 17.27.
26. On the symbolism of the dove, see Penco, "Simbolismo" 26.

rock-rabbits."²⁷ What is here meant by the mountains unless it be the high reaches of the Scriptures?²⁸ Those who are already able to make the great leap into contemplation climb to the heights of divine utterance as if they were mountain peaks. But since the weak are unable to reach these heights, it is properly said of them, "the rocks provide shelter for rock-rabbits," because high intelligence does not characterize those thus deprived, but they are humbly satisfied to rely on faith in Christ alone. It is also said in this passage, "In the coverts of the wall,"²⁹ because walls to enclose vineyards are usually made of stone, as Isaiah thus says: "My friend had a vineyard on a fertile hillside; he enclosed it with a wall and dug around it."³⁰ What should we understand by the wall made of stones unless it be the assistance and guardianship of the angels?³¹ By their aid, a soul engaged in combat is protected as they gather around it, and is sheltered from all the temptations of the spirits that oppose it. It says, moreover, in the words that follow: "Show me your face,"³² for the soul can be said to show its face to the heavenly bridegroom when by its innermost yearning it contemplates his image, as it were, face to face. "Let me hear your voice," he says, "for your voice is sweet and your face is beautiful."³³ O how sweet this relationship and how unspeakable the joy that wells up in the heart of man when creator and creature take their delight in mutual love, as the prophet puts it: "May my praise of him give him pleasure, for I will delight in the Lord."³⁴

That Anyone Who Would Despise the World Must Always Strive to Come to the Love of God

(6) This, moreover, should be the highest purpose of every holy soul unencumbered by worldly interests, and toward this it should strive, that through an increase of its good deeds it

---

27. Ps 103.18.
28. Cf. Augustine, *De civitate Dei* 18.32.623.
29. Cant 2.14. 30. Isa 5.1–2.
31. On which, see Ambrose, *Hexameron* 3.50.21.92.
32. Cant 2.14. 33. Cant 2.14.
34. Ps 103.34.

arrive at the love of God and finally find its peace in the delightful embrace of the true bridegroom. For as one is initiated into the various ecclesiastical orders that he might attain the goal of the priesthood, or rather (to apply the example to you), as a virgin is provided with a dowry that she might be married, so too all who leave the world must always endeavor to be united more intimately with their creator. Otherwise, what does it profit one to break the yoke of Egyptian slavery and to cross the Red Sea if it is never possible to enter the land flowing with milk and honey?[35] Now milk is the product of the flesh, while honey flows from above. And since our redeemer, in coming from heaven, took flesh from the Virgin, this is indeed the land of the living toward which we must always hasten, every step an act of love. Venerable sister, embrace this bridegroom with true affection and in this always find your delight. "Make the Lord your only joy," I say, "and he will give you what your heart desires."[36] Also, frequently receive his body and blood into your own mouth that you may deserve to hear him say, "Your lips, my promised one, distill wild honey, honey and milk are under your tongue."[37] For the adversary trembles to see the lips of a Christian red with the blood of Christ. At once he recognizes the mark of his damnation and cannot bear to see the instrument of God's victory by which he was taken captive and crushed. May Christ, therefore, by his mysterious sacrament be seen on your lips. May Christ by the warmth of his love always live in your heart, that the words of the bride in the Song of Songs may also apply to you: "My beloved is a sachet of myrrh, he shall lie between my breasts."[38] What is signified by myrrh, a kind of bitter spice with which the bodies of the dead are conditioned, unless it be the passion of Christ? And what is meant by the phrase "between my breasts" if not the location of the heart? And so, whoever constantly embraces Christ in the secret recesses of the heart, whoever continually meditates on the mystery of his passion with the purpose of imitating him, for such a one Christ surely becomes a sachet

35. Cf. Exod 3.
36. Ps 36.4.
37. Cant 4.11.
38. Cant 1.12.

of myrrh and, according to the words of sacred Scripture, Christ resides between her breasts. Similarly, the same bridegroom says to his bride, "Set me like a seal on your heart, like a seal on your arm."[39] Lest something that we wish to remember be overlooked, we often tie some reminder to our finger or to our arm so that, as we frequently take notice of this symbol, the thing that might be forgotten is always kept in mind. He, however, who seems to love Christ, but only appears to perform good deeds, in a way sets the bridegroom as a seal on his heart, but not on his arm. And he who is intent on doing good, but sluggishly remains cold, away from the fire of the love of God, he indeed sets the seal of sanctity on his arm, but as yet has not set the seal of Christ on his heart. Therefore, if the holy soul is to be marked in both places with the seal of Christ, it must set him as a seal on its heart so that it glows internally with the fire of his love. Let it further set the seal on its arm, so that it earnestly persist in good works. Paul had placed Jesus as a seal on his body, as it were, on his arm, since he said, "I bear the marks of Jesus on my body."[40] He had set Jesus as a seal on his heart, since in another passage he said with great joy, "As for me, the only thing I can boast about is the cross of our Lord Jesus Christ, through whom the world is crucified to me, and I to the world."[41] As he bore Christ's marks impressed on his body, so too he could rejoice to have his seal on his heart. The heavenly bridegroom, moreover, sets his seal on each of the elect, and is pleased in turn to take notice of it so as not to forget him. In this sense, he promised Zerubbabel, the high commissioner of Judah, "When that day comes, I will take you, Zerubbabel, my servant, and make you like my signet ring."[42] On the other hand, the Lord said of a certain wicked king, "Even if Jeconiah were the signet ring on my right hand, I would still wrench him off."[43]

---

39. Cant 8.6.
40. Gal 6.17.
41. Gal 6.14.
42. Hag 2.14.
43. Jer 22.24.

An Exhortation That She Always Repose in the Embrace of the Heavenly Bridegroom

(7) Therefore, venerable sister, always take care that the heavenly bridegroom also keeps you before his eyes through the grace of his love and that you do not, God forbid, look elsewhere by loving the things of time. And thus, as he looks attentively at you, not finding any remnant of sin, he is able to say, "You are wholly beautiful, my love, and without a blemish."[44] And you, unutterably burning with his love, may be able to say with feeling, "My beloved is white and ruddy, chosen from among thousands; his head is golden, purest gold, his throat is sweetness itself, he is altogether lovable."[45] The beloved is indeed white in his virginity, and ruddy by reason of his passion. White, because he says, "I am the lily of the valleys."[46] Ruddy, because John says of him, "Because he has washed away our sins in his blood."[47] Chosen from among thousands, because from among the multitude of all the saints, he alone was worthy to hear the words, "This is my beloved Son in whom I am well pleased."[48] Of whom Solomon says, "I have found one man in a thousand."[49] The number 1,000 is to be understood as meaning the totality of the whole human race,[50] among which our savior is like a lone bird on the roof.[51] His head is purest gold, because God is the head of Christ.[52] Indeed, as gold surpasses all metals, so without comparison does he exceed all creatures. His throat is said to be sweetness itself, because the hearts of those who hear him are bathed in sweetness by the honeyed softness of his words. "Your words," he says, "How sweet to my palate! They are sweeter than honey and the honeycomb to my mouth."[53] He is altogether lovable, because, as Peter testifies, the angels long to gaze on him;[54] or because the whole mystery of his humanity so excites desire in

---

44. Cant 4.7.
45. Cant 5.10–11, 16.
46. Cant 2.1.
47. Rev 1.5.
48. Matt 17.5.
49. Eccl 7.29.
50. See Gregory I, *Moralia* 9.3.3, 457 and 35.16.42, 1803.
51. Cf. Ps 101.8.
52. Cf. 1 Cor 11.3.
53. Ps 118.103.
54. Cf. 1 Pet 1.12.

the hearts of the elect that they are not only exalted by the glory of his resurrection, but through the ignominy of his passion are invited to imitate his example. He is lovable, because he is conspicuously outstanding in his remarkable birth, his life-giving death, his glorious resurrection, and his triumphant ascension. He is lovable as he speaks and as he works wonders. Therefore, venerable sister, always take delight in this your bridegroom, confide in him all your heart's desires, and in his embrace always find peace from all the senseless turmoil of this world.

He Cautions Her Always to Be on Her Guard against the Assault of Temptation

(8) But in the meantime, while you are in the embrace of the bridegroom, take special precautions against the adversary. You are still on the high seas and do not yet enjoy the peaceful quiet of the port. This life is the battle-readiness of camps, not the security of a walled town; it is the road, and not the fatherland. We are on our way and are not yet home. For "man's life on earth is temptation."[55] Wherefore, if you are free of the conflict of temptation, rejoice, to be sure, but do not on that account feel too secure, and be careful to prepare yourself against sudden and unexpected assaults of the enemy who lies in wait. It often happens that some who are converted from the world to God will, at the very beginning of their effort, experience a period of great quiet and tranquility in respect to carnal desires; but with the passing of time, they are worn out by the stiff trial of temptation. This happens, we know, according to the providence of God, so that they are not broken by the harshness of temptation at the very beginning of their new life. For if the bitterness of temptation were to overwhelm them while still inexperienced and ignorant of the inner struggle, they might easily return to what they had only recently abandoned. Regarding this it is written, "When Pharaoh had let the people go, the Lord did not lead them through the land of the Philistines, although that was the nearest way. He thought that the prospect of fighting would make the people

---

55. Cf. Job 7.1.

lose heart and turn back to Egypt."⁵⁶ Therefore, they who leave Egypt find that conflict has been removed from their lives, that is, that a certain peace and tranquility are given those who leave the world, so that by not being disturbed and terrified at the tender beginnings of their new life they do not return to those things on which they had turned their back. Consequently, at first they delight in sweet security and are sustained by peace and quiet. But after enjoying this sweetness, they are quite likely to bear the conflict of temptation, the more intimately they recognize in God the object of their love. And so, you should rejoice perhaps that everything is going well for you, but be on your guard against events that might later threaten. Always be cautious and circumspect, always be watchful that the enemy may never catch you yawning. For there is much that stands in league against you: your family ties, your youth, your beauty, and the memory of the wealth you left behind. To avoid surely the shafts of these encounters, there is no stronger shield, it seems to me, than meditation on death and the terror of the last judgment.

On the Soul and the Worrisome Sorrows That Confine It As It Leaves the Body

(9) When⁵⁷ the sinful soul is at the point of breaking free from the bonds of the body, one must indeed be aware of the bitter terror that buffets it, and of the biting stings of conscience with which it is afflicted. It recalls the forbidden acts that it has committed, and it beholds the commands that it negligently refused to fulfill. It laments its failure to appreciate the time when penance might have been practiced⁵⁸ and grieves that the immutable moment of strict accounting is unavoidably at hand. It yearns to remain, but is forced to go; it would like to recover lost opportunity, but is not heard. Looking back, it perceives the course of its past life to have been but one short

---

56. Exod 13.17.
57. This section, including the next two paragraphs, is frequently found in the MSS—generally anonymous—unrelated to *Letter* 66.
58. A rhythmic version of the following ideas is found in Damian's *Rhythmus de die mortis* (ed. Lokrantz, *L'opera* 88f.).

step along the way; and as it looks ahead, it beholds the span of unlimited existence. It is consequently distressed that in so short a time it was able to capture all the world's enjoyment; it weeps that because of this brief thrill of pleasure, it will forfeit the unspeakable delight of everlasting sweetness. It blushes to recall that for preferring a substance fated to be the food of worms it had neglected that which was destined to be borne aloft by choirs of angels. It peers into the future, viewing the glory of undying riches, and is dumbfounded in realizing that all this was lost because of its past improvidence. As it looks down at the base and loathsome darkness of this world and then marvels at the eternal brilliance above, it clearly grasps that what it had loved was indeed the night in all its blackness. Oh, if it were only possible to relive the time allotted to penance! How gladly it would follow the road of strict observance! How many and how great would be its promises! To what bonds of self-immolation it would submit!

(10) Meanwhile, as dimming eyes grow weaker, as it gasps for breath and hoarse cries escape from its throat, its teeth gradually darken and are discolored, as it were, with a kind of rust. Lips become pallid, all its members stiffen. As these and similar signs of approaching death make their appearance, all the words and deeds of the dying person are marshalled before him. His very thoughts, moreover, make their presence felt, and all these together bear bitter witness against him. All coalesce before his disapproving eyes and, as he turns to avoid them, he is forced to view them against his will. At one side, moreover, a frightening pack of demons takes its place, and, on the other, the angels stand in force. In him who lies between them, one can easily discern the winner who will claim his lot. For if signs of sanctity are seen in him, he is called by beckoning angels and invited to go forth accompanied by sweetly harmonious music. But if the black record and utter vileness of his deeds should decide that he stands on the left, he is buffeted by unbearable terror, brushed by a violent and sudden force, and is quickly seized and compelled to leave the confines of his miserable flesh and dragged in a flood of bitterness to everlasting torment. Then, when the soul has left the body, who can

count the armed host of evil spirits that lies in ambush, or the raging force, armed with deadly weapons, that blocks the way and, like legions deployed for battle, oppose the passage of a liberated soul? To meditate frequently on these and similar matters is to turn one's back on the enticements of this life, to repudiate the world, to crush the seductive movements of the flesh, and to guard inflexibly one's sole purpose of acquiring perfection.

Statements of the Scripture on the Day of Judgment

(11) To these thoughts should also be added the terror of the last judgment, so that one might turn his back on the false sweetness of this life by encountering this bitter happening. We will indeed courageously rise up to escape the vexations of the devil's attack if we foresightedly view the danger of this last agonizing experience. Surely, if we properly appraise this unexpected and terrible coming of Christ, what is there in this world that would delight even the foolish human mind? This is truly the day toward which the purpose and sum of all preceding ages conspire, in whose service all the volumes of sacred Scripture are recruited, and of which blessed Peter speaks in his effort to strike salutary terror in the hearts of his audience: "The day of the Lord will come like a thief, and then with a roar the sky will vanish, and the elements will catch fire and fall apart."[59] To this he quickly adds, "Since everything is coming to an end like this, you should be living holy and saintly lives while you wait and long for the day of the Lord to come, when the sky will dissolve in flames and the elements melt in the fire's heat."[60] And the Apostle Jude says of this subject, "I tell you, the Lord will come with his saints in the thousands to pronounce judgment on all mankind and to sentence the wicked for all the wicked things they have done, and for all the defiant things said against him by irreligious sinners."[61] In the book of Revelation John also says, "It is he who is coming on the clouds; everyone will see him, even those who pierced him,

59. 2 Pet 3.10.   60. 2 Pet 3.11–12.
61. Jude 14.15.

and all the races of the earth will mourn over him."[62] And Malachi says, "It is the Lord of hosts who is coming, and who will be able to think of the day of his coming? And who will remain standing to behold him?"[63] And a little later he adds, "For the day is coming now, burning like a furnace; and all the arrogant and the evildoers will be like stubble. The day that is coming is going to burn them up, leaving them neither root nor stalk."[64] And another prophet says, "A little while now, and I am going to shake the heavens and the earth, the sea and the dry land. I will shake all the nations and the Desired of all nations will come."[65] Likewise, another says, "The great day of the Lord is near, near, and coming with all speed. How bitter the sound of the day of the Lord, the day when the warrior utters cries of fear. A day of wrath, that day, a day of distress and agony, a day of ruin and devastation, a day of fog and whirlwinds, a day of trumpet blast and battle cry."[66]

(12) Here we should note how close the prophet considers the day of terrible judgment to be and how swiftly it is approaching and, to indicate this speed with greater emphasis he piles up words that express acceleration. Indeed, by employing amplification, he twice uses the word "near," followed by "coming with all speed," to teach us clearly that with the eyes of faith we behold already at the door that which the unbelieving and blind of heart think of as still far away. The former, as it were, stand trembling before the bench of justice, while the latter, through inattention every day of their lives, make light of the situation. Isaiah proclaims this day of final and irremediable urgency when he says, "The day of the Lord is coming, merciless, with wrath and fierce anger, to reduce the earth to desert and root out the sinners from it. For the stars and their brightness shall not send forth their light; the sun shall be dark when it rises, and the moon shall not shed her light. I will punish the world for its evil-doing, and the wicked for their crimes."[67] And again, "See," he says, "a strong and mighty Lord, like a storm of hail, a destroying tempest, like a storm of torrential, over-

62. Rev 1.7.
64. Mal 4.1.
66. Zeph 1.14–16.
63. Mal 3.1–2.
65. Hag 2.7–8.
67. Isa 13.9–11.

flowing waters, throwing them to the ground."[68] The same prophet says elsewhere, "See, the name of the Lord comes from afar, blazing is his anger, heavy his exaction. His lips brim with fury, his tongue is like a devouring fire. His breath is like a river in spate, to destroy the nations and reduce them to nothing."[69] And he continues, "Suddenly, unexpectedly, you shall be visited by the Lord of hosts with thunder, earthquake, mighty din, hurricane, tempest, flame of devouring fire."[70] Of this very fire Peter says, "By the same word, the present sky and earth are destined for fire, being kept until judgment day and the destruction of wicked men."[71] Of this also the prophet says, "The lord will make his majestic voice be heard and display his arm falling to strike, in the ferocity of his anger, in the glare of a devouring fire."[72] Speaking through Moses, the Lord further says this of the terrifying retribution, "My sword shall feed on flesh."[73] Jeremiah comments, "The sword of the Lord devours from one end of the land to the other; there is no peace for any living thing."[74]

(13) Now, it is said that the sword devours the land and that there is no peace for any living thing, because anyone who now lives according to the flesh or demonstrably strives inordinately for worldly things will surely be slain by the sword of final retribution. The Lord speaks of this sword by the mouth of Ezekiel: "My sword will leave its sheath to kill all flesh from south to north; all mankind is going to learn that I the Lord have drawn the sword from its sheath; it will not go back again."[75] The prophet Amos also speaks of this sword: "All the sinners of my people are going to perish by the sword, all those who say, 'No evil will ever overtake us, nor even come anywhere near us.'"[76] The terror of divine judgment had already afflicted the inner hearing of the prophet Nahum when he said, "The crack of the whip! The rumble of wheels! Galloping horse, jolting chariot, charging cavalry, flash of swords, gleam of spears,

68. Isa 28.2.
69. Isa 30.27–28.
70. Isa 29.6.
71. 2 Pet 3.7.
72. Isa 30.30.
73. Deut 32.42.
74. Jer 12.12.
75. Ezek 21.4–5.
76. Amos 9.10.

hosts of slain, utter catastrophe, dead bodies without end."[77] Moreover, what Daniel saw of God's judgment he clearly described when he says, "I watched until the thrones were set in place and the Ancient of Days took his seat. His robe was white as snow, the hair of his head as pure as wool. His throne was a blaze of flames, its wheels were a burning fire. A consuming stream of fire issued from his countenance." And shortly thereafter, "A court was held and the books were opened."[78] By these books we are to understand the saints whose worth is now hidden from them by their practice of humility, and lest they be read, are like a scroll that is not unrolled. But then, to enhance their reputation, they are opened for all to see, so that in them, as in an ordered piece of writing,[79] wrongdoers may read the commands of God's Law that they had refused to observe while they were still alive. They who now in their arrogance scorn hearing the word of God will then be compelled to read. Then they will realize that for the meek and patient the Lord's yoke is light and his burden is sweet,[80] a thing that they now, in their haughty pride, judge to be unbearable. There, everything that is proud will be confounded, and whatever was exalted, under the angry gaze of such majesty, will be laid low. Hence, Isaiah says, "Human pride will lower its eyes, and the arrogance of men will be humbled. The Lord alone shall be exalted on that day; for that will be the day of the Lord against all that is proud and lofty, against all that is arrogant, to bring it down; against all the cedars of Lebanon, high and towering, and against all the oaks of Bashan; against all the high mountains and all the soaring hills, against all the lofty towers, and against every fortified wall; against all the ships of Tarshesh, and against all that is beautiful to behold. And the haughtiness of man shall be humbled and the arrogance of men shall be brought low. The Lord alone will be exalted on that day, and all idols thrown down. And men shall enter into the hollows of the rocks, into the caverns of the earth, at the sight of the terror of the Lord,

---

77. Nah 3.2–3.   78. Dan 7.9–10.
79. See Tamassia, "Le opere di Pier Damiano" 666, who sees here a reference to the *Code of Justinian* or to the *Digest*.
80. Cf. Matt 11.30.

at the brilliance of his majesty, when he arises to shock the earth."[81]

(14) I should perhaps explain these words, step by step, but I am afraid that I might exceed the bounds of epistolary brevity. But this, I think, should be remarked in summary, that the day of divine judgment appears to be imminent for insensate things; yet we are to understand that, under the guise of irrational beings, the stupidity of evil men is indicated. The tall, towering cedars of Lebanon[82] are the powerful of this world, exalted, indeed, by the distinction accruing from their earthly dignity, but sterile in the production of good works. The oak indeed bears acorns, but these are unfit for human consumption, suited only to feed swine. Swine might be compared to unclean spirits who fatten on the foul deeds of sordid men. The high mountains and the soaring hills,[83] moreover, are the proud of every type, lifted up on high by the accumulation of arrogant thought; but they are lacking in grain with which the valleys abound and in all the fruit of spiritual effort. At the same time, the lofty tower and the fortified wall[84] signify those who, even though they are sinners, position themselves, as it were, behind defenses of innocence, covering themselves with protecting shields. They do not allow the arrows of their critics to reach them. Tarshish is said to mean "a seeking for happiness."[85] When the day of the Lord arrives, it will inflict sad and sorrowful troubles on anyone who seeks to enjoy himself in this world. By these he will be embittered forever. The day of the Lord will come, not for everything that is beautiful, but for all that appears to be beautiful; because he who, indeed, is rebuked by the inner ugliness of the hidden vices that assail him, but outwardly is covered over by a kind of beauty that attaches to spurious virtue or holiness, will be burdened with the weight of God's judgment.

(15) Yet, while much more could be said about these things, I must refrain from going into detail since I must avoid boring you with my prolix style. I have, moreover, omitted citing fur-

---

81. Isa 2.11–19.
82. Cf. Isa 2.13.
83. Cf. Isa 2.14, 30.25.
84. Cf. Isa 2.15.
85. Jerome, *Nom.hebr.* 43.26 (CC 72.113).

ther examples of the terror of divine judgment because while the total purpose of God's word lies in the service of this fearful trial, it is not proper that I burden the subject further by exaggeration. And should I go on at greater length, even if all the rest be left unsaid, these words of truth itself would suffice, in which he says, "In those days there will be such distress as, until now, has not been equalled since the beginning when God created the world; nor will it ever be again."[86]

Here He Advises That under the Guise of Family Affection One Should Not Return to the World

(16) Now, my lady—I call you my lady, or better, my queen, espoused to my Lord, the king of heaven, with the ring of a living faith and the pledge of the Holy Spirit[87]—carefully meditate and frequently read through these and similar items that relate to the severity of God's anger and displeasure. For these, as we note, await those who love this world. By this bitter antidote you may avoid the hissing of the ancient serpent and his death-dealing poison. I myself have often had the experience that, when these bitter thoughts had saturated my very being, the stomach of my mind was drained, as it were, of all the liquids of an evilly attractive world. Often, indeed, the wicked spirit, like a bird perched in the branches of a tree, sits on the tongue of the flatterer and seemingly by the tongue instills poison from mouth to mouth that lethally passes through the body of the listener. Close your ears to the seductive singing of the Sirens and prudently avoid shipwreck in the Scyllean whirlpool.[88] Let the terror of the judge confirm your will in its holy purpose so that the wind of fawning applause may never root it out. But using another tack, the ancient seducer,[89] who once used the serpent to spew his cunning poison into Eve, will still perhaps, as is his custom, hiss at you as at her daughter. "Go home," he says, "and still fulfill the purpose of your holy profession. Guide your family, live a life of virtue, observe a grave and modest regimen toward your son and others his age, af-

---

86. Mark 13.19.   87. Cf. Augustine, *Confessions* 7.21.
88. On the Sirens and Scylla, see Isidore, *Etymologies* 11.3.30–32.
89. Cf. Gen 3.1–5.

ford your insecure son the example of a mother who does not flaunt the law, and do not let him fall back into the company of flatterers." Therefore, in fabricating these ideas, the evil spirit hardly worries over the ruse to draw you back into the world, so long as he is sure that by a secular life he will dominate your thinking.

On the Monk Who Left the Hermitage to Return to the Monastery and Died after Sinning by Impurity

(17) Now, among many cases at hand, I think it proper to tell you about this event that happened to me just a few days ago. A certain simple monk of humble and modest behavior once came to me and asked to stay with us. For almost eight years he lived in our group as a hermit, not only observing chastity, but according to the testimony of all the brethren conducting himself in an exemplary way. Moreover, since he was skilled in writing, he produced many magnificent books for us. Recently, however, as he began to take on weight and appeared to be healthier than usual, he persisted in his demand that he be permitted to return to the monastery. That the evil adversary put this idea in his head is clear from what eventually happened. For soon after returning to his monastery as he had requested, he sinned by masturbating with another monk, a man old in his evil ways, equally skilled in letters, and also a scribe. And thus, by suddenly being caught up in this heinous crime, he spoiled the whole life that he had spent in purity. Nor did a fault so deserving of punishment pass without its just desert. For after a sudden attack of illness, he took to bed, and a few days later he died, troubled but confessing his sin. Thus it is "that he who is safe must be careful that he does not fall."[90] And he who, along with Lot's wife, is not deterred by the mere command to not look back should at least be terrified by the sight of the statue of salt[91] and by God's vengeance for this act.

On Sophia's Tomb

(18) But, on the other hand, perhaps, one might say that your very slim and delicate body was from earliest childhood

90. Cf. 1 Cor 10.12.   91. Cf. Gen 19.26.

tenderly nourished on choice and almost royal food; that now you cannot be content with the sisters' poor table, since you were formerly accustomed to magnificent courses; that you can hardly stand to smell, much less consume with them their common fare, since you were used to exquisitely delicate seafood stuffed with spices from the Indies. But now, as a disciple of the one who was crucified, you should prudently resist these soothing enticements to evil, or rather, these arrows daubed with honey that obviously fly from the devil's quiver, and repel them by earnest reflection on your state of life. Call to mind that the flesh that now is nourished by dainty food will in a little while be swarming with worms; that it will then become the meat of rodents, while at present it delights to be satisfied with pleasant fare; that it will emit an overwhelmingly fetid and putrifying odor proportionate to the gentle sweetness on which it was reared. As I write these things, I am now reminded of Sophia,[92] the sister of Count Uguzo and the daughter of Count Rainerius, who about six years ago, while still sound and in good health, requested the abbot of the monastery of St. Christopher the martyr[93] to build a tomb for her. When he resisted the idea, he noticed that she was greatly upset, so he more or less unwillingly consented. But after the tomb had been erected within the monastery enclosure, and just as the lady entered and saw it—I don't know how it happened—she suddenly took ill, and shortly after had a miscarriage and died. Now this tomb of hers that had been stuccoed and strengthened overall by the skilled efforts of the masons gave off such a malodorous stench for almost a year that one could hardly bear it, nor was it possible for the brethren to live peaceably in that entire half of the monastery. Many tombs had been erected on all sides, and even the smaller ones were of considerable size, yet none but this one was the cause of any offensive odor, so that it was clear as day that the more tenderly and delicately one treated the human body, the more wretchedly does it change into nauseous corruption. Consequently, when the brethren inquired of me why this had happened, I explained my opinion in these words:

92. On Sophia, see Reindel, *Briefe* 2 (1988) 268 n. 45.
93. Cf. Reindel, *Briefe* 2 (1988) 269 n. 46.

"It seems to me," I said, "that by God's design this had occurred for your benefit, that in this one body, which appeared to you so beautiful and charming, you might clearly understand how one should think of other women caught up in temptation to luxury. When that flesh attracted the critical eyes of onlookers, it was even then truly corruption, for it is now obvious what it was at that time. Indeed, all human flesh, which at present appears to be so vigorous, never of itself breeds corruption after death; but now it clearly states that it is only the festering mass that it had always been before."

*On the Wife of the Venetian Doge,
Formerly a Most Charming Lady, But Who Later Turned
into a Figure of Vile Corruption*

(19) And now, to confirm what I have just asserted, it is to my purpose also to cite an example of one who was still living. What I am about to relate I learned from a truthful and upright man. The Doge of Venice[94] had a wife from Constantinople, a lady who lived so delicately and fastidiously, and who pampered herself with such sumptuous and, I might add, such ingenious luxury, that she would not even condescend to wash with ordinary water. Her servants, however, strove to collect from all around dew from the heavens, and from this they laboriously provided a satisfactory bath. Moreover, she would not touch her food with her hands, but everything she ate had to be cut up into very small pieces by her eunuchs, which she then daintily raised to her lips with golden two- and three-pronged forks. At the same time, her room was perfumed by so many varieties of incense and spices, and the excess of it all so nauseates me in telling about it, that the hearer will hardly believe it.

(20) Now, from the punishment that followed, it becomes clear how detestable this woman's pride was to almighty God. With the sword of justice poised over her head, her whole body became so putrid that all its members began to decay, filling the entire room with an absolutely intolerable stench. No one

---

94. It seems most likely that Damian here refers to Mary, the niece of the emperor Basileios who in 1004 married the son of the doge Piero Orseolo II; see Kretschmayr, *Geschichte von Venedig* 1.142.

could bear such an attack on the sense of smell, including her cosmetician and her servant-lad. Only one maid, and she only with the aid of some fragrant essence, remained in her personal service. And even she would quickly approach her and then suddenly rush out. At length, wasted away by her sickness and suffering terribly, she died, to the great relief of her friends. And so let flesh itself teach us what flesh is made of, and that what it is in death is evident also in life.

On the Sufferings of the Damned

(21) O that temporal punishment would suffice for such as these and that hell also would not be their fate! There, indeed, a measure of torment is meted out in proportion to the sensual pleasure one has enjoyed; and the higher one is here exalted by a display of pride, the deeper will be the abyss of devouring fire that will there engulf its victim. And so, under the guise of the city of Babylon, this is said of the depraved soul: "As she glorified herself and played the wanton, so give her a like measure of torment and mourning."[95] And elsewhere, "Ruthless torment is reserved for the powerful, and the mighty shall be more mightily punished."[96] Those very carnal pleasures or other vices that in this life excited wicked men turn into pitch and rosin there and add to the roar of the avenging flames. There, indeed, as Scripture says, one finds the shadow of death, which surely refers to the gloom of dissension.[97] For every damned soul, as it burns in eternal fire, is cut off from interior light. It is of the nature of fire, however, that it gives off both light and heat; but this flame by which hardened vices are avenged possesses heat, although it is totally without light. And so it is that truth says of him whom he rejects, "Bind him hand and foot and throw him out into the dark."[98]

(22) Hence, if the fire that torments the reprobate were to have light, it would never be said that the outcast was committed to darkness. And so the psalmist states, "Fire has fallen on them, and they shall not see the sun."[99] Fire, indeed, falls upon the wicked. But as the fire falls, the sun is not visible because

95. Rev 18.7.
96. Wis 6.7–9.
97. Cf. Job 10.22.
98. Matt 22.13.
99. Ps 57.9.

the fire of hell blinds those whom it devours, depriving them of the true light. Thus as the pain of burning torments them physically, the punishment of blindness darkens them spiritually. It follows from this that those who have deserted their maker in body and soul are punished at once in body and soul; and those who in this life were slaves to their wanton pleasures on both accounts, now experience this twofold suffering. Hence, the prophet puts it well: "They went down into hell with their weapons."[100] Truly, the weapons of sinners are their bodily members with which they fulfill all the wicked desires they can devise. And Paul is right when he says, "Do not yield your members to sin as instruments of wickedness."[101] To go down into hell with their weapons is to endure the torments of eternal justice, possessed of those very members by which they glutted their voluptuous desires. Thus hereafter pain might entirely engulf those who now, as slaves to their pleasures, are completely at war with the Law of the just judge. Their agony, indeed, is such that it both tortures its victims beyond their endurance and suffices to end life itself. And yet, the sentence places such limits on life that the tortured will always live without end. Because of their torments, they come close to death, yet endure endlessly in a state of dying. The lot of these miserable creatures, therefore, is death without dying, an end without conclusion, dissolution that never ceases, because it is a death that goes on living, an end always beginning, and dissolution that never wanes.[102] So let those who now wallow in luxury go their way to live according to the dictates of their flesh, that later they may die in body and soul. Let them now drink to the full of worldly sweetness, that in the time to come, in their whole being, they may experience to the dregs the bitter absinth of perpetual torment.[103] It is the lot of those who have indulged in gluttony here to gnash their teeth hereafter; there they will mourn without respite, while here they laughed at their grossness; and just as they have enjoyed the scented

---

100. Ezek 32.27. 101. Rom 6.13.
102. See Damian's *Rhythmus de poenis inferni*, Strophe 14 (Lokrantz, *L'opera* 87).
103. Cf. Lam 3.15.

pleasures of perfume and sought the tartness of spices here, they will there be tortured in a sulphurous stench and enveloped in the gloom of pitch-black smoke. "They spend their days in prosperity and in an instant they go down into hell."[104]

That an Indifferent Monk Is a Worthless Plant, While One Who Is Fervent Is a Fruitful Vine

(23) While these ideas preoccupy us, may their overwhelming terror turn into a Red Sea that blocks a return to what was left behind in Egypt, to an ungenerous longing to be seated at the flesh pots.[105] I feel certain, venerable sister, that you who walk behind the animals of the gospel team with their heavenly wheels, whose feet are straight[106] and who did not turn back as they went will never follow Lot's wife[107] but rather, in your firm purpose, will imitate the virtue of Anna, whose countenance never changed again.[108] And since that which a flatterer praises is despised by authority within the Church, you should consider these two statements: "The sinner is praised for the desires of his heart, and he who does evil is blessed"[109] is the position of the flatterer; and "They are cursed who stray from your commandments"[110] is the voice of the Church. Since, as the prophet David states, the measure of the curse should be in proportion to the crime, so the Church imposed a thirtyfold curse on Judas Iscariot, who with sacrilegious greed sold the Lord for thirty pieces of silver. As the first part of the following states, "Set the sinner over him,"[111] so the final observation reads, "Let them be covered with their shame as if it were a double cloak."[112] If one carefully searches through the list of Psalms, it is clear that these ideas occur with regularity.

(24) Consequently, we should learn the sequence of events from the arrangement of the Scriptures. In the first place, the Law is set down, then one finds the history of the Judges, and finally we come to the book of Kings. In the first, therefore, we

104. Job 21.13.
106. Cf. Ezek 1.7.
108. Cf. 1 Sam 1.18.
110. Ps 118.21.
112. Ps 108.29.

105. Cf. Exod 16.3.
107. Cf. Gen 19.26.
109. Ps 10.3.
111. Ps 108.6.

embrace the commands of divine Law, and then arrive at the moment of judgment. In the end, if our case is not at odds with the Law, we reign forever with Christ. The produce from this crop should then be gathered and stored in heavenly barns. If the vine is rich in grapes, it is surely superior to all the trees in the orchard; on the other hand, if it is sterile, it is considered less valuable and meaner than other plants. In this connection, God spoke to the prophet: "Son of man, what shall be made of the wood of the vine in preference to all the wood from the branches of the forest trees? Do people use its wood to carve it into something? Do they make a peg out of it on which to hang any vessel?"[113] Obviously, this is how it is with a monk. If he is dedicated and fervent in producing fruit by his good works, nothing done by men will be thought superior to his achievement. But if he is indifferent, if he withers away unproductively and snores in his sleep, he will rightly be despised as a worthless weed and will not even be judged the equal of laymen. However, if one is fervent in his efforts to acquire perfection, but through weakness still unwillingly retains some tendency to vice from his former life, an ordinary layman, even though he proves to be holy and ascetical, can never be compared over all to him. Defective gold is certainly better than pure copper, and a raw pearl is more precious than Parian marble. Even a pale ruby is more lovely than a blue sapphire. And you, too, whose life, as it were, is only dawning, if you still experience something of the darkness of your former life, do not despair at arriving quickly at the fullness of light. Beware not only of relaxing in pampering the flesh, but be on your guard to exert yourself in works of religious discipline.

That Dominic Recited Twelve Psalters While Taking the Discipline, and Began a Thirteenth

(25) I wish it were now possible for you to observe my lord Dominic[114] who would more readily teach and direct you by the example of his outstanding life than anything I might achieve

---

113. Ezek 15.2–3.
114. On Dominicus Loricatus, see *Letter* 44 n. 31 and *Letter* 109.

by my unskilled words. For almost fifteen years now, this man wore an iron corselet next to his flesh, girded himself with two iron bands, and used two others that restricted his shoulders. Since, however, I have already related many things about him in my other works, I will now recount what he told me scarcely six days ago when he came to see me. On that occasion he said, "I happened to know that you wrote about me reciting nine psalters[115] in one day while taking the discipline. Indeed, when I heard this I began to tremble and worry, and, as my conscience rebuked me, began to weep. What a fool I am," I said. "Without my knowledge, look what was written about me, and I still don't know whether I can bring this off. So, let me try again and find out for certain whether I can do it. Therefore, on Wednesday I took off my clothes, and with a switch in both hands, stayed up the whole night and did not stop chanting and whipping myself until on the following day, after finishing twelve psalters in this fashion, I slowly dragged myself through the thirteenth up to the psalm, 'Blessed are they.'"[116] Let me further enlighten you with an example of what often seemed to me a harsh and difficult thing, but which he considered child's play and hardly worth noticing. A certain brother was terrified at beating himself and considered it a fearful burden to scourge himself and bear up under it. But at length he accepted the advice that the lord Dominic frequently gave him and kept on disciplining himself while chanting the entire psalter, to which he added fifty more psalms.

(26) This happened during the night preceding a Sunday, the feast of St. Michael.[117] The next morning, this brother went to the old man and, afraid that he might be thought guilty of indiscretion, related exactly what he had done. Dominic replied in these words: "Brother, don't be bashful and lose courage over your present weakness. God is surely strong enough to lift you up from lowly things to those that are higher and to toughen the milkfed days of your childhood till you grow to

---

115. In *Letter* 44 Damian reports that Dominic spoke of eight psalters, while in *Letter* 50 it was nine, but that he could never complete ten.
116. Ps 31.
117. 29 September, which in 1051, 1056, and 1062 fell on a Sunday.

manly strength." And he added, "I also began gradually, and even though weak and frail, I slowly reached the goal toward which God's goodness led me." And so it happened that he did not accuse him of excessive fervor, as the brother had feared, but rekindled his spirit, keeping him from despair for having done so little. Thus, by the example of this old man in taking the discipline, the custom spread in our area, so that not only men but even noble women eagerly took up this form of purgatory.[118] For the widow of Tethbaldus,[119] a woman of noble birth and high dignity, once told me that by taking the discipline according to a predetermined norm, she had satisfied 100 years of penance.

On the Everlasting Happiness of the Heavenly Jerusalem

(27) You should, therefore, always listen eagerly for an account of good men's deeds so that, on the one hand, if you are able to imitate them, they might earn for you a superabundance of never-ending reward. On the contrary, if you find them beyond your power, they will be more apt to preserve your humility. Let your soul be directed to the things that are promised in the fatherland so that as an exile you may minimize the difficulty that looms on the way. When one looks up and sees a lump of glittering gold, the burden of the journey grows lighter. When a crown is offered at the winner's circle, one readily runs the course. Call to mind, therefore, how fortunate is he who wins the right to enter the marriage banquet in the splendid company of the elect while a vast crowd of the damned is turned away. What an honor it is to be ever in attendance in sight of the creator; to contemplate the spectacle of truth most present before you; to behold God face to face, associated with angelic choirs. There those involved are so filled with attendant joys that they are never concerned about future hardships. There, while the soul enjoys to the full the quiet pleasure of unlimited light, it is unspeakably happy over the rewards of its companions. There the thirsty drink from

---

118. On this early use of *purgatorium* as a substantive see the *Introduction, supra* n. 118. The present letter was written in 1059–1060.

119. On the widow of Tethbald, see Reindel, *Briefe* 2 (1988) 276 n. 60.

the fount of life, and as they drink, they thirst for more.[120] There, indeed, it is impossible for either desire to beget lust or for gratification to turn into loathing. Because they are always in the service of the author of life, they derive from him the very essence of their happiness. Here one discovers the eternal greening of the bloom of youth, the charm of beauty, and the unceasing vigor of good health. In effect, from this eternal source they acquire the power to live forever and to rejoice ineffably and, what is far more important, to grow into the likeness of the creator himself. For, as John the Evangelist states, "When it is revealed, we shall be like him because we shall see him as he really is."[121] Then "death is swallowed up in victory,"[122] and all the corruption of human nature utterly falls away.

(28) Tobias, moreover, said of this city, "The gates of Jerusalem shall be built of sapphire and emerald, and the whole course of its walls of precious stones; all its streets shall be paved with clean white stones, and alleluia shall be sung along its ways."[123] And John says of it, "Each of its gates was made of a single pearl, and the streets of the city were pure gold, transparent as glass."[124] And at once he added, "The city did not need the sun nor the moon, since it was lit by the radiant glory of God, and the lamb was a lighted torch for it."[125] There, moreover, tainted human nature, cleansed of all the filth of passion, will leap for joy, and will endure unsullied in its moral purity and sincerity. In fact, as the body becomes spiritual, it will be in harmony with the soul,[126] and the whole man will in no way disagree with the will of its creator. Then will the words of the bridegroom to his bride be fulfilled: "Come, my spouse, the time of pruning is at hand."[127] For when a shoot is pruned, whatever is superfluous is cut away, leaving behind only what is useful. Consequently, all that the creator has made remains,

---

120. Cf. Damian, *Rhythmus de gaudio paradisi*, Strophe 1ff. (Lokrantz, *L'opera* 80).
121. 1 John 3.2. 122. 1 Cor 15.54.
123. Tob 13.21–22; cf. also Lokrantz, *L'opera* 81.
124. Rev 21.21. 125. Rev 21.23.
126. Cf. Lokrantz, *L'opera* 81. 127. Cant 2.12.

while whatever the devil has added is taken away. There each one's secrets will be laid bare before the eyes of all. There, with all hearts united by the bond of mutual love, none will differ from another in any way, but all will associate unanimously in a common exercise of will. When we celebrate a feast here, all others are omitted; there, however, one always experiences the collective happiness of all festivals, because they who are in fact the cause for celebration are present.

(29) In heaven there is an absence of ignorance and of impossibility, because, by their union with wisdom, the blessed know all things and, with omnipotence, they are able to do all things.[128] There we will be face to face with things revealed: how the Father ineffably begets the son, and how the Holy Spirit proceeds from both of them. There we will see how he who is nowhere absent is everywhere present—not in part but totally; also, how it is possible for him to observe the singular as if he were unconcerned about the universal, and how he beholds universals as if he took no notice of singular affairs; how he who is exalted over heavenly things supports the foundations of the deep; how he penetrates the hidden secrets of the world and yet encompasses all external things. The sweet odor of this place exceeds the powers of all perfumes, surpasses the fragrance of all spices.[129] There melodious instruments caress the ears of the blessed with sweet harmony.[130] There, amid green pastures that fill one with pleasant delight, snow-white lilies never wither and dark red roses and flowering crocus never waste away.[131] Certainly, the reality of the everlasting happiness of the heavenly Jerusalem is incomparably greater than the mind of man can ever conceive, and the mind grasps more than can ever be put in words.

(30) Now, what more can I say of the joys of these blessed inhabitants, since absolutely all the elements are at the service of their desire for utmost happiness and all things obey their every wish and command? For the statement is true that says,

---

128. Cf. Lokrantz, *L'opera* 82. 129. Cf. Lokrantz, *L'opera* 81.
130. Cf. Lokrantz, *L'opera* 83.
131. Cf. Lokrantz, *L'opera* 81, with reference to Prudentius, *Cathemerinon* 5.113–16.

"Whatever the Lord pleases, he does, in heaven and on earth, in the ocean and in the depths."[132] And whatever is said of the head is also worthy of belief in his members.

(31) Venerable sister, may almighty God admit you to these joys; may he who became the price of your redemption be your reward when he takes you to himself. Commend me to your guides, Moses and Aaron, namely, to the holy priests Vitalis and Rudolph.[133] They will know that, contrary to epistolary usage, I inserted titles here to relieve the double tedium of my unpolished and verbose style.

132. Ps 134.6.
133. See *Letter* 129, which was addressed to them. For attempts at their identification, see Reindel, *Briefe* 2 (1988) 280 n. 69.

LETTER 67

Peter Damian to Duke Godfrey of Tuscany. Communicating now by letter what he had often told the duke in person, Damian complained that the duke was neglecting his region, in which nearly 100,000 people lived, treating it as if it were some small country town. He should appoint a regent who would rule and administer the area in his name. But he is especially displeased by the duke's lenient attitude toward criminals, leading to an increase of violence. He attempts to change Godfrey's administration of justice by plying him with arguments from Scripture and by citing examples from secular history. In this letter, for the only time in all his writings, he refers to his birth date—scarcely five years after the death of the Emperor Otto III (+ 1002).

(1059–1063)[1]

TO HIS EXCELLENCE, Duke Godfrey,[2] the monk Peter the sinner sends greetings in the Lord.

(2) One who daily drinks wine, laced with spices and honey, will at length find the accustomed sweetness offensive to his taste, and will be happy to enjoy the tartness of a cheaper and less hearty wine. And, indeed, Solomon says that "a surfeit of honey is bad for a man."[3] Moreover, when eating food smothered with rich sauce, a green salad will inhibit squeamishness and will quiet the inner urge of a nauseated man to relieve himself by retching.

(3) Now, most eminent sir, you drink mead every day, mixed, as it were, with the flavor of nectar, when everyone who speaks to you says only what you wish to hear, and tries to suggest nothing but what will be flattering to your ear. He carefully composes beforehand whatever he must plainly tell you, hammering it out and polishing it as if he were using some work-

---

1. The dating follows Neukirch, *Das Leben* 101f. and Lucchesi, *Vita* no. 203 and 2.155; but see also Woody, *Damiani* 218.
2. On Godfrey, see Reindel, *Gottfried II* and *Briefe* 2 (1988) 280 n. 1.
3. Prov 25.27.

man's tools so that, whatever the subject, it is prompted by the speaker's underlying humility rather than freely spoken with authority. How unfortunate it is, and subject to deception, to be at the height of earthly dignity, for while people say what they think to other men, for the powerful of this world they put together their arguments in words that do not ring true. And rich men are compelled always to hold those suspect, who to others appear unsophisticated. Thus while worldly men drink only your excellency's honied wines, and suggest only what they think will please you; while you enjoy the sweet pleasure of daily flattery, you must not take amiss the bitterness of my words, since it is often a relief to have green and bitter herbs along with sweeter foods.

(4) And so, I now repeat in my letter what I have often said to you in person.[4] I am saying, indeed, that I am greatly displeased that you neglect this principality in which almost 100,000 people live, as if it were some little country town, and do not turn it over to a governor who will rule and administer it. Clearly, you owe an accounting to the severe judge for all over whom you preside by reason of your authority. And to the degree that it redounds to your glory to reach the heights of your power, so will it be the more difficult at the judgment, where you will be held accountable. Therefore, place the burden on someone else, and what you are unable to carry on your own shoulders, you will be strong enough to bear by employing another to whom you have given the task.

(5) This too I find no less displeasing, that in punishing crimes and restraining the daring efforts of evil men you appear to act more leniently than you should, and while you spare the sinner, you are guilty of increasing the number of sins. Surely, when the sternness of justice is weakened, the rule of law is destroyed. And when severe and avenging punishment is suppressed, one grants license to those who dare to commit crime. For inordinate compassion begets disloyalty, and the physician whose hand is uncertain enlarges his patient's wound. He causes the infection to grow, when instead of an incision he

---

4. On Damian's personal contacts with Godfrey, see Lucchesi, *Vita* no. 203.

daily handles it lightly, permitting the wound to be encrusted with a scab. The pharmacist, moreover, who does not mix pungent preparations with his soothing ointments will find that his remedy is of little use in drying up a tumor.

(6) All the members of the Church are not assigned the same office, for one duty is proper to a priest, another to a judge. The former must be the soul of compassion, fondling the Church's children like a forgiving mother, always gathering them to her breast and nourishing them with the richness of her teaching. But it is the duty of the latter to punish the guilty, snatching the innocent from their hands; to hew to the line of right order and justice and not grow slack in his zeal for imposing legal sanctions, not stray from the path of equity, and not weaken his inclination to impose the severity of the Law. He should always remember that the Apostle says, "You wish to have no fear of the authorities? Then continue to do right and you will have their approval, for they are God's agents working for your good. But if you are doing wrong, then you will have cause to fear them; it is not for nothing that they hold the power of the sword."[5] From these words you should understand that the prince's sword is quite different from priestly symbols of dignity. You do not buckle on your sword to stroke or caress the evil deeds of violent men, but to prepare to cut them down with your weapon's flashing blows. And so the Apostle continues, "For they are God's agents of punishment, for retribution on the offender."[6]

(7) Therefore, if the prince is God's agent who dispenses retribution to the offender, he who gently pats criminals and villains on the head is undoubtedly the agent of the devil. And just as he who punishes the wicked renders service to God, so he who handles evildoers lightly becomes the agent of the adversary, the devil. The sword will surely grow rusty if it is always left in the scabbard and is never bared to inflict vengeance. A sword becomes scabrous if it is not polished and is forever restrained from inflicting wounds.[7] On the other hand, Ezekiel

---

5. Rom 13.3–4.
6. Rom 13.4.
7. Cf. Lucanus 1.243.

says, "A sword is sharpened and burnished, sharpened to kill its victims, burnished to flash like lightning."[8] The judge's tribunal is truly far removed from the authority of the bishop. The former clearly carries a sword, that he may unsheath it to punish those who live to flaunt justice. The latter is satisfied with merely the staff of innocence, that he might quietly and peacefully keep watch over discipline. Nevertheless, if a bishop shows excessive leniency to his subjects, he too will deserve to be condemned by the sentence of God's anger. For it was the high priest Eli of whom God spoke to Samuel: "Because he knew of his sons' evil deeds and did not rebuke them, therefore I have sworn to the family of Eli that the wickedness of his house will never be expiated by sacrifices and offerings."[9] So let a judge continue being negligent in composing the cases and affairs of those in court, and spend the greater part of the day attending masses and saying prayers. But note that it was said above that not even the sin of a bishop can ever be expiated by sacrifices and offerings, because Eli did not punish the evil deeds of his sons.

(8) And think for a moment what kind of a sin it is to be negligent in regard to one's subjects, so that not even sacrifices and offerings that are primarily effective in washing away sins will be able to effect expiation.[10] There are many people who are deceived by the error of irregular compassion, foolishly thinking that they are pleasing to God; but in reality they violently fight against him, and for that reason they deserve his wrath, while they are of the opinion that they should receive his grace. As they bestow forgiveness on others, inspired by improper compassion, they themselves incur the force of God's anger.

(9) One of the company of the prophets ordered a certain man to strike him. But because he refused to do so, he was suddenly attacked by a lion, and died.[11] Ahab thought that he was pleasing God when in his kindness he called Ben-hadad,

---

8. Ezek 21.9–10.   9. 1 Sam 3.13–14.
10. Cf. Ryan, *Sources* 92 no. 176, citing Burchard, *Decretorum libri* 15.19, depending on Gregory I, *Reg.* 11.46 (MG Epist. 2.319); JE 1837.
11. Cf. 1 Kgs 20.35–36.

the king of Syria, his brother, even inviting him to sit in his chariot.[12] But note what his ill-advised mercy caused him to hear: "Because you let that man go," said the Lord, "a man who deserved to die, your life will be forfeit for his life, your people for his people."[13] Saul did not kill Agag, the king of the Amalekites, but after winning his victory, held him as his prisoner. For this act of compassion he deserved to be rewarded with these words: "Because you have rejected the word of the Lord, the Lord has rejected you as king."[14] The Israelites showed mercy to the Midianite women. But Moses said to them, "Why did you spare the women? Now kill all the men, also the boys, and kill every woman who has had intercourse with a man."[15]

(10) And again, after the figure of the bull-calf had been fashioned at Horeb, Moses said to the Levites, "Each of you kill his brother, his friend, his neighbor."[16] And after 23,000 men had been killed, he said, "Today you have consecrated yourselves to the Lord, because you have each turned against your own son and your own brother, and have brought a blessing upon yourselves."[17] When the Amalekite bragged that he had killed Saul, pretending that he had carried off, not the helmet, but the crown from the warrior's head, he was cut down by David's sword and died.[18] Also, those who had killed Ishbosheth, as they brought his head to David as if it were a gift, did not escape his sword.[19] They had hoped to receive a gift from him, but instead were met by the avenger of the murder they had committed.

(11) Peter, also, did not allow the lie of Ananias and Sapphira to go unpunished, but cut them down with the sword to cause terror in the hearts of others who might perhaps be tempted to do the same.[20] Paul, too, in trying to compel his disciples to avoid excesses, threatened to apply the rod to those who had committed sin.[21] Likewise, our savior, who appeared to be as meek

---

12. Cf. 1 Kgs 20.33.
13. 1 Kgs 20.42.
14. 1 Sam 15.23.
15. Num 31.15–17.
16. Exod 32.27.
17. Exod 32.29.
18. 2 Sam 1.1–15.
19. 2 Sam 4.8–12.
20. Cf. Acts 5.1–11.
21. Cf. 1 Cor 4.19–21.

as a lamb, soon after he had granted Peter power over heaven and earth, suddenly rebuked him in this stern fashion: "Away with you, Satan," he said, "you are a stumbling block to me, because you think as men think, not as God thinks."[22]

(12) Why is it that we so often find holy men attacking sinners, either with words of reproach or with avenging action, except that it might become perfectly obvious that in this mortal life one does not behave properly if he does not blend harshness with what is soft and agreeable. For where discipline is completely abandoned, where strict punishment prescribed by law is suppressed, it will follow that weak human nature, always prone to evil, will be inclined to act illicitly. And all the guilt of his subjects will certainly be heaped on the head of him whose duty it is to restrain them with the reins of discipline, so that they do not rush headlong into crime. What else can we call a prince's inordinate clemency, if not complete disorder for his people? For as he refrains from exercising the control of government, all his subjects, like unbridled horses, rush over the cliff. Let everyone do what he will, and then you will clearly see what was often said in the book of Judges: "In those days there was no king in Israel and every man did what was right in his own eyes."[23] Also that which was said by Michaiah in the time of the wicked King Ahab: "These men have no master, let each of them go home in peace."[24] In Saul's day it was also said that "the blades of the plowshares and mattocks and tridents and axes were blunted, right down to setting the goads."[25] The blades of utensils are indeed dull when the zeal and ardor of rulers are extinguished. Nor is there a goad that will pierce, when there is no one to correct the failings of sinners. Paul began to feel this goad piercing him when the voice of God spoke to him: "It is hard for you to kick against the goad."[26]

(13) What I am now about to tell you, I did not learn from reading history, but it was reported in simple words by Count Ubaldus, a well-spoken and prudent man. "The Emperor Theodosius,"[27] he said,

22. Matt 16.23.
23. Judg 17.6.
24. 1 Kgs 22.17.
25. 1 Sam 13.21.
26. Acts 9.5.
27. This narrative cannot be found in the sources. But it is recorded that

was accustomed to talk with a certain religious hermit, whose directions the emperor used to obey, and who revealed to him his innermost secrets of conscience. Now this servant of God, being a simple and honest man, almost unaware of the evils of this world, strictly warned the emperor that he should be merciful to lawbreakers; that he refrain from punishing the guilty; that he should not seek revenge on his brother, since he would beg forgiveness for himself from the heavenly judge. For as that judge will say, "Whatever measure you deal out to others will be dealt to you."[28]

(14) And so the emperor accepted the advice of the holy man, and began releasing criminals and evildoers without punishing their crimes, pardoning idolators and those who should have been chastised by law, and also forgiving all who had dared to usurp the rights of others. At these actions, the leading men of the realm complained, the officers in the royal administration predicted the imminent ruin of the world and declared that in every way it would be thrown into turmoil unless human affairs were remedied by a return to equity and justice. Finally, they deplored the widespread destruction and violence brought on by the lack of energy caused by this superstitious and silly piety, the dissolution of the ordinances of law, and the inciting of wicked and perverse men to commit every criminal and harmful act induced by this shameless grant of freedom. Disturbed by this list of complaints, the emperor despatched a courier to the man of God, earnestly pressed him for his advice on how he should reply to this dissension, and asked especially what he should do.

(15) After the man of God had carefully examined this message, and thinking over the possibility of changing his mind, he did not say a word, but replied by acting in a most mysterious way. While the bearer of the imperial message looked on, he began thoroughly combing his hair, and whatever fell into or covered his lap he at once threw into the fire. Then, taking up a hoe, he went into the garden. There he dug up whatever was harmful, removed dead plants and, weeding here and there, tended to the growing bushes and broke up the earth about the shrubs. Some, however, he pulled up so that, with their roots exposed, they would wither; others he nourished and cared for, so that they would mature to full growth. After finishing these tasks, rich with mystic meaning, and still holding his tongue, by sign he indicated

---

Theodosius had contact with hermits, from whom he received prophetic reports; cf. Lippold, *Theodosius* 37, 48.
28. Matt 7.2.

LETTER 67

that the messenger return to his lord and tell him in detail what he had seen.

(16) The latter returned quite angry, and began to grumble and protest that he had not been sent to a sane man, but rather to one who was psychotic and deranged. "I had hoped," he said, "that he would instruct me in fluent speech and, taking up my questions, would inform me about everything in a clearly phrased reply. But like a crazy man, completely out of his mind, he either combed his neglected hair, or taking a hoe began to chop up the garden, as if I should make a big issue of his lice and other parasitic guests, or as if I were looking for instruction in gardening."

(17) Then as the emperor listened carefully to what his courier had to say, and coming to the conclusion that what the hermit had done was of supreme importance, he replied that this was a thing not to be laughed at, but something quite profound, an answer in clear and certain terms to what he had sought. "The servant of God," he said, "gave me a better answer by his deeds than by his words, and by the twofold oracle of his actions solved the problems contained in my question. What could be clearer than combing his hair and then throwing what he had removed into the fire, as if he were saying, By the many teeth in the comb, that is, by careful and legitimate examination, whatever is good is made clean and remains behind. He wished, moreover, to repeat the same idea by caring for his garden, so that as he uprooted the noxious herbs with the soil around them, he cultivated the good plants that they might grow more luxuriously."

(18) When those who were present had heard this, they began to admire what previously they had taken to be the ridiculous nonsense of an old man as actually a profound mystery of spiritual wisdom. At that, the emperor, strengthened in his resolve as by a prophetic oracle, began to punish the violence of those who practiced injustice, to strike back with strict application of the law at those charged with crime, to restrain lawbreakers from attempting criminal acts, to put fear into the hearts of evildoers by using the power of his imperial authority, and to restore general peace. And thus the world, which through his inactivity had begun to fall apart, was revived through the rule of equity and justice.

(19) I have related this story, not that I take it as having happened just that way, but have presented here what was reported to me in the course of conversation while it is still fresh in my memory. Nevertheless, the ancients would not have passed on

to us this well-known case if they had not thought that this tale would serve to edify those who came after them.

(20) Scarcely five years before I was born, Otto III passed away, a man who had magnificently reigned as emperor and had vigorously ruled the Roman state.[29] When he was hardly more than twenty years of age, among other outstanding deeds, he put out the eyes of three leading men of the realm, namely, the counts Rodulfus, Raimundus, and Arimundus.[30] By this well-known act of justice he so terrified the plunderers of other men's property, and so established peace and security within the empire, that almost everyone within the confines of his realm lived in fear of him and never dared to overstep the limits of his own rights. And so it was that his fame spread from mouth to mouth. Six eyes were put out, and to a whole realm peace was restored. Three men were blinded, and the light of tranquility that they had sought was restored to all.

(21) You also, most splendid lord, should live by the example of holy princes who upheld the law. Let the idea of excessive compassion be totally foreign to you, and always take steps to safeguard justice in dealing with the people committed to your charge. For it is written, "Happy are they who act justly and do right at all times."[31] And Solomon says, "Love justice, you rulers of the earth."[32] Thus, always inflamed with zeal for right order, walk now on the path of justice that you may finally return to the author of justice himself, not to be judged, but to reap your reward.[33]

---

29. Otto died on 24 January 1002 (*Reg. Imp.* 2.3 [1956] no. 1450 IVa), whence we derive Damian's birth in 1007.
30. Cf. Reindel, *Briefe* 2 (1988) 288 n. 11.
31. Ps 105.3.   32. Wis 1.1.
33. Cf. Burchard, *Decretorum libri* 15.16 (PL 140.898A).

LETTER 68

Peter Damian to Duke Godfrey of Tuscany. The theme of his previous letter (*Letter* 67) is repeated: the duke's leniency is notorious; he must practice justice in punishing criminals so that the innocent will not suffer. He buttresses his argument with citations from the Greek and Latin Fathers, and at great length proposes the life of Godfrey's predecessor, the duke and marquis, Hugh of Tuscany, as his model. It comes somewhat as a surprise that an eleventh-century contemplative hermit, albeit a cardinal, should demonstrate so great an interest in the secular affairs of central Italy during the previous century.

(1059–1063)[1]

TO THE MOST excellent Marquis Godfrey,[2] the monk Peter the sinner sends his greetings.

(2) Messenger after messenger is often sent so that, at least by badgering requests, a matter that is highly important may be effected. For even the judge mentioned in the gospel,[3] but one who did not live by gospel precepts, a man who cared nothing for God nor man, at length acknowledged that he was worn out by a woman's untiring persistence. You, however, outstanding among your peers by reason of the decency of an upright life, and someone special in the sight of God because of your revered chastity, should not be led to reject my request as if I were some adversary quarreling with you, but rather as one whom you see proposing something that is to your benefit. Recently I sent you a letter on the strict application of justice, which I now repeat in writing, not retreating from the matter I formerly proposed.

(3) Therefore, most eminent sir, put the scales in equipoise, keep the tongue of the balance level, and always maintain the

---

1. For the dating, cf. *Letter* 67 n. 1.
2. On Godfrey, see *Letter* 67 n. 2.
3. Cf. Luke 18.1–8.

scales of legal sanctions swaying evenly before your eyes. But perhaps you will here object in the words of Solomon: "Do not be excessively just."[4] And, on the other hand, I will answer you: Do not be overcompassionate. For just as by unrestrained justice the irresolute are broken, so under too much compassion the spirit of license will boldly run to unbridled insolence. Was indiscreet kindness in evidence in the words, "If you take the stick to your son, you will preserve him from the jaws of death"?[5] Or again, "A father who spares the rod hates his son."[6] And elsewhere, "A man who loves his son will whip him often."[7] And that other advice, "An unbroken horse turns out stubborn, and an unchecked son turns out headstrong. Pamper a boy and he will shock you; play with him and he will grieve you. Do not share his laughter, for fear of sharing his pain. You will only end by grinding your teeth."[8] So, if a father should use correction and the rod on an only son, how much more should this be true of a prince with his people, so that a great number of them may not perish in their attempt to act with unbridled liberty. Hence the Scriptures have it, "A king untutored is the people's ruin, but wise rulers make a city fit to live in."[9]

(4) Therefore, that the people who are your subjects be kept from harm through the maintenance of a just regime, it is required that when you preside at the bench you dispense justice, and that you appoint men through whom you rule the provinces, that they strictly carry out the prescripts of the law. And so, as the wise man said, "A wise judge will judge his people, and the government of a sensible ruler will be sound." And he quickly added, "Like ruler, like ministers; and like leader of a city, like its inhabitants."[10] Clearly, what is more holy, more pleasing to God, or more preeminent in Christian living than to enforce justice and to oppose with the force of legitimate authority those who are about to act unlawfully, in which case it applies equally to criminals and to their victims? For the for-

4. Eccl 7.17.
6. Prov 13.24.
8. Sir 30.8–10.
10. Sir 10.1–2.

5. Prov 23.14.
7. Sir 30.1.
9. Sir 10.3.

mer, it serves to prevent them from incurring the punishment for violence; for the latter, to avoid the danger of future calamity; for the former, that they be content with what they have and do not seize another man's property; for the latter who are guaranteed public protection, that they do not lose what is theirs; for the former, that in doing harm to their neighbor they do not provoke the sword of divine anger; and for the latter, that always grateful that they are free from a climate of crime, they may rejoice in giving praise to God.

(5) Indeed, what sweeter sacrifice can one offer to God than to release orphans from the hands of violent men, to protect widows, to put the down and out on their feet again, and to restore the lost title to those who were robbed and cheated of their property? Therefore it was written, "In giving a verdict be a kind father to orphans and like a husband to their mother; then the Most High will call you his son, and his love for you will be greater than a mother's."[11] For what is greater, and in human affairs more preeminent, than that for which a mortal man becomes a child of God? God repays him from the depths of his love, not like a father but, what is still more significant, like a mother, so that he who stands and fights for orphans and widows against the crimes of the wicked may himself rest quietly like a nursing child at the comforting breast of God's goodness.

(6) All[12] speak with one voice and concur in expressing the same opinion, both the Fathers in the Old Testament and the holy doctors of the Church, in the matter of using the severity of the Law to punish the excesses of wicked men. For in the Law it is written, "You shall not allow criminals to live."[13] And the Apostle says among other things, "Submit yourselves, whether it be to the sovereign as supreme, or to the governors as his deputies for the punishment of criminals and the com-

---

11. Sir 4.10–11.
12. For a discussion of Damian's dependence here on Burchard, *Decretorum libri* 6.43 (PL 140.775f.), and for the identification of the biblical and patristic texts there cited, see Ryan, *Sources* 92f. no. 179; Reindel, *Briefe* 2 (1988) 291 n. 6.
13. Exod 22.18.

mendation of those who do right."[14] And St. Augustine says, "How out of touch with reality is it to spare one person and put everyone else in danger? For all are contaminated by the one sinner." And Jerome says, "He who strikes down the wicked because they are wicked, and has good reason to kill in cutting down evil men, is the agent of God." And elsewhere he says, "To punish murderers and idolators is not shedding blood." And St. Ambrose says, "To kill an enemy is a victory, a guilty man justice, an innocent man murder."

(7) These holy men would certainly not have said such things about penalizing criminals unless they had been convinced that capital punishment would also to some degree be good for their souls. On this point, passing over in the meantime what others had said, I will briefly cite here the opinion of Bishop Cyril of Jerusalem: "Death," he said, "which is imposed as a punishment for sin, wipes out the sin of him on whom it was inflicted by law."[15] Thus sin is absolved by the penalty of death, and nothing remains of this crime for which the victim must await the day of judgment and the punishment of eternal fire. When one willingly sins, and has it on his conscience, and it is not wiped out by some punishment or penalty, it goes along with him after death; and because he did not undergo temporal punishment here, he will pay for it with eternal suffering.

(8) Do you not see how much more serious it is to approve of sin than to suffer death? For here death is inflicted as a punishment, and the criminal is not sentenced twice by the just judge for the same crime.[16] But when sin is not absolved by punishment, it remains to be wiped away by eternal flames. Clearly, in this holy man's words it is asserted that the guilty man is absolved by temporal punishment but, by granting him immunity, he is made to suffer eternal torment.

(9) But, that I may give you an example close to home, or, as I might say, one that is local, no one better comes to mind than the duke and marquis Hugh of glorious memory, who

---

14. 1 Pet 2.13–14.
15. This citation could not be identified.
16. See Landau, "Ursprünge und Entwicklung."

came to rule the same territory that you now hold.[17] He came into possession of both principalities, I say, the one washed by the Tyrrhenian Sea, the other by the Adriatic. But when he considered that because of the violence of unjust men he was unable to rule both regions, he willingly ceded to the emperor the margravate of Camerino along with the duchy of Spoleto, but retained Tuscany for himself.

(10) If my memory serves me right, this was the time when the prince of Capua,[18] as he was removing his gloves, was suddenly surrounded by men who were conspiring against him, acting as if they would assist him. Suddenly they clapped both of his hands together and, unsheathing their swords, ran him through and killed him. As soon as that incomparably virtuous man, the marquis Hugh we spoke of before, heard the news, he did not waste a moment but at once surrounded the city of Capua with a goodly number of his troops. He did not break off the siege by his armed forces until he had taken the city by storm and killed his lord's murderers who rightly deserved to die.

(11) So many similar accounts of his many virtues are reported of him that with the passage of time his splendid reputation was never forgotten, but remained fresh and vivid, always reverently recalled when people came together. I could write of some of these accounts that would be greatly edifying to those who came after him. But since as they were told to me I neglected to take note of the words describing these events, and so that, God forbid, I do not mistakenly recount them, I will let them to be written down by others.

(12) Nevertheless, I shall recall one small event that I heard of him when he was still a boy. His father, the marquis Obertus,[19] the natural son of King Hugh, was married to Guilla, the daughter of the illustrious Marquis Boniface. Not long after his marriage he incurred the anger of Emperor Otto I and thereupon, leaving his wife, he fled as an exile to Pannonia.

17. On Hugh of Tuscany, see Reindel, *Briefe* 2 (1988) 293 n. 10.
18. On the events here described, see Reindel, *Briefe* 2 (1988) 293 nn. 11–12.
19. On whom, see Reindel, *Briefe* 2 (1988) 294 n. 13.

When after many years he was restored to the emperor's good graces, he returned, and was astounded to find his wife with a child now almost grown up. He denied that he was the father of the boy who stood there before him and, overcome by jealousy, he accused his wicked wife of committing an indecent crime. He stated that he was unaware of this unforeseen event, denied that he had any knowledge of how she had conceived, and declared it impossible that he was the father, since his wife had not been pregnant when he left.

(13) At that, the affair, now widely known, continued to be discussed, and this grave reproach could be laid to rest only by oath in open court. Both sides agreed to this solution, and an assembly of churchmen gathered in a large hall of their great house. As they took their places at length at the bench, only the boy stood before them. If he went up to his father whom he had never seen, he would undoubtedly clear his mother of all suspicion. And then what happened? Holy bishops were present, and along with monks and abbots, priests of lower rank were also in attendance. They cried and groaned and sighed, raised their eyes to heaven and sadly beat their breasts with their fists while bitter tears flowed down their cheeks. The boy was then set free, without help from his tutor or nurse, and he began to move about. The father sat with the crowd without any special seat to distinguish him from the rest and, bypassing everyone else, the boy promptly went up to him, and took hold of him as if attracted by one whom he knew very well.

(14) It was thus that he freed his mother of suspicion as he went to his father at the inspiration of God. And so, a mother's shame was swept away, a son was granted to his father, and the unaccustomed love of both parents for one another was restored by their child. All who were present, overwhelmed by such a miracle, celebrated with the joy they had hoped for, and happily gave proper thanks to God whose work it was.

(15) The same man, when he went riding, often used to leave behind the crowd from his court while he rode on far ahead, either alone or accompanied by just one companion. He would then urge on the farmers and shepherds with these words: "What do you think about that man they call the marquis? Isn't

he cruel and wicked in oppressing the poor, ruining the land, and wasting all the income from his property?" To which they replied, "Not at all," they said, "not at all. What you're saying, fellow, is totally false. There is no power anywhere on earth that so avoids violence and destruction, that rules the people under him with such peace and security. We hope he lives forever to take care of the poor, and may his years be long as he provides for all his subjects." Hearing that, the marquis praised the Lord. Then he would often say, "I always hope to act so kindly toward my subjects, especially the farmers, that the grain that falls from the foaming mouth of my horse when he is grazing may be picked up by the farmers' little pigs following right behind him."

(16) We might observe that when he inquired what others were saying about him, he was only imitating the example of our redeemer. Indeed, even though he certainly knew all things, like someone who was unaware he still asked his disciples, "Who do men say that the Son of Man is?"[20] When they told him of the various opinions that people had, he continued, "And you, who do you say I am?"[21] This he did, so that the king of the angels might set an example for the rulers of men, not that they should pay attention to the flattery that was used, but to inquire about what was thought of them when they were not present. Thus from this report they might correct what was deemed reprehensible, yet gladly improve on the good things they heard the people say of them.

(17) Now, to say a few words about the last days of the marquis. As he was in bed, afflicted with his last illness, and the light of his whole principality was burning low, amid the tears of a large gathering of his people of various rank, a certain venerable bishop, whose name I cannot at present recall, saw a piece of wood burning on the fire with the following words written on it: "The Marquis Hugh lived for fifty years." Those who were present took this to be a favorable omen and a sign that he would recover, thinking that there was still hope. But shortly thereafter the marquis passed away.

20. Matt 16.13.   21. Matt 16.15.

(18) I may also add that he built six monasteries belonging to his jurisdiction,[22] which with great liberality he endowed, not only with lands and serfs, but also with gold and silver vessels and various ecclesiastical ornaments. In one of these, especially observant and venerable, erected in the city of Florence to the honor of the Mother of God, his body lies buried.[23] When the Emperor Otto III,[24] who then ruled the Roman Empire, heard of his death, because he felt a certain amount of envy toward him, cried out with relief, "The fowler's trap is broken and we have escaped."[25] But shortly after, and that the same year, he too was dead. And so he who had so vilely rejoiced when another man died, met his own death, which he had not foreseen, not aware of what the wise man said, "Do not be smug over an enemy's death; remember that we must all die."[26]

(19) I think that it will also not be out of place to add something I often heard of his distinguished renown that flourished among the holy monks of that same monastery. They say that the marquis, of whom we have been speaking, appeared one night in a dream to the abbot Marinus[27] who then presided over that monastery, and told him that, as was customary, he should turn over his body so that it lay on its back and not face downward as it now reposed. Believing what had been told him in the vision, and wishing to verify it, the abbot actually found the body of this good man lying on its face, as it had been revealed to him. He therefore turned it over, as was only proper, so that it lay on the other side. We should not be surprised that this man wished to observe the burial customs, just as the head of all the elect wished them to be carried out in his own regard. For John the evangelist says, "Joseph and Nicodemus took the

---

22. On these six monastic foundations that Damian attributes to Hugh of Tuscany, see Reindel, *Briefe* 2 (1988) 296 n. 15.
23. On Hugh's grave in the Badia at Florence, see Davidsohn, *Forschungen* 31ff.
24. Hugh died on 21 December 1001 (cf. Falce, *Ugo di Tuscia* 162), Otto III on 24 January 1002 (see *supra*, Letter 67 n. 29). On Otto's citation of Ps 123, see Uhlirz, *Jahrbücher* 2.387.
25. Ps 123.7.   26. Sir 8.8.
27. On Abbot Marinus, see Falce, *Ugo di Tuscia* 70f.

body of Jesus and wrapped it, with the spices, in strips of linen cloth according to Jewish burial customs."[28]

(20) Most eminent sir, hold up this predecessor of yours before you as a mirror, and use as models the lives of others who checked the evil deeds of men by enforcing justice. Free the innocent from the hands of those who practice violence, and break the lofty necks of the proud and of those who act contrary to the prescripts of the Law. Let evil men see in you a prince, and not deride you as a priest. Tear out the roots of noxious weeds, so that fruitbearing plants may spread their leaves. Use the hoe of legitimate severity in such a way in cultivating the field that the Lord committed to you, so that you may deserve to bring to the heavenly barns a harvest that has grown a hundredfold, and to receive the financial reward from him who hired you.

28. John 19.40.

LETTER 69

Peter Damian to Boniface, cardinal bishop of Albano. He here returns to the classic theme that true renewal in the Church depends on the quality of the bishop. Damian speaks of the evil of simony and, in passing, of lay investiture, both of which lie at the root of the current problems of the Church. The cleric who buys his way to a prelacy is an obvious simonist; but he who achieves the same objective by prostituting himself at a royal or imperial court is worse, because the price in the sale is himself. Princes, too, are warned to avoid the practice of appointing sycophant clerics, so that they not be tarred with the same brush.

(ca. 1059–1060)[1]

TO THE MOST reverend bishop, Sir Boniface,[2] the monk Peter the sinner sends greetings.

(2) The wise man warns us, "Consult a buyer," he says, "about a sale, an envious man about gratitude, an unloving man about compassion, an honest man about honesty."[3] To which, moreover, he had previously added, "Consult a religious man about sanctity and a just man about justice."[4] And so, I cannot more aptly direct my remarks on bishops to anyone other than to a bishop. While many things about present day bishops displease me, venerable father, this is the most intolerable, I think: that as some of them feverishly seek after ecclesiastical honors, smoking like Mount Etna, they obscenely prostitute themselves like groveling slaves in vassalage to powerful men. They desert the churches as they hunger for churches, and while they seize tyrannical power over the citizens of a town, they scorn the idea, I might say, of being fellow citizens. They escape from military service that they might be

---

1. Dating follows Lucchesi, *Vita* 2.149.
2. On Boniface of Albano, see Hüls, *Kardinäle* 89f. and Zafarana, *Bonifacio* 113f.
3. Sir 37.12–13; on the variant from the Vulgate, cf. Sabatier 2.478.
4. Sir 37.12; Sabatier 2.478.

placed in command of knights, and while they are not ashamed to exchange a palace for the temple of God, they pass from the clerical state into the ranks of laymen. They lay down the arms of virtue, desert the forces of spiritual service, go over to the imperial court, and take on military obligations. They do not shy away from accepting the means of support along with the rest, and grasp only for the office of leadership or command. Indeed, as they do not enter by the door of the church, but rather through the secular postern gate, they become not shepherds of the flock, but thieves and robbers, as truth itself has said, "The man who does not enter the sheepfold by the door is nothing but a thief or a robber."[5]

(3) Moreover, a military commander is not brought in but is chosen from the ranks of the same army. Often one who is born in the same kingdom is promoted to royal estate. Finally, someone from among the serfs of the same estate is advanced to the office of steward. So then, why is it that only the Church of God is handed over to some outsider, some unknown man, as if it were some cheap tavern? If earthly things are distributed among members of the household, why is holy Church, which is the kingdom of God and the court of the heavenly empire, granted to strangers while its own members are turned down? From wherever he might come, if a person is chosen by those over whom he is to preside, he is not considered an outsider. But who would allow ecclesiastical authority to be granted to a man who deserts the Church to obtain possession of a church, and refuses to render service to his own, that he might claim for himself authority over others.

(4) Moreover, since the prophet says of the upright man, "that he snapped his fingers at every gift,"[6] who can protect him from the distribution of gifts, if he has turned over even himself to the authority of a stranger's service and is found guilty of lavishing his resources to finance campaigns of long duration? It is clear that the prophet's statement should be understood in this way, that there are three kinds of gifts, namely, a gift of the hand, a gift of service, and a gift of the

5. John 10.1.   6. Isa 33.15.

tongue. Obviously, a gift of the hand is money; a gift of service is the obedience required by vassalage; a gift of the tongue is flattering approbation.[7]

(5) If we properly consider these three types of gift, the one that is placed in the middle contains at once the first and the third. In the obedience required by vassalage, we consequently recognize both the gift of the hand, which is money, and the gift of the tongue, which is flattering approbation. For who has more obviously learned to spend money for acquiring honors than he who wastes such sums on horses and equipment, or to adorn himself in costly clothes? And in this he exceeds a man who spends money only once, because not being content to disburse only his wealth, he does not hesitate also to subject himself like a slave to the power of his lord.

(6) So who will argue that, given the occasion, he will smother his lord with affable words, that he will delight him with fawning flattery? And to win his good will, the clever observer searches for that which will please him most. Should his lord's eyes sparkle, or his attitude so indicate, he calmly pretends that it is a great festival. He watches every nod, as if he were awaiting his master's command like the voice of Phoebus speaking through the Sibylline oracle.[8] If he is commanded to go, he takes to his heels; if ordered to stay, he stands there petrified. If his lord gets excited, he begins to sweat; if he is warm, the latter complains of the heat. And if it becomes a bit cool, he must appear numb and shiver with the cold. If his master wishes to sleep, he must grow weary; if he has eaten his fill, he must do the belching. And thus, since he is not his own man, he may not say anything but what seems to please his lord.

(7) Isaiah spoke of similar people when he said, "They say to the seers, 'you shall not see,' and to the visionaries, 'you shall have no true visions; give us smooth words and seductive visions. Turn aside, leave the straight path, let the Holy One of Israel get out of my sight.'"[9] And thus, according to the psalm-

---

7. Cf. *Letter* 48 n. 17.
8. See Papias, *Vocabularium latinum* 268, 318; D. Detschew, "Apollon," RAC 1 (1950) 524–29.
9. Isa 30.10–11.

ist, as he heaps oily words of flattery upon him, he anoints his mind, which is the source of all thought. "My head," he says, "shall not be anointed with the oil of wicked men."[10] And Solomon states, "My son, if sinners should flatter you, do not agree with them."[11] For sinners use deceptive words when with flattery they suggest that something wicked be done, or praise you when you have done it.

(8) Now, with this evidence from Scripture it becomes clear that whoever indulges in flattery deserves especially to be called a sinner, indeed a great sinner. And when the psalmist says that "the sinner is praised because of his own desires"[12] and he is blessed who does evil, both he who praises and he who willingly accepts praise are forced to bear their guilt in common.

(9) Therefore, this kind of gift is a greater sin than the other gifts, and is more difficult to forgive, since the other two can easily be found in its absence. But without the other two, this type can scarcely ever be successfully given. For in the case of those who sell a church, if they are prompted by avarice, it suffices to consider its value in money; but if they are conceited, often only flattery will be accepted as a substitute for paying the price. But those who surrender themselves to earthly princes for the sake of acquiring preferment must both be lavish with their money and not forget to ingratiate themselves with their patrons by fondling them with fawning compliments. They will never refrain from giving money if they become a prince's vassal and ambitiously seek a prelacy. And if they serve him with the purpose of achieving power and acquiring wealth, they will offer themselves along with everything that they have. They will humble themselves so that later with impunity they may be proud; they will act like footmen to gain preferment, be worn thin by their efforts, so as later to rejoice; they will suffer poverty so that afterwards they may grow fat from continuous banqueting at the wedding feast; and like someone at the bargaining counter, they will mortgage

10. Ps 140.5. 11. Prov 1.10.
12. Ps 10.3.

their service to buy an empire. "They like to have places of honor at feasts and the chief seats in synagogues, to be greeted respectfully in the street, and to be addressed as 'rabbi.'"[13]

(10) Let others give a sum of senseless metal, let them weigh out a certain amount of stupid money; let them count the coins and consider the value in vessels carved in bas-relief. Let others, I say, give money; these men offer themselves as the price. Is not the unremitting service of vassalage a worthy price to pay?

(11) But now, moving from things of the spirit to marriage in the flesh, should we say that Jacob, who was in service for twenty years to earn his wives,[14] did not pay the price just because he did not give money to Laban, his father-in-law? But listen to what Scripture has to say about how his two wives complained. "Are we," they asked, "no longer to have any part or lot in our father's house?" And then they continued, "Does he not look on us as foreigners, now that he has sold us and used up the money that was paid for us?"[15] Obviously, since Jacob gave no money for his wives, but only tended his father-in-law's flocks, and as he worked for him as a shepherd, he was rewarded by marrying his two daughters. Do you wish to hear the price in Jacob's own words? "By day the heat consumed me and the frost by night, and sleep deserted me, and so for twenty years I worked for you in your household."[16] David, too, payed Saul nothing more for his daughter than service in his armed forces. So he sent messengers to his brother-in-law Ishbosheth and said, "Hand over to me my wife Michal to whom I was betrothed at the price of a hundred Philistine foreskins."[17] He considered the victory he had won by his effort to be worth the dowry, and Saul accepted it in lieu of some amount of money as the betrothal price. "Tell David this," he said, "all the king

---

13. Matt 23.6–7. This discussion is quite similar to that found in Atto of Vercelli, *Libellus de pressuris ecclesiasticis* 133f. See Reindel, *Briefe* 2 (1988) 301 n. 7. For a comparison of Atto and Damian, see Wemple, "Atto of Vercelli" *Temi e testi* 27 (1979) 145–68.
14. Cf. Gen 28 and 30.
15. Gen 31.14–15.
16. Gen 31.40–41.
17. 2 Sam 3.14.

wants as the bride-price is the foreskins of a hundred Philistines, by way of vengeance on the king's enemies."[18]

(12) Therefore Laban sold his daughters and consumed the price that was paid, not because he sequestered the money he had gained, but because he accepted payment in wearisome service. So Saul sought no gift of gold or silver in the marriage of his daughter, but accepted the effort of battle and the symbol of victory in place of the dowry; so he must be considered a seller of the Church, who pays for what he wickedly hopes to attain by giving his service in vassalage. And since he who receives the price may be said to sell the Church, he should more appropriately be thought of as selling it many times over, because he drags out the deal, once he entered it, by long, and I might say, protracted haggling. And the unhappy cleric, the more he serves with pretended humility, the greater sum of money he expends, as it were, since by his adulation in chasing after the title of bishop, he puts on the mask of a parasite. While ambitiously striving to be a bishop, he takes on the role of an actor; and so he must be called, not just some ordinary simonist, but a simonist through and through, because whatever could be done to sell the Church, he did by practicing threefold corruption. Nor should he brag that he had not payed out money, since what was still more precious, he offered himself in the deal. In doing so, he was lost in a shipwreck of hard labor, and at the same time wasted no small amount of his own substance.

(13) Let us imagine, for example, two clerics who own property of equal size worth 200 pounds. One of them goes to the royal court and gradually pays out for personal expenses what he had stashed away in a handkerchief; the other, like Jacob, stayed in his house and did not have to expand or contract his purse already bulging with money. At length, both of them were assigned a diocese. The one miserable monger gave all the money he had stored in his purse as the price for this sacrilegious deal, while the other who was in service at the court,

18. 1 Sam 18.25.

gave nothing extra, but took up his stewardship of his church as if he had obtained it for nothing. Which of these, I ask, paid the most for his church? Was it not he who, while handing over nothing to his patron, was so burdened with toil and trouble, and had spent all that he had during his long and oppressive service, while the other got his office cheaper and effortlessly paid his money to the trafficker? For it is reasonable to think that he who lost all that he possessed along with his effort, payed more than the man who quietly and leisurely payed the sum agreed upon.

(14) Moreover, since in civil law all curial service is forbidden to the clergy, this man has left the Church to take part in the court. And what unheard of folly it is to desert the clergy and become a courtier, so that he might rule over clerics. He becomes a slave to the world so that he might in the house of God usurp the power to rule and occupy the "seat of the scornful."[19] Once a man accepts investiture from the hands of a donor,[20] or in any other manner rises to the heights of authority that he has reached, just as soon as he discovers his group of flatterers, he hands out generous gifts from the property of the Church.

(15) In our own day a certain bishop came to office in the diocese of Bologna,[21] a courtier operating in just the way I have described. After he had alienated extensive holdings of the Church that lay around the city, he subsequently lost his voice. And thus, for the seven years he was yet alive, he lay paralyzed and speechless. This was surely just retribution by the heavenly judge, so that he who had used his tongue to carry on this sorry kind of dealing, should, along with his office, totally lose the power of speech. And so, every curial bishop attracts such people with gifts, grants them extensive benefices, and thus is chosen by those who did not elect him; and that nothing belonging to Simon is wanting to him, he sells the election itself in a sac-

19. Cf. Ps 1.1.
20. One of the few times Damian uses the term "investiture," although he frequently implies the practice elsewhere in his letters.
21. On Adalfredus, bishop of Bologna (1031–1055), see Schwartz, *Bistümer* 163; see also Lucchesi, *Vita* no. 52.

rilegious deal. And still in doing this he conceals the shamefulness of his crime, since under the guise of allegiance to the Church, he binds the members of his household with a solemn oath. No one harms the Church more severely than her own perfidious faithful, who are only too eager to expropriate her property. When, therefore, he puts such people in office, and when he compels them to take their oath specifically to him as if he were the Church, he is not acting in the welfare of the Church, but is quietly smoothing the way so that he may come to power. Whether he does this before consecration or afterwards, he must beware that, by squandering the property of the house of God, not for the good of the Church, but for the sake of his own confirmation, he not plunge into the whirlpool of simonist heresy as he strives for his honors, and thus crash to his ruin in the sight of God for having so arrogantly sought preeminence before men. For it is written, "As they were reaching for distinction, you drove them headlong into ruin."[22]

(16) Nor should I omit to say that he who reaches the heights of civil authority unwillingly, if then he undergoes difficulty and hardship, it will redound to the mounting total of his merits; and for the suffering that he bears, he will not hope in vain for the reward of eternal glory. So also he, who voluntarily seeks preferment or importunately pushes himself forward, will almost never be rewarded for the reverses he suffers while he is in authority. He should blame himself, therefore, for what he has to suffer, and ascribe it to his own account when he is abused. Let him recompense the effort he sustains with his honors, and consider the fruit of his labor to be the dignity he has achieved, rather than look hopefully for future reward, as the Lord declares when speaking of such people: "They have already received their reward."[23] For he has brought it upon himself that his spirit succumbs under the blows of such misfortune. But when one is drawn into government service unwillingly, and in fulfilling his office suffers reverses, his work will not go unrewarded. On the other hand, if he came into service by bribery or importuning, he is embarrassed to de-

22. Ps 72.18.   23. Matt 6.5.

mand payment for his efforts, especially when he remembers that he had used extortion and nagging incivility to come by his job.

(17) But I say all this so that those, who by serving princes and thus acquiring ecclesiastical dignity, should not boast that they had not practiced simony. Nor should they congratulate themselves on observing the norms of gratuitous promotion, since they are not unaware that they paid for what they got with hard labor.

(18) Princes also, and all others in charge of ecclesiastical appointments, should be especially careful not to grant holy places at their own whim or pleasure without taking divine justice into consideration, so that to their own confusion, they do not violate the precepts of God's Law and the statutes of the sacred canons.[24] For whoever exercises authority over the Church of God by use of power and not in accord with Law, will find that all the evil done by the candidate so promoted will be charged to the account of him who made the appointment. Thus, when that celebrated preacher said, "Do not be overly hasty in laying on hands in ordination," he promptly added, "or you may find yourself responsible for other people's misdeeds."[25] For whoever dares to promote an unworthy or wicked, and therefore a greedy man to office, is surely guilty of the sins of others. And since the Church of Christ, without stain or wrinkle,[26] is defiled by every offensive ordination, the whole infection brought on by this deadly disease is transfused into the soul of the minister of ordination.

(19) Now the history of the Romans[27] relates that when the Goths requested the Emperor Valens to send them bishops from whom they might learn the fundamentals of the faith, he sent them teachers who were not orthodox but of the Arian persuasion, and involved this uneducated people in the errors to which he had ascribed. But what a notable and awesome

---

24. See Ryan, *Sources* 119f. nos. 235, 258, citing Burchard, *Decretorum libri* 1.21 (PL 140.555A).
25. 1 Tim 5.22. 26. Cf. Eph 5.27.
27. Paulus Diaconus, *Historia Romana* 11.10–11, in Eutropius, *Breviarium* (MGH Auct.ant. 2.187).

judgment of God it was that followed. For when the Goths, who had already been driven from their former lands by the forces of the Huns, were affably settled by Valens on Roman territory south of the Danube without first entering into treaty with them, by the judgment of God they rose up in arms against Valens and defeated his army with great bloodshed. When Valens learned of this calamity, he left Antioch to engage the Goths with a great army he had assembled; but influenced by belated repentance, he ordered the holy bishops to be recalled from exile. He then went into battle, and lost. For at the first attack of the Goths, the Roman cavalry was thrown into disorder and fled, leaving the foot soldiers unprotected. They were quickly engulfed by the enemy's horse, overwhelmed by a storm of arrows, and in their flight, wandering here and there like madmen, they were cut to pieces by enemy swords. The emperor himself was wounded by an arrow, fell from his horse, and was brought by a soldier to a miserable hut. But when the Goths came upon it, he was horribly burned to death. Clearly, by the just sentence of God he was killed in the avenging flames by the same men whom he had burned with the fires of heresy, and so, according to the judgment of Scripture, fire came out of the thorn and burned up the cedars of Lebanon.[28]

(20) In this citation from Scripture that I have just used, this too appropriately comes to mind as I recall another passage from the same book of Judges. For while in this iron age those who are worthy to rule take flight, others who should rightly be banned, with no respect for the Law, make themselves available. Thus we see happening just what we read in this passage under the guise of a marvelous allegory. It says that "Jotham was standing on the summit of Mount Gerizim and cried at the top of his voice, 'Listen to me, you citizens of Shechem, and may God listen to you. Once upon a time the trees came to anoint a king, and they said to the olive tree, Be king over us. But the olive tree answered, What, leave my rich oil by which gods and men are honored, to come and hold sway over the trees?

---

28. Cf. Judg 9.15.

(21) "'So the trees said to the fig tree, Then will you come and be king over us? But the fig tree answered, What, leave my good fruit and all its sweetness, to come and hold sway over the trees?

(22) "'So the trees said to the vine, Then will you come and be king over us? But the vine answered, What, leave my wine which gladdens gods and men, to come and hold sway over the trees?'" With that Scripture continues, "'Then all the trees said to the thornbush, Will you then be king over us? And the thornbush said to the trees, If you really mean to anoint me as your king, then come under the protection of my shadow.'"[29]

(23) It would be tedious if I were to explain how Gideon was a type of the savior. In his many wives we should understand the various nations which were associated by faith; by his seventy sons, the same number of people of differing language. For the concubine, we should read the synagogue, and in Abimelech we should see the antichrist who will be a son of the synagogue.[30] And so in the Apocalypse this was said of those who were to believe in him: "They claim to be Jews but are not—they are Satan's synagogue."[31] And just as Abimelech killed his seventy brothers,[32] thus will Satan persecute all the nations that will not unite with him. And so, passing over those matters that would seem to require more extensive treatment that epistolary brevity will not suffer, let me shorten my explanation of the allegory, referring only to that which has bearing on the discussion I have begun.

(24) Whom should we understand by Jotham, which means 'complete' or 'perfect,'[33] if not every holy and learned preacher? He went up Mount Gerizim[34] and cried at the top of his voice. First he went up and then he shouted; first he climbed the mountain, and then raised his voice, for unless a teacher has first arrived at the height of virtue, he will cry out in vain. Just as Isaiah says, "You who bring Zion good news, up with you to the mountain top; lift up your voice and shout, you who bring

---

29. Judg 9.7–15.
30. Cf. Judg 8.29–31.
31. Rev 2.9.
32. Cf. Judg 9.5.
33. Jerome, *Nom.hebr.* 46.5 (CC 72.116).
34. Cf. Judg 9.7.

news to Jerusalem."³⁵ By Gerizim, however, we should understand holy Church, which is the school of all virtues, and abounds with the richness of heavenly produce. This is surely the mountain that was said by Moses to bestow blessings.³⁶ And the Church is the mountain of blessing, to whose children the Apostle says, "For a blessing is the inheritance to which you have been called."³⁷ We receive this inheritance from a widowed mother for whom her husband deigned to die, and of whom the psalmist says, "I will richly bless his widow."³⁸ It is proper that Gerizim, which means 'division' or 'stranger,'³⁹ should prefigure Holy Church. For the church of the gentiles, which was at first totally cut off from the Law of God, and when first called became a stranger, was later, through an increase of grace, made to feel completely at home. And so Paul said to the gentiles, now firmly rooted and, as it were, brought together into the city, "Thus you are no longer aliens in a foreign land, but fellow citizens with God's people, members of God's household."⁴⁰

(25) But now as I pass over many things, let me quickly run through what I proposed to do. The trees in the forest are proud and sterile men who deserve to burn in the avenging flames because they bore no fruit. "For every tree that fails to produce good fruit will be cut down and thrown in the fire."⁴¹ And what is meant by the olive tree, which spreads its leaves as a symbol of peace and produces rich oil, if not those who, anointed with the fullness of the Holy Spirit to spread the good news of peace, reconcile men to their creator? "How welcome," he says, "are the feet of the messengers of good news."⁴² The fig tree, however, is the figure of the holy Law; hence it says in the gospel, that "a certain land owner planted a vineyard in which he also planted a fig tree."⁴³ Now, "the vineyard of the Lord of Hosts is the house of Israel,"⁴⁴ in which God's hand

---

35. Isa 40.9.
36. Cf. Deut 11.29.
37. 1 Pet 3.9.
38. Ps 131.15.
39. Jerome, *Nom.hebr.* 18.24 (CC 72.82).
40. Eph 2.19.
41. Matt 3.10.
42. Rom 10.15; cf. Isa 52.7.
43. Matt 21.33; Luke 13.6.
44. Isa 5.7.

planted the Ten Commandments of the Law. But this fig tree first produced a people that were like unripe figs, shrivelled and useless, which it let fall; but then it brought forth a new growth to full maturity and sweetness, living by the Christian faith. Of these Jeremiah speaks, saying, "I am looking at figs; the good are very good, and the bad so bad that they are not fit to eat."[45]

(26) By the fig tree, therefore, we may rightly understand those who are well instructed in sacred jurisprudence. The vine, too, seems to mean about the same as the fig tree.[46] The Lord indeed says, "I am the true vine, and you the branches."[47] And since from the branches, vines are produced, why should we wonder that the holy doctors are called vines, so that what the savior of the world possessed by nature, they were privileged to have through grace? For as they incessantly preached of the triumph of the Lord's passion, they made our hearts drunk, as it were, on the wine of Christ's blood produced from the grapes of their teaching. Jacob spoke of this wine in referring allegorically to our savior when he said, "He will wash his cloak in wine, and his robe in the blood of grapes."[48] the cloak of Christ belonged to the apostles, while for other believers there was the synagogue. Also by his robe the gentile world is meant, concerning which he said of himself through the prophet: "As I live, says the Lord, you shall wear them as your jewels."[49] Christ, therefore, washes them in the blood of grapes, which was forced from him as he was ground in the winepress of the cross. Of this John says, "Who loved us and washed away our sins with his blood."[50]

(27) Therefore, since the olive tree, the fig tree, and the vine, that is, spiritual men, were unwilling to rule over the trees of the forest, that is, over worldly and carnal men, the thornbush presented itself, both to be destroyed by them, and to consume them by the example of an evil life, or in the fire of false doctrine. Now the thornbush bristles with formidable barbs, by

---

45. Jer 24.3.
46. Cf. Jerome, *Adversus Jovinianum* 1.30 (PL 23.252B).
47. John 15.5. 48. Gen 49.11.
49. Isa 49.18. 50. Rev 1.5.

which is meant any evil person who is thickly set with sins, as if they were sharp thistles. Thus it was said to the first man: "Your soil will grow thorns and thistles,"[51] that is, it will subject your body to the pricking pain of vice. And the Lord says in the words of the prophet, "They have surrounded me with the thorns of their sins."[52] While the trees, therefore, were seeking a king, that is, as wicked men anywhere are choosing a leader who will suit their carnal desires, the thornbush comes forward, that is, any reprobate who from their wickedness will increase within himself the fire of damnation, and who, in return, will consume them in the flames of his depraved life or teaching. And thus in the same book that I was citing, it says, "May fire come out of Abimelech and burn up the citizens of Shechem and all Beth-Millo: and let fire come out from the men of Shechem and all Beth-Millo and burn up Abimelech."[53] Jotham said all this as he stood on the summit of the mountain, because it is from holy preachers within the Church that we learn how to resist all perverse and wicked men who seek deceptive goals.

(28) And so, venerable brother, you asked for only one letter, but you have received a second one besides. And on my part I request that as the new one is sent with my affection, its twin also be returned to me, in keeping with the ethics of ancient disputation. But if you should enjoy hearing still more about curial bishops, you should take the trouble to look at the letter on the same theme I previously sent to your fellow cardinals.[54] This I will also add at the end of my letter, that henceforth, just as those who were promoted to serve the Church are normally called bishops, so also those who are advanced by acting as the servants of princes should, from the word curia, be called curials.

51. Gen 3.18.
52. This citation cannot be found in this form; perhaps Ps 117.12 suggested it.
53. Judg 9.20.   54. See *Letter* 48.

LETTER 70

Peter Damian to the cleric, Landulf Cotta of Milan. The theme of this letter, written after his reforming mission to that city, centers on the unfulfilled vow to enter the priesthood, made by Landulf when both he and Damian were weathering the riots brought on by their actions. Damian had warned him against rash promises made when fear for his life was upon him, but Landulf persisted. Now Damian holds him to his vow, arguing, as was his custom, by citing examples of those who had broken their promises. Of special interest is the autobiographical account, dealing with Damian's school days in Parma twenty-five years before this letter.

(after 1060)[1]

O THE CLERIC Landulf,[2] illustrious by reason of his senatorial family and his literary achievements, the monk Peter the sinner sends his greetings.

(2) I stood waiting for you, and I was certain that, according to your promise, you would enter the ranks of the religious life.[3] The king of Egypt had not treated you severely, putting you to work on clay and brickmaking;[4] Achish did not ask you to retire from service with his troops at the insistence of the other princes;[5] but it was rather the father-in-law of the girl from Bethlehem who detained you as he did the Levite from the hill-country of Ephraim, overwhelmed by love for his daughter, entertaining him with pleasant conversation and refreshments.[6] What was vowed to God and not to man, human foolishness has not fulfilled.

---

1. The dating follows Neukirch, *Das Leben* 99, Wilmart, "Une lettre," 132f., and Lucchesi, *Vita* no. 53; see also Reindel, *Briefe* 2 (1988) 310.
2. On Landulf, see Reindel, *Briefe* 2 (1988) 311 n. 1. and the literature there cited.
3. On the question of whether Damian refers to a vow to enter the priesthood or, as here presumed, to enter a monastery, see Somigli, "Pataria" 200f.
4. Cf. Exod 1.14.   5. Cf. 1 Sam 29.6–8.
6. Cf. Judg 19.1–7.

(3) I ask you, my brother, in your prudence what excuse can you allege? What argument can one offer that allows him not to fulfill what he promised to Christ the judge, with the angels as his witnesses? And that, since the Lord says through Moses, "When a man makes a vow to the Lord or swears an oath and so puts himself under a binding obligation, he must not break his word. Every word he has spoken, he must make good."[7] Will this, perhaps, clear you from lying, or will it appear as a suitable shelter for your defense, that the city of Milan was then involved in civil war, threatening sudden death for both of us? Is it the principle that what was occasioned by necessity, in the absence of free choice, will not stand? It is an opinion of canonical authority that if a ruler's widow, fearing violence, enters the convent with the purpose of not remaining in religion, she may not later go back on the promise she once made.[8]

(4) It is therefore out of the question that fear should free a man, when even in court it does not excuse women. This is especially true, since at the time when I objected to you obligating yourself with a vow of this kind out of fear for your life, unless you would later fulfill your promise by actually carrying it out, you swore that you would be liable to God's punishment if, after making this solemn promise, you should ever violate your oath. Let me tell you about a similar thing that happened, something that is common knowledge in our area.

(5) There was a man named Ardoinus,[9] a person renowned for his prudence, of an outstanding family and very rich. With undoubted devotion he had promised me that, if it were not possible at some earlier time, at least in ten years he would enter the monastery of St. Vincent that lies in the territory of Urbino.[10] At length, when the time agreed upon had elapsed, and I, like an earnest tax collector, pressured him with fawning and flattery, he indeed promised in words to do all that was right; but by using various kinds of subterfuge, he put off ac-

---

7. Num 30.3.
8. The substance of Damian's argument depends loosely on Burchard, *Decretorum libri* 8.85 (PL 140.798BC).
9. Cf. Palazzini, "Chiesa Marchigiana" 206f.
10. On San Vincenzo di Petra Pertusa, see *supra*, Letter 2 n. 7.

tually becoming a monk. Also, the abbot of this monastery encouraged his gifts, and dissuaded him from entering religion, since he was often supported by grants from the latter that were greatly needed. In the meantime, he fell seriously ill and, after confessing his sins, was absolved by the priest. He gave many bequests to the poor and to various churches, so that by so doing, and after properly arranging all his affairs, he could thus entreat his relatives and friends who were at his bedside: "I beg of you," he said, "by the love which is God himself, that none of you pray that I return to this mortal life, God forbid, so that sudden death may not later find me unprepared."

(6) Some time after his death, this man appeared to the aforementioned abbot in a dream during the dead of night. It seemed to him that the emperor, if I remember correctly, or some other powerful person, was standing in some extensive field with all the great men of his kingdom, together with a great army. As he looked about on all sides in astonishment, suddenly Ardoinus was brought forward by men who seemed to be guarding him. "Hey there," he cried, "not so fast! Stop and wait here a moment! Aren't you going to talk to me, Ardoinus? I say, brother, what's been happening to you? Are you enjoying yourself, or are you suffering? Are you in hell or in heaven?" To this Ardoinus sadly replied with many tears: "Why do you ask me about heaven," he said, "when I am being tortured with constant punishment, and not allowed, even for a moment, to catch my breath." The abbot said this to him: "What does St. Vincent say? Does he not help you in your need, you who were so earnest in working with the officials of his monastery?" At once he replied to the abbot: "St. Vincent," he said, "long ago led me to hope that I could talk with him. But, because he was busy just then, I did not get to see him. And now I am completely frustrated and have lost all hope."

(7) In all of this one should carefully note how straight is the line of divine justice, and how ingenious is the measure of God's punishment. This man, you will remember, when he was still alive, promised to become a monk in the blessed martyr's monastery, and always put it off. But now he always hoped for, and indeed was promised, a talk with the martyr; but he never

succeeded. It was also proper that the abbot should be the one who had this vision, since he had stood in the way of his becoming a monk.

(8) There was another man, also named Peter, a fellow citizen of mine in Ravenna,[11] a person of some distinction, skilled in the practice of the law and well educated in the discipline of the grammarians. He made an agreement with me that, if I left the world, he would do so also. But then what happened? At length, when I was going to the monastery, I urged him to carry out his pledge, but I was not successful. Indeed, happily he went ahead of me, but then stopped in his tracks and artfully held back. Not many days later, he became terribly angry with his brother-in-law, and in the encounter was unexpectedly struck on the hand by a sword, and the hand became stiff. And from that time on it remained numb and rigid, so that as he depended on his bailiff, he was more a burden than a help. Therefore, as he was now an invalid and cast aside by the world, he left the world; and now no longer lacking a hand, but ambidextrous, like Benjamin,[12] he persevered in the monastery until his death.

(9) As I recall these events, John, the bishop of Comacchio, comes to mind.[13] Since he procrastinated and put off entering the monastery for many years, it happened one day that he was staying on an estate he owned in a woodland region. While he was there, he ordered that a pig, which belonged to a certain widow and which she hoped to have for dinner, be caught, carefully prepared, and brought to him to grace his table. The poor widow, weeping and crying, begged him to give her something to eat in return for her attentiveness. But as the dear bishop, in providing for his own table, was more interested in his own stomach than in hers, he made light of the Lord's command given by the prophet, "Champion the oppressed, give the orphan his rights, and plead the widow's cause."[14] And as he

11. See Wilmart, "Une lettre" 131 n. 2; Cantin, "Saint Pierre Damien," esp. 250.
12. Cf. Gen 35.18; Judg 20.16.
13. On John of Comacchio (1003–1016), see Schwartz, *Bistümer* 169; Balboni, "San Pier Damiano," esp. 89.
14. Isa 1.17.

thought that the lawgiver was out of sight, he learned from the sentence he inflicted that he was right there. For as the bishop in his gluttony made sport of the widow's tears, he was suddenly struck in the throat and suffered a wound that as long as he lived defied the best efforts of the doctors.

(10) Since he was hampered by this illness, and since, according to Scripture, "only trouble will help us understand what we hear,"[15] he at length consented to sound advice, exchanged his episcopal attire for a monk's habit, and lived for many more years in the monastery of Pomposa[16] that had been built in honor of the blessed Mary ever virgin. Until his death he suffered from such throat trouble, that only with great difficulty could he swallow his food, so that he always sat at a separate table with brothers who came after him, and was hardly able to take enough food to satisfy his appetite.

(11) But as I remember this bishop, I am led to write about what happened also to the bishop of Chiusi.[17] On the Wednesday that is called the beginning of Lent, he had his servants prepare a great meal consisting of costly food, and to draw him a bath. Inviting many knights and a host of vassals, he spent a glorious day, and just as if they were all going to a wedding, they celebrated Lent with a nuptial banquet. This was so out of keeping with the rules of fasting that, while the ashes were still fresh on their heads, their stomachs swelled and they began to perspire from gorging themselves with meat and drink. But how the punishment of God hovers over us: Suddenly the face of the healthy and vigorous bishop was paralysed, becoming distorted about the eyes and mouth into something ugly. For the many years he still had to live, he bore this mark of God's judgment.

(12) And how can I overlook Adam, the bishop of Fossombrone?[18] He had often promised that he would become a monk, but had always made excuses, glossed with all sorts of specious

---

15. Isa 28.19.
16. On Pomposa, see the notes (*supra*) to *Letter* 6, *Letter* 24, and *Letter* 27.
17. On the various bishops of Chiusi (1049–1059) see Schwartz, *Bistümer* 204.
18. Cf. Schwartz, *Bistümer* 243.

arguments. One day he was under the weather with a slight fever, and he called me to visit him. When I then strongly urged him to become a monk, he admitted that he was indeed willing, and still, as one could almost read between the lines, he tried to delay the matter. Finally, and this made a good impression on me, he said, "I agree, father; anything that you tell me to do I will at once obey. But I want you to be aware that, as soon as I become a monk, this church will surely be subjected to immediate raids and plundering. Wicked men will totally destroy its lands and other possessions." When I heard this, and as I feared that I was being deceived about the fate of the church, I did not, unfortunately, make provision for his endangered soul. Yet as I left, I ordered him and his attendants that if the illness became any worse, they should at once send me a message, or immediately carry him to the monastery that was not far away.

(13) In the meantime, after I had left, his brother sent me the following by messenger: "My lord, as we had hoped, through God's goodness is recovering. But I advise that you come back to see him, observing this schedule: that next Sunday you stay at the monastery of St. Vincent, which is only about five miles from the cathedral. Get up early on Monday morning, and after a pleasant ride as you recite Lauds, you will be at our residence a little before dawn." And then he continued, "I beg you, please do not put off coming for, if you come, your effort on this trip will be adequately compensated."

(14) Upon hearing this last remark, I at once expressed my thorough displeasure, and absolutely denied that I had come looking for money as if I had hoped to receive a reward. By my word, I am not lying to you when I say that I gave him a good dressing down for being the bearer of this disgraceful message. But, on the other hand, as I thought it over, I began to fear that if the man died with this on his soul, my conscience would later torture me because of my negligence. What more can I say? I at length carried out everything he had told me to do and, just before dawn, arrived at the door of the church. But to my surprise, as everyone was running about making a

great disturbance, weeping and crying out, the dead body of the bishop lay there in its coffin, with no more than two boys attending him.

(15) We should note in this case, and consider most seriously, how much planning the clever and fraudulent devil uses as he lies in wait for unwary men who are in love with the things of this life. He had, indeed, accurately and artfully informed me by the messenger that was sent, of the exact moment I should come, just before the unforeseen death of the bishop, so that I should get there just after he died, and that my coming would be in vain. How are we benefitted when we are called to the grace of entering the religious life, if we always obstruct it with the defense of our excuses, and erect a barrier of things that we need to do, as if God could not see the reasons that lie within us? For since he will severely judge us when we unjustly take even small things, are we to believe that he will stand calmly by when a man takes away himself, namely, the most precious possession that he has?

(16) Let me tell you what old Guarimpotus,[19] a most upright man, superbly educated in the arts and in medicine, reported to me: "A certain man stole someone's hog and secretly hid it away in a cave. This man was unusually busy with works of mercy, and was particularly taken up with showing kindness to pilgrims and strangers. In the meantime, Jesus, who possesses all things, came along in the guise of a pauper and, as he appeared unsightly because of his long hair, was in need of a barber. At once, the man respectfully got to his feet and, besides serving him graciously in various other ways, began to cut his hair with a pair of scissors. But, as he was busy cutting away on all sides, he found two eyes hidden under the hair at the back of his head. The man was astounded, and in amazement began to tremble as he fearfully asked the meaning of what he saw. The stranger at once said to him, 'I am called Jesus, and I see all things everywhere. And these are the eyes with which I also saw the pig you recently hid in the cave.' And then he disappeared. Quickly coming to his senses, the man admitted to

19. On the identity of Guarimpotus, see Reindel, *Briefe* 2 (1988) 318 n. 14.

himself how good God had been to him, and did penance for what he had wickedly dared to do."

(17) But while engaging you in such gracious and brotherly familiarity, I beg you not to be annoyed, but to listen a bit to what I have to say. For it is just in this way that one demonstrates a fuller measure of sincere and trusting love, if when something comes to mind, he speaks of it, not in elegant but in simple words. Now there was a person named Pambo, a man of distinguished background, but in difficult circumstances, who stayed with me in a lodging in Rome at the time when the late King Henry received the imperial crown.[20] On Christmas Eve, just as it was getting dark, a large herd of swine was being driven through a long shed at the market. Waiting in the shadows of the vending stands, Pambo darted out and snatched one of the pigs, bound its mouth so that it could not grunt, and then, congratulating himself on his success, brought it to his friends to be roasted for the next day. When the holy day arrived, he enjoyed the results of his theft and, having satisfied his appetite, gloated that he had got by unpunished. But perhaps he thought that God had not noticed. Yet that same night he learned that divine retribution awaited him. For while he was asleep and had not taken proper precautions for his horse, a thief cleverly removed the rope that he had wrapped around his hand, and led the horse away together with its bridle and saddle. Upon awakening he realized that he had been punished in a very subtle way, for he saw that at a greater cost the horse had been taken from the same hand with which he had snatched the pig. But although in this case the punishment followed immediately upon the crime, it should not surprise us that for some guilty men the penalty is often delayed, allowing them to enjoy their misdeeds a bit longer. For as Scripture testifies, "They spend their days in prosperity, and in a twinkling of the eye they go to hell."[21]

(18) I clearly recall that when I was living in Parma,[22] going

20. Thus, Damian was living in Rome at the coronation of Emperor Henry III on 25 December 1046; cf. Steindorff, *Heinrich III* 1.315f.
21. Job 21.13.
22. On Damian's study years in Parma, see P. Riché, "Recherches sur l'instruction."

to school and studying the liberal arts, I was still a young man. Just as the first signs of a beard began to cover my face,[23] and feelings of sexuality unwillingly aroused my flesh, a certain cleric named Teuzolinus[24] had a mistress living with him in the student house next to mine, a woman, as they say, of lewd appearance, alluring in her shameless beauty. The cleric always appeared trim, attracting attention by his fine attire: he never wore anything on his head but a sable hat; he would tint his clothes—snow white and of the finest linen—with ocher, by the fuller's art; lastly, his shoes did not puff up to a curved point like an eagle's beak. His voice, moreover, was plain, but sweet and ringing, so that when he sang in church, he delighted the heart of those who heard him, and all the people present turned to see who was singing. Both had great charm and both were of ruddy complexion. Every day, in a holiday spirit, they greeted one another with wanton laughter, winking, and telling scurrilous jokes.

(19) From these passionate and abandoned goings-on, I could not distance myself mentally, because I was so physically near them. What could I do, since as I saw all this happening, I was so tempted by sexual excitement, that even after I came to the hermitage, the memory of this alluring scene often attacked me? I must confess that frequently the devilish enemy flashed these images before my eyes and tried to persuade me that people who live such delightful lives are the most happy and fortunate. But now that I have told of the beginning of this merry affair, let me also report on how it ended. Just last year, when the great fire destroyed that city,[25] after they had lived together in such wanton pleasure for almost twenty-five years, they were found in the house, dying together in the flames. And thus the heat of passion gained for them a fiery holocaust,

---

23. On Damian's age at this time, see Wilmart, "Une lettre" 129ff.
24. On Teuzolinus, see Botti, *Parma* 29ff.
25. The fire occurred in 1055; cf. *Annales Parmenses* 662; see also Lucchesi, *Vita* no. 53, where he assumes that the section of this letter on the fire in Parma was written in 1056, and that the two closing paragraphs were composed in or about 1060.

and a bitter ending, sad to say, demonstrated how much a carefree life was worth.

(20) But to return to those who vow to enter religious life and then go back on their promise. There was a priest named Marinus, who a few years ago sincerely came to me and told me with certainty that he would become a monk in our hermitage. Shortly after, however, he changed his mind and violated the pledge that through me he had made to God. But that his mental blindness would be evident in his flesh, and that the darkness that lurked in his heart should be clearly displayed on his face, an infection suddenly appeared in his eye, and as long as he lived it caused him to suffer an ugly deformity. Later when he was travelling to Rome on a pilgrimage, while crossing over a very narrow stream that the others had forded unharmed, his horse alone was suddenly noticed to be without a rider. They looked for him, and as they ran up and down the stream, they found his dead body deep in the water. And so, since he preferred this worthless wandering to his sacred promise, to his own disappointment he lost the reward of both undertakings.

(21) But, as I am enjoying your pleasant company and never come to an end in what I am writing, it is no secret that I have now exceeded the limits of epistolary brevity. Moreover, as an unpolished person, I do not admonish you who are so accomplished; I do not propose lessons from Scripture, but like a farmer relate only homespun things, that I might activate your appetite, dulled by its daily fare, by providing bran and green salad. I refer you, therefore, to your own mental archive, where certainly many pages of Scripture are preserved. There, in your wisdom you should investigate which is better: whether by paying your debt and entering the monastery, to sit with the judges;[26] or, by not paying, to stand before the court of the impartial judge and give answer to the charges. Of one thing I am sure: if by some argument you can be turned from the vanities of the world, you would certainly become God's

---

26. Cf. Matt 19.28.

spokesman, the herald of Christ, the trumpet of heavenly eloquence, the destroyer of the devil, and the builder of an edifice that will last forever. And finally, you would become a luminary of the Church and an impregnable fortress of Christian service.

LETTER 71

Peter Damian to the Empress Agnes, written in the name of the other cardinal bishops. The empress had communicated with the Holy See, asking that the pallium be sent to Archbishop Siegfried of Mainz. The letter is most deferential, but notes that traditionally a candidate for the pallium must first come to Rome, and there receive this symbol of his full estate.

(Early 1060)[1]

O THE MOST serene Empress A⟨gnes⟩,[2] Humbert[3] the archbishop and B⟨oniface⟩ of Albano[4] along with the other cardinal bishops send their allegiance and most amicable fidelity.

(2) For many years the Roman Church has not been in greater debt to anyone of imperial majesty than to your honor, from whose active and holy devotion it has received many great benefits. Thus, indeed, you are rightly called the daughter of blessed Peter, the prince of the apostles, and the faithful handmaiden of almighty God in the government that was committed to you. If, therefore, your majesty should request something of the Roman Church that might be contrary to canonical regulations, we do not ascribe it, God forbid, to malice, but rather impute it to the ignorance of your counselors.

(3) Now you have asked that the pallium be sent to the

---

1. Siegfried became archbishop on 6 January 1060, and this letter appears to have been written some weeks later.
2. On Agnes, see M. L. Bulst-Thiele, "Kaiserin Agnes," *Beiträge zur Kulturgeschichte des MA and der Renaissance* 52 (1933) 72f.
3. Anton Michel, "Die Anfänge," on stylistic grounds, attributed this letter to Cardinal Humbert. Lucchesi, *Vita* 2.155 also doubted Damian's authorship. But the chief MSS associate this letter with Damian's works, and MSS C1 and V2 ascribe it directly to him. The style, moreover, does not contradict his authorship.
4. On Boniface of Albano, see *supra*, Letter 69 n. 2.

elected archbishop of Mainz,[5] something that can undoubtedly be shown to be contrary to the decrees of the holy Fathers. Archbishops themselves, according to the practice of ancient tradition, must visit the tomb of the apostles, and there receive the symbol of their full dignity, without which they cannot be metropolitans.[6] But if, perhaps, one should object to this assertion by stating that the pallium was often sent by the Roman pontiffs to many places through nuncios, this affair would seem to be different, for the reason that at that time legates of the Roman Church functioned as the representatives of the pope in the provinces to which they were accredited. These men, therefore, examined those who were to be promoted to the head of the episcopate, and thus they obtained the pallium from the Apostolic See through nuncios.

(4) Therefore, let one example suffice to prove what we say. Brunhild,[7] the queen of the Franks, was able to obtain the pallium from the blessed Gregory for her brother Siagrius, the bishop of Autun, only in this way: He, although a good and upright man, had to travel to Candidus, the advocate, who held the office of plenipotentiary in that area, to be examined by him. Thus in receiving the pallium he paid proper reverence to the Roman pontiff in the person of his legate. Also, the emperor Maurice,[8] after petitioning the same Gregory for many years, was able to fulfill his request in the matter of the pallium only after Maximus, the bishop of Salona, had come to Ravenna and cleared himself under oath concerning the subjects that had been alleged against him, appearing before those who had been authorized to judge in this matter. For the blessed Pope Damasus[9] had already decreed that any metropolitan

---

5. Siegfried von Eppenstein (d. 16 February 1084) had been the abbot of Fulda, on whom Henry IV, 6 January 1060, bestowed the archbishopric of Mainz. For sources and literature, see Reindel, *Briefe* 2 (1988) 324 n. 4.

6. The regulation, that the pallium must be conferred on the recipient personally present in Rome, began during the pontificate of Alexander II; see Reindel, *Briefe* 2 (1988) 324 n. 5.

7. Cf. Gregory I, *Reg.* 8.4.1, 5–8.

8. Cf. Gregory I, *Reg.* 5.6.1, 285ff. to Sabinian, the deacon in Constantinople, on the involvement of the emperor Maurice in the case of Maximus of Salona. On later development of the problem, see Gregory I, *Reg.* 6.3.1, 382.

9. On the prescription that the metropolitan must appear in Rome within

who delayed beyond three months after his consecration to profess his faith to the Roman pontiff and request the pallium, would be deprived of the office committed to him.

(5) Wherefore, let your elected lord bishop of Mainz himself not postpone coming to the tomb of the apostles, and thus canonically and legally obtain the fullness of his dignity. For if it is necessary for us or our lord pope to act in favor of any mortal, we have no doubt that it will be done for the honor of your highness.

---

three months of his installation, see Burchard, *Decretorum libri* 1.25 (PL 140.555C–556A); JK 250.

LETTER 72

Peter Damian to Pope Nicholas II. Less than two years after his previous request for permission to abdicate from the episcopate (cf. *Letter* 57), Damian again writes to Nicholas asking for his consent to resign. His former bid, he notes, came at a time when the Church was in dire straits; but now times were better, and a man of his age and decrepitude should be given his release. To examples of abdication already cited, he adds many new cases, totalling thirty in all, and draws on patristic sources for further argument. On this occasion, Hildebrand is no longer considered his persecutor, but his own unworthiness is now put forward as a compelling reason for the pope to heed his request.

(December 1059–July 1061)[1]

TO HIS LORD, Nicholas,[2] the universal pope, the monk Peter the sinner offers his personal subservience.

(2) Your heart, which is the sanctuary of the Holy Spirit, is aware that unless the previous necessity of the Apostolic See had not compelled me, and unless the love that I have borne you for so long had not intervened, I would have completely divested myself of the office of bishop which was not canonically conferred on me and upon which I was forced to enter after the death of the lord Stephen[3] of blessed memory, your predecessor, indeed, but my persecutor. You remember, of course, my lord, how many times I complained of this in your presence, how many sighs and how much grief escaped from my very being, and how often I broke down in bitter tears. And yet I did not then obtain my dismissal from you because

---

1. The dating follows Lucchesi, *Vita* nos. 147, 149.
2. It should be noted that this letter was sent to the reigning Pope Nicholas II, while *Letter* 57, which perhaps was never sent, but from which *Letter* 72 heavily borrows, was addressed to the pope-elect and to Hildebrand. On this borrowing and on the likelihood that *Letter* 57 was never sent, see Lucchesi, *Vita* nos. 122, 126, 147.
3. Pope Stephen IX died on 29 March 1058. He is called Damian's persecutor because he appointed him Cardinal Bishop of Ostia; see K. Reindel, "Neue Literatur zu Petrus Damiani," DA 32 (1976) 405–44, esp. 414.

the needs of the Roman Church, which seemed threatened with ruin, did not allow it.

(3) But now that your hand is on the rudder of the ship of Peter,[4] the whole Church of Christ rejoices in peace and tranquility.[5] For winds and storms are repressed, the swells and foaming waves grow quiet, the seas are calm, and we again enjoy pleasant weather. Therefore, since during your holy pontificate the universal Church delights in this pleasant peace, I beg you to grant rest to my gray hair and advanced age. Wherefore, to gain the remission of all my sins which I so vilely committed, I give up the rights to the episcopal office, and by this ring—for you have already taken the staff—I renounce it and all future claim to its recovery. I also return both monasteries to you,[6] and implore you to allow an old veteran soldier to find a haven of peace.

(4) But perhaps I will hear the objection[7] that once authority has been accepted, one is not permitted to lay it down. To this I will briefly speak my mind: There are many who have not deserted the rights enjoyed by bishops and are found to be on the judge's left,[8] and there are those of whom we read who have renounced their rights with a proper intention yet have every reason to hope that they will eternally enjoy Christ's company. And yet I do not say these things so that one might lightly desert the episcopate, but only in the case where some necessity or reasonable cause intervenes.

Of Valerius the Bishop of Hippo[9]

(5) The blessed Bishop Valerius, indeed, while providing for a successor, enthroned the great Augustine as bishop of the Church of Hippo.

---

4. The usage of *sagena*, meaning a 'ship' and not a net, is almost uniquely Peter Damian's. For other occasions when he used this word, see *Letter* 48 n. 6.

5. Lucchesi, *Vita* 1.150 n. 28 concludes from these remarks that the troubles caused by antipope Benedict X had ended.

6. One of these was surely Fonte Avellana, where Damian was prior since 1043. About the other there is no certainty.

7. From here onward, through the nine next examples, the text repeats almost *verbatim* the examples cited in *Letter* 57.

8. Cf. Matt 25.41.

9. On Valerius, see *Letter* 57 n. 18.

Of Lucidus the Bishop of Ficoclae[10]

(6) When Lucidus the bishop of Ficoclae became aware that his death was imminent, he took shelter with a cenobite order and exchanged the trappings of episcopal dignity for the monastic garb. And that you might know what this conversion bestowed on him, the authentic record of his collected letters relates that, when he was at the point of death, the grace of the Holy Spirit was reflected on his happy face. Before he died, moreover, the blessed Apostle Andrew appeared to him and told him the hour at which he would pass away.

Of the Blessed Bishop Adalbert[11]

(7) What shall I say of blessed Adalbert the martyr? Because he deserted the authority of the Church of Bohemia and became a monk, he was found worthy to wear the triumphant crown of martyrdom.

Of Genebald the Bishop of Lodi[12]

(8) As I purposely pass over others in silence, a certain holy penitent comes to mind, but for the moment I forget his name. After he had given up the episcopal office in Gaul before finishing seven years of service, an angel came to him and commanded him to return to his see. But he refused until, at the warning of the same angel, the blessed Remigius suddenly appeared. And so, fearing even things that seemed safe, lest perhaps he become the victim of deception, he yielded to human command while at first refusing to budge at the word of an angel.

Of Lawrence the Bishop of Sabina[13]

(9) The bishop of Sabina also deserted his pontifical throne after turning his back on the episcopal dignity, and then he built the monastery of Farfa. Ancient tradition, which honors

---

10. On Lucidus, see *Letter* 57 n. 19.
11. On Adalbert, see *Letter* 57 n. 20.
12. On Genebald of Lodi, see *Letter* 57 n. 21. His name appears here only in the superscription; cf. Reindel, *Briefe* 2 (1988) 168 n. 22.
13. On Lawrence, see *Letter* 57 n. 23.

the deeds of his sanctity, bears witness to the nobility of this man of Christ, and present devotion is also at hand to hold his memory in benediction. Many there were, before and after his time, that remained in that see until the end of their days, but never did they produce such bounteous fruit for the Lord.

Of the Bishop Bonitus[14]

(10) Nor do I forget you, blessed Bonitus, who despised your church, and suddenly retired to a life of solitude because you happened to receive your see from the hand of the king, namely, from a lay person.

Of Gaudentius the Bishop of Ossero[15]

(11) Also, the venerable Bishop Gaudentius of Ossero, with whom I had the good fortune to be acquainted and through whom God had performed a great miracle, gave up his episcopal office. He went by sea to Italy from the kingdom of Slavonia, landed on the coast at the city of Ancona, and there, a little over two years ago, he died happily.

Of Bishop Paulinus of Nola[16]

(12) Then there was Paulinus, head of the Church of Nola, who resigned the episcopal ministry to help a widow locate her son, and who worked like a common slave in the service of a tyrant.

Of Martirius the Bishop of Antioch[17]

(13) I remember reading in the ecclesiastical history written by a Roman archivist that Martirius the bishop of Antioch resigned his see because his fractious people would not obey. There it is stated: "When Martirius returned to Antioch and found the people, abetted by Zeno, in revolt, he renounced his episcopal office in the presence of the people, saying, 'With the

---

14. On Bonitus, see *Letter* 57 n. 24.
15. On Gaudentius, see Reindel, *Briefe* 2 (1988) 172 n. 28.
16. Cf. Gregory I, *Dialogi*, ed. A. de Vogüe, SC 251, 260, 265 (1978–1980) 3.1, vol. 2.258.
17. On the source of this narrative, cf. Reindel, *Briefe* 2 (1988) 330 n. 16.

clergy out of hand, the people in revolt, and the church in a deplorable state, I resign, but still retain the dignity of the episcopate.'" In the same work one finds also this tale included: Because he was a prudent man, a patrician named Appio, who during the reign of the wicked Anastasius was ordained a priest through violence in the city of Nicea, was created pretorian prefect by decree of the gracious emperor Justin, who succeeded Anastasius in office. And thus imperial piety corrected what had been assumed in the violent days of the tyrant. I have purposely referred to this case because, since I myself was violently dragged into office, one can gather what may be rightly thought of me in the light of this ancient authority. Nevertheless, it appears to be another's business to decide whether the fact that he was made pretorian prefect after becoming a priest is to be charged to authority or to a wrongful act.

What the Blessed Gregory and Jerome Thought about Giving up the Episcopal Office

(14) Now in addition, the blessed Pope Gregory also did not forbid bishops to resign from their dignity if necessity seemed to demand it. But it will be sufficient for me to cite the title of this item, lest I be guilty of drawing out this letter through redundant verbosity. He who arranged the volume of his register had this to say: "Gregory in no way refused to appoint successors to bishops who had voluntarily renounced their sees, but ordered that they be properly provided for from the income of the church they had left," and the rest that is added there at greater length.[18] And so it was that the same outstanding pope, in the following citation, published his decision to the bishop of the first see of Justinian, who suffered from headache: "If, however," he said, "the most reverend John should perhaps petition that he be allowed to resign the honor of his episcopal office as a remedy for his illness, after putting his request in writing, his wish should be granted."[19]

18. Cf. John the Deacon, *Sancti Gregorii magni vita* 4.39 (PL 75.202 B).
19. Cf. John the Deacon, *Sancti Gregorii magni vita* 4.39 (PL 75.202 A).

(15) St. Jerome, moreover, when treating of the lazy head of a church, had this to say: "Immediately he heard the bruising reply of the angry master: 'You wicked servant, why did you not put my money in the bank, so that on my return I could have drawn it out with interest?'"[20] And explaining this, the same doctor said, "That is, deposit at the altar what you were unable to bear. For while you, the lazy manager, were holding the money, you were occupying the place of another who could have doubled the sum."[21]

Of Justus the Bishop of Lyons[22]

(16) What shall I report of the bishop of Lyons, whose name Justus reflects also his life, and who in a praiseworthy manner directed the affairs of his episcopal office and laid it down in a similar manner? Once a certain man possessed by a devil burst on the scene in such a wild fury that he violently struck everyone he met, wounding some with his blows, dismembering others, and finally killing others still. One day, as a large crowd of people attacked him, he broke into the church and took sanctuary there. But then, as he was being hounded to death and necessity had taught him to return to his senses, suddenly the holy bishop sprang between him and the crowd and stood there as the defender of the one who had sought refuge in the church. Those, however, whose relatives were dead or mutilated, vehemently objected and tried to rush the guilty man and lynch him. But to finish the story, it was agreed at length that the good bishop would be given security, that the murderer would not be killed, and, as a symbol of their victory, he turned the man over to them. But as soon as they got him in their hands, they killed him. At that, the man of God grew pale and trembled as if he had been the author of this murder, resigned his church, and afterwards became a hermit in Egypt. I have set this down in writing just as that servant of God, Sir Stephen,[23] who is busy in your service, reported it to me.

20. Luke 19.23.
21. Jerome, *Epistula* 14, c. 8.1.57.
22. On Justus of Lyons, see his anonymous *vita*, AA SS Sept. 1. 373f.
23. On Stephen, see *Letter* 49 n. 1 in Reindel, *Briefe* 2 (1988) 62 n. 1.

Of Peter the Archbishop of Ravenna[24]

(17) Archbishop Peter also resigned from the Church of Ravenna and, while still alive, was succeeded by Honestus[25] during the reign of Otto I.

Of Gregory the Bishop of Nazianzus[26]

(18) It is also a matter of record that the celebrated Gregory of Nazianzus, whom historians call the Theologian, gave up the see of Constantinople during the reign of the religious and Catholic emperor Theodosius. If I perhaps am not thought credible in this matter, the words of his history are recounted here: "Since he had labored much and had rid the city of the scourge of heresy, the holy synod confirmed Gregory, the Theologian, as bishop of Constantinople and placed him on the throne against his will. But when this wise and holy man had learned that certain people in Egypt were envious at what had happened, after explaining in an address how this thing had come about, he freely left the throne from which he had ruled the city. At his refusal of the throne, the emperor and the synod promoted Nectarius.[27] These are not my words, but those found in his own history.

That Souls Condemned to the Pains of Hell Enjoy Respite on Sundays

(19) I think that we should speak of a subject that I heard about from Archbishop Humbert,[28] a man of great authority. After returning from the region of Apulia, he told me of a mountain range of rugged rock near Puteoli that rose from dark and ill-smelling waters. From these steaming waters, small birds are usually seen rising, and from Saturday evening until Monday morning they are ordinarily visible to humans. During

---

24. Cf. Schwartz, *Bistümer* 151. He was in office from 927 to 971.
25. On Archbishop Honestus (971–983), see Schwartz, *Bistümer* 151.
26. On Gregory, see Hefele-Leclercq, *Histoire* 2.1–10; J. T. Cummings, "Gregory of Nazianzus, St.," NCE 6 (1967) 791–94.
27. This citation cannot be found in the sources, including Gregory's own *Apologeticus*.
28. On Humbert's inclination to cite miraculous accounts, see H. G. Krause, "Über den Verfasser der *Vita Leonis IX papae*," DA 32 (1976) 49–85.

this time of grace, they are seen freely walking here and there about the mountain as if they had been liberated from their bonds. They stretch their wings, comb their feathers with their extended beaks and, as far as one can tell, peacefully relax during the refreshing time allotted them. These birds are never seen eating, nor is it possible to catch them with any sort of snare.[29]

(20) But at dawn on Monday a great raven that looks like a vulture begins with arched neck to croak at the birds, and at once they hide from him by diving into the water and are not seen again by human eyes until they emerge from the depths of these sulphurous waters on Saturday evening. So it is that some say that these are the souls of men that have been condemned to the fierce pains of hell, and that on Sunday and during the nights before and after they enjoy refreshing respite in honor of the Lord's resurrection. To this story the noble poet Prudentius also attests in his published poems.[30] But just as I had written this account of the birds and the raven appearing and disappearing in the waters, Desiderius, the abbot of the monks at Monte Cassino, came along and totally denied that these things ever take place. After I had talked with him for a while, and with Humbert, who had related this story, Humbert said, "I certainly do not vouch for the evidence of this account, but simply tell you what I heard from the people who live in that area." Yet since both these men, Desiderius and Humbert, are so trustworthy that neither can be denied credibility, I too am unwilling to affirm this account out of hand but think that it should be left to the investigation of the reader to discover whether it is true or not.

Of the Bishop of Capri[31]

(21) Now to apply this event to the subject we have been discussing. The bishop who presided at Capri, if I remember cor-

---

29. For the literature on this legendary phenomenon, see Reindel, *Briefe* 2 (1988) 335 n. 27.
30. Prudentius, *Cathemerinon* 5.125–28.27. On this legend, see also A. H. Krappe, "An Italian Legend in Pierre Damian," *The Romanic Review* 15 (1924) 94–99.
31. P. B. Gams, *Series episcoporum* 1 (1873) 867.

rectly, saw the great Pope Benedict,[32] who had died some time before, riding a black horse. As he saw him going on his way, he shouted, "Hello there, aren't you Pope Benedict who all of us know is dead?" And he said, "Yes, unhappily it is I." Then the other asked, "How is it with you, Father?" "I suffer heavy torments," he replied, "yet I am hopeful that with others' help I will win a reprieve. But go, I ask you, to my brother John,[33] who now presides over the Apostolic See, and tell him to act in my name and, for the benefit of my soul, to distribute to the poor the great sum of money he will find hidden in the safe. And let him know that by the decree of God's mercy this is how I can be helped. For all other sums that are given to the needy on my behalf are of no benefit to me since they were acquired through plunder and injustice." On hearing this, the bishop quickly travelled to Rome and reported to Pope John what his deceased brother had said. Soon after he laid aside the burdens of his episcopal office, became a monk, and thus, from the calamity that had befallen others, provided for his own salvation.

Of Pope Benedict[34]

(22) Humbert also told me this story about the pope who bore the same name as this Benedict, his nephew who occupied Rome by force, the next to succeed John, the immediate successor. He reported that a certain lord en route somewhere happened to ride past a mill. Suddenly he saw a huge monster and he was so terrified at the sight of it that he began to quake in horror. The monster appeared to have the ears and tail of an ass, while the rest of it was the body of a bear. When the traveller froze in terror at the approach of this strange creature and, in fear, began to think of running away, the hideous thing began to speak in a human voice: "Do not be afraid, my good sir," it said, "please be assured that I was once a man just as

---

32. Benedict VIII (d. 9 April 1024); see G. Tellenbach, "Benedetto VIII," *Dizionario biografico degli Italiani* 8 (1966) 350–54.
33. On John XIX (1024–1032), see Herrmann, "Tusculanerpapsttum" 166f., 180f.
34. Benedict IX; see O. Capitani, "Benedetto IX," *Dizionario biografico degli Italiani* 8 (1966) 354–366; V. Gellhaus, "Benedict IX," NCE 2 (1967) 274–275.

you are. But because I lived like an animal, I was rewarded after death by being made to look like an animal." Then, when the traveller asked him who he was, he said, "I had only the name Benedict, he who recently came into possession of the Apostolic See unworthily." When asked about the kind of punishment he had received, he replied, "Now, indeed, and until the day of judgment, I am dragged and forced along through filthy places filled with thorns, through burned regions that are ill-smelling and sulphurous. But after the last judgment, the boiling cauldron in the depths of hell, from which there is no escape, will swallow me up and subject me, body and soul, to irremediable torture, so that for me no hope remains that it will ever end." After he had said these things, he disappeared. But as I seek for a reason why he was seen in this form, I find no mystery behind this vision. For, since this man lived at the very height of luxury from the beginning of his calamitous pontificate until the end, it is proper that he appear to have the ears and tail of an ass. Now the ass is a wanton animal, as the prophet indicates when speaking of those who surrender to carnal impurity: "Their flesh is like the flesh of asses."[35] To explain why in his other parts he had the form of a bear, I have learned that at all times he lived a sensuous life. For, as we learn from the natural philosophers, when a bear gives birth, it does not bear a whelp like other animals, but produces a piece of flesh. As soon as it comes forth, the bear quickly licks and fondles it, and thus with its tongue forms it into a creature after its own likeness.[36] So it is right that one who has lived a wanton and carnal life should be matched in form with an ass and a bear. Surely it is evident to all how much better it would have been had he renounced the episcopal office and done penance, than to continue in office until the end of his days and completely lose his true life.[37]

(23) But as I sadly relate this story, I will add another tale about a miracle of divine goodness which I also learned from Humbert. But this one has a happy ending.

35. Cf. Ezek 23.20.
36. Cf. Ambrose, *Hexameron* 6.4.214; Isidore, *Etymologies* 12.2.22.
37. See Herrmann, "Tusculanerpapsttum" 165.

Of the Monk Who Was Condemned to Hell and Was Later Set Free
(24) In the monastery of St. Sylvester, he reported, which lies in the territory of Urbino,[38] a certain monk died and, from early dawn until about eight o'clock in the morning, the corpse, washed and bound in the usual manner,[39] lay on its bier, with the brothers standing about chanting psalms. When Mass was almost over and they had sung the *Agnus Dei* as prescribed, suddenly the dead man lying in their midst came to life and sat up. The brothers were stunned and frightened by this unusual event, since he whom they were burying with full funeral rites was once again alive. When they came closer and eagerly tried to hear what he was saying, my God! he began to curse and swear, using the blessed name of our savior in blasphemy. And when the crucifix, that symbol of life, was handed him to kiss, he sacrilegiously spat on it. At the same time, he did not hesitate to abuse the inviolate Mother of God with vile and disgraceful language. "Why are you chanting for me," he said, "and why do you try to say Mass for my soul? I have gone down into the fiery depths of hell, for it is there that my lord and master, Lucifer,[40] has sent me forever. He has placed on my brow a crown of bronze that always glows with inextinguishable fire, and has clothed me with a cloak of metal, the same that he was wearing. The mantle was so long that it reached to the heels, and so fiercely hot that it seemed to be molten, and from it flowed drops of fire." When the brethren as one man exhorted him to do penance and confess his secret sins, he again began to curse and blaspheme and, in mad and sacrilegious words, condemned not only works of penance but all the mysteries of our redemption.

(25) The monks, however, never tired of using the ever successful weapon of prayer and, shedding their habits, began to beat their bodies with switches, to strike their chests with their fists, and never gave up chanting and reciting every prayer they

38. See Palazzini, "Chiesa Marchigiana" 220.
39. See Theodomar of Monte Cassino, *Epistula ad Theodoricum* 32, ed. K. Hallinger, *Corpus Consuetudinum Monasticarum* 1 (1963), 135.
40. On Lucifer, see Isa 14.12 and Jerome, *In Esaiam* 5.12/14.168f.

knew. With all the brothers engaged in mournful prayer and fasting and eagerly awaiting the goodness of God, finally the brightness of God's power appeared. For suddenly, the desperate man whom the yawning depths had swallowed up became conscious, praised the omnipotence of God our savior, renounced the evil delusions of Satan, venerated the cross, and eagerly requested a penance. Then he confessed that after leaving the world he had sinned through fornication and had never revealed it in confession. And so, praising and blessing God, he lived until the next day, and thus marvellously restored to his creator, he left this world acknowledging the goodness of God. Thus, indeed, did fraternal prayer bear fruit by snatching a victim from the very bowels of hell, and from the quickly extinguished flames, it took a living stone to place in the structure of the heavenly Jerusalem. These things were told me by Humbert, whose words seem to be grounded in apostolic truth.

(26) Now if he who had fallen in monastic life and who must answer only for his own soul deserved to receive such a terrible sentence, how can an unworthy bishop like me be secure when he is guilty of so many souls who are lost through his negligence and bad example? Since it is evident that there were many who shed their episcopal responsibilities for the slightest of reasons, it will suffice here to include one such case taken from the history that Cassiodorus translated from Greek into Latin.[41] I will merely transcribe the words of this history so as to remove all doubt from those who might hesitate to accept this story.

Of Silvanus the Bishop of Philippopolis

(27) The report says that "Silvanus was a rhetorician, at first a student of Troilus, the sophist; a perfect Christian who also held the monastic life in high regard. Nor did he ever appear wearing the doctor's mantle. Some time later the Bishop Atticus befriended him and consecrated him bishop of Philippopolis. But after spending three years in Thrace and, because

---

41. Cassiodorus, *Historia tripartita* 12.8.21–25, 675f.

he was in frail and delicate health, he could not bear the cold, he asked Atticus to send him to another place, saying that the cold climate was the only reason that he wished to leave. After another candidate had been consecrated in his stead, Silvanus stayed in Constantinople where he lived the monastic life to perfection, and was such a humble man that he went about despised among the great population of the city because he wore sandals. Some time later the bishop of the Church of Troy died, and the Trojans came asking for a bishop. While Atticus was thinking about whom he should consecrate, it happened that Silvanus came to pay him a visit. When the former saw him, his deliberations were at an end. He then said to Silvanus, 'You have no further reason for avoiding the burden of ecclesiastical office. Troy is not a place that has cold weather and, with the help of God, a spot has turned up that is suited to your health. Therefore, get ready and travel to Troy.' And Silvanus went."

(28) But if someone should perhaps accuse him of indiscretion and condemn him for going elsewhere to enjoy his comfort after despising his former position because of the cold, let him take note of the miracle that happened afterwards because of him, and at least stop heaping blame on this good man. For the story of his life continues: "After that, I will report the miracle that took place on his account. A large ship, equipped with great masts, was being built on the shore near Troy, and when the shipwrights wished to launch it with the help of many people tugging at the lines, it would not move. As this had happened for several days, they suspected that the ship was possessed by the devil. They then went to Bishop Silvanus and asked him to say a prayer at the site in the belief that the ship could thus be launched. But in humble words he told them that he was a sinner, stating that this was a task for a just man and not for him. But at their request, he went to the shore and, after saying a prayer, touched a rope and ordered them to get on with the work. After a short tug, the ship slipped quickly into the sea."[42]

42. Cassiodorus, *Historia tripartita* 12.8.26–27, 676.

(29) This miracle caused all the people of the province to revere this man. For if Silvanus had sinned by resigning his episcopal office and by going to another see, he would have appeared not as a wonderworker but as one who was pitied for his guilt. For the power to work miracles is a sign of sanctity. Moreover, if, as is said, one is not allowed to resign an episcopal see for any reason, how is it that we find so many holy bishops in our histories transferring from one see to another, for certainly they had first to abandon their own sees before going elsewhere? Most of them, moreover, when turning their backs on the position given them, had no idea that they would be transferred to another.

(30) Certainly it stands to reason that it is a smaller matter when one simply abandons his episcopal office than when he moves from one see to another. Present-day cleverness, therefore, will not dissuade me from that to which the example of our venerable Fathers invites me. For if blessed Silvanus, only because of physical discomfort from the cold, could desert his office without blame, why should I be held guilty of fault for turning my back on pastoral duties, since in my daily involvement in secular affairs I am growing lukewarm in my love of God and begin to feel the deadly cold of a languid spirit? For as Scripture says, "As a well keeps its water cold, so does wickedness keep the soul cold."[43] I remember often being so on fire with the love of God[44] that I then wished to break the bonds of my flesh, and free, as it were, of the filth and darkness of my prison, I began to yearn with all my being for the light of eternity. Then it seemed to me, as the Lord promised in the words of the prophet, that my heart of flesh had been made of wax.[45] The fire of heavenly desire would cause my yearning to melt away and would often bathe my face in floods of tears. I stand in horror, on the other hand, when I hear my many words that were not conducive to leading anyone to Christ— all the nonsense and trifling worldly speech that I uttered, like the barking of a dog or the bite of a serpent. Often, in a most

---

43. Jer 6.7.
44. Damian here seems to speak of personal mystical experiences.
45. Cf. Ezek 11.19.

existential insight, I beheld Christ pierced with nails, hanging on the cross, and with my mouth I eagerly tried to catch the dripping blood.

(31) If, moreover, I should attempt to put in writing the sights I beheld in contemplation, whether of the sacred humanity of our redeemer or the unspeakable beauty of the glory of heaven, it would take me days to explain them all. But now I am as hard as stone since I am constantly exhausted with external affairs and never experience the tears of deep compunction.[46] Often I place my hand upon my breast as if to show the physician of souls the wound that festers there, crying aloud and exclaiming with deepest supplication: You who illumined the caverns of hell with the rays of your divinity, remove this darkness from my soul and peacefully shed on it the light of your truth. Once Jesus stopped as the blind man along the way cried out to him, and he restored light to his eyes;[47] but another time he passed by as if he had not heard those idle cries, and so the miserable sightless man continued in his blindness. But I, alas, like another Samson shorn of his seven locks,[48] weep at the loss of the sevenfold gifts of the Holy Spirit; and with eyes torn, not from my head but from my heart, reel under the weight of secular cares. I am that Zedekiah[49] whom the king of Babylon first deprived of his good works, that is, who first slaughtered his sons, and then put out his eyes, cutting off the light of intimate contemplation.

(32) Therefore, if that holy man, Silvanus, did not hesitate to give up Thrace solely because of bodily inconvenience, why cannot I desert Rome to avoid such great wounds to my soul? However, it is not altogether harmless to my body since it is the site of constant fevers. And so I remember once composing this quatrain:

> Rome, the devourer of men, bends their necks with arduous burdens:
> Rome, rich in feverish fumes, its harvest of death is yet richer.

46. Cf. *Letter* 50 n. 74.
47. Cf. Luke 18.35–43.
48. Cf. Judg 16.19.
49. Cf. 2 Kgs 25.6–7.

For him who can stand to the wind, the fevers of
Rome are his consort.
Him whom they once infest, while he lives is always
their victim.[50]

Permit him, therefore, who is bound, body and soul, by adversity to return as a fugitive to his master; and after turning his back on the swine and the husks they eat, let the son go back to his father's embrace;[51] with his locks again grown long, let Samson again glow with his former vigor,[52] so that he may again wear the cloak he had lost and, with his strength renewed, overthrow those who had previously been the victors.

Of the Simonist Bishop Who Could Not Pronounce the Name of the Holy Spirit.

(33) Along with other matters, I think it worthwhile to insert among these accounts the story I heard from Hildebrand, the archdeacon of the Roman Church. When he was still serving only as subdeacon,[53] he was sent by Pope Victor as a plenipotentiary to Gaul, and there he convened a synod.[54] With the authority of the Apostolic See, he there deposed six bishops involved in various kinds of crime. Among these was a certain bishop, who, because he had insinuated himself into the episcopal office through the heresy of simony, was not able, no matter how hard he tried, to pronounce the name of the Holy Spirit.[55] Indeed, he experienced no difficulty and easily pronounced the names of Father and Son, but when he came to the Holy Spirit, he began to stutter and his tongue remained rigid. And so he deserved to lose the Holy Spirit whom he had bought: He who was excluded from his soul could also find no place on his tongue. Convicted, therefore, because of this dif-

50. See Lokrantz, *L'opera*, nos. 34, 57.
51. Cf. Luke 15.15–20.
52. Cf. Judg 16.22.
53. Jasper, *Das Papstwahldekret von 1059* 34ff., doubts the dating of this event (23 Aug.–14 Oct. 1059) by Borino, "L'arcidiaconato" 513.
54. On this legation, see Hefele-Leclercq, *Histoire* 4.1120f.
55. On the literature of this anecdote, in which the simonist bishop is identified as Hugh of Embrun, see Reindel, *Briefe* 2 (1988) 345 n. 51.

ficulty, he abandoned his episcopal office. But in no way do I consider him worthy to be numbered among those holy men who, for love of Christ, deserted their pontifical dignities.

Of a Count Who Was Damned because of a Church That He Possessed

(34) And now, since I already mentioned this most prudent man, I will not hesitate to tell of another outstanding example related by him, even though it has little to do with our present theme. For while he was speaking in the Church of Arezzo[56] on the subject of unjust possession of church property, and you, venerable father, were present on that occasion, he included this very appropriate story. In Germany, he said, there was a certain rich and powerful count who died almost ten years ago and, although it is almost a miracle for men of this rank, he was a man of good reputation and unsullied life, as far as one can humanly judge. After his death, a certain religious descended in spirit into hell and there saw our count standing on the top rung of a ladder. Now it happened that this ladder appeared to rise from the midst of crackling flames of avenging fire, and was meant to receive all those who were descendants from the same line of counts. The place was one of loathsome darkness, an immense abyss that extended without limit in all directions, and from the deepest point rose the ladder that was placed there. The line of heirs was arranged in such a way that when one of them was newly arrived, he occupied the topmost rung on the ladder, and he who had been there before, and all the others who were near him, went lower. When, with the passing of time, one after another of that family found his place after death on this ladder, the others moved down to lower levels by reason of the inevitable judgment that had been passed on them.

(35) When the man who had beheld these things inquired about the cause of this horrible damnation, and especially why this count was punished, who in his time had lived so justly, decently, and honestly, he heard that it was on account of a

---

56. See Lucchesi, *Vita* no. 145, who dates this event for Oct.–Nov. 1059.

piece of land that belonged to the Church of Metz,[57] which his great-grandfather had taken from blessed Stephen. He was now the tenth heir to succeed to this inheritance, and all heirs were condemned to the same punishment, for since the same kind of avarice had united them in sinning, so also a common torture would be theirs in suffering the penalty of this fierce fire.

(36) Unjust possessors of ecclesiastical property should take notice and carefully beware that while they satisfy themselves with the profits of others, afterward they do not feed the devouring flames with their very beings. Now since I am of a mind not to be so strict in observing the rules of writing as I am to edify my brothers, I have inserted here several items that are extraneous to the purpose of this work, so that, in a way, I might tightly bind with the cord of my writing that which bobs about on the waves, lest it be completely forgotten. For when one goes fishing, if luck comes his way, he suddenly captures an animal or a bird, even though he had never intended to hunt or go fowling.

(37) Moreover, to bolster my assertions also with the authority of the gospel, when our savior went to the house of the official of the synagogue to raise his daughter to life, he healed the woman suffering from a hemorrhage,[58] just as if he were doing so without first intending it. Who should wonder, then, if when writing we should sometimes pause in our appointed task and insert something that we think will serve to edify? Even so, this too does not run counter to my purpose, for if this man perished for possessing a small piece of church land, what should be thought of him who, as bishop, unworthily presides over an entire church and does not relinquish it? But now, after this digression, let me return to the topic.

---

57. On the cathedral in Metz, cf. E. Lesne, *Histoire de la propriété ecclésiastique en France* 1 (1910) 89. See also the *Vita sancti Arnulfi*, c. 14, 347f. for an account of this theft.

58. Cf. Matt 9.18–25.

Of Milesius the Martyr

(38) I will also report what the *Tripartite History*[59] has to say about the blessed martyr, Milesius, and, so that my readers may think it more credible, I will use the very words of that *History* in my account. "Then also," it says, "a bishop named Milesius won the crown of martyrdom. First, however, he was in the army in Persia, but afterwards he left the service and became eager to lead an apostolic life. For it is said that after he was consecrated as bishop in a Persian city he suffered many difficulties. He was wounded and dragged about, but bore all his trials like a man. When, however, he could not persuade anyone there to become a Christian, he was greatly displeased, cursed the city, and departed. Some time later, when the lords of that place had offended the king, an army came with 300 elephants and destroyed the city and turned it into a wasteland, fit only for farming. But the Bishop Milesius, carrying only a bag that contained a book of the holy Gospels, travelled to Jerusalem to pray, and then to Egypt to visit the monks who lived there. The Syrians are witnesses of this man's holiness and of the miracles that he performed, and have written his acts and life." Notice that he, who abandoned the title to the see that had been given him, not only did not incur the guilt of crime but, what is more, obtained the power of working miracles.

Of Arnulf the Bishop of Metz

(39) Indeed, as I peruse the expanse of history, as if looking curiously at the face of the heavens, blessed Arnulf,[60] the bishop of the Church of Metz, flashes upon the scene like a golden star. By the brightness of his example he drives away the darkness of our ignorance, adds insuperable strength to my assertions, and unties every knot of doubt in this argument. In fact, as I learned from the reliable account of my brethren who assuredly have read his history, he performed the duties

---

59. Cassiodorus, *Historia tripartita* 3.2.35–38, 137f.
60. Arnulf of Metz (614–629) was neither the father of Pepin nor the grandfather of Carloman. His history is reported by Paul the Deacon, *Liber de episcopis Mettensibus* 264.

of the office of duke in Lorraine, not far from Flanders. He was, moreover, the father of King Pepin and the grandfather of Carloman. Consumed with the ardor of the Holy Spirit, and putting aside his love for his wife and children, he exchanged the pomp of earthly splendor for the glorious poverty of Christ, and led the life of a hermit. It happened that he came to a river known as the Mosel and, wishing to cross, he arrived at the middle of the bridge where the rushing waters were deepest. There he threw away his ring and made this bargain with himself. If, he said, I again recover this ring from the swirling waters, I will then know that without a doubt I have been absolved from all my sins. Soon after this event he went into a hermitage where he lived for a while, dead to himself and to the world.

(40) In the meantime, at the death of the bishop of the Church of Metz, divine providence disposed that blessed Arnulf be promoted to govern that see. Since in the hermitage he was not accustomed to eating meat, he continued to abstain from it also as bishop. Once a fish was brought to him as a gift. When the cook was cleaning and preparing it, he found a ring in its entrails; at once he happily brought it to his master. On seeing the ring, the bishop recognized it immediately and wondered not so much at the brilliance of its shining metal, but at this—that by the grace of God he had won pardon for his sins. And what makes one wonder the more is that it is a two-day journey from the bridge where the ring was flung away to the place where the fish was presented to the venerable bishop. Then the man of God, in that he had been absolved from his sins, was filled with still greater fear of God, and thought himself to be the more in God's debt the more he beheld the goodness of heavenly mercy shown in his behalf. Therefore, after selecting a successor, he again repaired to the hermitage, and after giving up his pastoral duties, lived there until he died a happy death. By what he did, this famous man taught us what we also should do.

Of Farulfus the Bishop of Cisterna

(41) Again, it was scarcely fifteen days ago that I witnessed the venerable man, Farulfus,[61] willingly give up the administration of his church. In his see in Cisterna, a city in Apulia, which he now resigned, he bound two iron hoops about his chest and stomach with which now for almost seven years he has punished himself. He almost never drinks wine and mortifies himself with frequent fasts. Such a man has exhorted me to renounce the episcopacy no less by his words than by his example.

Of Hildulfus the Archbishop of Trier

(42) The whole West, moreover, is aware of the holiness of Hildulfus, the archbishop of Trier,[62] and of the wonderful life that he led. As the history of his life attests, he begged the bishop of the city of Jacob Leuchae, now known as Toul, to provide him a place of solitude where he might properly live. First, however, he chose a successor and, after building a monastery, he walked the path of strict monastic discipline. In that life, the many miracles performed by him are clear evidence that in giving up his see this man of the Lord not only was not guilty of any fault, but offered to God a sacrifice acceptable to him.

Of Deodatus, Also an Archbishop of Trier

(43) What can I report of Deodatus,[63] a man of great sanctity who was also bishop of the same Church of Trier? As his authentic history relates, he obtained from Girbaldus, the holy bishop of Leucha, a place in a valley of the Vosges mountains

---

61. Neither Farulfus nor the see of Cisterna in Apulia can be identified. There was a city of Cisterna in the province of Bari, but it had never been an episcopal see.

62. Despite the *vita* of Hildulfus by Valcandus (BHL 3947–49), and the work of Anton Michel (ZKG 64 [1952/53] 225–59), grave doubt exists that Hildulfus was ever bishop of Trier.

63. There is also much confusion in Valcandus (cf. n. 62 *supra*), over Deodatus, who is called the bishop of Nevers, and who also appears in the eleventh-century lists of bishops for Nevers.

where, renouncing the world, he lived a praiseworthy life, founded monasteries and, after long service in the militia of Christ, victoriously entered the select assembly of the blessed.

Of Gondebertus the Archbishop of Sens

(44) And what of Gondebertus,[64] the celebrated archbishop of Sens? Clearly aflame with heavenly desire, he abandoned the church that had been entrusted to him, and in a place called Grandiavium he built the monastery of Sens, which took its name from the church he had left behind. I had intended not to exceed twenty in my list, but I cannot overlook that which is right before our eyes.

Of Lambert the Bishop of Florence

(45) And last of all, omitting still others, let us come to an example close to home. Lambert,[65] of blessed memory, who before your time presided as the third bishop of the Church of Florence, subjected himself to monastic discipline, turning his back on his pontifical office. Your exalted holiness is not unaware that this man's splendid reputation is on everyone's lips, and that the sweet odor of his fame is there for all to observe.

Of Nonnus the Bishop

(46) The blessed martyr Nonnus,[66] who is also known as Hippolytus, comes to mind and should not be overlooked. After winning more than 30,000 Saracens to faith in Christ by his most efficacious preaching, and after calling blessed Pelagia from a life of ill repute to the purity of the Church, and finally, after composing several volumes on sacred doctrine, he at last abandoned his bishopric. He left the area of Antioch where he originated and travelled to Rome. When blessed Aurea was martyred near the city of Ostia by being thrown into the sea

---

64. See Richer, *Gesta Senoniensis ecclesiae* 1.1–3.257ff.
65. On Lambert of Florence (1025–1032), see Gams, *Series episcoporum* 747; Davidsohn, *Geschichte* 1.150.
66. On Nonnus-Hippolytus, see *De S. Hippolyto* 2.11–12, AA SS August 4.506, where Damian's account is found. Nonnus is the patron of Ostia, Damian's episcopal see; cf. Lucchesi, *Vita* no. 113.

with a stone tied about her neck, blessed Nonnus devotedly retrieved her holy remains and carefully buried them. Soon afterwards, the same persecutor, named Ulpius, ordered him to be drowned near the Tiber in a ditch filled with water and, after his triumphant martyrdom, his body was buried with Christian devotion in the city of Porto. At that spot, for the space of an hour, a voice was heard like that of children calling, "Thanks be to God." It is perfectly clear, therefore, that he who deserved such an ending to his life did not appear to have offended God because he deserted his diocese.

Of the Bishop of Penna

(47) In our own day, moreover, the bishop of Penna[67] freely gave up his pontifical title and with sincere devotion willingly entered the service of his successor. Indeed, his successor told me that he was so submissive and showed such obedience and humility that he seemed never to remember that he had been placed in authority over others.

Of the Bishop of Cagli

(48) Also in our own time, Liutulfus, the bishop of Cagli,[68] divested himself of his episcopal dignity, handed over his church to his successor who is now in office, and thus, if his spirit does not weaken, won the opportunity of doing penance. Fortunate, indeed, is he who so arranges his life in these mortal days that he is able through repentance to deplore his sins. Fortunate, I say, is he who in time disposes of whatever might be standing in his way as an obstacle to truth. For whatever we have committed in this life must here be corrected through penance according to the measure of our sins, or, without doubt, it will be left to the retribution of punishment in the life to come.

---

67. See Schwartz, *Bistümer* 238, who notes a bishop Bernard of Penna-Pescara, who resigned his see in 1055.
68. On Liutulfus and the diocese of Cagli, see Schwartz, *Bistümer* 241; Lucchesi, *Vita* no. 32.

Of the Lay Brother Who Was Beaten by St. Andrew and St. Gregory

(49) In reference to what I have been saying, it is not out of place to insert here briefly what I heard from the reliable account of my brethren. In the monastery known as Clivus Scauri,[69] which St. Gregory built within the walls of Rome, a certain boy was presented as an oblate by his parents that he might henceforth serve God. Afterwards, when he grew up, he left the monastery and returned to the world and married. As a young man, by the judgment of God, he was suddenly afflicted with a throat disease, and as the sickness grew in intensity, he was at the point of death. Finally the wicked fugitive asked to be carried to the monastery; there he accepted a penance for his evil deeds and received the habit. While his wife and several others were standing at his bedside, he began to groan and cry aloud, and to scream at the top of his voice as if he were delirious. When they earnestly asked him why he was making such a commotion, he replied, "Don't you see the blessed Andrew the apostle and St. Gregory together beating me with their sharp whips?" Moaning again and crying bitterly, he then breathed deeply and said, "They have now been beating me because I left the monastery and took a wife." Again, after much weeping and wailing, he quieted down and said, "Now they are afflicting me because, not only did I give nothing to poor beggars, especially the Scots, but what is worse, I often made fun of them." Continuing to cry and lament, he admitted that he had borrowed six pennies from a poor widow and refused to return them. "And now I am receiving as many blows at the hand of these saints who are beating me as the woman took steps in coming to me asking for her money. And that you may know that I am not lying, the day after tomorrow I am going to die at noon."

(50) It was then Friday. While it was still dark the following Sunday morning—it was Palm Sunday—all marvelled as he quickly jumped out of bed, snatching his scapular and hairshirt that were lying nearby, and rushed in a frenzy into the

---

69. On which, see John the Deacon, *Sancti Gregorii magni vita* 1.6 (PL 75.65 AB).

church of St. Andrew. There, lying on the ground, he said to the brethren who were present, "Now that I have been flogged by the saints' blows, I leave my body as pure as when I came from the baptismal font." During the celebration of the Mass, just as the reading of the Passion of our Lord was completed, at the hour that he had predicted, he gave up his spirit to God. When the body was stripped for washing, as was the custom, they saw on his limbs such welts and cuts as if his body had been scourged with material whips.

Of the Little Dog That Was Killed before the Couch of St. Gregory

(51) But why should we wonder that the saints of God, who are to be judges of the world, should punish a man who has the use of reason, since sometimes, as we also learn, they vent their anger on a senseless animal? Now in that same monastery there is a grotto said to have been St. Gregory's. In it there is a spring where he used to drink that gushes clear cold water; so too there is a stone couch that can still be seen, where he used to rest in the summer time. Once a little pregnant dog entered the grotto by chance, either to drink because of the heat, or rather, perhaps, to give birth to her pups in that place. But she did not reach the water, for as soon as she came near the couch, she fell over dead. With what dread, therefore, should we consider God's judgments toward men when he visits such terrible punishments on animals that are without the use of reason. For if almighty God would not allow that innocent little dog to even touch the ordinary water in that holy place, what disgust must he feel when an evil person approaches the sacred altar to receive his Body and Blood? But when a wicked man provokes and irritates God with his foul deeds, divine patience does not at once impose retribution, but holds him accountable for everlasting punishment.

Of the Princes Pandulf and John Who Were Condemned to Hell

(52) As I was in the process of composing this piece, Desiderius, the abbot of the monks of Monte Cassino, arrived.[70] Since he is related to the blessed Daniel by reason of his name,

---

70. On Damian's meeting with Desiderius in Florence, January 1060, cf. JL 4426.

he is also[71] like him in his statement of truth. And so he is the source of a story that, I am persuaded, should here be written down. He told me of a servant of God in the area around Naples, who lived alone in a rugged cave near the main road. While he was chanting his psalms one night, he opened the window of his cell to see what time it was, when he saw many black men, who looked like Ethiopians,[72] passing along the way, driving a long line of pack animals laden with hay. When out of curiosity he asked them who they were and for what purpose they were transporting this fodder, they answered, "We are evil spirits and we are getting this ready not as food for cattle, but rather as fuel to burn men. We are waiting here in the neighborhood for Prince Pandulf of Capua[73] who has just died, and for John, the commander of the troops in Naples, who is ill but still alive."[74] At once the man of God quickly went to visit John and faithfully told him everything that he had seen and heard. At that time the Emperor Otto II had come to Calabria to fight against the Saracens.[75] When John heard these things, he said, "Now it is necessary for me as a vassal to meet with the emperor and to discuss with him the state of affairs in this region. But I swear that after the emperor's departure I shall leave the world and become a monk."

(53) But to make sure that what this man had told him was true, he at once sent a messenger to the fortress of Capua where he found that Pandulf was already dead. But John, the commander of the troops, even before the emperor had arrived in his territory, lived for only fifteen more days. At his death, Mount Vesuvius, from which hell frequently breaks loose,[76] erupted in flames; so it was obviously proved that the

---

71. See Dan 9.23, 10.11, 19, where Daniel is called a *vir desideriorum*.
72. On black Ethiopians, see Isidore, *Etymologies* 14.5.14. Damian refers to Ethiopians also in *Letter* 109 (PL 144.1020A). For a negative view of these people, cf. Zeph 2.12.
73. Peter the Deacon uses this account in his revision of the *Chronicle of Monte Cassino*, referring to Pandulf IV (d. 1049): *Chronica monasterii Casinensis* 327f.
74. On John, see K. and M. Uhlirz, *Jahrbücher des deutschen Reiches unter Otto II. und Otto III.* 1 (1954) 172.
75. Cf. Uhlirz, *Jahrbücher* 1.174–83.
76. Similarly, according to Isidore, *Etymologies* 14.8.14, Mt. Etna is the entrance to hell.

hay that had been prepared by the demons was nothing else but fuel for the fierce fire that awaits evil and reprobate men. For whenever a wicked rich man dies in that region, fire is seen to erupt from that mountain; and such a mass of sulphurous resin suddenly flows from Vesuvius that it forms into a flood rushing down into the sea. Here, indeed, one can physically see what John in Revelations says of the wicked: "But their legacy will be the second death in the lake burning with fire and brimstone."[77]

(54) In the same context, the prince of Salerno, the grandfather of prince Waimar,[78] who a few years ago was killed by the swords of his own men for his many acts of violence and oppression, when looking out one day and seeing black smoke and sulphurous flames escaping from far off Mount Vesuvius, at once concluded, "Surely some rich criminal is at the point of death and is about to go to hell." Oh the blindness of a wicked man and, what is more, how terrible the judgment of the creator in regard to our deeds! A few nights later, while securely sleeping with a whore, he died. As she later reported, not knowing what had happened, she stayed with him for some time, and then she repulsed him—not a man but a lifeless corpse.

(55) Also, a certain priest from the area of Naples, wanting to learn more of this phenomenon, which he should not have done, decided with much daring and presumption to approach the place where this hellish pit was most active. Therefore he said Mass, and thus prepared and armed, he began his trip. But since this rash investigator came closer than others usually go, he was unable to turn back and was never seen again.

(56) Another priest, too, left his sick mother in Benevento, and while accompanying his lord near the area of Naples, saw the escaping flames and heard the cry of someone in pain, which, without doubt, he recognized as the voice of his mother. He noted the hour and learned for sure that it was then that his mother had died.

77. Rev 21.8.
78. This is the grandfather of Waimar V, assassinated by his own men in 1052; see *Chronica monasterii Casinensis* 2.82, 329.

Of the Twenty-Four Elders

(57) But to return to the subject we have been discussing: It will suffice that we have listed two dozen bishops who decided to relinquish their administrations with burning love for God, so that, freed of earthly duties, they might depend more closely and familiarly on God. Truly, these venerable pontiffs, like the twenty-four elders, prostrate themselves before the one sitting on the throne, and worship the one who lives forever and ever, casting their crowns before the throne of the Lord.[79] They indeed place their crowns before the Lord's throne as they put away the adornments proper to their dignity for his love. Like them also, they have golden vials full of incense made up of the prayers of the saints,[80] so that they might be able to offer God a sweeter and purer odor of prayer as they strive to set themselves apart from the affairs of this world.

(58) Surely, unless I were avoiding the distaste of prolixity, I should also quite properly include Athanasius[81] among these men. Under the Arian Emperor Constantius he deserted his church and betook himself to a solitary workshop belonging to a holy woman. There he hid for six years, unknown to all except to the woman who lived there. I could also add blessed Martin[82] to their number, who in part gave up the rights of his episcopal office during most of the last fifteen years of his life, completely absenting himself from councils and synods so that he might live closer to God.

Of the Holy Bishops Gaudiosus, Quodvultdeus, Sergius, and Three Others Who, on the Authority of Blessed Gregory, Deserted Their Churches

(59) I might also add blessed Gaudiosus,[83] who was given the charge of the church of Abitina,[84] a diocese in Africa. As the Vandals were invading Africa he, together with St. Quodvult-

---

79. Cf. Rev 4.10.
80. Cf. Rev 5.8.
81. See *Epistola Palladii episcopi Cappadociae* 51 (PL 74.334C–335C).
82. On Martin, see Sulpicius Severus, *Vita sancti Martini* 9.3 and 10.2, ed. J. Fontaine, SC 133 (1967) 270–74.
83. See R. Aubert, "Gaudiosus . . . ," DHGE 20 (1982) 47.
84. Cf. A. Audollent, "Abitinae," DHGE 1 (1912) 129–31.

deus and other bishops, fled and founded a monastery in the city of Parthenope.[85] If he could flee to avoid the swords of the Vandals, how much more should I fly from the snares of eternal death?

(60) Sergius the metropolitan of Damascus[86] could also conveniently be added here, since for the love of Christ he left his church and travelled as a pilgrim to Rome. Finding the basilica of blessed Boniface and Alexius[87] almost devoid of priestly service, he went to Benedict[88] the bishop of the see of Rome and begged to be allowed to set up the monastic life in that church. Having lived in that place as a religious for many years, he there ended his days.

(61) Blessed Gregory, moreover, as one can find in the history contained in his register, allowed three bishops—one of the first see of Justinian, another of Rimini, and a third only because of a head ailment—to freely leave their sees, taking with them a necessary stipend from the churches they had deserted. And he permitted them to appoint successors. Anyone who has read the letters to Anatolius the subdeacon of Constantinople, and to the bishops Marinianus and Etherius of Ravenna will not doubt this.[89]

(62) So now, if we join to the twenty-four bishops I mentioned above these three, who left their churches by permission of blessed Gregory; and moreover, if we add to all of them blessed Gaudiosus, Quodvultdeus, and Sergius the metropolitan of Damascus, we clearly find thirty bishops who renounced their sees for the love of God. Let the investigator of the past, the researcher into histories and annals, tell me whether any pontiff of the Apostolic See had ever objected to so many holy Fathers turning their backs on pastoral care. Who of them

---

85. On which, see Victor of Vita, *Historia persecutionis Africanae provinciae* 1.15.8.

86. On Sergius, see Duchesne, *Mélanges d'archéologie et d'histoire* 10.225–50.

87. On which, see B. Hamilton, "The Monastic Revival in Tenth-Century Rome," *Studia monastica* 4 (1962) 35–68.

88. Benedict VII (974–983); see P. Delagu, *Dizionario biografico degli italiani* 8 (1966) 346–50.

89. See John the Deacon, *Sancti Gregorii magni vita* 4.39 (PL 75.201D–203D); Ryan, *Sources* 72f., no. 129.

ever reprehended one of these men through rescripts sent to him, or condemned him by synodal action? Let him speak, or since he is unable to find a thing to report, let him bite his impudent tongue and stop disparaging me with unjust detractions.

(63) Did not the lesser Pope Benedict,[90] to whom we referred above, give up the administration of the Apostolic See and establish Gregory, who was called Gratian, as his successor in the Roman Church?[91] Later, when the council[92] had debated these events with the emperor Henry present, since payment had intervened, he who accepted the money was deposed, and he who abdicated was not excommunicated.

(64) As an example for imitation we can also bring forward St. Benedict, who like some great pontiff did not hesitate to abdicate the government committed to him.

(65) Leo, the abbot of Nonantula, also comes to mind.[93] While he was still a cleric and, having satisfied his devotion, was returning from Jerusalem, he began his career possessed of nothing else but a donkey. With it he wandered about every day in the woodlands and fields, gathering material that would serve the brethren to wipe themselves after they had taken care of the needs of nature.[94] Having performed manual tasks of this kind that were to his glory while practicing saying the psalter, he at length was promoted as a holy priest to offering the sacred mysteries to God with many tears. Later, however, when he was compelled to accept the government of the monastery, he stated that he was frequently unhappy. "Jesus, I beg you," he said, "I grasp your feet and, now miserable and blind, I turn

90. Most reports of Benedict IX speak, as Damian does, of a voluntary retirement; see Herrmann, "Tusculanerpapsttum" 151–55.
91. On the problem of the deposition of Gregory VI, see F. J. Schmale, "Die 'Absetzung' Gregors VI. in Sutri und die synodale Tradition," *Annuarium historiae conciliorum* 11 (1979) 55–103, esp. 92 nn. 134–35.
92. On the synods of Sutri and Rome, see Hefele-Leclercq, *Histoire* 4.981–94.
93. The problem of the identity of Leo of Nonantula and of other personalities here referred to is fully discussed in Reindel, *Briefe* 2 (1988) 364–65 nn. 92, 94.
94. See also *Letter* 50 n. 69, where the same word, *anitergium*, is used; cf. also DuCange 1.256.

the mills of the world." Scarcely two years had passed when he restored his pastoral staff to the hands of Otto who was then ruling the empire. Then while staying at St. Boniface in Rome, he kept busy for the rest of his days with nothing but what would win him a reward in eternal life. Afterwards, a blind man came to his tomb and, as is claimed, his sight was restored.

(66) While there has been no lack of bishops—and it may be observed that I went to examples of abbots, which are less apt—so that I do not introduce a new classification, I mention Leo the archbishop of Ravenna, who when afflicted with paralysis of the mouth, gave up his see, and thus lived on in private life for almost four years. While Otto the Third was happily reigning, Frederick[95] became his successor and gave him ample goods of the Church whereby he might support himself.

Conclusion of the Foregoing Discussion

(67) Supported by the authority of these and other Fathers, I irrevocably return my episcopal office and the monasteries into your holy hands, and I renounce all right whereby I might in the future reopen the issue and reclaim them. And since I am not worthy to remain in ecclesiastical office because of my innumerable sins, may divine mercy grant through your holy prayers, venerable father, that I may persist in lamenting and penance for as long as I may yet live. For I confess that I came to this honor as a criminal and as a sinful person, and not without blame; and I have lived reprehensibly in this office. Therefore it seems right to me that you should of your own volition depose me, rather than have me undergo the sentence of deposition and eternal damnation before the tribunal of the tremendous judge in the sight of angels and men.

(68) But let this now suffice: May almighty God, who by the counsel of his inscrutable providence has deposed me from any ambition to govern and has raised you to the heights of ecclesiastical office, inspire you to issue me such commands by your holy letters that will conform to my pleading and desire.

---

95. On Archbishop Frederick of Ravenna, see Schwartz, *Bistümer* 154.

LETTER 73

Peter Damian to Albert, bishop of Velletri or administrator of Ostia. He strongly warns his colleague against involvement in worldly affairs; that the tithes and alms of the people should be fairly divided, so that all the clergy receive their share, and Damian not be given a greater portion; that bread and wine be equally distributed among the poor of the church to which they belong; and that tainted money not be accepted, even under the guise of using it for charitable purposes.

(Lent 1060)[1]

BESEECH YOU as an experienced man, venerable brother Albert,[2] and with the authority of paternal vigor I command you not to be so preoccupied with temporal affairs that you will not sufficiently watch over the souls that have been committed to us. To us, I say, have these souls been committed, because as they were given by God to me, so have I entrusted them to you, and thus both of us must undoubtedly give an account to God alone. You should therefore strive, my brother, to lead a religious life and safeguard your reputation. If you live a holy life, it will be to your honor and to mine; and, indeed, not only to us, but also to those entrusted to us. For if your name should suffer from an evil reputation, God forbid, it will also redound to my dishonor; and like a cancerous example, it will spread to those whom we are obligated to mold in virtue. Hence, after Peter had first remarked, "Let your behavior be such that even pagans can recognize it as good, so that even if they malign you as criminals now, they will then come to see for themselves that you live good lives, and they will give glory to God on the day when he comes to hold as-

---

1. The dating follows Lucchesi, *Vita* nos. 60, 148.
2. In the circumstances to which Damian refers, the addressee can be only the bishop of Ostia or Velletri; see Lucchesi, *Vita* nos. 60, 133, and 148; see also Schwartz, *Bistümer* 276.

size."³ He added a little further on, "With modesty and respect, keep your conscience clear so that, when you are abused, those who malign your Christian conduct may be put to shame."⁴ And Paul also wrote this to Timothy: "A bishop must have a good reputation with the non-Christian public, so that he may not be exposed to scandal and get caught in the devil's snare."⁵

(2) You should, moreover, dear brother, earnestly be on your guard and diligently see to it that when you allot tithes or any other offerings of the faithful among the churches, you presume not to lessen the amount to be given to my fellow priests, so that out of fidelity to me, as it were, you might increase the amount that should be mine. God forbid that anything that belongs to someone else should benefit me, and that what is made sacred by the intention of the donors should become sacrilegious as it is handled by priests. For as the Apostle says, "I have everything—far more than everything,"⁶ and I do not wish by my authority or by cunning to deprive my brothers of that which God has given for our common use. It is my duty to them to be an example of Christ's simplicity and humility, and I must evidently appear to bear the mark of Christ's poverty in their sight. Let it not be said of me that I have used their poverty for my own benefit, so that with the same Apostle in good conscience I may humbly boast in their presence, "I have learned," he said, "to find resources in myself whatever my circumstances. I know what it is to be brought low, and I know what it is to have plenty. I have been very thoroughly initiated into the human lot with all its ups and downs—fullness and hunger, plenty and want. I have strength for anything through him who gives me power."⁷

(3) I wish, moreover, that in those churches of the diocese in which bread is offered on more solemn feasts, and if there be other occasions when food and drink are given, that these be

---

3. 1 Pet 2.12. 4. 1 Pet 3.16.
5. 1 Tim 3.7. For the introduction of the word "bishop" into the text, see *Beuron* 25 (1975–1982) 497, with reference to Gregory I, *In librum primum regum* 5.27.436.
6. Phil 4.18. For this variant from the Vulgate, see *Beuron* 24.2 (1966) 252.
7. Phil 4.11–13.

distributed to the poor. In gathering these things to be given to other poor persons, we should not offer people who judge us to be avaricious in stuffing our own pockets an opportunity for detraction. For certainly it is proper that Christ's poor receive help particularly from the congregation of that church to which they belong.

(4) Be careful also that as some, I will not say shepherds, but workers, are accustomed to do, you do not accuse any one of the priests of wrongdoing under the guise of making money so that, after suspending him from office, you restore him to the privileges of his rank for the sake of your own profit. For it was Gehazi, you will remember, who deserved to become a leper because he changed his mind out of love for money.[8] He who derives a profit from restoring an office will not be able to avoid the oral barb that Peter hurled at Simon.[9]

(5) Anyone who grants the dignity of the priestly office for a price will be forced to endure the itching leprosy of simony.[10] And in general, I will provide you with this rule of thumb: Whenever you are aware that any money or profit is unjustly or reprehensibly acquired, I forbid with the authority of almighty God that this filthy gain ever accrue to my account, that it ever redound to my financial profit. While not fearing to sin because we are compassionately concerned in feeding the poor, we should not cruelly offend God under the guise of mercy; and it should not happen that our offenses are increased from that by which they might be destroyed, as we pretend to offer as a work of mercy something that is detestable; nor that what appears to be unleavened bread is actually leavened.

(6) Now, as you go from place to place, as you travel anywhere, or indeed when you are doing anything that must be done, let some verses from Scripture be always on your lips and, as a mortar grinding the psalms like aromatic spices, may they give forth a fragrant sweetness. Let your lips grow pale with fasting, and may your tongue, not in words but by rational

---

8. Cf. 2 Kgs 5.27.   9. Cf. Acts 8.20.
10. Beginning with this sentence, the letter breaks off in MS C2. It continues to the end only in MS Vat. Chigi A. V 145, fol. 4ᵛ–5. This conclusion, therefore, was unknown to C. Gaetani, the first editor.

intention, display your inner gravity and mortification. Let your scant interest in your attire reflect the humility of Christ. And that I may bring all this to an end in a few words, let me apply to brother Albert what the Apostle said to Titus: "In your teaching, you must show integrity and high principle, and use wholesome speech that will shame any opponent when he cannot find a word to say to our discredit."[11]

(7) May almighty God, dear brother, lead you along the path of such a holy life and, after you have carried out the duties of your stewardship, may he associate you in the pleasures of the heavenly kingdom with those who have served him well.

11. Titus 2.7–8.

LETTER 74

Peter Damian to Bishop V⟨ ⟩ on the question of alienation of Church property. The goods of the Church were given by penitents to relieve the burden of their guilt. He who in any way disposes of these properties must himself assume the guilt. Widows, orphans, pilgrims, and the poor depend on the charity of the Church. He who deprives the needy of sustenance, causing them to die of hunger, is to be charged with multiple homicide.

(Lent 1060)[1]

TO THE MOST reverend bishop, Sir V⟨ ⟩,[2] the monk Peter the sinner sends greetings.

(2) I would have you know, venerable brother, that word has got about, far and wide, charging that you have alienated property belonging to your diocese, and lately this notoriety has caused me to suffer great sadness. Have you forgotten that only about five years ago,[3] Victor, the bishop of the Apostolic See, in plenary council held in Florence, at which the emperor Henry[4] was also present, forbade such a thing under pain of excommunication? Are you unaware that lands are given to the Church so that the poor may be supported from their income, that the needy may be fed, and that from them assistance be provided for widows and orphans? From the very beginning, when the Church was still a young institution, the custom took root that those who came to the faith would dis-

1. For the above date, see *infra* n. 3.
2. At the time of this letter, both Gubbio and Assisi had a bishop named Ugo; cf. Lucchesi, *Vita* no. 62. Nine years later in *Letter* 157 to bishop Mainardus of Gubbio, Damian was still concerned with the expropriation of Church property, indicating, perhaps, that the present letter was addressed to Ugo of Gubbio.
3. This statement helps to date the present letter, since the Council of Florence took place in 1055; cf. Hefele-Leclercq, *Histoire* 4.2.1117; Ryan, *Sources* 73 no. 130.
4. On the presence of Henry III, cf. Steindorff, *Heinrich III*. 1.305ff.

pose of their possessions and would place the price they had received for them at the feet of the apostles.[5] And so we read in their Acts, "All who had property in land or houses," they said, "sold it, brought the proceeds of the sale, and laid the money at the feet of the apostles."[6] As time passed, however, it seemed proper to the leaders of the Church that these possessions should instead be handed over to the churches.[7] From them, therefore, the Church was able to support not only clerics who functioned in their sacred offices, but could also give relief to various needy folk and to those who suffered in poverty.

(3) Carefully consider, therefore, venerable brother, how many murders on the day of judgment will be charged to him who now deprives this great number of widows, orphans, and various poor people of their livelihood. What will be the state of his conscience when he comes before the tribunal of him who has a special love for the poor, before him who declared that he is fed when one feeds the poor, that he is hungry when the poor are hungry; when he comes before the tribunal of him who stated that taking food from the poor is the same as taking it from him?[8] If he is to be damned who kills only one man with his sword, what will be the sentence pronounced against one who, by wasting the goods of the Church, kills many people by the sword of hunger and want? The voice of God already spoke of such as these, when he said to every evil vendor, "Your brother's blood is crying out to me from the ground."[9] And the former, indeed, slew his brother out of envy, because his sacrifice, disapproved by God, was not accepted. These latter often do something similar out of greed for money, "which is the service of idols."[10]

(4) But because I bring action against you and reprimand

---

5. See Ryan, *Sources* 73 no. 131, citing Burchard, *Decretorum libri* 3.2 (PL 140.673f.) in dependence on Pseudo-Isidore (Hinschius 144). See Fuhrmann, *Fälschungen* 99 n. 120, 184, 369ff., and 884f.
6. Acts 4.34–35.
7. See Ryan, *Sources* no. 132, citing Burchard, *Decretorum libri* 3.3 (PL 140.674B); JK 87.
8. Cf. Matt 25.35. 9. Gen 4.10.
10. Eph 5.5.

you in these matters with the severity that they deserve, you have replied that it was only something small that was given away, and that it was not done in the manner brought to me by popular report. To which I have this to say: At times a liquid flows out drop by drop, but at length the vessel is totally empty; also a full storeroom, from which a little is taken every day, will finally be found bare. So the very thing that you call small and very minor will not escape the attention of him who judges all things. Listen to what Jeremiah had to say: "The word of the Lord came to me: 'Hanamel, son of your uncle Shallum, is coming to see you and will say, Buy my field at Anathoth; you have the right, as next of kin, to buy it.'"[11] And a little further on he added, "I knew that this was the Lord's message; so I bought the field at Anathoth from Hanamel, the son of my uncle, and weighed out the price, seven staters and ten pieces of silver."[12] Notice how meager, how small this field appeared to be, that it could be bought for only ten pieces of silver and seven staters, and still the prophet reported that the Lord had spoken to him over this matter. For this small piece of land was of such value to Jeremiah that he would say, "I signed and sealed the deed and had it witnessed; then I weighed out the money on the scales, and I took the deed of purchase that had been sealed, with the agreements, signatures, and seals on the outside,"[13] and much more that I will not cite, so that it does not become tedious for the readers.

(5) Since, therefore, such a small piece of property was bought by the prophet with so much attention, and was even prescribed by the word of God, with what fear should we approach the sale of any possessions belonging to the Church, by which Christ himself in his poor must be supported? But why do I speak of selling,[14] when not only those properties that are rented by the contract of emphyteusis, or let by mortgage, or granted by a longterm lease, but also those that laymen receive under the simple term of benefice, can never be recalled or

11. Jer 32.6–7. 12. Jer 32.8–9.
13. Jer 32.10–11.
14. See Ryan, *Sources* 73 no. 133; C. Boyd, *Tithes and Parishes in Medieval Italy* (Ithaca, 1952) 105f.

restored to the churches?¹⁵ Thus, indeed, the hands of plunderers are besmeared with the glue of diabolic tenacity. In whatever way they may have received them, they never agree to return their property to the churches; they not only hold on to them with a quasi-proprietary right while they are alive, but they also pass them on to their descendants to be held by them far into the future. Laymen beg you for ecclesiastical property, they make themselves obnoxious, they persist in their urging. And they do this not according to the stipulations of a charter, but only, perhaps, under the guise of a benefice that, indeed, is just as if they had been written on bronze tablets with a stylus of hardened steel. And so they come to you, using the words of Ahab, the king of Samaria: "Let me have your vineyard for a garden, for it is close to my palace."¹⁶ But you should answer at once, as did Naboth, the Israelite, "The Lord forbid that I should let you have land that has always been in my family."¹⁷

(6) Moreover, you are not unaware that when we accept lands from penitents, we remit an amount of their penance in proportion to their gift, as it is written, "A rich man's wealth is his release."¹⁸ Think about this, therefore, and give it proper consideration: just as he who gives lands to churches deservedly has the amount of his penance lightened, so he who disposes of such lands is required to carry the like amount of penance. For if the donor is absolved, it follows that the predator will be bound by his obligation. He will be held responsible for so much of the debt as the former had still to pay. And so, whoever wastes Church property will have all this evil on his own head. For on God's fearful day of judgment, the saints, whose honor is lessened by the poverty of clerics, will be angered; the poor, widows, orphans, and pilgrims will cry out that they were put to the sword. And thus, he who perhaps never shed blood will be guilty of multiple homicide.

(7) There are also those who hand over parish churches to laymen; these sin more gravely in that they are guilty of com-

---

15. In general, see Pierucci, "San Pier Damiano" 303.
16. 1 Kgs 21.2.   17. 1 Kgs 21.3.
18. Prov 13.8.

mitting sacrilege because they profane sacred places; while appearing to grant favors to the people, they instead hand them a deadly poison to drink. For what is converting tithes to secular use, if not exposing people to lethal poison whereby they will perish?[19] To this we may add that members of a parish are given good reason to withhold obedience to their parish churches by not paying them their legal tithes, which are truly the principal income of a bishop, and by so doing deprive the churches of their rights, turn what is given into spiritual disaster for the beneficiary, and cause the people to fall away from the practice of Christianity.[20]

(8) My dear brother, have nothing to do with such sacrilegious grants, and always use great care and foresight in avoiding these abominable and profane contracts. Always apply such watchful attention to supervising, first of all, the souls entrusted to you, and then also the property of the Church, so that after you have finished the course of your stewardship, you will not be called, God forbid, the despoiler of the Church, but will be known far and wide as its guardian and shepherd.

(9) I would hope, my brother, that this reprimand does not appear harsh to you. For since you are aware that it was by my doing that you were promoted to the episcopate, it is only proper that as you had me as your patron, you should also at times bear with me as one who rebukes you. Indeed, the Lord himself first placed Peter in command of the universal Church, and then struck him down with serious censure. For after saying to him, "I will give you the keys of the kingdom of heaven, and whatever you bind or loose on earth will be bound and loosed in heaven,"[21] he shortly afterward reprimanded him severely when he said, "Away with you, Satan; you are a stumbling block to me. You think as men think, not as God thinks."[22] By

---

19. See Ryan, *Sources* 74f. no. 134, citing *Capitulare Ravennas* (898) c. 10, ed. A. Boretius and V. Krause, MGH Capit. 2 (1897) 110.
20. See Ryan, *Sources* 75 no. 135, citing Kurtscheid, *Historia iuris canonici* 286ff., who discusses the *bannus parochialis*, which intimately bound the people to the parish church.
21. Matt 16.19.   22. Matt 16.23.

this, to be sure, he provided us an example, that those whom we raise to the highest honors, we should always restrain by the rule of discipline. And so that such men, flattered by their prestige, not immortalize themselves as proud tyrants, their masters should hold them in check with goading supervision.

LETTER 75

Peter Damian to the archdeacon Hildebrand. A lament over the latter's silence and his apparent lack of interest in one who would be his friend, this letter is in sharp contrast with *Letter* 160, which one may doubt was ever sent to the archdeacon. Of special interest is the autobiographical note, revealing self-consciously his own satisfaction with the high quality of his writing. Noteworthy also is Damian's regard for the authority of the tough little man who would later, as Gregory VII, disturb the *status quo* existing between the *sacerdotium* and *imperium*.

(1060)[1]

TO SIR HILDEBRAND, the archdeacon,[2] the monk Peter the sinner sends his allegiance.

(2) I marvel, venerable brother, that your holy disposition can find no opportunity to be less severe with me, that especially when I am absent, you do not send me even a single word or ever speak of me, a thing that would seem to involve the obligation of charity.[3] But whenever a message is sent to me, or when in your presence I, perhaps, have something to say, my name, for all its insignificance, is hooted at, my reputation is spat upon, my lightheartedness is ridiculed, and such things are said about me as to cause my enemies to take me as a joke and to evoke sad embarrassment.

(3) Certainly, after I came under obligation to the Roman Church,[4] I willingly strove always to obey both God and Peter and to submit to whatever you had planned or undertaken. And in all your struggles and victories I have acted not just like

---

1. The dating follows Lucchesi, *Vita* nos. 122 and 148.
2. On Hildebrand and his appointment as archdeacon, see *Letter* 72 n. 53.
3. Lucchesi, *Vita* no. 122 conjectures that Damian's lament may well relate to his *Letter* 57 and *Letter* 72, in which he begs to be relieved of his episcopal duties. See also Lucchesi, *Vita* no. 148.
4. On Damian's appointment as cardinal and his other episcopal duties, see *Letter* 57 n. 7.

some comrade or footsoldier, but have thrown myself into the enterprise like some thunderbolt. In what conflict were you ever involved in which I did not at once become both prosecutor and judge? In every instance I followed no other canonical authority but the decision of your will, and your will alone was for me the authority of the canons. Nor did I ever reach a conclusion that seemed correct to me, but only one that was approved by you. If you should like to know, moreover, just how highly I regard you, inquire of the abbot of Cluny,[5] with whom you are well acquainted. For one day when your name came up in conversation, he said, "He is not aware that you esteem his friendship so highly, for if he were, he would be more than ready to show great affection for you."

(4) But why do I go on with this letter, since I have no hope that you will ever read it? Certainly, there is no one alive to whom I would rather write, if only you would condescend to read it. But since there is little chance of that, notice how careful and polished is my style, how flowery my eloquence, how glittering and elegant is my diction. But whether you take note of it or not, by this letter I return to you the diocese you have given me,[6] and cut off every right and all authority that came to me in its regard.

  5. The possibility of Hildebrand's meeting with Abbot Hugh of Cluny was likely in 1055 in Florence, and in 1058 in Rome or in Florence; see Lucchesi, *Vita* nos. 101, 117, 118, 123.
  6. Lucchesi, *Vita* 151, is certain that Damian here refers to Ostia; but see *Letter* 57 and *Letter* 72.

LETTER 76

Peter Damian to Dominic Loricatus and to his brothers in the hermitage of Suavicinum. He exhorts his brethren to bear external difficulties with patience, following the advice of sacred Scripture and the example of the saints. They should rather be ill at ease when all goes physically well with them, rejoicing at the loss of temporal goods and fearful when they receive a gift. The latter point he illustrates by an example from his recent experience in Milan, when a local abbot offered him the gift of a silver vase. Assured that the gift was only an expression of friendship, and not a bribe, Damian eventually accepted it for one of his monasteries, not yet fully equipped. Later, however, his conscience continued to trouble him, and he returned the vase. By this experience he advised that among monks the expression of friendship should be free of gift-giving.

(First half of 1060)[1]

TO SIR DOMINIC[2] and to the other brothers living in the hermitage near Mount Suavicinum,[3] the monk Peter the sinner sends his highest allegiance in the Lord.

(2) You have written to me, my dear brothers, that such ill will from evil and violent men has overwhelmed you that unless I come at once to your aid, you will abandon this monastery and build another that will be free of this plundering and other trouble. I must say that when I heard this report, I was greatly disturbed, and your timidity saddened me more than these hostile attacks. For since you are obviously diligent in reading the word of God, I marvel that you are still unaware that patience is the queen of virtues, and all the books of Scripture are in accord with this. "For," as the Apostle says, "all the Scriptures were written for our instruction."[4] But how do they serve as instruction for us? Were they written that we might know

---

1. The dating follows Lucchesi, *Vita* nos. 142 and 144.
2. On Dominic, see his short *vita* in *Letter* 109. He died on 14 October 1060.
3. For Suavicinum, see *Letter* 50 n. 30 and *Letter* 109.
4. Rom 15.4.

how to lay syllogistic snares, to adorn our thundering and carefully constructed words with a variety of rhetorical flourishes, to set them to sweet and harmonious music played on the organ, or, as they say, to acquaint ourselves with the mathematician's measuring rod to indicate the constellations of the stars? For such investigations we were surely not instructed in sacred Scripture, but rather that through them we might become models of patience. And so the Apostle quickly added, "That through patience and the encouragement of Scripture we may maintain our hope."[5]

(3) The same Scriptures, moreover, while instructing us in the practice of patience, also sustain us with consoling hope. For as they tell how God's chosen ones must undergo great suffering and hardship, they show also what reward they shall receive because of them. The physician, indeed, applies leeches[6] to the swollen parts of the sick man's body and allows them to suck the poison from the internal organs, along with the blood; but the doctor and the leech act with differing purpose. The latter has no other objective but to drink blood; the former intends the sick man to recover. The leech sucks until it is full, and then dies; but as the sick man is bled he becomes well again. The former is satisfied and is happy to die; but as the sick man endures the leech's wound, he regains his health.

(4) Why should we wonder, then, that almighty God, who is the physician of souls, controls us in such hidden ways that from wounds inflicted by others he prepares medication for us? In so doing, as we suffer from a wound inflicted by the enemy, he provides us with a most powerful antidote for our well-being from it. The *thirus*[7] belongs to the genus snake, and from its blood we procure a remedy for snake bite, which cures deadly infection in those who have been poisoned.

(5) If, therefore, men know how to resist poison with poison, how much more marvellously can God provide for our welfare by using the calamities caused by others? What else do we read in the lives of the saints, but how they had to undergo suffering

---

5. Rom 15.4.
6. On phlebotomy in general, see Zimmermann, *Ordensleben* 180–83.
7. Cf. Isidore, *Etymologies* 4.9.8; DuCange 8.101.

and attack from the disturbances of wicked men? Our redeemer also was unable to enter his heavenly kingdom with the servile body he had taken from the inviolate Virgin, until he had undergone all the torments of derision and suffering of which Scripture speaks. What is novel about sinful man losing all his external possessions, when he who could never sin bore the suffering of the cross in his own body?[8] According to the Apostle, "You have not yet resisted to the point of shedding your blood."[9] Would that this at least could be said of you, using the words he spoke of those who suffered patiently: "You cheerfully accepted the seizure of your possessions."[10] And hence another apostle said, "My brothers, count yourselves supremely happy whenever you have to face trials of many kinds."[11]

(6) Now there are two things by which, if we pay close attention to them, we will easily overcome arrogant violation of every description and vexatious injustices, namely, precept and example. For holy Scripture exhorts us to patience, and all the saints bore with patience whatever could be done to them by the raging members of the devil. That we are aided by divine admonition and by the example of those who went before us, and are rescued from the depths of trouble inflicted on us, is indicated by the prophet Jeremiah when he was hoisted from the pit. As Scripture relates,[12] they threw him into a pit in which there was no water, but only mud. Afterwards, so that he could be lifted from the pit, a rope and cast-off clothes were let down to him. What is the significance of the ropes if not the precepts of the Lord? These commands, since they both convict us and liberate us when we do evil, bind us, as it were, and lead us on; they confine us and lift us up. But that we should not fall when we are lifted up by the ropes that bind us, old clothes are let down to us at the same time. So that God's commands do not terrify us, the example of the ancient Fathers strengthens us, so that by comparing ourselves to them, we may

---

8. Cf. 1 Pet 2.22–24.
9. Heb 12.4.
10. Heb 10.34.
11. Jas 1.2.
12. Cf. Jer 38.6–13.

dare to think it possible to do what, because of our weakness, we would fear to undertake.

(7) If, therefore, we would hurry to be lifted from the depths of this troubled life, we should wrap these ropes about us, that is, we should be bound by the precepts of the Lord. Old clothes are also handy, so that the ropes may bind less painfully; that is, we should be encouraged by the example of those who preceded us, so that these precise laws, as they lift us up, will not injure us who are weak and fearful. The Apostle Paul, as it were, added the use of old clothes when he adapted the example of the ancients to his spiritual precepts to encourage his disciples, when he said, "Holy men had to face jeers and flogging, even fetters and prison bars. They were stoned, they were sawn in two, they were tempted, they were put to the sword."[13] And a little further on, he said, "since we are surrounded by this cloud of witnesses, we must throw off every encumbrance, every sin that encompasses us, and run with resolution the race we have entered."[14] And again, "Remember your leaders, those who first spoke God's message to you; and reflecting upon the outcome of their life and work, follow the example of their faith."[15] First of all, as he spoke of spiritual guidelines, he provided them, as it were, with ropes. But then, calling to mind the lives of our ancestors, he used them like old clothes. Truly, the servant of God must be fearful when he receives something of temporal value, and must rejoice when he loses it. For he who proposes to scale the heights of heaven undoubtedly climbs more easily when he is devoid of everything than when he is encumbered.

(8) Now let me tell you what recently happened to me. I had gone to Milan, serving as a legate for the lord Pope Nicholas.[16] While I was there, the abbot of the monastery of St. Simplicianus[17] sent me a silver vase as a gift. After one quick look at what had been given me, my first reaction was to refuse it and to inquire diplomatically why he was presenting me with

---

13. Heb 11.36–37.
14. Heb 12.1.
15. Heb 13.7.
16. See *Letter* 65 n. 9.
17. On this Milanese monastery, see Cottineau, *Répertoire topo-bibliographique des abbayes et prieurés* 2.1.1851.

this gift; for I suspected that perhaps he had some business to conduct with me, and to prepare the way, he would engage in a bit of bribery. Now it is customary for us who act as ministers of the Apostolic See to accept absolutely nothing from those whose affairs are still in process; but from those whose business has been completely cleared, it is customary not to refuse if they wish to make an offering. This rule does not apply to all of us, but only to those who would somewhat better guard against avarice.

(9) To make a long story short, we met for an open discussion, I asked why the gift had been offered, and I inquired whether he had any action before the Apostolic See. It was found that he had discharged all his business, and was free of all restraint, so that he could truly say, "I am content where I am, among my own people."[18] I asked him further whether he was perhaps aware of any financial deals that had taken place as he was advanced to ecclesiastical orders, or when he accepted the office of abbot. After he had denied that anything like that had taken place and had stated that his offer had been made for no such reasons, but only that he might facilitate our friendship, I replied that he should take back what was his, that he should not pay for my friendship as people in the world do, but that he could have it freely, as is proper among fellow monks.

(10) As all this was taking place, and I tell you this confidentially, I was of such a mind that if, after careful inquiry, I found that everything in the case was straightforward and he still insisted on giving me this gift, his urging would in no way offend me. It was my intention that force be used on me, and that I be compelled to agree unwillingly. When he absolutely refused to take back what once he had given, and would listen to nothing I had to say, now that I was sure and felt more bold in the matter, I pressed him still harder to take back what he had offered.

(11) In the meantime, a day went by. When during the night I was engaged in prayer, reciting the psalms for the office, my

---

18. 2 Kgs 4.13.

conscience began to torment me most sharply, demanding, as it were, an account from me: "If, as it seems, he is a good man, why do you wish to take money from an innocent man, since there are no grounds for you to expect him to help you. Moreover, if he has business at the curia, it is improper for you to put a price on your verbal intervention regarding this holy brother, which, as something that is in the service of either side, should be rendered freely to his benefit as well as yours." And as he persisted in pushing his point against me, and as I was unable to endure the clash of my disturbing thoughts, with darkness disappearing, I quickly went to him the next morning and revealed to him my wounded and troubled conscience.

(12) While both of us argued our positions, he asserting that he would not take back what he had given, and I stating that I would not keep it, I finally put an end to our friendly encounter in this way: "I have two new monasteries," I said, "one, with the help of God, already completed, while the other still awaits consecration by the bishop.[19] If you like, you can help in furnishing these sacred places. Send either one, your gift as a token of your esteem, and it will be to your spiritual benefit." By this means I justified my shameful cupidity and cleverly accepted the gift by acting as if I had not taken it.

(13) But later, upon returning to the hermitage, I indeed promptly went to my cell, but could hardly bring myself to enter it. I was just not myself, and by my own fault, so to speak, I found it most difficult to pull myself together. Among other things, I was so confused by the cloud that hung over me because of this gift, which, like a mass of worms, never ceased gnawing at my innards, that in all conscience I would have preferred to be struck down with leprosy than bear the wound inflicted by this present. On the one hand, moreover, I considered the great generosity of this brother who, while owing me nothing, still offered me this gift and, on the other, my avarice, which accepted it while doing nothing to deserve it.

(14) I was disgusted that I had forgotten what the wise man

---

19. The two monasteries cannot be identified.

had said: "Do not keep your hand open to receive and close it when it is your turn to give."[20] And since, according to the Apostle, "happiness lies more in giving than in receiving,"[21] I judged him, indeed, to be happy, while I myself was miserable. "Woe is me," I said. "Since Scripture commands that we restrain our hand from accepting gifts,[22] do you really pull back and reject them, or rather hold out your hand to receive; do you compel it to grasp, or withdraw it that you may conceal what you possess?" Truly, avarice is glue on the hands of him who receives, not allowing one to shake off whatever has been offered, but, like pitch, causing it to hold fast.

(15) So what was I to do? No longer able to bear this mental torture, I decided to return the gift to the holy brother. And from now on, with God's help, I will be more careful in regard to sordid gifts.

(16) Note what I said above, that the servant of God should be fearful when he receives anything of temporal value, and should rejoice when he loses it. Henceforth, neither for the purpose of building a monastery, nor to take care of the necessities of the servants of God will I keep something that seems respectable. May I be strong enough to control the forces of greed! It is like one who is eager to break the bonds of chastity and gets married that he might produce heirs. Under the guise of begetting children he becomes a slave to lustful pleasures. Thus some, while not content to live deprived of all things like Christ and the apostles, are happy to be involved in governing or in some other occupation, so that in satisfying their own cupidity they may appear to be engaged in necessary works of charity.

(17) But we, my dear brothers, should always be glad to bear patiently any injuries that come our way, and be of service to those who do us harm. Let us be cautious and suspicious of receiving favors, but as far as possible be kind in granting them. Be fearful in times of prosperity, but untroubled in adversity. When one performs good works and bears up under

20. Sir 4.36.   21. Acts 20.35.
22. Cf. Isa 33.15.

persecution, then undoubtedly he will be sure that he can be counted among the members of Christ. For when one lives virtuously and suffers affliction in this life, he will in a double sense be following in the footsteps of Christ, and in the life to come will not be excluded from his company.

LETTER 77

Peter Damian to the archdeacon Almericus. Testifying to a great affection for his correspondent, he deplored the recent appearance of a certain hermit who, he thought, would truly benefit from entering organized religious life. He hinted that many of his writings did not reach an audience and, if they did, his literary production would equal that of Demosthenes or Cicero. He asked for the return of one of his works, and requested a gift of fish for Christmas, which in that year fell on a Monday.

(1060)[1]

TO SIR ALMERICUS, the archdeacon,[2] the monk P⟨eter⟩ the sinner sends his affection in fraternal charity.

(2) May the Holy Spirit, the source of all charity, make known to your genuine disposition, my dear son, how great is the affection I bear you, and how constantly and steadfastly I always remember you. To this my conscience bears witness, and I am not lying, that my love for you exceeds even that for those to whom I am bound by blood relationship. Certainly it is proper that spiritual love should be greater than that of the flesh.

(3) However, it is deplorable that the fragrant shoot that recently sprouted among pebbles on a sandy shore, we now see striking deep roots in the same soil. But were it transplanted from the sterile sand in which it now grows to the garden of the monastery, it would, without doubt, begin to bud and, according to the statement of the opening psalm,[3] would not lose even a single leaf, much less its fruit. It would always remain green like the cedar of Lebanon or like the palm tree,[4] and as the fruitful olive tree in the house of the Lord,[5] would blossom in abiding beauty. But on this subject I have said enough.

1. The dating follows Lucchesi, *Vita* 2.151.
2. Cf. Mittarelli-Costadoni, *Annales Camaldulenses* 2.149.
3. Cf. Ps 1.3.
4. Cf. Ps 91.13.
5. Cf. Ps 51.10.

(4) It is indeed wearisome for a writer to work at his craft when he is aware that there is no one who is eager to listen when it is read aloud.[6] And while the subject matter quickens the heart of the hearer, a long-winded piece fails to give pleasure. Nevertheless, if I knew that you were gladly listening to what I write, it seems to me that I could easily equal Demosthenes or Cicero in my output. Return my little book to me. And since we do not eat meat on Mondays,[7] I ask you to send us some fish to celebrate Christmas, so that what is given to the brothers may also benefit both of your parents. For while a meal refreshes the monks here on earth, the latter may offer votive prayers for them. Send my greetings to my dearly beloved brothers Julian and Fuscard, and to the Lord's distinguished nightingale, Corbuo, all of whom so generously supplied me with food, and tell them that my love for them is as warm as ever.

6. Damian speaks here of a "hearer" of his letters, because in the eleventh century reading was apparently still done aloud.

7. This reference to the prohibition of eating meat on Mondays is curious, since Damian totally forbade meat except for those who were sick; see *Letter* 50 n. 56; *Benedicti Regula* c. 39, 11, 110, where meat is defined as "the flesh of four-footed animals." Damian never departs from this definition, nor does he ever refer to fowl of any kind in the diet of his hermits. But perhaps fish, too, was so rare a delicacy that it properly enhanced the celebration of Christmas. On the harsh diet prescribed by Damian, and its surprisingly beneficial effect on the monks' life expectancy (ca. 65 years versus the average 30 years in the eleventh century), see C. Lohmer, "Ausgewählte Aspekte der mittelalterlichen Ernährung für Mönche, untersucht am Beispiel der monastischen Bestimmungen des Petrus Damiani," *Aktuelle Ernährungsmedizin* 13 (1988) 179–182.

LETTER 78

Peter Damian to John of Lodi. In this letter he interprets allegorically the ten plagues of Egypt, equating them with ten vices or temptations to vice. Against such spiritual plagues the decalogue is the appropriate antidote, prescribed for the Hebrew people, and since then for all true Israelites in spirit.

(1060)[1]

O MY BELOVED brother John, no longer of Lodi[2] and therefore a laudable man, the monk Peter the sinner sends the affection of his paternal love.

(2) Only recently, my dear son, did you turn your back on Pharaoh, and at the same time abhor the slavery of this proud and tyrannical king of Egypt. It is, therefore, necessary for you now to undergo many kinds of temptation as you proceed through the desert, to suffer the deprivations of hunger and thirst, and thus, by living with danger in the wilderness and with hardship in various forms, arrive at the promised land.[3] Along with the Hebrew people, you should, therefore, hurry on toward Mount Sinai, there to receive the commandments of God's Law, so that armed with them as with weapons and cuirass, you may repel the arrows of an attacking foe and not fall victim to the chance assaults of adversity.

(3) Now this Law was given to the people on the fiftieth day after they had departed from Egypt.[4] The number fifty is made sacred by its reference to penance, as we can gather from many

---

1. The dating follows Lucchesi, *Vita* 2.153.
2. On John, see G. Lucchesi, "Giovanni da Lodi, il discepolo," *San Pier Damiano nel IX centenario della morte (1072–1972)* 4 (1978) 7–66.
3. Damian here generally depends on the thought of Augustine; see Augustine, *Quaestiones in Heptateuchum* 2.19–40, 77–85, and esp. *Sermo* 8.79–99.
4. Cf. Exod 16.1.

passages in Scripture. It denotes the year of jubilee,[5] and Psalm 50 which David wrote to lament his sins. And there were the two debtors mentioned in the gospel,[6] one who owed 500 silver pieces, and the other fifty. Also the man who owed 100 jars of oil and was told to write fifty.[7] All of these give off the healthy odor of penance, if only we had an intelligent sense of smell that could keenly detect the fragrance of mystery.

(4) And so, to be worthy to receive the commands of divine Law, discipline yourself through penance, confess the evils of past sin and thus, by enrolling among the ranks of penitents, you may come to the mountain of God by acknowledging your sins. All of this aptly agrees with the notion that this mountain is called "Sinai," which is interpreted to mean a 'bush.'[8] For by the bush that is armed with thorns is meant the sharpness of our sins that are annoying to God. And thus Jeremiah said, "This people has encompassed me with the thorns of their sins."[9] And we read in Revelations that "every eye shall see him, and among them those who pierced him; and all the peoples of the world shall lament in remorse."[10] This mountain prefigures the holy Church in which there are both confession and the remission of sins. For Moses saw the Lord in the bush, and the bush signifies the Church in which we behold God. And thus Moses petitioned the Lord, saying, "If I have indeed won your favor, clearly show yourself to me that I may see you."[11] And he received the answer that he should take his stand on the rock, and from there he would see the Lord's back.[12] Now the rock is the faith upon which the Catholic Church is built, from which it sees God.

(5) From this mountain you must accept the remedies that will heal the sickness you contracted in Egypt. For the plagues that occurred in Egypt are nothing but wounds. And what was

---

5. On this interpretation, using Lev 25.11 and Num 36.4, see Isidore, *Etymologies* 6.18.4–5.
6. Cf. Luke 7.41. 7. Cf. Luke 16.6.
8. Cf. Jerome, *Nom.hebr.* 15.1 (CC 72.77).
9. A reputed saying of Jeremiah, frequently cited by medieval writers, esp. Isidore of Seville, *De fide catholica* 1.31 (PL 83.482 C).
10. Rev 1.7. 11. Exod 33.13; cf. Sabatier 1.203.
12. Cf. Exod 33.22–23.

this heavenly Law if not medicine for these wounds? Consequently, by confession the sinner must discharge the impurities of his guilt, and thus drink from the cup of penance filled from the vessel of God's Law. Here one takes the antidote that will heal the sickness of our ailing soul. Moreover, souls that are dissipated by carnal pleasure run loose over the fields and meadows of their earthly desires, and frolic like unbroken horses amid the delights of alluring wantonness. They urge one another on, as the book of Wisdom relates, and say, "Come then, let us enjoy the good things while we can, and make full use of the creation, with all the eagerness of youth. Let us have costly wines and perfumes to our heart's content, and let no flower of spring escape us. Let us crown ourselves with roses before they can wither. Let no broad field escape our pleasure, let none of us miss his share of the good things that are ours; who cares what traces our revelry leaves behind?"[13] Now the healthier and fatter these playful and whinnying horses are, the more we know that within them they suffer from the last stages of disease. And when the bridle of God's Law is put on them, what else can be done but apply laces and harness to their rotting members, so that what is about to split apart and run forth may be held together by the bonds of heavenly precepts?

(6) So it was that the Samaritan in the gospel,[14] when coming upon the man who had been hurt by robbers, bandaged his wounds, applying oil and wine. And to this point Ezekiel promised, "I will search for the lost, recover the straggler, bandage what was broken, and strengthen the sick."[15] Plagues, therefore, occurred in Egypt because man's soul is wounded in the world. And so, it is necessary for those who are wounded to come to Mount Sinai, that is, to the Church, to bind up their wounds with heavenly precepts. For there were just as many commandments made known by God as there were plagues, that for the same number of spiritual afflictions a similar number of remedies could be applied to them.

(7) But before discussing this numerical agreement between

---

13. Wis 2.6–9.
15. Ezek 34.16.
14. Cf. Luke 10.34.

the plagues and the commandments of the Law, it must be remarked that as we read that the Hebrew people received the decalogue on the fiftieth day[16] after the paschal lamb had been slain, so too the Holy Spirit appeared to the apostles in various tongues on the fiftieth day after the Lord's resurrection.[17] There it was stated that the Law was written by the finger of God, and the Holy Spirit, who was given to the apostles on Pentecost, was called the finger of God, as the Lord himself thus says: "But if it is by the finger of God that I drive out devils, then be sure the kingdom of God has already come upon you."[18] There the people heard voices, peals of thunder, and the sounds of a blaring trumpet; it saw flaming torches, lightning flashes, and the smoking mountain.[19] The voices and thunder and the trumpet blasts all signify the impetuous sound of preachers; but in the torches and lightning we see the brilliance of miracles.

(8) All of this was achieved by the power of the Holy Spirit by which the inspired apostles burst forth in various tongues and radiated with the splendor of their miraculous powers. That the Lord, moreover, came down in fire and smoke[20] has the mystic significance that as he illumines the faithful by the light of his knowledge, so too, as it were, he dulls the vision of unbelievers, through the smoky darkness of error. And thus the Lord said in the gospel, "I have come into this world to give light to the sightless and to blind those who see."[21] And in Isaiah it is said, "Wicked men have been set ablaze like a fire, fed with briars and thorns, kindled in the forest thickets; they are wrapped in smoking pride."[22]

(9) But since these mysteries are not adapted to the brief range of a letter, and can hardly be explained even in lengthy volumes, let us return to the plagues of Egypt[23] and to the commandments of the Law, and see on the one hand our wounds

---

16. Cf. Exod 19–20, but the number fifty is not found in the Vulgate.
17. Cf. Acts 2.1–4.   18. Luke 11.20.
19. Cf. Exod 19.16.   20. Cf. Exod 19.18.
21. John 9.39.   22. Isa 9.18.
23. On the Egyptian plagues, see M. J. Redle, "Plagues of Egypt," NCE 11 (1967) 422–24.

and, on the other, the heavenly remedies for them; the same number of each, realizing that there are just as many antidotes as there are diseases. Thus as the poultice of salvation is applied to each of our wounds, the soul of man may then be restored to the healthy status it once enjoyed. Moreover, since by a flood of licentiousness the soul is dissipated, it is in need of the bonds of God's Law. And when it is held fast by the fetters of heavenly commandments, it is restored to a healthy condition by the opposing warmth produced by its wounds.

(10) So let us begin. The first plague was the turning of the waters into blood.[24] These plagues, moreover, occurred only in Egypt, that is, in an obscure heart overcome by the gloom of blindness.[25] For such waters are turned into blood when the mind, blind to its own condition, disturbs and violates the purity of the true faith. And as all plant life emerges from the depths of the earth because of water, thus too spiritual food is produced by faith. To be sure, water is turned into blood when the senseless heart is obscured by the blindness of unbelief. As the Apostle says of certain people, "Knowing God, they have refused to honor him as God, or to render him thanks. Hence all their thinking has ended in futility, and their misguided minds are plunged in darkness."[26] Against this first plague, that is, to counter this pestilential wound, we must at once use the remedy of the first commandment, "Hear, O Israel, the Lord your God is one God."[27] This is, indeed, the healing bandage which must be applied to the wounds of unbelief, that after hearing these words you must worship only one God and not spread the corruption of a decaying belief in many gods. And deservedly by God's decision it happened literally that the Egyptians drank of that same river of blood in which originally Hebrew boys had been killed.[28]

(11) Now the second plague was a swarm of frogs. The frog is a noisy animal, and it usually croaks in muddy swamps. We

---

24. Cf. Exod 7.17–20.
25. Cf. Jerome, *Nom.hebr.* 66.28 (CC 72.143).
26. Rom 1.21.
27. Deut 6.4; for this variant, cf. Sabatier 1.340.
28. Cf. Exod 1.22.

consider heretics and philosophers to be like them, those who, as it were, utter mocking reproach against Christ on the banks of the marshes, that is, among the masses soiled by the filth of unbelief. While by their fallacious arguments they never give up chattering nonsense, they produce emptiness and disgust in their audience, but fail to offer them food for the life of their souls. For this disease, which is a lethal bane to the soul, we have the second commandment providing us with the cup of salvation. For the second commandment reads, "You shall not misuse the name of the Lord your God."[29] Now he misuses the name of Christ who believes that Christ is not the creator but only a creature. Every creature is subject to folly. Consequently, such men are surely lacking in reality who, by twisting the truth about God into lies, give credence to this unreality.

(12) Gnats made up the third plague.[30] This animal is indeed so small and insignificant that when it hangs in the air and restlessly flies here and there in pathless patterns, its flight escapes the eye. But when it settles on the body it stings us, so that while you are unable to see them as they move, you are forced to feel them when they bite. As they fly about making a nuisance of themselves, they are always attacking us about the face and they give us no rest. This plague, then, clearly illustrates the vice of idle wandering and restlessness. Those who suffer from this disease uselessly move from place to place, and like those afflicted by the evil of Vertumnus,[31] never rest because of their lack of patience.

(13) But because these gnats are so tiny and harmful and seemingly have no substance but their bite, those who, like gnats, are subject to the vice of restless wandering make light of sin as something insignificant, and are stung by the barb of guilt that is not without significance. It is not the weight that bothers us, but rather the bite that pricks us, because the more they make light of this vice, the deeper will the sting of sin penetrate the depths of a soul that is ill. For this sickness, the medicine of the third commandment is provided, when the

---

29. Exod 20.7.   30. Cf. Exod 8.16.
31. Vertumnus, the god of changeableness, is referred to in Horace, *Sat.* 2.7.14; see also W. Eisenhut, "Vertumnus," RE 2.8.1 (1958) 1669–87.

Lord said, "Remember to keep the sabbath day holy."[32] For us the word "sabbath" means 'rest.'[33] When we keep the sabbath day holy, the Spirit of God is surely present. And so it is written, "On whom does my spirit rest, if not on the man who is humble and quiet, one who reveres my words?"[34] You must meditate on these words, because if the Holy Spirit rests only on the quiet man, he will desert one who is restless. And just as the second commandment has reference to the Son, so the third pertains to the Holy Spirit who is, indeed, the third person in the holy Trinity. Remember that it was the magicians who ascribed the third plague to the Holy Spirit, since they had failed to produce gnats, and said to Pharaoh, "It is the finger of God."[35]

(14) The Apostle exhorted his disciple to venerate the sabbath when he said, "Pay heed to your reading and your teaching."[36] And elsewhere he said, "Pray continuously."[37] Through the prophet, God called us to honor the sabbath when he stated, "Take pains to learn that I am God,"[38] as if he were saying, Celebrate a spiritual sabbath and avoid the restlessness of idle wandering so that, enjoying stability by the grace of the Holy Spirit, the gnats will not disturb you, and you may be made holy by observing the spiritual sabbath.

(15) We should note, moreover, that only three commandments were inscribed on the first tablet, while the other seven were written on the second.[39] The former are concerned with the love of God, while the latter pertain to the love of neighbor. And so there were no more than two tablets because they are distinct in expressing the two kinds of love. That the three commandments were inscribed on one tablet and the seven on the

---

32. Exod 20.8.
33. Jerome, *Nom.hebr.* 75.29 (CC 72.154).
34. Isa 66.2.
35. Exod 8.19. For this variant from the *Vulgate*, cf. Augustine, *Quaestiones in Heptateuchum* 2.25, 79.
36. 1 Tim 4.16. 37. 1 Thess 5.17.
38. Ps 45.11.
39. For the arrangement of the Ten Commandments on the two stone tablets, not mentioned in the Old Testament, see Augustine, *Quaestiones in Heptateuchum* 2.71.2, 103.

other, we learn especially from what the Apostle said to the Ephesians: "Children, obey your parents in the Lord, for it is right that you should. 'Honor your father and mother' is the first commandment with a promise attached, expressed in the words, 'that it may be well with you and that you may live long in the land.'"[40] Why is this called the first commandment if not for the reason that it is placed at the beginning of the second tablet? The words "with a promise" are used, which are found with no other commandment, because the promise of longevity follows this commandment. For after saying, "Honor your father and mother," it then continues, "that it may be well with you and that you may live long in the land." So this commandment, which is the fourth in the total number of precepts, is placed first on the second tablet.

(16) Opposed to it is the fourth plague, the fly, which is called the dog-flea.[41] Nothing is more dog-like than to disregard one's parents and not to show respect for those who begot us. Dog-like qualities, just like infesting fleas, irritate them, and since they do not know how to honor their parents, they are fickle and inconstant and wanting in natural dignity. Their bad manners bite them like dog-fleas, as they snarl and bark at their parents and torment them with impatience. Therefore, a remedy for this plague is proper respect for one's parents.

(17) The fifth plague was the death of cattle.[42] Of all those who desert their own marriage to pollute themselves by shameful deeds with other women and continuously abandon themselves to the currents of obscene passion, what else can we say but that they are dumb animals, completely devoid of rationality and spiritual understanding? They have become "like a horse or mule, unreasoning creatures."[43] And in Jeremiah it is said, "I gave them all they needed, yet they preferred adultery, and haunted the brothels; each neighs after his neighbor's wife, like lusty stallions consorting with the mares."[44] These animals will become totally extinct unless they are treated with

---

40. Eph 6.1–3; Exod 20.12.
41. Cf. Exod 8.21; cf. Isidore, *Etymologies* 12.8.12.
42. Cf. Exod 9.6.   43. Ps 31.9.
44. Jer 5.7–8.

the medicine of God's Law. And so it was said, "You shall not commit adultery."[45] This, the fifth commandment, is applied like a medical bandage to heal the fifth plague, so that as one is forced to be content with his own marriage, he will not reach out with intemperate and unbridled lust for carnal embrace with others.

(18) The sixth plague consisted of wounds and festering, swelling boils.[46] By the wounds we may understand the cunning and purulent malice of hatred; by the boils, swelling and inflated pride; by the festering, burning anger and the insanity of flaming fury. There are some people with homicidal tendencies, in whom these pestilential qualities rise to the surface and become viciously acute, and unless they shed human blood, they can never be at peace. And so for this furious disease, this monstrous savagery, the sixth commandment is applied like a remedy from heaven, whereby it is said, "You shall not kill,"[47] so that everyone who hears these words will repress within himself the rising fury of ill will, not allowing the brewing poison of a malicious conscience to break loose in spilling blood.

(19) Next came the plague of hail,[48] in which both hail and fiery flashes occurred. Yet these two are opposites, cold in the hail and heat in the fire. Thus those who steal the property of others are both frozen in regard to fraternal charity and on fire with the ardor of their cupidity. It was also stated that thunder and lightning came together with the hail. What else is meant by thunder and lightning but unbearable fear? And this is proper to thieves, that they have a visceral dread of being caught and then punished, yet still never hold back, and continue with the evil deeds they had planned from the start. Truly these plagues, that is, hail and fire, lightning and thunder, devastate the hearts of those who secretly filch from others as if they were corn fields, and destroy all the crops of good will that might be growing there. The remedy of the seventh commandment applies to this dreadful sickness, as it is said, "You

---

45. Exod 20.14; cf. Deut 5.18.
47. Exod 20.13; Deut 5.17.
46. Cf. Exod 9.9.
48. Cf. Exod 9.24.

shall not steal,"[49] so that one who is aware of this command will not find the crops proceeding from his heart destroyed by this multiple calamity, but will see the granary of his soul filled with the produce of good works, fulfilling this apostolic admonition: "The thief must give up stealing, and instead work hard and honestly with his own hands, so that he may have something to share with the needy."[50]

(20) Locusts were the eighth plague.[51] To whom can we better compare these animals that destroy young plants and devour the crops with their ravaging teeth than to those who slander their brothers and falsely accuse them of crime? They consume, as it were, another's growing crops when they not only suppress the good deeds of their brothers, which they should be proclaiming, but, what is more, defame them by bringing specious charges against them. They disparage them, not only by enviously covering up the truth about their good deeds, but also by branding them with the stigma of fictitious wickedness. Did not those gnaw like locusts, of whom the Apostle said, "If you go on fighting one another, tooth and nail, all you can expect is mutual destruction"?[52] The commandment that states "You shall not give false evidence,"[53] aptly opposes this plague. So that every giver of false witness (who will not go unpunished) may refrain from defaming another's life, he must discard the teeth of the locust and not gnaw away at the growing crops in another's field.

(21) We now come to the ninth plague, extensive darkness.[54] No one is immersed in greater interior darkness than he who proves unfaithful to his marriage vows and seeks to have access to the wife of another. But the brightness of God's Law illumines this darkness, nourished by a heart addicted to lust, when this is said: "You shall not covet your neighbor's wife."[55] We should here note that it was not said, You shall not go off with, or You shall not defile, but what is more important, "You

---

49. Exod 20.15. For this variant, see Sabatier 1.175.
50. Eph 4.28. See *Beuron* 24.1 (1962–1964) 196.
51. Cf. Exod 10.13.   52. Gal 5.15.
53. Exod 20.16; Deut 5.20; for variant, cf. Sabatier 1.175.
54. Cf. Exod 10.21.   55. Deut 5.21; cf. Exod 20.17.

shall not covet your neighbor's wife." First, indeed, it was said, "You shall not commit adultery."[56] Here it is stated, "You shall not covet your neighbor's wife." And thus, regarding this one subject, there seem to be two commandments. On the one hand, we have the prohibition against adultery, the effect of violating another's marriage right and, on the other, the desire to do so. First of all, impure and illicit intercourse in adultery is condemned, and then, a restraint is placed on hungering after adulterous lust. And, to be sure, this desire to invade another's marriage is adultery, as the Lord says: "If a man looks on another's wife with a lustful eye, he has already committed adultery with her in his heart."[57] One must, therefore, not lust after another's wife lest his heart be filled with a darkness that can be felt. But if he already suffers from such darkness, he should let in the brilliant light of this commandment that he might be able to expel the gloom of a blinded conscience.

(22) Lastly, we come to the tenth plague, the death of the firstborn.[58] A man has two sons, the first when he is engaged in matters that refer to this life; the second when he performs a spiritual task whose objective is life everlasting. But the spiritual achievement must enjoy first place in our efforts as if it were our firstborn. Hence the Lord says, "Set your mind on God's kingdom before anything else, and all the rest will come to you as well."[59] As if he meant to say, Bear spiritual fruit, which will indeed be your firstborn; but that which is necessary for this life should be the second in succession. To this firstborn, along with Jacob, there will come a blessing.[60] But of Esau, and of others like him, Scripture says, "If you begin by piling up property in haste, it will bring you no blessing in the end."[61] Deuteronomy spoke figuratively of these two offspring: "When a man has two wives, one loved and the other unloved, if they both bear him sons, and the son of the unloved wife is the elder, when the day comes for him to divide his property among his sons, he shall not treat the son of the loved wife as his firstborn in contempt of his true firstborn, the son of the

---

56. Exod 20.14; cf. Deut 5.18.
57. Matt 5.28.
58. Cf. Exod 11.5.
59. Matt 6.33; Luke 12.31.
60. Cf. Gen 27.27–29.
61. Prov 20.21.

unloved wife. He shall recognize the rights of his firstborn, the son of the unloved wife, and give him a double share of all that he possesses; for he was the firstfruit of his manhood, and the right of the firstborn is his."[62]

(23) About this long quotation I am inclined to offer only this comment, that the loved wife is the life of ease, that which is delicate and carnal. But the unloved wife refers to the spiritual life, that which is inflexible, severe, and totally at odds with the pleasures of carnal desire. To her son belong the rights of the firstborn, because he who deserved to have the fruits of the spiritual life as his reward is, according to John, the "firstborn from the dead and ruler of the kings of the earth, who loved us and washed away our sins with his life's blood."[63] But without doubt this firstborn, that is, this spiritual fruit, becomes something deadly for him who is not content with what is his and desires the property of others; who yearns for what belongs to his brother and burns with avaricious lust for the goods of his neighbor. But the tenth commandment of the Law is this: "You shall not covet what belongs to your neighbor."[64] Therefore, he should pay close attention to this commandment so as not to lose the rights of the firstborn and, that he may enjoy his birthright, he must never desire what belongs to another.

(24) These, then, my dear son, are the commandments of God's Law; from them flow all the writings of sacred Scripture, and on them depends the whole structure of the religious life. These are surely the bandages for our festering wounds, these are the salutary medicine for feeble souls. On Mount Sinai, that is, on the heights of a holy way of life, we must heal all these plagues that we endured in Egypt, all the internal forms of disease that we had contracted on the even ground of the secular life. Remain constant in observing these commandments, diligently meditate on them and, I might say, continuously pound these condiments or spices in the mortar of your mind. Never leave your fragrant cell, but there carefully look into

62. Deut 21.15–17.
63. Rev 1.5.
64. Exod 20.17; cf. Sabatier 1.175.

every hidden recess of your soul, examine all the secrets of your heart, apply to your wounds the remedies that appear proper to each of them, and after recovering from your illness, closely guard your health by every means at your disposal. For a relapse is worse than the previous fever and, as the doctors say, you should pay no less attention to your diet than to the prescribed cure. You should avoid food that does not agree with you and refuse, as you would a deadly poison, whatever is harmful or is found opposed to accepted remedies. This is indeed the ten-stringed lyre that we are urged to strike with frequent blows of the mallet,[65] that is, with holy deeds, to sound as many strings as there are commandments.

(25) And so, having neatly put all this in order, ascend the mountain with Moses, take up the practice of the eremitical life, that you may deserve, as he did, to hear this message: "Go, and tell them to return to their tents, but you yourself stand here beside me, and I will set forth to you all the commandments, the rites, and the laws."[66] As you turn your back on the world, remain always at God's side and be ready to serve in his presence. For he did not say, Sit here, or Recline at my side, but Stand here with me that you may realize that spiritual repose consists in constant effort. Therefore, stand at the Lord's side on the mountain, that you may always wage implacable warfare against the evil spirits, that you may forcefully break the seductive wantonness of carnal passions. So fight against the barbarous attack of vice, so that with Joshua you may be victorious over the rebellious kings. Then he may invite you in triumph to put your feet on the necks of these kings.[67] Thus enriched with enemy spoils and arrayed with the banners of victory, like a conqueror you may enter the promised land and, indeed, with every true Israelite, possess forever by right of inheritance the land of the living.

---

65. Cf. Ps 91.4; 143.9.
66. Deut 5.30–31.
67. Cf. Josh 19.24–25.

LETTER 79

Peter Damian to Pope Nicholas II and to Hildebrand, the archdeacon. Since the pope and his archdeacon had taken away his episcopal and monastic benefices, together with their income, he takes this occasion to request that they also allow him to resign from his episcopal office. He pleads his case with examples from the Old Testament and from the history of the early Church.

(Between Fall 1060 and July 1061)[1]

O THE BLESSED Pope Nicholas[2] and to the venerable archdeacon Hildebrand,[3] the monk Peter the sinner sends his proper service.

(2) Blessed be almighty God, since what once had been given me as a benefice has now been taken away, and since even my episcopal attire has been removed, I now see certain indications that I shall very soon be completely divested of the episcopal office.[4] Indeed, when Jacob's sons had decided to kill their brother Joseph, they first stripped him of his long, multicolored tunic.[5] And again, when the Lord ordained that the high priest Aaron was to die, he said to Moses, "Aaron shall be gathered to his father's kin."[6] And then he added, "After you have stripped the father of his robes, invest Eleazar his son with them, for Aaron shall be taken from you: he shall die there."[7] Thus, when God wished anyone to abdicate his episcopal office, he first deprived him of his sacred vestments and, by putting them on his son, he ordained that he should serve in place

---

1. The dating follows Lucchesi, *Vita* 2.148.
2. Pope Nicholas II (6 Dec. [?] 1058 to 19–27 July 1061).
3. On Hildebrand as archdeacon, see *Letter* 72 n. 53.
4. See *Letter* 57 and *Letter* 72.
5. Cf. Gen 37.23.
6. Num 20.24.   7. Num 20.26.

of his father. Consequently, the taking away of vesture clearly indicates the removal from office.

(3) We also find in the *Tripartite History*[8] that when famine broke out in the province of Jerusalem, the people looked to Cyril who then presided over Jerusalem as their bishop, when in their necessity they were without food. Since there was no money to help them, he sold the sacred vessels and church vestments. By so doing he was able to be of service to the people who were in terrible need. Because of this the emperor Constantius became angry, especially since he was aware that Acacius, the bishop of Caesarea in Palestine, was plotting against Cyril. The former claimed that Cyril had sold the sacred vestment which the celebrated emperor Constantine had given to Macarius, the bishop of Jerusalem, out of reverence for that church. The garment, which he could use when administering sacred baptism, was woven of silk and golden thread. It was bought by a certain theatrical dancer. As he related, when the dancer put on the vestment and performed his usual dance, he suddenly fell, struck down by the punishment of God, and died. After Acacius had accused Cyril of this crime, he forced him to step down from his episcopal office. If, therefore, these eminent pontiffs, Aaron and Cyril, after being deprived of their vestments lost also the dignity of the priesthood, what else can this mean for me, an insignificant and unworthy man, but that when I am forced to put off the attire of a bishop I am undoubtedly deposed from the episcopal office?

(4) You have, moreover, by occupying and confiscating the monastery, cut off its revenues. And you have also spent what little profit there was deriving from the diocese. What else remains to be done but that the knight, no longer fit for service, divest himself of this cloak and also of his military rank, since he has already lost the grant of his military stipend? Let the diocese, together with the monasteries,[9] be forfeited to your own use, and let no one in the future ever suggest to me the

---

8. Cassiodorus, *Historia tripartita* 5.37 (CSEL 71.279–80).

9. This reference is so general that the diocese and monasteries cannot be identified.

empty word benefice, but let it be perfectly clear to you and yours that I have been stripped of everything that belongs to you. Both of you, kind sirs, must now be aware that I am so irrevocably returning this office to you that so long as life is still in me, I shall never again hold it.

LETTER 80

Peter Damian to an unidentified Bishop V⟨   ⟩. After noting the bishop's recovery from serious illness, he commends him also for his spiritual renewal to a life of peace and forgiveness in the face of provocation from his enemies. He takes occasion to discuss the ascetical and psychological ravages of anger, fortifying his essay with several examples drawn from his own experience and from stories told him by Archbishop Alfanus of Salerno and Abbot Desiderius of Monte Cassino. He concludes with an autobiographical admission of his own proneness to attacks of anger and lust.

(After 1060)[1]

TO THE MOST reverend bishop, Sir V⟨   ⟩,[2] the monk Peter the sinner sends greetings in the Lord.

(2) Truly God's provident will must be praised, since when he cuts, he cures, when he strikes, he instructs, and when he wounds, he restores us to health. It was for this purpose, venerable father, that divine severity afflicted you with blows of bodily chastisement, that he might restrain you like a docile youth from acting frivolously; so struck you with the hammer of punishment that, like a useful vessel in the house of the Lord, he might scour you, cleaning away the filth of scabrous dross or enveloping rust. This is why he spoke of incorrigible and undisciplined men in the words of the prophet: "You struck them down, but they did not grieve; you pierced them to the heart, but they refused to be corrected."[3] And again he said, "In vain does the refiner smelt the ore; their wicked deeds are not consumed."[4] And elsewhere by the prophet God's voice spoke of such men: "To me all Israel has been turned into

---

1. The dating follows Lucchesi, *Vita* no. 34. Neukirch, *Das Leben* 109 dates this letter between 1060 and 1068; Woody, *Damiani* 212ff. in 1068.
2. The contents give no clue to the identity of this Bishop V⟨   ⟩.
3. Jer 5.3.   4. Jer 6.29.

dross."⁵ All Israel was then converted into dross when the sinner, after being struck down by the punishment of God, either falls into the abyss of despair or, through impatience, revolts against the authority of him who justly chastised him. On the other hand, with the metal remaining intact, the dross[6] disappears under the blows inflicted by divine punishment, as the penitent, lashed by the scourge of God, throws off the rust of his bristling vices and glows with the brilliance of reviving virtues, shining with the splendor of an exemplary life.

(3) All this we clearly see fulfilled in you as a result of God's grace, as you forgave all your enemies and caused the Church to rejoice at your spiritual recovery and at your return to bodily health. And so with David you must thankfully sing to God, "The Lord did indeed chasten me, but he did not surrender me to Death."[7] And with Jonah, "As my senses failed me, I remembered the Lord, and my prayer reached you in your holy temple."[8] Therefore, with the same prophet you must give thanks for this special purpose: "I will offer you sacrifice with words of praise, whatever I have promised I will pay to the Lord for my rescue."[9]

(4) May we too, who were found worthy through the goodness of God to have you back after it seemed we had lost you, offer him, like bullocks, a sacrifice proceeding from our lips, and with Sarah, the daughter of Raguel, let us say, "God of our fathers, blessed be your name, for when you were angry you showed us your mercy, and in time of trouble you forgave the sins of those who called upon you."[10] Acting as intercessory, I often tried to have you live in peace again with your enemies, that in priestly fashion you might forgive those who hated you and unjustly did you harm. But while it was impossible for a conciliator to soothe your ruffled spirit, the Lord's severity stepped in and subdued it and, so to speak, placated your anger by being furious with you. Indeed, he wished to be severe

---

5. Ezek 22.18.
6. Cf. Isidore, *Etymologies* 16.21.6.
7. Ps 117.18.
8. Jonah 2.8.
9. Jonah 2.10.
10. Tob 3.13.

with you to remove your rage; he displayed a vengeful spirit that he might rebuild in you a spirit of meekness.

(5) Your prudent judgment will now clearly be able to decide how carefully one must avoid the vice of anger. For with those who formerly seemed so bitter toward you and totally unworthy of close relations with you, you now get along most pleasantly and are secure in enjoying their friendship. You would then have been correct in saying, "My eyes are worn out with anger,"[11] but now you can sing lightheartedly, "The precepts of the Lord are right and gladden the heart; the commandment of the Lord shines clear and gives light to the eyes."[12] Love is indeed enjoined by the Lord. "This is my commandment," he said, "that you love one another."[13] This precept truly gives light to the eyes of the heart, just as ill will and hatred, on the contrary, blind them. For as John says, "One who hates his brother is in darkness; he walks in the dark and has no idea where he is going, because the darkness has made him blind."[14] But, on the other hand, the Lord says, "I have come into this world as light, so that no one who has faith in me should remain in darkness."[15] Now if one who believes in Christ will not remain in darkness, and if, according to John's words, everyone who hates his brother is in the dark, it follows that he surely does not believe in Christ who is blinded by the darkness of deadly anger.

(6) Therefore, we can reasonably conclude from these apostolic and gospel statements that whoever is struck blind with hatred has no right to be numbered among Christ's faithful, and whoever is filled with hate is consequently an infidel and has no faith in God because he has abandoned the love of neighbor commanded by God. That alone can be called the true faith that is active in love.[16] Anger, therefore, must be

---

11. Ps 6.8. In place of "fury" in the Vulgate, Damian has "anger"; on this see Gregory I, *Moralia* 5.45.82.279, which, throughout this letter, Damian uses not only for the thought content, but also for the Scripture citations in their variant form.
12. Ps 18.9.   13. John 15.12.
14. 1 John 2.11.
15. John 12.46; cf. Sabatier 3.452.
16. Cf. Gal 5.6.

barred from the minds of the elect. Anger generates hatred that befogs the eyes of the heart and causes them to go blind because of its poisonous offspring. Every angry man truly destroys himself as he eagerly seeks to injure his neighbor, or what is still more horrible, longs to kill him. And so it is written, "Anger kills the foolish man, and envy slays the little one."[17] And since it was also written, "But you, O Lord, judge with serenity,"[18] so often as we patiently restrain the violent movements of the soul, we are striving to model ourselves on our creator. For while anger pounds on the quiet of the mind, it thoroughly shatters it and tears it to pieces so that it can hardly be recognized; like rushing waters, it throws its internal structure into confusion; as anger, like a seething flood, violently disturbs a heart already in flux, its image no longer agrees with what it was before. Finally, by anger wisdom is destroyed, so that one knows not what to do or how to do it. And so it was written, "Resentment is nursed by fools."[19] And elsewhere we read of the same topic: "Anger destroys even the wise,"[20] since a confused mind, even though it is able to understand subtleties, can never get down to the task because it is burdened with the weight of deadly vice. It is also true that he who is subject to frequent outbursts of anger can never achieve justification. Someone, perhaps, might accuse me of lying if the Apostle had not written in his letter, "A man's anger cannot promote the justice of God."[21] For while a disturbed mind upsets the judgment of reason, one accepts as proper not what God commands, but that which his fury suggests.

(7) The enormity of anger's contagion becomes clear from this, that we are prevented from associating with an angry man, that he seems to be struck down, I might say, by a kind of excommunication based on the sentence of some ancient law that excludes him from the company of his fellows. For Solomon said, "Never make friends with an angry man, be careful not to learn his ways, or you will find yourself caught in a

17. Job 5.2.
18. Wis 12.18.
19. Eccl 7.10.
20. Cf. Prov 15.1.
21. Jas 1.20.

trap."[22] And again, "Better to live in a corner of the housetop than to live with a nagging wife."[23] Hence, one who does not restrain himself like a human being must live alone like an animal. Obviously, harmony is disrupted by anger, the very thing that often destroys human society. Just as it is written, "A man prone to anger provokes a quarrel and a hothead uncovers sins."[24] It is said that a hothead uncovers sins, because as he provokes evil men to insane fury, he compels them by impatience to become worse than they were before.

(8) By anger, moreover, one loses the light of truth, and the rays of the never-setting sun are hidden from the view of a befuddled mind. Hence the Apostle says, "Do not let sunset find you still nursing your anger."[25] For when anger brings on the darkness of mental confusion, God hides from him the light of his knowledge. It is certain that through anger the splendor of the Holy Spirit is dispelled, because the soul of the reprobate no longer deserves to be his dwelling place. And so the prophet says, "On whom does my spirit rest, if not on the man who is humble and quiet, on one who reveres my words?"[26] When he speaks of a humble man he then inserts the word "quiet" because as anger robs the mind of peace and humility, it promptly slams the door on the Holy Spirit, and as he becomes arrogant in his furious madness, forbidding entrance to the Holy Spirit, the mind condemns itself, as it were, to live behind bolted doors. We should also be aware that anger frequently takes on the appearance of calmness, pretending a superficial placidity. While openly not flying into a rage, internally it burns more fiercely than a furnace and, although outwardly silent, it is shouting aloud so that only the angry man can hear it. And so Solomon says, "We expect fury from wicked men."[27] And a certain wise man said, "The thoughts of an angry man are a generation of vipers; they consume the mind that gave them birth."[28]

(9) Natural philosophers tell us that the human soul has

22. Prov 22.24–25.
23. Prov 21.9.
24. Prov 29.22.
25. Eph 4.26.
26. Isa 66.2.
27. Prov 11.23.
28. Cf. Gregory I, *Moralia* 5.45.79.278.

three dimensions: it is rational, they say, irascible, and lustful.²⁹ Therefore, that which does not occur accidentally but is rooted in our nature can be controlled only with great effort. Yet we should never despair, for just as we can win the battle against lust we can overcome this vice. To be sure, our nature, in which these qualities are said to be innate, was degraded by the sin of our first parents, but through the grace of our redeemer it was restored to its original state of health. And although the law of our flesh is in conflict with the Law of the spirit, our soul can readily overcome this ancient darkness if it continues to enjoy the renewed vigor of God's grace. To this the Apostle says, "In Christ Jesus, the life-giving Law of the spirit has set me free from the law of sin and death."³⁰ And then he continued, "What the Law could never do, because our lower nature robbed it of all potency, God has done by sending his own Son in a form like that of our sinful nature, and to deal with sin, he has passed judgment against sin within that very nature, so that the Law's justification might find fulfillment in us."³¹ Moreover, if anger or lust, which are said to be an intimate part of our nature, could not be conquered by the force of the spirit, this same eminent preacher would never have commanded the impossible. For he said, "But now you must yourselves lay aside all anger and malice."³² And to the Ephesians he also said, "Have done with spite and passion, all angry shouting and cursing, and bad feeling of every kind."³³ Concerning lust, however, it is superfluous to cite examples, since the Old Law forbids it and every opinion of sacred Scripture condemns it.

(10) Therefore, by divine grace it is possible to overcome whatever we are commanded to surmount by God's Law. What could be worse than anger, which is spewed forth with the venom of the ancient dragon, and like a deadly poison ravages the heart of every madman? "Anger," as it is written, "is possessed by a devil."³⁴ This we will be able to prove if we carefully

---

29. Cf. Aristotle, *Topica* 4.5; but especially *De anima* 9.25, where he cites this opinion as that of older authors. See also Plato, *Tim.* 41E–43E, and 69C–70A.
30. Rom 8.2.   31. Rom 8.34.
32. Col 3.8.   33. Eph 4.31.
34. A presumed citation, not found in Scripture; cf. *Letter* 54 n. 22.

study the history of the irascible Saul. For Scripture says that "when the women of the Israelites, playing on their tambourines, sang joyfully to the accompaniment of their timbrels,

> Saul made havoc among thousands
> but David among tens of thousands,

Saul was furious and the words rankled." And then it continues, "Next day an evil spirit from God seized upon Saul, and he fell into a frenzy in his house."[35] Here we may clearly observe what we read above, that "anger indeed is possessed by a devil." First, anger entered Saul's heart and let in the spirit of iniquity; following that, his raving flared up into a passion of insane fury and incited him to kill David in whom the Holy Spirit dwelt. For according to Scripture, "Saul had his spear in his hand, and he hurled it at David, meaning to pin him to the wall."[36] The inspiring spirit of anger was enraged within its host, causing him to seethe with the wildest envy because of this blameless man.

(11) Something just about like this took place some ten years ago in the principality of Urbino.[37] It came to my attention as the news began to spread, almost at the very time it happened. One day, late in the afternoon, sunset found the hearts of two priests still filled with anger,[38] and the provoking spirit of discord incited them to mutual insults and threats of bodily injury. As one of the priests heaped slurs and indignities on the other, and both exchanged taunts and offensive epithets, one of them menacingly snatched up his spear and went on his way gnashing his teeth. His home was some distance away, and his fury accompanied him with every step. As he went along, night overtook him, and his interior darkness grew deeper in his heart. Suddenly five black riders on equally black horses met him on the road, and the one who appeared to be their leader insolently spoke to him: "I have often urged you," he said, "to enter my service and to come along with my followers. Just as often you made some excuse, but now you will find it impos-

---

35. 1 Sam 18.6–10. 36. 1 Sam 18.10–11.
37. On Damian's relations with Urbino, see Lucchesi, *Vita* no. 34.
38. Cf. Eph 4.26.

sible to evade my authority." He seemed to be a nobleman named Romanus, who had frequently approached him to become his subject.

(12) The priest was struck with a horrible fear, clapped his hands together as the leader commanded him and, kissing the other's hand as was customary for those swearing homage, bound himself by feudal oath to the service of his lord. This was indeed in keeping with what Solomon said: "Hand in hand, an evil man shall not escape punishment."[39] Suddenly the man asked him, "Do you know who I am?" And the priest at once replied, "Are you not my lord Romanus?" The other answered, "Not at all," he said, "not at all. I am the devil to whom you have just sworn homage and bound yourself by inseparable ties. Remain faithful in your fealty and carry out what you promised." And after all this was said and done, the devil promptly disappeared.

(13) Trembling at this encounter, the priest in horror and confusion arrived at his home, overwhelmed with fear. Shortly after, while I was present, he approached his bishop of blessed memory, whose name was Teuzo,[40] and begged for a penance. He was at once deprived of his priestly rank. As the heat of summer was upon us and it was almost time for the harvest, I ordered that he be jailed and observe a Lenten fast of forty days; I prescribed with due moderation the years of penance he should perform, and I exhorted him that he should not despair of returning to good health. In this event we obviously see that an angry man, burning with a frenzy of unbridled fury, as Scripture says, is possessed by the devil.[41] Does not an angry man act under the influence of the devil, when at times he is led to attack an innocent man who has done him no harm, rather than one who does his bidding? Besides, since he is lacking in clear judgment, he even takes out his spite by assaulting inanimate objects.

(14) And indeed, Cyrus, the king of Persia, is known to have

39. Prov 11.21.
40. Perhaps Teuzo of Orvieto, for whom there is evidence in 1054 and 1059; cf. Schwartz, *Bistümer* 260.
41. Cf. 1 Sam 18.10.

done just that, as we learn from Orosius in his history of antiquity.[42] As Cyrus was about to cross the Gyndes river with his great army, one of the king's cavalry, who was outstanding for his shining armor and noble appearance, entered the white water where the swelling eddies were rushing over the ford and was suddenly swept away and drowned in the swirling rapids. The king then became terribly angry and decided to punish the river, declaring that he would make it so passable that it would hardly ever come up to the knees of the women. As far as we can estimate, he spent a whole year on this ridiculous project, and because he considered the river guilty of *lèse majesté*, by digging many collateral drainage ditches on both sides, he seemed to be inflicting on it an equal number of wounds. He subdivided the river into 460 smaller channels, making his enemy, as it were, lose an enormous amount of blood. He punished the richly flowing waters, with which the tyrant was so enraged, by forcing them to become a poor insignificant stream.

(15) Do you not see how anger makes a man insane? He who carries out what impatience suggests exposes himself to mockery and ridicule. The poison of our ancient enemy in various forms flows into our miserable souls by every vice with which men are afflicted. But with pestilential anger, the serpent strikes at our very heart, pouring into it all his bitter gall, thus causing a prudent man to go out of his mind, turning rationality into madness and innate cleverness into insanity. He deprives these poor souls of their reason and compels them to rave like madmen. Even though this vice is totally disallowed to all Christians, it must be especially avoided by priests. For since truth itself commands all the faithful in general that if anyone is nursing a grudge, he should leave his gift where it is before the altar and not dare offer his gift until he has made peace with his brother,[43] how much more should a priest be inclined to act in this way? For he is not about to offer some amount of gold or silver, or some perishable pearls, or even

---

42. Orosius, *Adversus paganos* 2.6.112.
43. Cf. Matt 5.23–24.

sheaves of grain, but the life-giving sacrament of the Eucharist. And since this unique sacrifice should be offered especially for our enemies, as the Apostle observed when he said, "When we were God's enemies, we were reconciled to him through the death of his Son,"[44] how can a priest dare approach this tremendous sacrament, with what audacity can he presume to participate in this heavenly banquet, if he refuses to pardon his brother while celebrating this very mystery of reconciliation? Here an enemy is offering a sacrifice that should remove enmity; he approaches this mystery of peace while he is not at peace, but it would be better for a sinner to forego celebrating than offer this sacrifice of praise, since God is more readily appeased by the holocaust of one's good will than by the sacrament where another is the victim.

(16) After all of this, it will not be out of place, I think, if I should here insert the outstanding case that several people reported to me.[45] There was a certain man, they said, who had killed a person more eminent than himself, from whose son he had to defend himself by frequent warlike action. This was customary in secular affairs and not in keeping with the Law of the gospel. In avenging his father's death, the son caused much destruction and often engaged in plundering raids. While this was happening, the murderer found himself in great difficulty, so he decided to travel to the imperial court and, if possible, to seek a remedy for all these calamities. Discovering this plan, the man who was out to avenge the blood of his father went after him with the idea of either taking him to court or, by never giving up his pursuit, to surprise and attack him with his swordsmen. Now at that time the emperor was staying in Germany.

(17) And so, as the first man rode along at a moderate pace without fear of any difficulty and his pursuer moved more quickly, it happened at last that they came upon one another in mutual confrontation. But since the man who was guilty of murder had scarcely four or five armed men who could help

---

44. Rom 5.10.
45. The same account is told of John Gualberti; cf. *Vita Johannis Gualberti* c. 2–3.1080.

him, while the murdered man's son was accompanied by almost thirty knights, he advised four of his guard to take off. But as he saw that he could not escape from his pursuers, he begged for mercy and surrendered. After throwing away his weapons, stretching out his arms in the form of a cross, he prostrated himself on the ground and asked that they either pardon him or kill him. The latter, however, now that he had won, held back from striking him out of reverence for the cross, and also restrained his men from killing him. After coming to terms, in honor of the holy and life-giving cross, he not only spared his life, but forgave him for killing his father.

(18) After this significant victory, by which he overcame not only the other man but also himself and was, I might say, the master of both his enemy and his own soul, he arrived at the imperial court, which was now close by. But, as he entered the church to say a prayer, a wondrous and astounding thing happened: the figure of the savior that was attached to the cross was seen bowing to him three times.[46] Oh what a glorious and outstanding distinction it was for him who out of reverence for Christ had not sought vengeance, that he was found worthy to be greeted with respect by the author of mercy himself; and that he who for his own salvation had not taken revenge should be so honored by him. When soon thereafter the emperor[47] heard of these events, he received him with honor and friendly affection, as he deserved, and with great liberality rewarded him with gifts. Oh, if only this man had been a priest! How confidently he could have come forward to offer sacrifice to God, since he had been deemed worthy of such a singular greeting by his God! On the other hand, how pernicious and disastrous it is for one to approach the holy altar if he stores up a blend of anger and hatred in his heart! That which was meant to provide eternal rest becomes for him the source of everlasting fire.

(19) To the same purpose, the following seems recently to have happened to one of his priests as reported by Alfanus,

---

46. In the *Vita Gualberti*, c. 3.1080, the church is identified as that of San Miniato al Monte.

47. Conrad II; cf. Woody, *Damiani* 213f.

the venerable archbishop of Salerno.[48] Now this priest was particularly greedy in gathering money, took interest on the capital that he lent, and in general lived a very carnal life. One day as he was celebrating Mass, just as he was breaking the host, the body of the Lord, three sparks of fire suddenly sprang from this heavenly sacrament and terrified the celebrant as they struck him in the chest. But what this could have been will be left to the judgment of anyone who would care to investigate.

(20) It also seems to me that I should not here pass over in silence what the same archbishop of Salerno and Desiderius,[49] the most dedicated and truthful abbot of Monte Cassino, told me, using, I might say, practically the same words. It happened that as a bishop, whose name I cannot now recall, was about to consecrate the church in a certain fortified town, he received a request from the bishop-elect of Benevento for the relics of the blessed Barbatus.[50] Complying with this fraternal appeal, he procured the relics in their richly ornamented reliquary, properly sealed it, and on the day assigned sent the bishop the enclosed gift, employing the services of a trustworthy monk. But, when the seal was broken and the container opened, it was found to be completely empty. The bearer was astounded as he discovered that the relics he thought to be inside were missing. Disappointed, the bishop was frustrated in that his expectations had not been fulfilled. Nevertheless, because of the urgency of the situation, the church was dedicated. The courier returned carrying the reliquary, which he now thought to be empty. But, as he walked along, to his surprise he felt something moving within the casket. Quickly he opened it and found that what he had been asked to carry was now filled with these marvelously venerable relics. Somewhat later, however, this church was totally destroyed along with the fortified town in which it stood. But whether this occurred because of that bishop, or for some other divine purpose, I have no way of knowing.

(21) There was also this other judgment of God about which

48. On Alfanus, see *Letter* 49 and *Letter* 59.
49. On Desiderius of Monte Cassino, see *Letter* 82 n. 2.
50. On Barbatus, see L. Jadin, "Barbatus," DHGE 6 (1932) 622f.

the brothers had little doubt. It seems that a certain priest had sinned with another man's wife but, after later becoming a monk at Monte Cassino, he lived an upright life. In the very week in which it was his turn to celebrate Mass, as he was chanting Prime with the community, he was suddenly struck by lightning, and to everyone's horror it killed him.

(22) I also recall another story that the same archbishop of Salerno reported as happening to one of the citizens of his city. As he was caught in a storm at sea, the man solemnly swore that he would become a monk but, after his rescue from the shipwreck, he failed to fulfill his vow because of his attachment to a worldly life. A year had passed, and on the very day he had promised the Lord to enter the monastery, on the first of January it was, as he walked about here and there leading a group of boys, playing and laughing and singing some silly lighthearted songs, a stone from the roof suddenly fell on him and crushed him. And so this unlucky man who of his own accord had refused to leave the world unwillingly lost it, and he who out of love for the flesh had lied to the truth itself was deprived of the deceitful pleasures of the flesh. Thus, what was said in Scripture applied to him: "Pride comes before disaster."[51] And in the words of the Apostle, "It is a terrible thing to fall into the hands of the living God."[52]

(23) But, if the anger of the living God is something to be feared by all sinners, it must certainly be a greater source of dread to him who is afflicted with the vice of ungovernable fury. For as he allows this storm of a vexatious spirit to brew within his heart, he brings down upon himself the full measure of God's wrath by his anger. Nothing is more in keeping with justice than that anger is answered by anger, and that vengeance breeds vengeance in return. And so the wise man says, "The vengeful man will face the vengeance of God, who keeps a strict account of his sins."[53] On the other hand, he gives us a wholesome warning when he says, "Suffer your neighbor when he does harm to you; then, when you pray, your sins will be

---

51. Prov 16.18.
52. Heb 10.31.
53. Eccl 28.1.

forgiven."[54] Following that as if still pursuing the argument, he continues, "If a man harbors a grudge against another, is he to expect healing from God? If he has no mercy on his fellow man, is he still to ask forgiveness for his own sins?"[55] To this, as if still irked over the subject, he added, "If a mere mortal cherishes rage, can he look to God for pardon?"[56] Then, as if he were saying that prayer for an angry man will not be heard while he continues in his wrath, he consistently remarked, "Who will beg forgiveness for his sins?"[57]

(24) Since we must promptly repress the urge to anger as we become aware that death is quickly catching up with us, the wise man aptly observed, "Think of the end that awaits you, and put away your hatred; think of the fear of the Lord, and do not be enraged at your neighbor."[58] Therefore, you must curb the anger that is in your heart so that it will never be able to erupt in words, as it is said in Ecclesiastes: "Banish anger from your mind, and shake off malice from your flesh."[59] The Lord proposed an angry flood that sweeps everything before it, when he commanded us to check our wrath with self-restraint: The first is in the mind, the second in the throat, and the last in the voice. "Anyone," he says, "who nurses anger against his brother must be brought to judgment"; here he would have us restrain the mind. "If he uses the abusive term *racha*, he must answer for it to the court"; here we have a barrier to the throat. "If he calls him 'fool,' he will have to answer for it in the fires of hell";[60] here, then, is an obstacle to the voice. These are the obstructions, like hurdles and masses of rubble, that at God's command block the assault of anger and fury; so that they do not destroy everything in their path like a raging torrent, they should be held in check by the decision of rational discipline. Our mind must not be like glass that breaks at the very first blow, but rather like a vein of precious metal that is purified by the pounding hammer. Glass would indeed be far superior to all glittering metal if it were not shattered by every

54. Eccl 28.2.
55. Eccl 28.3–4.
56. Eccl 28.5.
57. Eccl 28.5.
58. Eccl 28.6–8.
59. Eccl 11.10.
60. Matt 5.22.

little blow, if by its own natural strength it did not break on impact. But since it is so fragile, it is thought to be inferior and of less value than all other kinds of metal. Glass, as we know, is made of sand, the product of man's art and industry,[61] and so by its very nature it is bound to be fragile.

(25) Now history[62] relates that a certain workman in the time of the emperor Tiberius invented a mixture by which glass would become malleable and flexible, and like any other metal remain solid and unbroken when pounded. After being admitted to the royal court, the artisan gave the emperor a goblet made according to the formula that he had discovered. Angered by the gift, the emperor promptly threw the goblet to the floor. Yet it did not break, but like some bronze or silver vessel was only dented on one side. The artisan at once picked up the goblet from the floor, took a hammer from his pocket, and repaired the vessel, which had not been broken but only bent, just as if it were made of metal. The emperor was greatly surprised at seeing him do this, and he said to the artisan, "Is there anyone besides you who knows how to make glass of this kind?" The workman swore that no one on earth other than himself knew the secret. When the emperor heard this, he at once ordered the man to be beheaded, reckoning that if the fine quality achieved by this method should become common knowledge, gold would be thought as worthless as clay, and every other kind of metal would lose its value. Surely, if glass were to lose its fragility and be made malleable, and could be made to withstand pounding, who would ever think that shining metal was equal to the clearness of glass?

(26) But now to return to the subject. Just as its fragile quality causes glass to be valued less, and just as their strength and solidity recommend other metals, thus does the whole fabric of other virtues fall to pieces because of anger; but through the majesty of imperial patience we fashion ourselves into God's dwelling place that glitters with the splendor of brilliant jewels. For while the former pulls out virtues by the roots, the latter stimulates their growth.

61. Cf. Isidore, *Etymologies* 16.16.2.
62. Cf. Petronius, *Satyricon* 51–52; Isidore, *Etymologies* 16.16.

(27) It is also true of me, who will still write about this matter, that a natural disposition to anger arouses me, and often the slightest offense disturbs my peace of mind, so that frequently I seem to be pierced by a fiery spear and not just lightly pricked by some thorn or needle. I consider a slight scourge to be rather a bullwhip, and when I take the blow, I groan as if the lash were weighted with lead. But this is only my inner disposition; when it comes to external behavior, anger can say what it will. It can rage and howl and gnash its teeth but, in everything it might secretly suggest to me, as far as I can counteract it, there will be no cooperation from me. Even though it well up within me, unleash its fury, rant and rave and rise up with pride, I will not lend my members to its service that it might use them as weapons to achieve its purpose. "You must no longer put the body's several parts at sin's disposal,"[63] the Apostle says. I will not move a hand, that with my help it might strike or take something by force. Neither my tongue nor my lips will I move, allowing it to use them to spew out its bitter gall.

(28) And as I completely deny assistance to this savage anger, like a flame without nourishment it must soon grow weak and die, or like a wind that lacks an obstacle against which it may blow, it will harmlessly move through space. Exhausted, it will strike back against itself, as it is frustrated at not finding anything combustible on which it can feed. Thus I reply to anger and to the enticement of lust as well. At times lustful desire is enkindled and flares up within me, agitates my whole being, causing my genitalia to grow hard. But in all of this, passion can be satisfied that it is doing what it can, since it will never find me cooperating with it. Anger may clamor, and I may hear it; lust may grow hot, and I may experience it; but at these disturbances I never lift a finger to help them, nor provide fuel for these raging fires. With anger I never bring myself to add to its fury, and with lust I never blow on the embers, causing them to burst into flames. By so doing, anger will necessarily rise in vain, and thus grow weaker, and the fires of lust will

---

63. Rom 6.13.

burn themselves out for lack of fuel. I can, indeed, quell nature by bringing reason to bear, but am never able to destroy it; I can soften its impact, but can never totally annul it. Let everyone do to me what he will; I must look for patience within myself. Nor can I hope for reward from someone else's virtue, for where there are no battles to challenge us, we will never find an opportunity to win victories. In vain do we hide behind a shield when spears and swords are never brandished against us. If the fire in the furnace is extinguished, the metal's purity is never tested. And so, another man's meekness will not make me patient, but within myself I must build up defenses that will ward off and repel the volley of assaulting missiles.

(29) All of this, venerable father, I have written for you in unskilled fashion, not that I might instruct you, who by God's help are already a teacher in the Church, but that by taking the occasion to address you in this agitated manner, I might benefit myself and others like me. Nor do I fear that your holy prudence will take it amiss that someone younger than you should humbly presume to call these things to your attention, since we know that the Lord, using the prophet's words, said, "Come now and reprove me."[64] And we know that the Lord's servant, Moses, patiently listened to Jethro, who was of alien birth, when he said, "Like a fool you are wearing yourself out."[65]

(30) May almighty God, venerable sir, who has kept you out of harm's way for us, likewise help you to avoid the filth of all vice and, as his vessel baked in the fire, produce in you the splendor of spiritual virtues.

64. Isa 1.18.   65. Exod 18.18.

LETTER 81

Peter Damian to Ambrose, who had recently entered the monastic life. A specimen of Damian's theological thinking, this primer of Catholic belief, marvelous in its clarity, was written to serve as an introduction to theology for a young monk who had asked for instruction. Stressing first the importance of the virtue of faith, Damian then concentrates on the doctrine of the Trinity, on Christology, and on the Holy Spirit, with passing reference to Mary, the mother of God. Damian gives special attention to the procession of the Holy Spirit, basing his teaching on both Greek and Latin Fathers. While he does mention a contemporary schism between the Greek and Latin churches over this issue, he does not refer to Michael Cerularius, the Greek patriarch, the supposed author of the schism.

(After 1060)[1]

O AMBROSE,[2] my dear son in blessed hope, the monk Peter the sinner sends the truth of the orthodox faith.

(2) Dearest son, you request that I compose something for you on the Catholic faith and briefly discuss at least a few of the things that were explained at greater length by the Fathers. For, as you say, you hope to be more efficiently instructed, and this lesson may be more tenaciously impressed on your memory, if what was published in the pages of the ancient doctors should now proceed from my lips, as from our own library.

(3) For although that which is blended comes from the same cask, it is, however, more acceptable when served by a hand from the household. And often medicine is more useful to us when given by those who recognize the discomfort of our ill-

---

1. Dating follows Neukirch, *Das Leben* 113; Gaudenzi, *Il codice* 306, dates this letter for 1056/57, and claims that it was written in Acereta.
2. Ambrose was also the addressee of *Letter* 128. In the Gaetani edition 3 (1615) 1, this letter was entitled "On the Catholic Faith," without support in MS C2, the sole MS for this letter.

ness by the constant familiarity of living with us. Now because you are well known to me through the brotherly love that makes us one in mind, you are confident that I will apply a strong poultice of salvation to the spot where I am aware that the nerves of your faith waver away somewhat weakly from a healthy certitude. And thus what you do is beyond reproach, so that you may build, as it were, the foundation of faith at the very beginning of your recent conversion, on which the scaffold of your future deeds, like a spiritual edifice, may rise, never to collapse.

(4) Your request is certainly praiseworthy, and what is asked is not frivolous but particularly necessary. And thus, the holy eagerness of your devotion, because it earnestly solicits something worthwhile, does not, for its importuning, deserve to be repulsed. Truly, without faith we can neither live in Christ nor please God at all by any activity. To this, both apostolic and prophetic authority at once attest. For these are the words of the Apostle: "Without faith it is impossible to please God."[3] And by the prophet it is said, "The just man lives by faith;[4] but if he draws back, he shall not please my soul."[5]

(5) And so, according to both statements, it is impossible to please God unless we hold to the correct norms of the true faith. Faith is the beginning of virtues, faith is the foundation of good works, faith is the preamble of all human salvation. Whoever does not cautiously walk the line of this narrow path will of necessity be caught in the trap of error. Thus, if anyone appears to espouse the cause of good works but is without proper faith, he can in no way be counted among the company of the sons of God. And he who does not know how to walk by faith will find it impossible to reach the sight of God; and putting it all briefly, without the right faith, one neither acquires the grace of justification nor merits eternal life. Now, therefore, let us proceed to the quick of things, to the core of the matter here proposed, with him of whom we speak as our guide.

(6) First of all, therefore, whoever wishes to be a true and

---

3. Heb 11.6.   4. Hab 2.4.
5. Heb 10.38; cf. Sabatier 2.964.

perfect Catholic must believe[6] in God the Father almighty, the maker of all that is seen and unseen. Let him also believe in his only-begotten Son, namely, in the Word, the power and the wisdom by whom all things were created. He was not created, but begotten before all ages: true God in all things like the Father, and of one substance with the Father, even though he is possessed of another person. He is neither later in time nor inferior in dignity, nor weaker in power; the begotten is altogether as great as he who begot. And even though we state that the Son was born of the Father, still nothing temporal is attributed to him, just as it is not ascribed to the Father. For he who professes the Father to be eternal must also admit that the Son is coeternal with him, that is, that the Father who always existed before all ages, utterly without beginning, also always had a Son. He could not have been the Father from all eternity if he had not been eternally possessed of a Son. One must also believe in the Holy Spirit, also true God, proceeding at once from the Father and from the Son, always equal to both in substance, power, will, and eternity. Certainly he does not proceed from the Father to the Son, and then proceed from the Son to sanctify the creature, as some wickedly and infectiously observe, but proceeds simultaneously from both. For the Father begot the Son in such a way that the spirit of truth proceeds from the Son just as he proceeds from the Father.

(7) Therefore, my dear son, be constant and firm in the belief that the Father and the Son and the Holy Spirit are the one, only, and true God—omnipotent, eternal, immutable, independent of external agency. For there is only one substance or essence that is immutable and totally without change or inconstancy, and that is God. Indeed, being itself, from which the word "essence" is derived, especially and most truly pertains to him. To this highest and unique substance alone belongs the noun that the Greeks call "ὤν," 'being,' and the Latin "est," 'is.' Hence the Apostle states, "There did not exist in him being and non-being, but there is in him only being."[7] And the Lord

---

6. On the *Nicene Creed* and other creedal declarations, see F. X. Murphy, "Creed," NCE 4 (1967) 432–38.
7. 2 Cor 1.18–19.

also said to Moses, "I AM who am," and, "This is what you shall tell the children of Israel: 'I AM sent me to you.'"[8] Nevertheless, while we speak of the one, simple, and indivisible substance of God, we should distinguish the Trinity by names, and should profess that one God the Father and the Son and the Holy Spirit must be recognized, because each one of these is God; and that the one God is all of these together. Each one of these is the full, perfect, and eternal substance, and all of them together are likewise one simple substance. Hence the Father and the Son and the Holy Spirit spoken of together are not something greater or fuller than when speaking of each single person of this same holy Trinity. For the omnipotent God, by the immensity of his nature, both fills and contains all creation, and therefore the Father fills the totality of being, as does the Son and the Holy Spirit, because by nature God is one in the Father and in the Son and in the Holy Spirit.

(8) Thus, my son, when you happen to be occupied with litanies or prayers, do not do what certain simple people do, more out of ignorance than through unbelief. For they invoke the name of the Father or the Son or the Holy Spirit not only once, but to promote greater reverence, they repeat the name of the holy Trinity often, as if it were something more; so that as a multitude of saints is something more than one saint, so too, God forbid, the whole Trinity is something greater than one person of the same holy Trinity. The piety of the faithful rejects this, nor does the rule of orthodox faith admit it. Without any doubt we must believe that the Father is the whole and perfect God; that the Son is the whole and perfect God; and that the Holy Spirit is the whole and perfect God. And still there are not three gods, Father, Son, and Holy Spirit, but one God, whole and perfect. Nor do the three named together, Father, Son, and Holy Spirit, indicate something greater than each of them, even if Father, Son, or Holy Spirit is called upon singly. Indeed, there is the same greatness in each person cited singly as exists in the entire Trinity called upon in common. Otherwise, when we rightly say God the Father, God the Son,

---

8. Exod 3.14.

and God the Holy Spirit, each of them would be an imperfect God if God were more fully seen in three rather than in a single person. But God forbid that this should apply to the piety of the faithful, who do not ascribe anything greater or lesser to the simple nature of the godhead.

(9) Since, therefore, the Father alone, or the Son alone, or the Holy Spirit alone is just as great as the Father, the Son, and the Holy Spirit together, God should never be called threefold; while he cannot be diminished, there is also nothing by which the ever existing perfection of the supreme Trinity may be increased. Therefore, God is whole and perfect, whether he is singly called Father, or Son, or Holy Spirit, and the whole and perfect God is simultaneously Father, Son, and Holy Spirit. And so, God must be called triune, and not threefold.

(10) There is in this holy Trinity, moreover, no degree of time, no distinction of greatness, no variety of dignity. For there is nothing here that is older in time, nothing that differs in quantity, nothing that exceeds in honor. But the total divine essence is of such a simple nature that, with the exception of words that indicate personal quality, whatever can be essentially said of one person can also be understood without distinction of the three. It should be noted that man was created, not in the likeness of one person, but of the whole Trinity. Hence we do not read, "I will make man in my image," but "let us make man," he says, "in our image."[9]

(11) Also, as we shame Arius[10] by professing the substance of the entire Trinity to be one and the same, so too, avoiding the godlessness of Sabellius,[11] we distinguish, under the proper qualities of each, three unconfused and individually expressed persons. Nor, indeed, as devised by godless heresy, do we say that, when he wishes, God the Father is Father; when he wishes, he is the Son; when he wishes, he is the Holy Spirit. But each person is so distinguished from the others by certain properties that the Father is always the Father and never the Son or the Holy Spirit; that the Son is always the Son and is never the

---

9. Gen 1.26.
10. See V. C. DeClercq, "Arianism," NCE 1 (1967) 791–94.
11. See P. Lebeau, "Sabellianism," NCE 12 (1967) 783.

Father or the Holy Spirit; and the Holy Spirit is never the Father or the Son, but always the Holy Spirit. We should note, therefore, not only the bare difference in name, but subtly distinguish that which is proper to the person.

(12) The Father, therefore, has this as his own, that of all things that are, he is unique in that he does not derive from another; and because of this, he alone is acknowledged to exist in the person of paternity, but is not unique in the essence of divinity. But the only-begotten Son of God has this as his own, that he alone was consubstantially and coessentially born of the unique one, that is, from the Father; and this is the property of the Son. It is proper to the Holy Spirit, however, that he simultaneously proceeds from the Father and the Son, and is the Spirit of both; indeed, consubstantial and coeternal, of the same immensity and power, of the same will and inseparable nature. He is in no way less in anything than they from whom he proceeds, but together with them is worshiped as the true omnipotent God, and with them is equally adored. For he abides entirely in the Father, entirely in the Son; he proceeds entirely from the Father and proceeds entirely from the Son. He so abides in them that he always proceeds from both; he so proceeds that he always inseparably abides in them. With them, indeed, he possesses naturally and coessentially both the totality of unity and the unity of totality. He is, moreover, that highest charity, by which the begotten is loved by his Father and loves his Father. And therefore there are not more than three, essentially undivided and distinct in their threefold properties: one loving him who is from him; one loving him from whom he is; and that very love itself, of which it is said "that God is love."[12]

(13) And this is the highest, ineffable, and incomprehensible Trinity, I will not say of one God, but the one God. Nor is one turned or changed into the other; but what he is, without any change, he always remains unimpaired. For the prophet says, "From my mouth will go forth the word of justice, and it will not return."[13] What is the meaning of "it will not return"? A

---

12. 1 John 4.8.   13. Isa 45.23.

Sabellian should not say that he is the Father who is also the Son; nor should a Patripassian[14] say that, when he wills, he is the Father and, when he wills, he is the Son. Therefore, when the Word has gone forth it does not return, because the Father is always the Father, and the Son is always the Son.

On the Mystery of the Lord's Incarnation

(14) We also believe that the Son of God, whom God the Father begot before the ages from his own substance, put on true humanity according to our nature and came forth from his mother's womb without defiling her virginity. For he who was God from God, omnipotent from the omnipotent, not later in time, not inferior in majesty, certainly not dissimilar in glory, not divided in essence, he the everlasting only-begotten of the everlasting Father was born of the Holy Spirit and of the Virgin Mary. Because he so assumed human nature that he did not change his divinity into something else, he substantially so counited true flesh and true soul with himself, that according to his humanity he might destroy death by dying, and overcome the devil who had power over death. This uniquely wonderful and wonderfully unique generation is not to be so understood so that what was proper to the race should be destroyed by the novelty of creation. For indeed, the Holy Spirit imparted fruitfulness to the virginal womb, but the reality of the body proceeded from the pregnancy of the mother, which the spirit of rational life ensouled.

(15) And so we condemn Apollinaris,[15] who claims that the savior did not receive a human soul, but only a soul that lacked reason. For he propounded as dogma that only divinity could suffice to give the soul and infuse the judgment of rational wisdom, which, undoubtedly, is the same as saying our redeemer was not man, but had only the members of a human body. Brute animals also possess soul and body, but they do not have reason, which is proper to the mind.

---

14. See P. Lebeau, "Patripassianism," NCE 10 (1967) 1102.
15. See J. Bentivegna, "Apollinaris of Laodicea," NCE 1 (1967) 667f.; F. Chiovaro, "Apollinarianism," NCE 1 (1967) 665–66.

(16) Yet if we must detest Manicheans[16] who deny that he possessed a true body, which is the lowest part of man, how much more should they be condemned who affirm that he did not have that which in man is superior? God forbid, therefore, that we should believe what rash blindness and proud loquacity invent. God forbid, I say, that the Son of God should receive something less of human nature, and that in becoming man he was unlike us in flesh, or in soul, or in sensation. We must profess that, except for the blemish of sin that is natural to those for whom he became man, he was completely like us. For this reason he is called the mediator between God and men,[17] since he is true God as he is also true man; in his divinity, having the same nature with the Father, and differing in nothing from his mother in his human substance; having from us until death the penalty of our wickedness, possessing from God the Father incomparable justice; "who was crucified for our infirmity, but lives by his own power."[18] By participating in the human condition, he experienced death, which he freely accepted, not losing the power of his nature by which he enlivens all. He indeed is the agent and the product of the agent, because as a priest he offered himself in sacrifice, and it was he himself who hung on the cross as a pleasing victim. Keeping in mind what is proper to both natures joined together in one person, humility was received from his majesty, weakness from his power, and mortality from his eternity. To pay the debt of our human condition, his nature that was capable of suffering was united to his invulnerable nature, so that one and the same mediator between God and men could both die, on the one hand, and be incapable of dying, on the other.

(17) But now, my son, perhaps you are taken aback by the thought that may be occasioned by what follows from this thinking. While the Son is of one substance with the Father and is believed to be inseparable in nature, how could the Son without the Father put on human form, or alone undergo the rigors of the passion? For that which is divine and unapproachable,

---

16. See J. Ries, "Manichaeism," NCE 9 (1967) 153–60.
17. Cf. 1 Tim 2.5.   18. Cf. 2 Cor 13.4.

and cannot be comprehended from evident signs of his unutterable being, is often explained by Catholic doctors through examples of visible things. Thus the blessed Augustine says, "The soul is one thing, the intellect is another, yet intellect is in the soul. The soul, indeed, is one, but the soul performs one thing and intellect another. For the soul lives, the intellect understands, and life belongs to the soul while wisdom belongs to the intellect. And still there is no soul without intellect, nor an intellect without a soul. And while they are one, the soul alone received life and the intellect alone received wisdom. Thus, even though both Father and Son are one, and God is one, flesh belongs to Christ alone, just as wisdom belongs to the intellect alone, even though it is not separate from the soul."[19] And again he gives another example: "In the sun, heat and light are in one ray, but heat dries while light illumines. And while heat does one thing and light another, still they cannot be separated from one another. And thus the Son took on flesh and did not desert the Father. Also in the case of the zither, since there is no doubt that art, hand, and string work together, only one sound is heard. Art directs, the hand plucks, and the string sounds. The three work together, but only the string sounds what is heard. Thus the Father, the Son, and the Holy Spirit all combined in the humanity of Christ, but only the Son took on humanity."[20]

(18) But if, perhaps, this too concerns you—how it was that the true body of Christ could come forth from his mother's womb while preserving her virginity—turn your eyes to that which is easy, and from little things grasp what is boundless. A ray of the sun penetrates a window in such a way that with imperceptible subtlety it passes through its barrier. Yet it does not cause even a small crack but appears to be the same inside and out. And neither when it enters nor when it comes out does it destroy, for in its entrance and exit the window remains whole. If the sun's ray does not break the window, is it not possible for the omnipotence of the redeemer at his birth to pre-

19. Pseudo-Augustine, *Sermo* 245 (PL 39.2196.2); cf. E. Dekkers, *Clavis patrum Latinorum* 91.
20. Pseudo-Augustine, *Sermo* 245 (PL 39.2197).

serve the integrity of the Virgin?[21] For the virginal integrity gave birth unimpaired just as it conceived without being violated. Indeed he, who was born of her, is the true and entire God just as he is a true and entire man. And there is nothing deceitful in this unity, for both the humility of man and the sublimity of the godhead are joined to one another. Just as the nature of God is not diminished by bowing low, so the nature of man is not destroyed by elevation. Let each nature, therefore, do what is proper to it, the Word performing what belongs to the Word, and flesh naturally carrying out what belongs to the flesh. The one is resplendent with miracles, the other is subject to indignity. But neither is the creature changed into divinity, nor divinity turned into a creature. For the person of the mediator between God and men so subsists of both and in both natures that, after the Son of God was made man, the fullness of divinity in no way destroyed the human nature, as impious heresy blasphemously states, nor did divinity change into the essence of humanity. For when God assumed human nature, his divine nature remained completely unchangeable and incapable of suffering. He consists, therefore, of two natures because he united both indivisibly; but he exists in two natures, because he preserved both intact.

(19) Hence, the only-begotten Son of God, in taking a perfect human soul and body, is both consubstantial to the Father in the form of God, and consubstantial to his mother in the form of a slave. But in assuming partnership with human infirmity he did not, therefore, participate in our sins. For in assuming the form of a slave without contracting servile contagion, he did not diminish divinity, but enhanced humanity. Indeed, the nature was taken from the mother of the Lord, but not the fault.[22] Nor was he able to commit sins of his own, since he came to wash away the sins of others. And thus we know that the individual quality of the human and divine nature persists in him, so that as we observe in him that the Word is by nature

---

21. Cf. Pseudo-Augustine, *Sermo* 245 (PL 39.2197.4); see also G. M. Roschini, "La Mariologia di S. Pier Damiano," *San Pier Damiano nel IX centenario della morte (1072–1972)*, 1 (1972) 195–237, esp. 223.

22. Cf. Roschini, "Mariologia" 218.

something quite different from the flesh, we still profess that the one Son of God is both Word and flesh. He is, indeed, true God and true man, namely, God in that "in the beginning was the Word, and the Word was with God, and the Word was God";[23] but he was man in that "the Word became flesh and made his dwelling among us."[24] He was God in that "through him all things came into being, and apart from him nothing came to be";[25] he was man in that "he was born of a woman, born under the law."[26] The infancy of the little one is observed in the lowliness of the crib, the sublimity of the Most High is proclaimed by the voices of angels.

(20) It is necessary, moreover, for the investigator of this high problem both to observe discreet caution and to weigh the matter circumspectly. We are compelled surely to distinguish persons in the divinity, since we dare not divide the divine substance. So we believe that the Father, the Son, and the Holy Spirit are three persons, while professing that they are of only one, simple, and entirely inseparable essence. But, on the other hand, we ascribe to Christ two complete and perfect substances, divinity and humanity, while we assert that he is possessed of only one person. Nor is it proper to say of the Father, or of the Son, or of the Holy Spirit that each is something else— for in all of them there is one and the same nature—but only that each is someone else, since without doubt there is in them a diversity of persons. In Christ, however, there is no other, since in God and man there is only one person; but one must say that he is something else, for the twin natures are of different substance. On the contrary, Bishop Nestorius[27] and the archimandrite Eutyches[28] together with Dioscorus[29] disputed with one another with this difference: the former contended that Christ was only man, while the latter two ascribed to him

23. John 1.1.
24. John 1.14.
25. John 1.3.
26. Gal 4.4.
27. Patriarch of Constantinople, d. after 451, who attacked the title of Mary as the *theotokos*; cf. P. T. Camelot, "Nestorius," NCE 10 (1967) 348.
28. The father of Monophysitism, d. 454; cf. P. T. Camelot, "Eutyches," NCE 5 (1967) 642.
29. Patriarch of Alexandria, d. 454; cf. F. X. Murphy, "Dioscorus," NCE 4 (1967) 879.

only a divine nature. Rightly did Holy Church manage to close its doors on these men so that they were compelled to dispute with one another outside the fold, without causing disaster to others. But we so unhesitatingly understand the mystery of the Lord's incarnation that, even though believing that there is one true person of God and man, we still contend that there is not in him one nature, divine and human. Nor is the divinity of Christ the same as his flesh, nor could the flesh be the same as his divinity; both natures of divinity and humanity nevertheless remained unchangeable and unconfused in their proper quality. We profess, therefore, that the human substance, that is, true flesh and true rational soul were received by the Son of God in the unity of person, but not in the unity of nature.

(21) And thus, the mystery of the Lord's incarnation, while not producing in Christ a duality of person, does not cause the reception of human nature to be something common to the blessed Trinity: for while simply retaining the permanent quality of both substances, the individual unity of the person nevertheless remains always intact. This acceptance of servile form pertains only to the person of the Son, from whom, however, it removed nothing of the fullness of divinity, nor deprived him in the slightest of inexhaustible majesty. So it is that in one and the same redeemer of ours, the truth of human nature was manifest and, at the same time, the eternal immutability of divine power persisted. Therefore, in Christ we say that there is a diversity of natures but not of person; yet in the blessed Trinity we profess that there is a distinction of persons, but not of nature. For even though, as man, he might have been concealed under the deficiencies of one small body, as the God of all things, however, he ruled over visible and invisible creatures. Nor is he now the one by whom all things were created, and someone else who was made man; he is at once creator and creature, at once physician and medicine, at once priest and victim. Clearly, the immensity of divine greatness is that by which we understand him to be within all things, but not enclosed; outside all things, but not excluded. He is, therefore, within in that he contains all things, without in that he confines all things by the immensity of his unlimited magnitude. By the

external, he is seen as the creator; by the internal, he proves to be the governor and director of all things.

(22) However, there are some who, while striving to investigate the mystery of divine generation, are deceived by the phantoms of bodily thought. Did the omnipotent God, they ask, take a wife because he gave birth to a son? But from our very weakness we can gather what needs to be considered in the secret depths of God's work. For first a plan is born in the mind of the architect so that the structure of the future home may be built. Therefore, the mind that lies hidden gives birth to the plan, that the building might arise with all its features of walls and corners. Hence the plan is somewhat like the son of the human mind; it comes forth both to construct the external edifice and yet remains totally in the mind of the thinker. If, therefore, the structure of the house is built because of the plan, as if it were the son of the mind, do we not consider the Son of God, namely, the Word, to be like this, by whom all things were created? Therefore, since the mind of man has the power to give birth to a plan without a mother, how much greater was the power of the Father to produce ineffably the Word from himself alone? When he received human form, he in no way abandoned the hidden secrets of the Father's divinity; when clothed with the veil of our flesh, he was received into the virginal womb, but was not enclosed by it. And why should we marvel at this in the Word of God, since the words that we speak with the human tongue so fruitfully influence the senses that the ear of the audience grasps them, but does not contain them? For unless they were grasped, they would instruct no one; if they were contained, they would not reach out to others.

(23) Therefore the Son of God comes to us in the mystery of the incarnation much more fully and, so to speak, more ineffably, and nonetheless persists with the Father in his divinity. He who took on true flesh from the virginal womb so willed to unite both natures that he who was true man was also true God, and he who was man was doubtless also God. For this acceptance was such that it made God man and man God. Therefore, when the form of God took on the form of a slave, both were God, both were true man because of the reception

of human nature. Hence, even though one of the great saints might be worthy to receive a special grace from God, no one can be united with God in one person. Indeed, only the soul together with the body of Christ together with the Word is the one Christ, the one Son. The blessed Apostle, therefore, to show the difference between all the saints together and the cause of the saints and of all sanctity, said, "In times past, God spoke in sundry and varied ways to our fathers through the prophets; in this, the final age, he has spoken to us through his Son, whom he has made heir of all things and through whom he created the universe."[30] But it is one thing for God to speak by the mouths of the prophets, quite another through the Word, coeternal and consubstantial to him before all ages. The word of the flesh is one thing, but the Word made flesh is something different. It is one thing for God to be in man, something else again to be the God-Man. To be a minister of the word is quite different from being its master. It is not the same to be called the author of faith as to be known as its preacher. Moreover, to receive the Holy Spirit by the grace of a prophet is different from possessing him substantially by nature. For even though the Holy Spirit would descend upon Christ in the form of a dove,[31] still the divinity of the redeemer could not receive him, for in the essence of divinity the Father, and the Son, and the Holy Spirit are one God.

(24) It follows, therefore, that Christ received the Holy Spirit in his human soul and not in his divinity, and by this he is one in nature with the same Holy Spirit. Therefore, the eternal divinity of the Son with his total humanity and the same total humanity of the Son with his eternal divinity is one person in the blessed Trinity, not by adoption but as his own; not nominally but coessentially and perfectly. And totally in his divinity and humanity he is the only-begotten and true Son of God; totally in his divinity and in his humanity he is the true Son of Man, not indeed in name, as the Spanish heresy[32] presumes to

30. Heb 1.1–2.
31. Cf. Matt 3.16; Mark 1.10; Luke 3.12; John 1.32.
32. An obvious reference to Adoptionism, promoted by Elipandus of Toledo and Felix of Urgel, first condemned at Regensburg in 792; cf. S. J. McKenna, "Adoptionism," NCE 1 (1967) 140–41.

assert with wicked daring. For this heresy claims the Son of God to be true God in his divine nature, nominally and by adoption in his human nature, so that, as it were, there appear to be two persons in Christ: by his divinity he is the true Son of God, but in his humanity he is adopted. Indeed, it is certain according to the norms of Catholic faith that the only-begotten Son of God assumed human nature into his unity, preserving, however, what belonged to each substance, but completely retaining the undivided and simple unity of the person. Consequently, there are not two Christs, or two Sons, but God and man; there is one Christ, there is only one Son. It was not by local motion that the divinity of the Word came to the blessed Virgin, but by the ineffable mystery of his power that the Son of God at his conception filled the womb of his mother and nonetheless endured in the unity of the Father's divinity. He came to us that he might take from us what he found in us, and that he might offer for us what he took from us. Nor can the divinity of the Word be either divided into parts or separated from the Father; it is everywhere total, everywhere perfect. Thus he did not desert the Father when he came down to the Virgin, just as he did not desert the world when as victor over death he ascended into heaven. Hence he said, "No one has gone up to heaven except the one who came down from heaven, the Son of man who is in heaven."[33] He speaks, indeed, on earth, and he states that he is in heaven, because when he came down from heaven he nevertheless remained in heaven. And just as it is the Son of Man who is said to have come down from heaven, so it is the Son of God who is seen bodily in the flesh.

(25) In Christ, therefore, there exist both unity of person and two natures with unconfused and always distinct properties. Thus, there is in him one nature that takes its origin from the virginal womb, and the other that, without any beginning at all, is coeternal with God the Father: One that cried in the cradle, the other in which he was adored by the Magi;[34] one

---

33. John 3.13.   34. Cf. Matt 2.11.

that grew in age and wisdom,[35] the other by which he is the very power and wisdom of God;[36] one by which, after fasting continuously for forty days, he was hungry,[37] the other, to which the highest angels in their office of ministry at once gave service;[38] one by which he slept in the boat and was awakened by the disciples,[39] the other by which he commanded the winds and tempestuous waves. One that, with a flow of tears, wept at the death of his friend; the other by which he recalls his soul from hell and raises his body, dead for four days, intact from the tomb.[40] There is one nature by which he was filled with sorrow to the point of death,[41] another by which he stated that he had the power to lay down his life and take it up again;[42] one by which he could walk with dry feet on the swells and rough waves of the sea,[43] another by which, in fleeing into Egypt, he avoided the cruelty of Herod.[44] There is one by which he shone like the sun, transfigured on the mountain,[45] there is another by which, with the disappearance of the vision, only the form of human weakness remained. There is in him, moreover, one nature, by which he is addressed: "You are my Son, today I have begotten you,"[46] and another of which, according to the testimony of another prophet, it was said, "You are my servant, for through you I show my glory."[47] And according to another text, there is the voice that says, "From the womb, before the daystar, I have begotten you";[48] and according to another, this statement: "It is too little, he says, for you to be my servant, to raise up the tribes of Jacob and to convert the lands of Israel."[49]

(26) There is, therefore, in Christ one hypostasis[50] or person,

---

35. Cf. Luke 2.52.
36. Cf. 1 Cor 1.24.
37. Cf. Matt 4.2.
38. Cf. Luke 22.45.
39. Cf. Mark 4.38.
40. Cf. John 11.17, 43–44.
41. Cf. Mark 14.34.
42. Cf. John 10.18.
43. Cf. Matt 14.24–26.
44. Cf. Matt 2.13–17.
45. Cf. Matt 17.2.
46. Ps 2.7.
47. Isa 49.3.
48. Ps 109.3.
49. Isa 49.6.
50. At this point Gaetani 3 (1615) 6A = PL 145.30D, has *substantia*. MS C2, however, reads *subsistentia*, translated here as 'hypostasis,' a synonym for person.

but not one substance or nature, so that even though the divine nature is one substance and the human nature another, still in Christ we in no way believe that the Son of Man is other than the Son of God. Truly, from the very beginning of the Lord's incarnation, God passed into man and man into God, so that both he who was born of the Father before the ages is at once the true Son of Man and true man, and he who at the end of the ages was born of the Virgin is truly both the Son of God and without doubt true God.

(27) We, therefore, rightly profess two nativities in Christ: one from the begetting Father, without beginning and without temporality, everlasting and coeternal; the other from the substance of his mother in the course of time. For in Christ divinity and the human condition came together so that the Word might become flesh and that flesh might pass into God, allowing the one Emmanuel[51] to come forth from both substances, who would be the proper mediator between God and men. In him, indeed, would the natural rights of each activity be preserved, both the sublimity of the Godhead and the humility of the flesh. There are, consequently, not two, but one and the same that carried out dual functions, and each form or nature operates in conjunction with the other according to its own properties: namely, divinity taking part in the functions of the flesh, and flesh participating in the functions of divinity. Hence, there is the same God and man in one hypostasis or person preserving the twin properties of each substance, nature remaining intact, so that it neither divides the two nor, after the union, confuses them. For the Word is the Word and not flesh, and the flesh is flesh and not the Word. But the function of the flesh and of the Word is one, because the person of both God and man is one. Hence John states, "What was," he says, "from the beginning, what we have heard, what we have seen, what we have looked upon and our hands have touched of the Word of life."[52] Yet, if it were not for the mystery of the union with man, no one would be able to see God or, what is still more impossible, to touch him with his hands. For divinity

51. Cf. Isa 7.14.   52. 1 John 1.1.

is so inseparably united with humanity that after it once received humanity into the unity of the person, divinity did not afterwards in the slightest withdraw from it. For God as man came forth from his mother's womb; God as man hung from the wood of the cross. But the same God-Man, only in the flesh, lay in the tomb, and the same God-Man, only in his soul, descended into the depths of hell. Thus, divinity that at the conception received both, clearly did not detach itself in death from the two human components it had received.

(28) Who is it, then, by whom the world was made? Christ Jesus, but in the form of God. Who is it by whom the world was redeemed? Christ Jesus, but in the form of a slave. Who was it who was not abandoned in hell? Christ Jesus, but only in his soul. Before his resurrection, who was it who lay for three days in the tomb? Christ Jesus, but only in the flesh. Therefore, in each of these there is Christ, and in all of them there are not two, but one Christ. Thus, we behold one and the same, thriving in his dual nature and naturally operating according to both substances; each substance, in communion with the other, performing what belongs to it, that is, in accord with the innate essential quality or natural properties of each. And thus we should weigh all of these things cautiously, so that we believe, on the one hand, that full humanity was assumed by God, and understand, on the other, that full divinity was united to man: but in such a way that we render to God what belongs to God, and to man what is proper to man.[53]

(29) Since, therefore, there is often much questioning about this topic, there is a great difference between the acceptance of the dove,[54] in which form the Holy Spirit was seen, and that in which the Son of God deigned to appear in the reality of the flesh. For some have tried to convince us that the Son of God was not born of a woman,[55] just as the Holy Spirit was not born of a dove. This dove, they say, was not hatched from an egg, even though it was seen bodily by human eyes. But, indeed, true believers reply that in the same source in which we read

---

53. Cf. Matt 22.21; Luke 20.25.
54. Cf. Matt 3.16; Mark 1.10; Luke 3.22; John 1.32.
55. Cf. Gal 4.4.

that the Holy Spirit appeared to John in the form of a dove,[56] we also find that Christ was born of a woman.[57] And it is not correct to believe one part of the gospel and not to believe another. For if we believe from the gospel that the Holy Spirit was seen in the form of a dove, we must also believe that our redeemer was born of a virgin. But why was the Holy Spirit not born of a dove if we acknowledge that Christ was born of a woman? It is for this reason, undoubtedly: the Holy Spirit did not come to redeem doves by his appearance, but to represent visibly by this figure spiritual love and innocence. But the Son of God, who came to lift up our fallen human nature and to renew it, rooted in original sin, had to assume naturally and essentially in the unity of his person what he came to liberate by the mystery of his passion and resurrection.

(30) Nor do we say this to indicate that only our redeemer assumed true flesh, while the Holy Spirit took on an imaginary form. For just as it was not becoming for the Son of God to deceive the eyes of men, so too it was in no way proper that the Holy Spirit should counterfeit something with a lie. It is clear that, while the former is truth, the latter is also the spirit of truth. Hence both bodies, the dove's and the human's, were in truth the substance seen by human eyes. But the appearance of the dove, after serving the useful purpose at hand, ceased to exist, while the Lord's body always continued on in the stable unity of the Word who assumed it. We must, therefore, profess that Emmanuel, the true God, distinctly and invisibly exists in two substances; therefore we assert that the blessed Virgin is truly the mother, not only of man but also of God. For naturally and carnally she gave birth to the flesh that became the Word of God. We should also admit that the Word, naturally counited to the flesh according to its hypostasis [person],[58] is also the one Christ with his own flesh, at once God and man, the redeemer of the human race. Nor must we say that Christ is a man bearing God in himself, but rather with the very flesh to-

---

56. Cf. John 1.32–34. 57. Cf. Luke 2.6–7.
58. Again the text of Gaetani 3 (1615) 7A and PL 145.32D is defective, reading *substantia* in place of *subsistentia*, and actually omitting a sentence and a half of the text, which is translated here.

gether with the soul he is true God and truly the unique and natural Son of God. Nor may we by any means presume to assert that the human nature he assumed is to be co-adored and glorified along with God the Word, as if one were to be venerated in the other. For we should be convinced that this *co-* must be understood as an added syllable. We should rather adore Emmanuel with one, simple adoration, namely, as true God and man. This is found also included in the *Anathemas* of St. Cyril.[59]

(31) Nor must we say that God so works in man that he is one who is seen externally and another who functions interiorly. But we should rather venerate one God: the one who is perceived by the eyes as man, and the majesty that lies hidden within. Hence, he is indeed the mediator, for he is at the same time true God and true man, having the same nature of divinity with the Father and the substance of humanity no different from that of his mother. In each nature he is the same Son of God, receiving what is ours and not losing what is his own—in man renewing man, in himself always remaining unchanged. According to the form of God it was said, "Before all the hills he brought me forth,"[60] that is, before all the sublimity of the angels, and "before the daystar I begot you,"[61] that is, before all time and temporal things. In keeping with the form of a slave, however, it was said, "The Lord created me in the beginning of his ways."[62] According to the form of God he said, "I am the truth and the life";[63] according to the form of a slave, "I am the way."[64] In saying, "The Word was made flesh,"[65] it does not mean that the divine nature was changed into flesh, but that by the Word flesh was taken up into union with the person. Bodily nativity from his mother, of course, took away nothing from divine majesty; it conferred nothing upon it, it changed nothing from her into something else. It was thus im-

---

59. Ryan, *Sources*, no. 259 cites Cyril of Alexandria (d. 444), *Anathemata* 8, ed. E. Schwartz, *Acta conciliorum oecumenicorum* 1.5.2 (1924–1926) 271; cf. M. E. Williams, "Anathemas of Cyril," NCE 1 (1967) 481–82.
60. Prov 8.25.
61. Ps 109.3.
62. Prov 8.22; cf. Sabatier 2.309f.
63. John 14.6.
64. John 14.6.
65. John 1.14.

possible for unchangeable substance to be converted into something different, just as it could not be diminished or increased.

(32) Therefore, recognizing the marks of each nature, we adore the Word in Christ the man, and Christ the man in the Word. For after the Word became flesh, the one Christ exists in two essences whereby, surely, there is nothing in either nature that does not belong to both. He is the same in the form of God as he is seen in the form of a slave—at once subject to suffering in our weakness, yet invulnerable in his divine power; at once remaining incorporeal but taking to himself a body. He is the same one who remains at the throne of his Father's majesty and yet was crucified on the tree by the wicked ones. It is clear, then, that both substances concurred in one person, and thus he is one and the same victor over death, rising above the heights of heaven and not abandoning the whole Church to the end of time. In both natures, enduring indeed in their own qualities, such a common unity was achieved; that whatever there is that belongs to God is not taken from man, and whatever belongs to man is not removed from the godhead. Once he was conceived in the womb of the Virgin, nothing of the power of the Word was wanting to either soul or body for even a moment in time; nor was it lacking before the vesture, with which the most high King endowed himself, was formed or ensouled, but by him and in him began that temple of the human body that the Son of God essentially united with himself. At the point of being conceived, the Son of God approached the Virgin's womb and there, as it is written, "wisdom built the house of his body."[66]

(33) At the time of creation, therefore, nothing of the future child was there begun, but after the coming of the Word into his oneness, the new man had his beginning. With the two natures coming together in the one person of Christ, there would be in him both divine power to perform wondrous deeds, and human weakness for undergoing suffering. But both were God because of the power of the receiver, both were man because of the lowliness received.

66. Prov 9.1.

(34) We must be careful, therefore, not to believe that the Son's majesty is unequal to that of the Father, taken up with the things that refer to his slave status, which is indeed the human form. We must show that the Son of God in himself is not a distinct or alternate person, and that in this person he at once says, "The Father is greater than I,"[67] and at the same time, "I and the Father are one."[68] God indeed says, "The Father is greater than I," but because of our weakness; and man says, "I and the Father are one," but because of divine power.

(35) But since it is believed that the Son of God did not receive a diminished humanity, but the whole and integral man, it is asked why we assert that God-Man had only one person. For how did he take on the whole man if he did not receive a human person? Or if the Son of God, who is one person in the Trinity, is joined with the person of a man, how do we assert that the substance of both God and man came together in one person? As I carefully researched this and diligently explored what was defined by the Fathers on this topic, I found that Alcuin wrote to the Emperor Charles that "the Son of God did not receive a human person, but a human nature."[69] According to this statement it is clear that the person of the Son received the human essence without receiving a human person. And Leo the Great, the bishop of the Church of Rome and a most productive doctor of the Christian faith, used these words in one of his sermons: "This wonderful birth of the holy Virgin," he said, "brought forth in the child one person truly human and truly divine. For the double substance did not possess its properties in such a way that there could be a distinction of persons in them, nor was the creature so taken up into union with its creator that he might be the dweller and it the dwelling, but in such a way that the nature of one was mixed together with the nature of the other."[70] This statement is both well said and weighed in a most careful balance of words. For Emman-

---

67. John 14.28.
68. John 10.30 and 14.28.
69. Alcuin, *De fide ad Carolum* 3.9 (PL 101.44A).
70. Leo I, *Tractatus 23*, ed. A. Chavasse, CC 138.1 (1973) 102f. The first part of the statement lends itself to misunderstanding. But from the context it is clear that Leo excludes the possibility of a dual personality.

uel, God with us, is always one person in the blessed Trinity, which, since it can never be diminished in the plenitude of its power, cannot be increased by its connection with the humanity it receives. Such, then, is the person, but it may be left to your diligence to propose parallel statements and to discover whether one of the Catholic doctors has written more elaborately on the subject.

(36) This epilogue introduces new material in such a way that one may understand what was said above. But since in matters secret and profound, verbosity of style may blunt the unskilled minds of the audience, and because when one tries to enlighten the mind one often confuses it, I remain aware of your status as a novice, my dear son, and I do not wish you to be drawn further into these matters. Rather, after running through this brief summary you may grasp them more firmly. For although you are energetic and possess a lively disposition, one must keep in mind that your conversion is recent; indeed by placing the burden of a long disputation on your shoulders, your more delicate strength may weaken under the charge before it learns to bear its weight. And looking also to your weakness, I append an epilogue that you may now find, reduced to one statement, what was said at greater length before, that you may more easily grasp it, not just as a repetition but as an addition.

(37) Therefore, my son, believe that the omnipotent God is substantially one and personally threefold. The persons however, even though they are distinct in quality, are still not separate in their operation. We are never more clearly aware of the distinction of persons than when we recall the baptism of the Lord. Let us observe, then, as the waters of the river Jordan behold, as it were, the divine spectacle there displayed of the undivided Trinity of divine persons presented to us. For as "the lamb, who takes away the sins of the world,"[71] was baptized, suddenly the heavens were opened and the Holy Spirit came down upon him in the appearance of a dove. With that, the voice of the Father spoke: "This is my beloved Son," he said,

---

71. John 1.29.

"in whom I am well pleased."[72] We have, therefore, a clearly defined Trinity: in the voice, the Father; in the man, the son; and in the dove, the Holy Spirit.

(38) And so, this blessed Trinity, just as it is distinguishable by name, so too it is seen in this place to be literally distinct in its operations. For it is not possible to say that the Son, who was seen in the form of a slave, is the Father or the Holy Spirit; nor that the voice, which sounded from heaven, is that of the Son or of the Holy Spirit; nor that the dove was the Father's or the Son's, for the gospel itself testifies "that the Holy Spirit came down upon him in the form of a dove."[73] But the correct faith, the true faith, is not uncertain by reason of presumed opinion, but is bolstered by the testimony of the text. Nor does it fluctuate with heretical temerity but, based rather on apostolic truth, it clearly attests that whatever is performed by God is done by the entire, inseparable blessed Trinity. For while alone the Son was born of the Virgin Mary, alone hung on the cross, and alone rose from the dead, still the Father, the Son, and the Holy Spirit together accomplished the mystery of the divine incarnation, passion, and resurrection. That it was the Father who sent him, that is, ordained that he become incarnate, the Apostle here says: "For when the fullness of time had come, God sent his Son made of a woman, made under the Law."[74] And so, the Father sent the Son, and the Holy Spirit also sent him. The Son himself gave witness of this, saying through the prophet, "The Spirit of the Lord is upon me, because he has anointed me; he has sent me to bring glad tidings to the lowly, to heal the broken-hearted, to proclaim liberty to the captives, and release to the prisoners."[75] And the Apostle says of the Son, "Though he was in the form of God, he did not deem equality with God something to be grasped at. Rather he emptied himself, taking the form of a slave."[76]

(39) While, therefore, only the Son became incarnate, the Father, the Son, and the Holy Spirit cooperated in the Son's incarnation. The Father acted also in the Son's passion, as it is

---

72. Matt 3.17; cf. Sabatier 3.15f.
73. Matt 3.16.
74. Gal 4.4.
75. Isa 61.1.
76. Phil 2.6–7.

said: "Who did not spare his own Son, but handed him over for the sake of us all."[77] The Son also took part, as it is said, "Who loved me and gave himself for me."[78] The Holy Spirit, too, was involved, of whom it is written: "For the spirit of wisdom is benevolent, and did not acquit the accursed one from his lips."[79] Christ, to be sure, was called the accursed one because he hung on the cross. Of this the Apostle says, "To free us from the curse of the Law, Christ became accursed."[80] Hence, the Spirit did not acquit the accursed one from his lips because he permitted Christ to undergo all the sufferings of the passion and death, which he foretold through the lips of the prophets. The Father also caused the resurrection of the Son, as it is said: "Because of this he exalted him and bestowed on him the name above every other name."[81]

(40) The Father, therefore, revived the Son, awakening him from the dead, and especially exalted him above all. But Christ also revived himself, as he says, speaking figuratively of his body: "Destroy this temple, and in three days I will raise it up."[82] To clearly show, moreover, that he is the author of his passion and resurrection, he summed it up in one brief statement: "I have power," he said, "to lay down my life, and I have power to take it up again."[83] And he asserted this a second time when he said, "No one takes it from me, but I lay it down and I take it up again."[84] That the Holy Spirit also, with the Father and the Son, is the author of the resurrection is attested by the Apostle who says, "If the Spirit of him who raised Jesus from the dead dwells in you, then he who raised Jesus Christ from the dead will bring your mortal bodies to life also, through his Spirit dwelling in you."[85] Thus, if at the end we are to be given life because of the Spirit dwelling in us, it follows that the Holy Spirit has already done for the head of the Church what in the future he will achieve in the body.

77. Rom 8.32; for this variant, cf. Sabatier 3.625.
78. Gal 2.20.
79. Wis 1.6; cf. Sabatier 2.392f.
80. Gal 3.13.
81. Phil 2.9.
82. John 2.19; cf. Sabatier 3.394.
83. John 10.18; cf. Sabatier 3.439.
84. John 10.17–18.
85. Rom 8.11.

(41) The same must be held also of miracles or of any other deeds, so that we are to believe that the entire Trinity performs whatever appears to belong specifically to one person. For it was the Father, the Son, and the Holy Spirit who inseparably worked the signs and wonders that Christ performed. Thus we have this statement: "It is the Father living in me who accomplishes the works."[86] He says of the Holy Spirit also, "If it is by the finger of God that I cast out devils, then the reign of God has come upon you."[87] Therefore, no limits of brevity contain this incomprehensible Trinity, nor expansion in space; it is never absent, it is always and everywhere inseparably present. It is not partly greater, partly less, but everywhere total, always undivided. The Father is from no one, the Son is from the Father alone, the Holy Spirit from both. Very many of the Greeks think that the Holy Spirit proceeds from the Father alone and not from the Son, because they cannot find, as they think, clear evidence in the Lord's words. St. Jerome also, following their teaching, so states in his explanation of the faith, "We also believe in the Holy Spirit, true God, who proceeds from the Father,"[88] in which he was silent on whether he proceeded from the Son. Also in the *Creed* of the Council of Nicea we find: "We also believe in the Holy Spirit, who proceeds properly from the Father, and like the Son is true God."[89]

---

86. John 14.10.   87. Luke 11.20.
88. This citation cannot be found in Jerome. It derives from Pseudo-Jerome, *Epistola 17 seu Explanatio fidei ad Cyrillum* (PL 30.176 D; 179 C–D). But in both texts the word *proprie*, 'properly,' occurs and in the second the author states, "The Holy Spirit properly and truly proceeds from the Father *and from the Son.*" It would seem, therefore, that Damian is not citing directly from this text, but is using some, as yet, undetected source. Nevertheless, in *Letter* 91 (PL 145.639C–D) Damian quotes Jerome as saying, "The Spirit who proceeds from the Father and from the Son," a text that Ryan, *Sources* 128 no. 278 attributes to Smaragdus, *Libellus de processione sancti Spiritus*, ed. A. Werminghoff, MGH Conc. 2.1 (1906) 238. See also J. Gill, "Filioque," NCE 5 (1967) 913–14.

89. This is not found in the generally accepted text of the *Nicene Creed*. But the citation, without attribution to Nicea, is in Pseudo-Jerome, *Epistola 17* (PL 30.176D).

That without Doubt the Holy Spirit Proceeds from the Son, Just As from the Father.

(42) But since I am instructed by the teachings of the blessed doctors Augustine[90] and Gregory[91] and other Catholic Fathers, I am compelled to believe that the Holy Spirit proceeds from the Father and also from the Son. And that in the future the faith of believers not be forced to waver, I would not find it burdensome to produce a few items of evidence from the Scriptures. And so, both prophetic announcements and apostolic authority give witness and profess that the Holy Spirit proceeds from the Father and from the Son. For Isaiah says of the Son, "He shall strike the earth with the rod of his mouth, and with the spirit of his lips he shall slay the wicked."[92] And the Apostle says of him, "And the Lord Jesus Christ will kill him with the spirit of his mouth, and destroy him by manifesting his own coming."[93] The savior clearly stated that the Spirit indeed proceeds from him when he breathed on his disciples about him. "Receive," he said, "the Holy Spirit."[94] And John says in Revelation that "a sharp, two-edged sword came out of the mouth of Jesus."[95] And so, the Spirit that there he breathed from his lips is, indeed, the sword that here came forth from his mouth. Through the prophet the Father also says to the Son, "My Spirit, which is in you, and my words, which I have put in you, shall never leave your mouth, nor the mouths of your children from now on and forever."[96] And the Apostle says, "If anyone does not have the Spirit of Christ, he does not belong to him."[97] And to the Galatians, "Since you are the sons of God," he says, "God has sent forth into your hearts the Spirit of his Son, which cries out, 'Abba, Father.' "[98]

(43) St. Peter, too, indicates that the Holy Spirit is of the Son

---

90. See Augustine, *De trinitate* 15.17, ed. W. J. Moutain and F. Glorie, CC 50 (1968) 503.
91. See John the Deacon, *S. Gregorii magni vita* 2.2 (PL 75.87f.).
92. Isa 11.4.
93. 2 Thess 2.8; for the addition of "Christ," cf. Sabatier 3.860.
94. John 20.22.
95. Rev 1.16; cf. Sabatier 3.993.
96. Isa 59.21.
97. Rom 8.9.
98. Gal 4.6.

just as he is also of the Father when he says, "Of which salvation the prophets carefully searched out and examined, who prophesied of the glory that was to be yours, investigating the times and the circumstances that the Spirit of Christ within them was pointing to, predicting the sufferings that are in Christ and the glories that would follow."[99] And the Lord said in the gospel, "When the Paraclete comes, the Spirit of truth, who comes from the Father."[100] Now, since Christ himself is the truth, he taught that the Spirit was his when he declared him to be the spirit of truth. And John says, "The way we know we remain in him and he in us is that he has given us of his Spirit."[101] We read also in the book of blessed Job: "And he shall attentively hear the terror of his voice, and the sound that comes out of his mouth."[102] Here, indeed, the mouth of the Father must undoubtedly be understood as the Son, but the sound proceeding from his mouth is the Holy Spirit, who is rightly called the sound, because with a noise he came upon the apostles, and from the heart that he filled he at once broke forth in words of sacred eloquence.[103] Moreover, the psalmist is witness that the mouth of the Father is truly to be understood as the Son, and that the Holy Spirit comes forth from this mouth when he says, "By the word of the Lord the heavens were made, and by the Spirit of his mouth all their host."[104]

(44) Now I judge it superfluous to give examples of the Holy Spirit proceeding from the Father, since we observe such an abundance of them throughout many pages of the Scriptures, such as in this text: "You yourselves will not be the speakers, but the Holy Spirit of your Father who will be speaking in you."[105] And in the second letter to the Corinthians the Apostle says, "God is the one who firmly establishes us along with you in Christ; it is he who anointed us and has sealed us and given the pledge of the Spirit in our hearts."[106] And in the first letter to the Thessalonians, "Hence whoever rejects not man, but God, who also sent his Holy Spirit upon us."[107] That the Father,

99. 1 Pet 1.10–11.
100. John 15.26.
101. 1 John 4.13.
102. Job 37.2.
103. Cf. Acts 2.4.
104. Ps 32.6.
105. Matt 10.20.
106. 2 Cor 1.21.
107. 1 Thess 4.8.

moreover, poured forth the Holy Spirit upon the disciples is written in the letter that was sent to Titus: "Through the baptism of new birth and renewal of the Holy Spirit, whom he lavished on us through Jesus Christ our savior."[108] In the Acts of the Apostles it is written that the Son also poured forth the same Spirit. For Peter says of Christ, "Exalted at God's right hand, and having received from the Father the promised Holy Spirit, he poured forth this gift, which you see and hear."[109] Through the testimony of Joel the voice of both of them states that the Father and the Son together pour forth the same Spirit: "I will pour out my Spirit upon all flesh."[110]

(45) But even though, as I said, many of the Greeks do not believe that the Holy Spirit proceeds from the Son as from the Father, the blessed Athanasius, bishop of the see of Alexandria, said among other things in the book he wrote against Arius, "I believe that the Son is in the Father and the Father in the Son; I believe also that the Spirit, the Paraclete, who proceeds from the Father is of both the Son and the Father, because he also proceeds from the Son, as it is written in the gospel that, by his breathing, he would give the Holy Spirit to his disciples, saying, 'Receive the Holy Spirit.'"[111] Against the Nestorians, Cyril also says of this same procession of the Holy Spirit, "For although his Spirit is of his substance," without doubt, that is, of the Father, "we may understand that what belongs to the person is the Spirit and not the Son, although he is no stranger to the latter. For he is called the Spirit of truth, and Christ is the truth. And so, he also proceeds from him just as he does from God the Father."[112] And among other things, St. Ambrose spoke thus: "The Spirit, indeed, is not sent from

---

108. Titus 3.5–6.   109. Acts 2.33.
110. Joel 2.28; cf. Sabatier 2.915.
111. John 20.22–23. Ryan, *Sources* 120f. no. 260, following Gaudenzi, *Il codice* 306, points to Smaragdus, *Libellus* 238 as the source of this quotation. Gaudenzi, *Il codice* 306f. notes that *Codex Vat. Ottob. lat.* 339 contained the work of Smaragdus, and that Damian's visit to the monastery of S. Giovani di Acereta in 1057–1058, which owned this codex, allowed him to cite Smaragdus in *Letter* 81.
112. Smaragdus, *Libellus* 238.25; cf. Ryan, *Sources* 121 no. 261. See Damian, *Letter* 91 (PL 145.640A), where this text is also cited.

a place, as it were, nor does he proceed from a place when he proceeds from the Son."[113] Augustine also writes against the heretic Maximus: "You inquire of me," he said, "if the Son is of the substance of the Father and the Holy Spirit is also of the substance of the Father, why is the one the Son and the other not the Son?" And he quickly replied, "Hear my answer, whether you understand or do not understand: The Son is from the Father and the Holy Spirit is from the Father, but the former is begotten, the latter proceeds. Hence the former is the Son of the Father, of whom he is begotten; the latter, however, is the Spirit of both, because he proceeds from both."[114] And a little farther on, "He is, therefore, the Spirit of both proceeding from both."[115]

(46) And so, concluding my statement based on the authority of the same illustrious doctor, there is in the blessed Trinity one Father, who of himself alone begot a Son essentially unique; one Son, who alone was essentially begotten of one Father; and one Spirit, who alone essentially proceeds from the Father and the Son. But since by far the greatest number of ancient and recent authors agree on the procession of the Spirit from the Father and the Son, and since examples from almost every page of Scripture abound in sufficient number, I think it superfluous to compound the accumulation, in that you can find here more than enough to satisfy.

(47) Therefore, my dear son, this discussion on the Catholic faith is suitable enough both for me, now almost finished running the race, and for you, who have recently entered training in the spiritual army. Given the depths of such incomprehensible and incomparable material, just as a new knight at the outset of his apprenticeship in warfare must be inquisitive, so also unless one is polished and experienced in sacred Scripture, he should not easily reply. The latter, to be sure, so as to build a foundation for correct faith on which he may construct the edifice of good works; the former, that he might subtly discern the secret of the heavenly mystery by lifelong dedication

113. Smaragdus, *Libellus* 238.30.
114. Smaragdus, *Libellus* 239.1.
115. Smaragdus, *Libellus* 239.6.

to duty. For faith is both the beginning for those who perform good deeds and the perfection of virtue achieved. Just as the Apostle said of Christ, "No one can lay a foundation other than the one that has been laid, namely Jesus Christ."[116] On the contrary, for it is also said of him by the prophet, "The stone which the builders rejected has become the cornerstone."[117] For he, who for our support is set at the foundation as the base of the edifice, presides as the peak and the cardinal point of the Church.

(48) May almighty God, my dear son, so place your feet on the rock of the Catholic faith that he may lift the sight of your mind to the heights of his contemplation.

116. 1 Cor 3.11.   117. Ps 117.22.

LETTER 82

Peter Damian to Desiderius, the abbot of Monte Cassino. It is an exhortatory letter to this wise and creative abbot, advising him to disregard the applause that might accompany his achievements. Among his many duties as abbot, he should not neglect his own spiritual growth in the art of contemplation, the better to advise and direct the monks in his prestigious monastery.

(Lent 1061)[1]

TO THE VENERABLE abbot, Sir Desiderius,[2] the monk Peter the sinner sends his service.

(2) Fire attacks everything that lies in its path, and by its very nature, it reaches up beyond itself and attempts always to go higher. Fraternal love also, burning within me in your regard, is never content to find its objective in you alone, but through you is referred to our common creator. For love that is so preoccupied with one's neighbor that it does not also include God is useless, arid, and insipid; for the love of God is primary. Still, by loving our neighbor whom we see, we arrive at the love of God whom we do not see.[3]

(3) In the meantime, therefore, as I love you whom I see in person, at all times I lift my eyes to him whom I always desire to attain along with you. Consequently, let us unite and join hands and spur one another on with mutual exhortation, that we might lighten the burden of our journey. But since you are weighed down with the task of governing your prestigious

---

1. Dating follows Lucchesi, *Vita* no. 161.
2. Damian also sent to Desiderius *Letter* 86, *Letter* 90, *Letter* 95, *Letter* 102, *Letter* 106, *Letter* 109, and *Letter* 159. On this distinguished man, named cardinal priest of St. Caecilia, and later elected Pope Victor III, see H. E. J. Cowdrey, *The Age of Abbot Desiderius, Montecassino, the Papacy and the Normans in the Eleventh and Early Twelfth Centuries* (Oxford, 1983); Herbert Bloch, *Monte Cassino in the Middle Ages* 1 (Cambridge, MA, 1986) 40–110.
3. Cf. 1 John 4.7–8.

monastery, beware that amid the labor entailed in this form of life, fainthearted weariness not impede you, and that the soothing words of flatterers do not sap the strength of your spirit that too readily agrees with them.

(4) Therefore, call to mind what the Scriptures have to say about that upright man, Tobias: "It happened one day that, worn out from burying the dead, he lay down to sleep by the courtyard wall when, from a swallow's nest, warm droppings fell into his eyes while he slept and he was blinded."[4] Worn out from burying the dead, he lost his sight as he lay down, exhausted by the effort. But one who perseveres incessantly in performing good works will surely keep the eyes of his soul out of harm's way; when he weakly succumbs to fatigue, he deservedly loses his sight. And so it was written, "Woe to those who have given up the struggle."[5] Therefore Paul says, "Be alert, stand firm in the faith, be valiant and strong."[6] What is meant by gently flying swallows but the easy morals of flatterers and those of charming words? While they stroke us with the sweetness of their soothing speech and anoint the head of the listener with the oil of their flattery, they blind the eyes of the spirit, depriving them of their accustomed light. "The just man shall buffet me," says the psalmist, "and in his mercy he will reprove me, but my head shall not be anointed with the oil of wicked men."[7] It is, moreover, like putting dung into one's eyes as they anoint us with soft-spoken and beguiling speech. These people will often say, "Live while you can, and pamper your body with rich food, lest by severely wearing yourself out, your weak body should soon succumb from such oppressive effort. Adorn yourself with more becoming garments, that you might continue to enjoy the splendor of the office that you hold. Let a host of clients crowd in on you from all sides like troops drawn up for battle so that, while this crowd of supporters looks after you, the high dignity of your position may not grow stale." But if the bitterness of this devilish mischief be exposed for us, the darkness of temptation imposed on us will disap-

---

4. Tob 2.10–11.   5. Sir 2.16.
6. 1 Cor 16.13.   7. Ps 140.5.

pear. And so the text cited above continues, "Then Tobias took the fish gall, spread it on his father's eyes, and quickly the white patches were peeled from his eyes like the membrane of an egg, and he at once recovered his sight."[8] Now the fish's gall is the malice of Behemoth,[9] who is the source and beginning of all wickedness. And so fish gall is applied to the blind man, and at once his blindness disappears, for when the bitterness of the devil's cunning is held up for us to see, the darkness is at once thrown off, and our inner light that had, as it were, undergone this eclipse is restored.

(5) We should note what was said, namely, that white patches were first removed from his eyes, and thus light was at once restored. He, indeed, has white patches in his eyes who thinks that he is holy. Anyone, therefore, who would recover his sight should first cut away the white patches of pretense and not deny that he is a sinner, if he would avoid the blindness of sin. "Blessed are the pure of heart, for they shall see God."[10] These are the eyes of which it is said in the Song of Songs, "Your eyes are like doves, not revealing that which lies hidden within."[11] For although the saints now look upon their creator through the grace of contemplation, there is still something great that, in our corruptible flesh, the vision of the human mind cannot attain. And then the text continues, "Your hair is like a flock of goats climbing up Mount Gilead."[12] Just as the eyes denote the doctors of the Church, who are placed at the head of lesser members that they might see higher spiritual truth, so too by the hair and the flocks of goats are meant the simple and the subordinate.[13] Even though in their simplicity they are unable to understand mystical and higher things, still they adorn Holy Church as hair embellishes the head because of their great number and disposition. The goat is the figure of sin, since it is often burnt in sacrifice for sin. And by Gilead is meant a "multitude of witnesses."[14] In Gilead we should therefore see

8. Tob 11.13–15.
9. Cf. Job 40.10.
10. Matt 5.8.
11. Cant 4.1.
12. Cant 4.1.
13. See Cornelius a Lapide, *Commentaria in scripturam sacram*, 2d ed. 24 vols. (1874–1877) 8.34.
14. Jerome, *Nom.hebr.* 7.4 (CC 72.67).

Christ to whom the assembly of all the saints bears witness, but by the hair or the flocks of goats we should understand the multitude of Christ's subjects. Now the flocks of goats climb up Mount Gilead, which means that the great number of all the saints strive in Christ, on whom they build their foundation, to climb to the heights of virtue. But why do I emphasize this citation if not to help you understand that insofar as the eyes are separated from the hair, so too in the practice of contemplation there must be almost the same distinction between religious leaders and their subjects? Insofar as you are the eye for those entrusted to your direction, you should engage in the pursuit of spiritual goals and take care to provide not only for yourself but also for them. In consequence, you will frequently be overwhelmed by sorrow and experience the salutary compunction of tears.[15]

(6) Thus we read in Genesis: "This is the Onam," it says, "who found hot springs in the wilderness while he was tending the asses of his father Zibeon."[16] Taken literally, this statement seems to be empty and of little meaning. To what purpose should sacred Scripture report that one tending asses had discovered water in the desert? But when the literal meaning appears to be useless, the mind must seek out its spiritual significance. What should we understand by the figure of Onam[17] tending his father's asses in the wilderness, if not a spiritual man, for whom God is the father, caring for his untutored brethren by restoring primitive discipline? And what is meant by finding hot springs, but shedding tears of compunction, evoked by the fervor of the Holy Spirit? At the same time, an interpretation of the names used in this figure should not escape our attention. Onam may be interpreted 'their sorrow' or 'sadness,' or also 'grumbling' or 'murmuring.'[18] For whoever is afflicted with the sorrow of compunction is compelled to grumble and complain, and to be ill at ease with his

---

15. On the "compunction of tears," cf. *Letter* 44 n. 39 and *Letter* 50 n. 74.
16. Gen 36.24. Damian's *Onam* differs from the *Ana* of the Vulgate; cf. *Beuron Latina Vetus* 2 (1951–1954) 378.
17. Cf. Cornelius a Lapide, *Commentaria* 1.334.
18. Jerome, *Nom.hebr.* 9.28 (CC 72.83).

wicked life. Zibeon has the meaning of 'practicing equity,'[19] which everyone knows is proper to God. He, indeed, is primarily governed by equity who is never compelled to deviate from the rule of justice. So it was that Onam discovered hot springs while tending the asses of his father Zibeon in the desert. For whoever shows himself to be a child of God by the uprightness of his life and is heartily sorry for his sins, as he seeks to practice ever watchful solicitude for his brothers, he will receive the grace of tears as a gift from God.

(7) That blessed sinner who first anointed the Lord's feet and later also poured a bottle of very costly perfume over his head as he reclined at table was in the same context.[20] The head of Christ is God, and the feet of Christ are the servants of God. For just as she offered this service to the humanity of Christ and was thus found worthy to reach an understanding of his divinity, so it is with a teacher in the Church who, by his solicitude for the members of Christ, receives the grace to contemplate the divinity of Christ. There are, moreover, certain uneducated brothers who are ignorant of the meaning of contemplation and are therefore totally unable to participate in the study of spirituality. But as they utterly cut themselves off from this world, as they strive to wear themselves out in various chores commanded them by obedience and zealously follow the wishes of their superiors in all things, they gain such familiarity with almighty God that at times miraculous deeds of virtue take place through them.

(8) Just yesterday at sundown, a certain brother by the name of John came to me and told of a wondrous thing that happened to him some time ago, a deed that certainly should be remembered. "When I was living in the monastery at Chiazerna,"[21] he said, "where it was my duty to take care of the treasure room housing the sacred things used in divine service,

---

19. Jerome, *Nom.hebr.* 11.1–2 (CC 72.72).
20. Cf. Matt 26.7; Mark 14.3; John 12.3.
21. The editor of the Latin edition (Reindel, *Briefe* 2 [1988] 446 n. 11) resolved this place name (Classerna) as a reference to S. Apollinare in Classe. I would prefer to see it as Chiazerna, the Benedictine abbey of St. Angelo in the diocese of Gubbio, duchy of Urbino; see L. H. Cottineau, *Répertoire topo-bibliographique des abbayes et prieurés* 1A (1935–1939) 769.

one day after Compline I returned the liturgical books to the archive, inserted the key as was my custom, and locked it. But as it later became apparent, a spark blew from the candle I was carrying and, unbeknownst to me, ignited the cloth that covered one of the books. The next morning when I opened the chest to take out the books, smoke and heat struck me in the face. Shocked and terrified, I at once took pains to see if any of the books remained undamaged. But what an inconceivable marvel of God's power! While nearly all twenty of the cloth covers in which the books were enclosed were burned and reduced to ashes, the books themselves were untouched. The fire, moreover, had ignited the chest and left a large area burned out of the bottom. When the brothers heard this, they praised God's power; for just as he had protected the Hebrew boys in the Chaldean furnace,[22] he also saved his books from the fire in the blazing chest." The brother who told me these things is an uneducated person,[23] but a man of such devoted obedience and purity of life that it was in no way unbecoming that God should deign to work a miracle because of him.

(9) You too, venerable brother, should so watch over God's house along with the flock committed to you that you never allow yourself to become careless; so imitate the fruitfulness of Leah[24] in bearing children, that you do not neglect the embraces of the beautiful Rachel. Never become so attached to the charming words of falterers that, while taking delight in the empty words of fickle men, the droppings of swallows cover over the eyes of your soul, as they did to Tobias.[25] If someone in friendly fashion should correct you, kindly listen to him; but turn away from the former as if you were nauseated or forced to vomit, lest Solomon's words should apply to you: "A man who is still stubborn after much reproof will suddenly be broken past mending."[26] And of such Isaiah says, "For they are a

---

22. Cf. Dan 2.
23. Damian here uses the Latin word *idiota* to denote 'an uneducated person' or *conversus*, 'lay brother'; cf. DuCange 4.284. He uses the word also in *Letter* 44 and *Letter* 109.
24. Cf. Gen 29.   25. Cf. Tob 2.11.
26. Prov 29.1.

race of rebels, disloyal sons, sons who will not listen to the Lord's instruction. They say to the seers, 'You shall have no true visions'; they give us smooth words and seductive visions. Turn aside, leave my straight path, and rid me forever of the Holy One of Israel."[27]

(10) Therefore, as I said above, let us boldly approach the throne of our gracious God,[28] put behind us the darkness of this world, and let the gloom of earthly concupiscence be removed from our eyes that, when the night of carnal passion has lifted, the splendor of the true sun may emerge for us. Let us yearn for him who "dwells in unapproachable light,"[29] and in the intimate depths of our heart come near to him, the author of true light who waits for us. If we make the effort to find hot springs in the desert, we shall find them. Then, as we withdraw from the world, the fervor of the Holy Spirit may inflame us and the tears of salutary compunction may wash us clean, as Isaiah says: "The Lord will satisfy your soul with his splendor, he will give you strength of limb; you will be like a well-watered garden, like a spring whose waters never fail."[30] And when this comes to pass, man's soul becomes a paradise and is truly made into a garden of delights.[31] Then will the love of this world be turned into bitterness; the mind, freed from the chains of carnal desire, will be lifted up to the heights, and will find its delight only in the ineffable association with its creator, as it was said by the same prophet: "Then you shall find your joy in the Lord, and I will set you riding on the heights of the earth, and the patrimony of your father Jacob shall be yours to enjoy."[32]

(11) Most dear brother, let us strive to reach the banquet where we shall be intimately refreshed and never cease to hunger for the delights of heavenly food, so that as we partake, as it were, of this meager breakfast we may be nourished at the table of the heavenly marriage feast and not grow weak on the way. And even though you are burdened with various duties

27. Isa 30.9–11.
28. Cf. Heb 4.16.
29. 1 Tim 6.16.
30. Isa 58.11.
31. For further use of this figure, see *Letter* 49 n. 60.
32. Isa 58.14.

inherent in your office as abbot, let your soul retreat to the haven of solitary quiet whenever possible, imitating Moses who frequently paid short visits to the tabernacle of the covenant.[33] What is meant by these frequent visits to the tabernacle but that we should be taught by this example: that he who in God's presence is carried away by contemplation should, upon leaving it, be constantly occupied with the affairs of his weaker brothers; that within that presence he should meditate on the high secrets of God, but when leaving it he should bear the burdens of others who are flesh and bone. He who always comes to this tabernacle with his doubts, and consults the Lord before the ark of the covenant, undoubtedly provides an example for those in authority. Thus, when they are away from God and are uncertain in their actions, they may always retreat into themselves as into a tabernacle, to seek advice of the Lord, as it were, before the ark of the covenant, and to search the pages of sacred Scripture in solitude for answers to their doubts. This the very truth demonstrated by assuming our lowly nature. He spent his nights in prayer in the mountains, but by day he brilliantly performed miraculous deeds in the towns, thus showing the way that good leaders might imitate. For if they are now engaged in the contemplation of the highest truth, they may still be compassionately involved in the needs of their weak brothers, because charity will wondrously scale the heights when it reaches down in mercy to the lowly needs of our neighbor; and the more benevolently it belittles itself in unpretentious tasks, the stronger will it be when returning to the highest good.

33. Cf. Exod 33.

LETTER 83

Peter Damian to the senator, Peter. He writes to chide the senator for discontinuing the construction of a monastery he had proposed to build. Responding to those who contend that there is no profit in erecting an ecclesiastical structure, he cited the example of Solomon and the later restorers of the temple in Jerusalem, and then *exempla* taken from more recent times. The letter is incomplete in its one surviving manuscript.

(Between June 1061 and November 1062)[1]

TO SIR PETER, a man of senatorial rank,[2] the monk Peter the sinner sends greetings in the Lord.

(2) It is common to both the chosen and the reprobate that they equally undertake good deeds, but it is the special quality of the chosen to carry them through successfully. The former, indeed, persevere unalterably in what they have begun, while the latter are fickle and inconsistent and quickly change their minds. So it is written, "A fool is as changeable as the moon."[3]

(3) My dear friend, you indeed began building a monastery, but before the walls were scarcely a foot and a half high, you stopped construction. One might rightly scoff at this by quoting the statement in the gospel, "There is the man who started to build and could not finish."[4] Or he might cite what Tobiah the Ammonite in the book of Nehemiah derisively said of Jerusalem as it was being rebuilt: "Whatever it is they are building, if a fox climbs up their stone walls, it will break them down."[5] For while the walls stand there half demolished and

---

1. Dating follows Lucchesi, *Vita* 2.157.
2. This senator Peter cannot be found in other sources; cf. Mittarelli-Costadoni, *Annales Camaldulenses* 2.335.
3. Sir 27.12.
4. Luke 14.30.
5. 2 Ezra 4.3.

disgracefully unfinished, they might more properly be called a ruin rather than a monastery.[6]

(4) Or do you think, as some people, like bleating sheep, are crazy enough to say, that it is unprofitable and produces no yield to engage in building ecclesiastical structures? Are you unaware that after the temple was finished, the Lord appeared to Solomon in a dream and not only granted him wisdom beyond all human capacity, but gave him also an incomparable amount of riches? "I have given you wisdom and understanding. I will further give you such wealth and riches so that no king before your time nor since can match you."[7] Indeed, if almighty God despises the efforts of those who build his churches, how is it that he commanded that a tabernacle be constructed for him with such great care in the desert?[8] Was he speaking to Moses in a belittling or off-handed way when he said this? "I have specially chosen Bezalel, son of Hur, of the tribe of Judah. I have filled him with the spirit of God, making him skillful and ingenious, expert in every craft, and a master of design, whether in gold, silver, copper, or in marble or gems or various kinds of wood. Further, I have appointed Oholiab, son of Ahisamach of the tribe of Dan to help him, and I have endowed every skilled craftsman with the skill that he has. They shall make everything that I have commanded you."[9]

(5) Moreover, if he ordered such meticulous care in constructing a tabernacle that he knew would soon be abandoned, how much greater is his concern in building the Church, which for the salvation of all men will stand unmoved to the end of time? The tabernacle erected in the desert and the temple constructed in the reign of Solomon were shadows and figures of that Church that now stands so brilliantly among the Christian people. And so it was said to Moses, "As you were shown on the mountain, so shall it be made."[10] For the architect and builder of this Church is Christ, who is the true king and

---

6. The Latin text here uses the word *ecclesia*, which may mean either 'church' or 'monastery.' The context suggests the latter word.
7. 2 Chr. 1.12. 8. Cf. Exod 25.
9. Exod 31.2–6.
10. Exod 27.8, freely cited by Damian from the Vulgate.

priest.¹¹ But that temple, as it was restored after its previous destruction, had Zerubbabel, who was of the royal tribe of Judah, and Jesus, the son of Jehozadak, the high priest, as its directors in the restoration. Thus it was that the prophet Haggai said, "Then the Lord stirred up the spirit of Zerubbabel son of Shealtiel, governor of Judah, and the spirit of Jesus son of Jehozadak, the high priest, and the rest of the people; they came and began work on the house of the Lord of Hosts, their God."¹² Of this restoration he spoke in the words of Isaiah: "Ancient ruins shall be rebuilt and sites long desolate restored; they shall repair the ruined cities and restore what has long lain desolate."¹³ And again he spoke of this subject: "Watch and I will restore the fortunes of the clans of Jacob and show my love for all his dwellings. Every city shall be rebuilt and the temple will be restored in keeping with its plans."¹⁴ There can be little doubt that he who takes pains to build the physical structure of a church to the honor of almighty God has a part in erecting this spiritual temple.

(6) In addition, you should not be exhorted by words alone to follow through with what you have so well begun, but you might be moved also by external signs of the power of God. Alphanus, the archbishop of Salerno,¹⁵ a truthful and prudent man, reported that he had heard the following in the city of Constantinople. "It happened," he said, "that the emperor"—whose name he had forgotten—"was at one time afflicted with blindness, which no medical care was able to remedy. As it was impossible to overcome this malady by any human means, he undertook to seek relief from God in prayer. He had heard in a dream that if he visited the church of St. Lawrence the martyr,¹⁶ he would regain his sight with God's help. He therefore made a vow to travel to Rome, and at once ordered a ship to

---

11. On this idea, see J. Leclercq, "L'idée de la royauté du Christ au moyen âge," *Unam Sanctam* 32 (1959).
12. Hag 1.14.
13. Isa 61.4.
14. Jer 30.18.
15. On Alfanus of Salerno, see *Letter* 59 n. 1; on his stay in Constantinople between June 1061 and November 1062, see Lucchesi, *Vita* 2.157.
16. The reference is to S. Lorenzo al Verano; cf. *Monasticon Italiae 1: Roma e Lazio*, ed. F. Garaffa, No. 91 (1981) 58.

stand by so that he could promptly begin his trip. But his wife, anxious about losing control of the empire while her sons were still small, and fearing that her husband's authority would collapse if he suffered shipwreck, had recourse to the following pious fraud.

(7) "She gave orders to the oarsmen that they should not go directly to Rome, but only pretend to make the journey by stopping at various ports and hold up the ship at likely harbors along the way. As the sailors, according to instructions, deceived the emperor by changing the names of places they had reached, moving to ports they had already visited, zigzagging back and forth over the same route they had once taken, the empress employed a host of stonecutters and masons and built an imposing and wondrous church in honor of St. Lawrence, constructed exactly according to the size of the basilica erected for this martyr in the suburbs of Rome. For she said that if her husband should recover his sight through the intercession of St. Lawrence, whatever God could do in Rome, he could also perform here.

(8) "A year passed while the emperor was led by a circuitous route, moving from one port to another, and while many artisans worked at home on the basilica, completing the construction and marvelous ornamentation. After all this had taken place, the emperor was brought back to the walled city of Constantinople, which, according to the reports of his shipmates, he took to be the city of Rome. They made careful provision and saw to it that only those who spoke Latin should accompany him, the latter persuading him that this was Rome and that he was visiting the church of St. Lawrence the martyr. As they led him by the hand the emperor entered the church and at once recovered his sight; and he was greatly surprised at seeing his wife, his retainers, and his servants standing there about him."

(9) The following story that I am now putting in writing, I learned from Desiderius, the venerable abbot of Monte Cassino.[17] "There was a nun," he said, "whose name was Bella,

---

17. Desiderius of Monte Cassino, *Dialogi de miraculis sancti Benedicti*, ed. G.

living in the monastery of blessed Peter the apostle that stands within the walls of Benevento.[18] As long as she lived, she did not abandon the religious life. Moreover, at the time she was espoused, in keeping with her well-placed lineage, to a man of outstanding family, she turned her back on earthly marriage that she might receive a heavenly bridegroom.[19] She therefore broke off the agreement, written up in the nuptial documents, and as she received the monastic veil, was wed to the author of perpetual virginity and unsullied purity. From the very beginning of her holy conversion she obliged herself to lead a life of mortification with high purpose. Putting aside every kind of indulgence in bodily pleasure by a severe and rigid regimen, she overcame her body that was used to quite different treatment so that often, weakened by fasting, she threw herself onto the bare pavement and sought for herself no other bed but the ground."

(10) But for the moment passing over her life, let me briefly continue with what the Abbot [Desiderius] had to say of her teacher, named Offa, who had been the occasion of her entering the order of nuns and had given her a splendid education. He said that "one night she rose early in the still of night, as was her custom, and while occupied with her many prayers was preparing to walk about the altar to envelop it with the odor of burning incense. She took the censer and went to the place where the incense was kept. But, as it happened, whether the incense had fallen or had been removed, she did not find it as she had hoped. And then the light in her lamp went out because of the wind that had risen as it began to storm. As the nun carefully looked here and there and was still unable to find the scent to put into the censer, suddenly someone came up in the dark and handed her the incense she had sought." We can readily believe that this could have been done by an angel.

(11) Desiderius further stated that a marvelous thing hap-

Schwartz and A. Hofmeister, MGH SS 30.2.3.9 (1934) 1149f., gives the same account.

18. Cf. *ItPont* 9.101.
19. A similar legend is found in Gregory I, *Dialogi* 3.14, ed. A. de Vogüe, 3 vols., SC 251.2 (1978–1980) 302.

pened as her spiritual mother, of whom we have been speaking, lay suffering from the illness of which she shortly died, in the sight of the people who stood there close to the bed. Suddenly her whole body rose in the air and remained suspended until she had completed the prayer she had begun. After her happy death, her holy body was buried in the church. A certain farmer[20] placed a sack full of grain on her tomb and promptly, by divine intervention, it was blown aside by a violent wind. And so this clumsy and ignorant bumpkin had to gather up his grain lying there in the dust, since he had not shown proper reverence for the grave that held this holy body. Since . . .[21]

20. For a similar legend about the grave of St. Equitius, cf. Gregory I, *Dialogi* 1.4, 2.56.
21. MS Monte Cassino 359 (C2), the only source for this letter, breaks off at this point.

LETTER 84

Peter Damian, writing in the name of Pope Alexander II, to the clergy and people of Milan. Ghost-written shortly after Alexander's election, this letter expresses the pope's spiritual concern for his native city. Exhorting the Milanese people to a life of virtue, he programmatically hopes for an improvement in clerical morality during the time of his pontificate.

(October 1061)[1]

LEXANDER THE BISHOP,[2] servant of the servants of God, to all the Milanese, both clergy and people, sends his greetings and apostolic benediction.

(2) It has been ordained in God's good judgment that I, a son of the Church of Milan, nourished since childhood at Ambrosian sources,[3] should rise unworthily to the service of the Apostolic See, and devote myself with pastoral solicitude to the mother of all the churches.[4] And while concern for the universal Church is no light burden on my shoulders, nature itself compels me to show special interest in you, so that I might increasingly be occupied in fostering the eternal welfare of that city in which I began my earthly career. For a fire more readily ignites the forest in which it started; a spring before all else saturates the earth from which it has its source.

(3) Thus, my dear friends, with deep paternal love I exhort you to lift your sights to heaven, despise the deceitful and perishable values of earthly things, prudently free yourselves from the befouling love of this world, and deeply burn with desire

---

1. The dating follows Lucchesi, *Vita* no. 159. One may also take note of the superscription of MSS Ch2 and U1: "A letter from Pope Alexander sent to the people of Milan in the week of his ordination."
2. Cf. JL 4469; Schmidt, "Alexander II" 179ff.
3. On the Milanese origins of Anselm of Baggio (Alexander II), see Schmidt, "Alexander II" 1ff.
4. For the dependence of the Church of Milan on Rome, see *Letter* 65.

for your creator. "You are indeed," as the blessed Apostle says, "a holy nation, a people claimed by God for his own, to proclaim the triumphs of him who has called you out of darkness into his marvelous light."[5] Of those, therefore, whose undefiled and imperishable inheritance resides in heaven, let it not be said that their hearts were engaged in the love of earthly things.

(4) Indeed, as I am speaking to ordinary folk, I am happy to cite for you a well known text from Scripture. Call to mind, my brothers, the words you use in the Lord's Prayer: "Our Father, who art in heaven."[6] We should therefore be totally absorbed in quickly reaching the inheritance of him whom we call our Father. Of our earthly inheritance, moreover, it was written, "The inheritance which at the first you so eagerly sought will bring you no blessing in the end."[7] Why is it, therefore, that when we say "Our Father," we at once add, "who art in heaven," and not rather, who art on earth, which, indeed, is better known to us? Or, who art in the waters or in the depths, since God is everywhere, and nothing is devoid of his omnipotence? But when we say, "Our Father," we further say, "who art in heaven," that we might lift our minds to our inheritance in heaven, and after being united with such a sublime source, need not basely seek for anything on earth to become God's heir.

(5) Now Abraham, the father of faith, had several sons, but only the one born of his wife was of distinguished birth. Those, however, whom he had from lowborn concubines were excluded, we know, from succeeding to their father's inheritance. Yet all those whom Abraham supported were known as the sons of Abraham. But when it came to inclusion in his will, it was clearly seen who was the legitimate heir, and who would be disinherited. For as Scripture states, "Abraham gave all that he had to his son Isaac, but gave presents to the sons of his concubines, and sent them away from his son Isaac."[8] Note,

---

5. 1 Pet 2.9.
6. Matt 6.9.
7. Prov 20.21.
8. Gen 25.5–6. On variants from the Vulgate in this citation, see the *Beuron* 2 (1951–1954) 362; cf. Sabatier 1.70.

therefore, that all were called his sons, but not all obtained rights to their father's inheritance. In the same way, my brothers, there are many today who bear the title of Christian, who are unworthy of being included in the inheritance of Christ, and who never come to inherit paternal property, because, like lowborn sons, they meanly seek the goods of this earth and not the things of heaven.

(6) Now you, my dear friends, who are my members and the very depths of my soul, try to walk along the path of our heavenly mandate in such a way that my heart may always deserve to rejoice over the holy life of my blood brothers. In him who deigned to be born of the Virgin, may I dare to hope that in the days of my ministry holy chastity may be exalted among the clergy and that the lust of the incontinent will be destroyed along with other heresies.

(7) My dear brothers, may almighty God guard you from all evil and lead you along the path of justice to the kingdom of heaven.

LETTER 85

Peter Damian to Albert, a nobleman. He here demonstrates his somewhat academic interest in family problems. Not revealing the source of his information, he chastises the nobleman for despising his mother in deference to his wife, refusing to allow her any voice in domestic affairs. Filial piety extends also to married children, who should remember that to their parents they owe their very existence. He cites copiously from the Old Testament in pursuing his argument, and finally appeals to an *exemplum* he overheard in conversation with Pope Alexander II. He hopes that this narrative will soften Albert's attitude toward his mother, and his wife's regard for her mother-in-law.

(October 1061–1071)[1]

TO ALBERT, a distinguished man,[2] the monk Peter the sinner sends greetings in the Lord.

(2) One who makes little of honoring his parents stands in contempt of the commands of the Law of God. One who does not obey those who bore him will not receive a share of the inheritance in the land of the living. On the contrary, God spoke through Moses and commanded, "Honor your father and your mother, that you may live long on earth."[3] And the wise man also says, "He who honors his father will have a long life, and he who obeys his father comforts his mother."[4] Then he adds, "He who fears the Lord honors his parents, and in word and deed and with great patience will obey those who bore him as though he was their slave."[5]

(3) It normally happens, moreover, according to the just plan of God, that he who is humbly subject to his parents will enjoy the obedience of his own children when he too becomes a par-

1. The dating follow Neukirch, *Das Leben* 113.
2. See Mittarelli-Costadoni, *Annales Camaldulenses* 2.336.
3. Exod 20.12.   4. Sir 3.7.
5. Sir 3.8–9.

ent. And so it is written that "a son who respects his father will be made happy by his own children; when he prays, he will be heard."[6] He who listens to God's command and is subject to the regulations of his parents indeed deserves to have God listen to his prayers. Moreover, just as he who curses his parents is deserving of the death penalty, so he who reverently obeys will be rewarded by the blessing of God. And so it was written in the Law: "When any man reviles his father or his mother, he shall be put to death."[7] And elsewhere it is also written, "Honor your father so that you may receive the Lord's blessing, that his blessing may be yours forever."[8] And then the text continues, "For a father's blessing strengthens his children's houses, but a mother's curse uproots their foundations."[9] Therefore, if the children's house is destroyed by the parents' curse, and is strengthened by their blessing, we must beware that in offending our parents we do not destroy the children who will come after us.

(4) It has come to my attention, most noble sir, that out of love for your wife you are despising and slighting your holy mother, and that you give her no authority in directing the ordinary affairs of your household. By such actions you appear to be only imitating the qualities of fire, which consumes the wood as it rises from it, turning it to ashes, yet it bakes stones and makes them glow. By consuming the wood from which it comes it destroys, as it were, the mother who gave it birth. But in the case of stones that put it out, it makes them glow and turn as white as lime. Now since fire burns when set to wood, but merely bakes the stones, it has opposite effects regarding things that are not opposed. For while stone and wood differ, they are not opposed as white is to black, the first of which shows up in stone, while the other appears in wood. The former it makes white, but the latter it turns black, just as by the stones it would be totally extinguished unless it were fed by the wood. And so the wise man puts it well: "Honor your father and do not forget your mother's birth pangs; remember that

---

6. Sir 3.6.
7. Lev 20.9.
8. Sir 3.9–10.
9. Sir 3.11.

were it not for them you would not have been born, and repay them for what they have done for you."[10]

(5) Think for a moment how cruel it is to snub and despise those from whom you have your very being, and with what great humility you should submit to those who gave you birth and to whom you are indebted for what you essentially are by nature. Since you cannot be in doubt of what you received from them as a boy, how much more should you repay them with gratitude now that they are older? Accordingly it was written, "My son, look after your father in his old age; do nothing to vex him as long as he lives. Even if his mind fails, make allowances for him, and do not despise him because you are in your prime."[11]

(6) But perhaps you will say, "My mother often exasperates me, disturbing me and my wife with her harsh words. We cannot bear such reproach and insult and will not tolerate her abuse and disgusting scolding." Yet in all this you will be more richly rewarded if, while suffering annoyance, you accept it with gratitude and, amid all her sarcastic censuring, you humbly reply with courtesy. To this point it was written, "If you support your father it will never be forgotten, and because of the sins of your mother good is returned to you."[12] Since, therefore, for your mother's sin only good things will happen to you, why do you not put up with it when she is harsh or unjustly offends you? These are certainly terrifying words that Scripture uses: "What an infamous thing it is to leave your father in the lurch, and he who provokes his mother's anger calls down God's curse."[13] Will he, moreover, who dishonors his parents, since he is rejected by God, not suffer for it even in this life? But listen to what Scripture says: "A man is honored if his father is honored, and it brings dishonor to a son if his father is discredited."[14] But in gathering texts from the Old Testament, I find it also apropos to include an event of recent vintage, so that at least the sight of God's vindictive justice may

10. Sir 7.29–30.
11. Sir 3.14–15.
12. Sir 3.15–16.
13. Sir 3.18.
14. Sir 3.13.

terrify those who are not restrained by the bonds of his commands.

(7) Yesterday afternoon I happened to hear the following story from the lips of the venerable Pope Alexander.[15] "As Ardericus, a native of Milan was celebrating his wedding," he said, "a waiter complained that the food had not been properly seasoned. When the groom informed his mother of this charge, getting into a heated argument, he angrily and stubbornly asked her why this lack of condiment had occurred. His mother retorted that she had provided the servants with all the spices they needed. Finally, in a violent fit of anger, the groom dared to raise his hand against his mother, and in a mad fury disrespectfully struck her in the face. But how undisturbedly divine justice can punish our anger, how quietly it can vent its rage on human frenzy and remain tranquil as it avenges our senseless display of viciousness. And so Solomon says, 'But you, with strength at your command, judge with equanimity and rule us in great forbearance.'[16] Suddenly, the left side of the assailant's jaw became numb and began to cause him great pain. And as the numbness steadily increased and wore him out with such excruciating torment that he could hardly bear it, compelling him to moan and gnash his teeth, his mother who might have felt that only a stepson could strike her so, treated him like her real son and did not act like a stepmother, as he deserved, but demonstrated the depths of her maternal love. In the meantime, the flesh around the jaw began to swell and putrify, while pus and poison oozed from a hollow cavity in the wound.

(8) "As the horrible stench from his rotting flesh and the deep pain frightfully bore down on the man, causing him to regret the marriage he had just contracted, he feared that his wife might look for another husband. As he observed the wife he had just married, he now thought of her as someone married to another man. And yet his mother did not think of turning on her son who was in this dangerous state but, overcome

---

15. This meeting with Pope Alexander cannot be dated exactly. But on their close relationship, see Schmidt, "Alexander II" 179ff.
16. Wis 12.18.

with heartfelt love, went to the church of the blessed martyr Nazarius.[17] There she vowed to do everything she could, and offered gifts at his shrine. Prostrate on the ground she prayed and begged him with tears to win forgiveness for her offending son. And so divine mercy takes note of the prayers of this mother, and as God had inspired her to plead for the son who had done her harm, he heard her request that he should also mercifully care for him in his affliction. Shortly after, as the putrid flesh came loose and bone fell away from his jaw, all pain quickly disappeared and a thick scab formed over the spot, and divine compassion restored the desperate man to his former good health. In this way the sign of God's mercy was seen on the face of this man, and at the same time it showed the mark of human failing. For while one saw a face from which a bone had been removed, it clearly appeared healed. One could observe the just results of a furious son's anger, and at the same time note what a mother's love could achieve as she pleaded for him at the court of God's goodness."

(9) Therefore, most noble sir, let this evidence of God's power be a warning to you, let this disaster befalling one who assaults his mother terrify you and restrain you and your lovely wife from every offense to her mother-in-law. Thus, as you honor your parents, which is the first commandment that bears a promise,[18] having once passed through the desert, may you deserve to enter the land of the living along with those who are true Israelites.

17. This church is currently known as San Nazaro Maggiore; cf. *Milano e il suo territorio* 2 [1844, reprint 1975] 351.
18. Cf. Exod 20.12; Deut 5.16; Matt 15.4.

LETTER 86

Peter Damian to Desiderius, the abbot of Monte Cassino, and to his community. He deplores the wretched condition of the contemporary world and its rulers, while congratulating the monks of Monte Cassino for whom the Lord had prepared their monastic ark against the current flood. He also sees their cloistered refuge as a Cassiodorean *vivarium*, filled with fish and fowl and animals of all kinds. These he proceeds to interpret mystically, adapting their natures to human vices and virtues. His chief source, the *Physiologus*, is much in evidence. This work was composed in Rome.

(October–November 1061)[1]

TO SIR DESIDERIUS, the archangel of monks,[2] and to his holy community, the monk Peter the sinner offers his service.

(2) You who are not unaware of the crimes that occur in this mad age would be wise to consider that, having left the world, you should be deeply grateful to your God for having rescued you. Decency and right living have all but disappeared and, as vigorous church discipline gradually collapses, a pestilential flood of vice and depravity of every kind grows deeper day by day. It would seem that the prophet's statement has come true, especially in our age: "There is no good faith or compassion, no knowledge of God in the land. We are compelled to endure a flood of cursing and lying, of killing and robbing and adultery."[3] And since royal authority does not curb these events but gladly permits them to occur and favorably assents to them, causing people to laugh when rightfully they should weep with fury and impatience, the prophet properly continues, "They

---

1. The dating follows Lucchesi, *Vita* no. 161.
2. On Desiderius of Monte Cassino as the recipient of this work, see Cowdrey, *Desiderius* 35. The abbot is called "the archangel of monks" also in *Letter* 106.
3. Hos 4.1–2.

win over the king with their wickedness and princes with their treachery, lecherous all of them, hot as an oven over the baker's fire."[4] And since the flames of avarice or passion have first engulfed the timbered ceilings and paneled walls of princes, and then spread through their subjects, raging at ground level, the prophet added shortly thereafter, "They all grow feverish, hot as an oven, and devour their rulers. King after king falls from power, but not one of them calls upon me."[5]

(3) And since a wicked people does not deserve good rulers, and thus the whole world, like a single body, is shot through with a continuing criminal disease, the voice of God makes this charge through the prophet when he says, "Where now, O Israel, is your king that he may save you in all your cities, or your rulers for whom you asked me, 'Give me a king and princes'"?[6] And then he promptly continues, "I will give you a king in my anger, and in my fury I will take him away."[7] Thus it happens that while the world's rulers are more interested in wealth than in law, they fail to use legal sanctions to curb their subjects who are prone to evil. In our day the world is in pain, as Isaiah says: "Your head is a mass of sores, and every one of you is sick at heart, from head to foot there is not a sound spot in you."[8]

(4) Therefore, my dear friends, you must take special care always to be immensely grateful to God that, in this age, you were chosen to live apart from the world in which it is obviously difficult for anyone to be saved. You have fulfilled what God loudly proclaimed in the words of Zechariah: "Away, away; flee from the land of the north." And again, "Escape, you people of Zion who live with the daughter of Babylon."[9] And truth itself said to them, "I have chosen you out of the world, and because you do not belong to the world, for that reason the world hates you."[10] For just as the shepherd rescues an only sheep from the ravenous jaws of the attacking beast if it has sunk its teeth into one of the weaklings in the flock, so too has Christ rescued you from the mouth of the cruel plunderer who

4. Hos 7.3–4.
5. Hos 7.7.
6. Hos 13.10.
7. Hos 13.11.
8. Isa 1.5–6.
9. Zech 2.6, 7.
10. John 15.19.

sought to have you serve him as the world was falling apart. And so we find these words in the writings of the prophet Amos: "As a shepherd rescues out of the jaws of a lion two shinbones or the tip of an ear, so shall the Israelites who live in Samaria be rescued."[11]

(5) Thus there can be no doubt that you were granted an abundant gift of grace, of which the same prophet spoke in another chapter: "I would send rain on one city and no rain on another; rain would fall on one field, and another would be parched for lack of it."[12] For hearts that are carnal and attached to this world grow arid from neglect amid an extended dry spell, because they are not watered by heavenly grace and the rains of compunction. Of such land the voice of God says, "I shall command the clouds to send no more rain upon it."[13] But, on the other hand, Isaiah says of the soul that truly thirsts after God and with unceasing desire seeks for the fountain of wisdom, "I will pour down rain on a thirsty land, showers on dry ground. I will pour out my spirit on your offspring and my blessings on your children. They shall spring up amid desert shrubs like willows by a flowing stream."[14]

(6) Therefore, since almighty God withdrew you from the world and ordained that you should serve him by observing the monastic *Rule,* it was as if he had chosen your small number from among the many who were about to perish in the flood, and brought you into the refuge of the ark, coated with pitch, that you might live.[15] For the monastic enclosure is a *vivarium* of souls.[16] There, indeed, you will find fish that have fins, as approved by the Law,[17] furnishing delicacies for the table of the Israelites that they might be changed into the body of Christ. Now fish that have scaly fins can be seen leaping out of the water.[18] Fin-bearing fish are the symbol of those chosen souls that alone are transformed into the body of the heavenly

11. Amos 3.12.
12. Amos 4.7.
13. Isa 5.6.
14. Isa 44.3–4.
15. Cf. Gen 7.
16. Cassiodorus, *Institutiones* 1.29.3, 74f.
17. Cf. Lev 11.9; Deut 14.19.
18. Ambrose, *Hexameron* 5.11.34,168.

Church, because now that they are endowed with the fins of virtue, they are able to leap with desire for heaven, striving for higher things through contemplation, even though of themselves they will again fall back because of their mortal flesh.

(7) In pursuing our spiritual interpretation, is it more proper to call the monastic enclosure only a *vivarium* or weir for fish, as we have done above, or also a haven for heavenly animals, or even an aviary? These three types of animals are spoken of by the psalmist when he says, "The cattle in the field, the birds in the air, and the fish in the sea."[19] Hosea the prophet also speaks of them: "With the wild beasts and the birds of the air and the fish in the sea shall they be gathered together."[20] Which of these three words best expresses the idea of a monastery? Obviously, all three are appropriately used in describing a monastic enclosure, since a variety of spiritual animals is found in it, enflamed by the fire of harmonious and indivisible charity.

(8) There too, as was said above, live spiritual fish continuously swimming in the rivers of sacred Scripture. Were there not this spiritual haven where heavenly and otherworldly fish could spiritually live, the Lord would not have spoken figuratively to blessed Job of the skin of the behemoth: "Can you fill a net with his skin or a fish-weir with his head?"[21] There you have cattle in the field of which Jacob spoke: "Ah! the smell of my son is like the smell of bounteous fields blessed by the Lord."[22] And of those chosen animals, living in the harmony of holy love, Isaiah says, "Then the wolf shall live with the lamb, and the leopard lie down with the kid; the calf and the young lion and the sheep shall grow up together."[23] Because of the depth of this holy love, the wolf will live with the lamb, since those who were robbers in the world now rest peacefully with those who are meek and mild-mannered. The leopard lies with the kid, because he who was spotted with the stains of his sins is now in humble agreement with him who despises himself and acknowledges that he is a sinner. Moreover, the calf and

19. Ps 8.8–9.
20. Hos 4.3.
21. Job 40.26.
22. Gen 27.27.
23. Isa 11.6.

the lion and the sheep grow up together, because the one with a contrite heart who prepares himself to be offered as a daily sacrifice to God, and the other, whose cruel fury is like that of a lion, and he too who is always as simple and innocent as a lamb come together in the haven of holy Church. One will also find there the birds of the air, namely those who rise above all difficulties with the wings of virtue and, from the heights their souls have achieved, look down upon all earthly affairs that pass beneath them. And while they refuse to grovel among the things of this earth under the yoke of carnal desire, they seek freedom in the air and soar to the heavens on the wings of mental prayer.

(9) The Lord indeed spoke of these birds in the gospel when he declared that the mustard seed would grow up to be a tree: "But when it has grown," he says, "it is bigger than any garden plant; it becomes a tree, big enough for the birds to come and roost among its branches."[24] Nor should we wonder that man can be figuratively compared to the animals in the field, the birds in the heavens, and the fish in the sea, since man himself, for whose benefit all these were created, is called "the whole creation": "Go forth," said the Lord, "to every part of the world, and proclaim the gospel to the whole creation."[25] Thus by employing mystical interpretation we can discern human behavior in the natural acts of animals, just as in men we find something pertaining to the functions of the angels.

(10) Just as almighty God, the creator of all things, put the whole earth at the disposal of men, so too by these natural powers and necessary functions with which he endowed dumb animals he took pains to look after man and instruct him. Thus in the animals man might discover what should be imitated and what avoided; what he might find useful in borrowing from them, and what he should properly disregard. In so doing, as rational man is instructed by things that lack reason, he may always move unencumbered toward his creator along the road of wisdom. But that what I say may become clearer, I shall gladly here discuss the qualities of animals, and briefly indicate

24. Matt 13.32. 25. Mark 16.15.

how they might be adapted to human behavior, doing so summarily and insofar as epistolary brevity will allow. Nor do I, as one who has experience in the matter, claim to know these things myself, but have decided to insert in my work, irrevocably and without further examination, only what has come down to us from those who have spent much effort in researching the nature of things.[26]

On the Nature of the Lion

(11) Now the lion, since it is the bravest of all animals and, as Scripture states, "does not turn tail for anyone,"[27] seems also to have a certain subtlety. For when it is sought by the hunters, catching their scent at once, it cleverly contrives a new kind of deceit so as to throw its pursuers off the track. With its tail moving along the ground, it covers over all its tracks, and thus eludes the snares of the hunters and is not caught.[28] Clearly, those who hunt men are the evil spirits who, like hunters, search for meat as they fiercely strive to have men of every kind live according to the flesh. But whoever is like the lion, of which Jacob says, "Judah, you lion's whelp,"[29] catches the hunter's scent, because he detects the snares of the clever enemy. He, indeed, craftily caught this scent who said, "We are not ignorant of his cunning."[30] On the other hand, there are those who are not aware, of whom John says, "They had no experience of the deep secrets of Satan."[31] The lion also covers its tracks

---

26. See *Letter* 57, opening paragraph, where Damian also refers to specialists in natural history. Here, besides the *Hexameron* of Ambrose and the *Etymologies* of Isidore, he uses various traditions of the *Physiologus*, especially the following: *Physiologus latinus versio B* (=*Physiol. lat. B*), ed. F. J. Carmody (1939); *Physiologus latinus versio c* (=*Physiol. lat. c*) =*Physiologus Bernensis*, commentary by C. von Steiger and O. Homburger (1964); and the *Physiologus latinus versio Y* (=*Physiol. lat. Y*), ed. F. J. Carmody, University of Californa, *Publications in Classical Philology* 12 (1941) 95–134. When a source citation was necessary, the translator chose *versio Y* in the notes, reflecting his use of this version when editing *Letter* 86. Damian also seems to have had in hand *De bestiis et aliis rebus libri quatuor* (PL 177.9–164). For further bibliographical discussion of this source problem, see Reindel, *Briefe* 2 (1988) 464–65 n. 5.
27. Cf. Prov 30.30.
28. Cf. Isidore, *Etymologies* 12.2. 5; *Physiol. lat. c* 52; *Physiol. lat. Y* 1.103.
29. Gen 49.9.
30. 2 Cor 4.2, a variation on the Vulgate.
31. Rev 2.24.

with its tail, which is the extreme part of the body, because it hides the wickedness of its former life with the covering of a new form of living, as it is said: "Blessed are they whose wickedness is forgiven and whose sins are covered up."[32] And elsewhere, "You have forgiven the guilt of your people and covered over all their sins."[33] And so the tail of the lion wipes out the tracks it had made when the cover of a good life in latter days conceals one's earlier life.

(12) At this point we should note that the lion turns up its nose at yesterday's food and refuses to eat the leftovers of its own meal.[34] And you, O man, now that you have had your fill, thoroughly detest sin, so that you will not be found returning to your own vomit like a dog.[35] We may further add that the lion sleeps with open eyes.[36] You too should be so asleep to the world that you always remain wide awake for the Lord, as it is written, "I sleep but my heart is awake."[37] The lioness gives birth to dead young, and the cub remains dead for three days until, on the third day, the male comes and breathes into its face, and then at once it comes to life.[38] The contemplative life also begets you dead to this world, and the omnipotent Father sends you his life-giving Spirit. In this way, he who on the third day raised up the lion's whelp of the tribe of Judah, within the three days of faith, hope, and charity will cause you to come to life, not to the world but to himself, that with the Apostle you may freely sing out, "The life I now live is not my life, but the life that Christ lives in me."[39]

The Antelope[40]

(13) The antelope, moreover, is such a fierce and violent animal that a hunter cannot approach it, nor any enemy come near it. It has long horns, formed like a saw, with which it is

32. Ps 31.1.
33. Ps 84.3.
34. Cf. Ambrose, *Hexameron* 6.3.14, 212.
35. Cf. Prov 26.11; 2 Pet 2.22.
36. Cf. *Physiol. lat. Y* 1.103; Isidore, *Etymologies* 12.2.5.
37. Cant 5.2.
38. Cf. *Physiol. lat. Y* 1.103; Isidore, *Etymologies* 12.2.5.
39. Gal 2.20.
40. Cf. *Physiol. lat. Y* 2.104; *Physiol. lat. B* 2.12f.

able to cut through great trees, causing them to fall to the ground. But when it is thirsty, it comes to the Euphrates to drink. On the banks of this river there is a certain kind of shrub, bearing the name *gericina*, having fine and dense tendrils. When the antelope approaches the *gericina*, it becomes playful and frisky, and its horns are ensnared in the wild growth. Continuing to struggle and completely unable to get loose, it begins to cry out at the top of its voice. Attracted by the sound, the hunter comes up and kills the antelope, held fast by its own fetters.

(14) You too, O servant of God, admonished by the two Testaments, are invincibly armed, as it were, with as many horns, by which you are strong enough to protect yourself against all danger and forcefully ward off attacking spirits. When to your credit you begin to thirst after God, the living fountain, after you have drunk from the mighty Euphrates, that is, the waters of God's word, do not concern yourself with secular affairs. Do not ensnare yourself like a frisky animal in the thickets of carnal pleasures. For, as they hold you fast, the evil adversary may suddenly attack you and inflict a deadly wound as did the wicked hunter. When the flames of passion excite you, they are the clamor that arouses the hunter. There is no crime that cries more loudly to heaven. Of this Abraham said, "There is great outcry from Sodom and Gomorrah; their sin is very grave. I must go down and see whether their deeds warrant the outcry that has reached me."[41] But so that temptations to impurity may lose their effectiveness, you must undoubtedly avoid associating with women.

On the Nature of the Pyrobolus

(15) On a certain mountain in the East there are fiery stones that are both male and female, and are called *pyroboli*.[42] When they are apart from one another they do not burn; but if the female stone approaches the male, fire suddenly erupts from them, so that everything near the mountain is consumed by

---

41. Gen 18.20–21.
42. Cf. *Physiol. lat. B* 3.13f.; *Physiol. lat. Y* 3.104.

the smoking flames. From these stones we should learn that if we are not to be engulfed by the fire of lust, we should avoid looking at women. For, in seeing them, flames may be ignited and cause in us a brush fire, not on the mountain, but in our very soul.

The Beaver

(16) Moreover, that we might extinguish temptations to impurity, it is also worth imitating the example of the beaver,[43] whose testicles are most useful for medicinal purposes. For when the beaver becomes aware that it is being followed by the hunter because of its genitalia, it bites them off with its teeth and throws them at the hunter. The latter at once gives up the chase, since he has what he wanted in following the beast. But should it happen that another hunter take after him, despairing of ever getting away, the beaver senses the dangerous situation and exposes himself to the hunter, showing him that the genitalia for which he is being sought are missing. By thus demonstrating that he no longer has what the hunter is looking for, he is in no further danger from the spear of his pursuer.

(17) If you would also elude the snares of the hunter within you, take special care to cut away all enticements to carnal desire. Excise from your heart every intention to engage in sexual pleasure, and thus, as it were, rid yourself of your private parts, the root of all impurity, as you utterly reject every act of lust and every desire in that regard. And as the evil spirit, like the wicked hunter, releases the arrows of lust in your direction, rise up at once like a man and show that your testicles, the means of lusting, are missing, and say to him, "Why do you follow me? Why do you try to ensnare me and take away what I no longer possess? See, my private parts are missing; having cut away the seeds of lust, I now inviolably observe my vow of chastity." My Lord speaks to me in the words of Isaiah: "The eunuch must not say, 'I am nothing but a barren tree.' For these are the words of the Lord: 'The eunuchs who keep my sabbaths, who

---

43. Cf. Pliny, *Naturalis historia* 8.47.109; Isidore, *Etymologies* 12.2.21 and 19.27.4; *Physiol. lat.* Y 36.128–29.

choose to do my will and hold fast to my covenant, shall receive from me something better than sons and daughters, a memorial and a name in my own house and within my walls.'"[44] I am one of those of whom he himself said in the gospel, "There are eunuchs who have castrated themselves for the sake of the kingdom of heaven."[45] In this way we should be on guard so that the crafty enemy with the shafts of his temptations may not pierce us through the heart, and by artful design pluck the fruit of chastity or of other good works.

The Hedgehog[46]

(18) The hedgehog also presents this symbol, in that as its entire body is covered with sharp bristles, it goes into the vineyard at vintage time and attacks the very best grapes it can find. It shakes the vines with such force that all the grapes fall to the ground and then, coming down out of the vines, it rolls about among the grapes until all of them have been transfixed by his bristles. Thus covered with grapes, it then leaves and brings food to its young. And so, the vineyard of good works must be guarded so the ancient enemy cannot attack it and tear down the rich growth of spiritual virtues, piercing the ripe grapes with the spines of its temptations, to bring them as food to wild beasts, that is, to the powers of evil opposing us. And thus a man, weakened and frustrated in his work will groan, using the words found in the Song of Songs: "They sent me to watch over the vineyards, but I did not watch over my own vineyard."[47] Just as the vines are stripped of their grapes by the hedgehog, so too every careless person is deprived of his good works by the devil. The sly spirit of evil will always use a thousand tricks and new devices not only to strip us bare, but also to wholly devour those whom he deceives.

44. Isa 56.3–5.
45. Matt 19.12.
46. Cf. Jerome, *In Esaiam* 6.14, 249; Isidore, *Etymologies* 12.3.7; *Physiol. lat.* Y 16.114.
47. Cant 1.5.

The Fox[48]

(19) The fox, too, acts in nearly the same way when, by pretending to be dead, it is actually the cause of death to the birds. When he is hungry and, after anxiously searching, has nothing to eat, he looks around for some red earth. When he finds it, he rolls around in it, covering his whole body so that it appears to be raw and bloody flesh. Then he stretches out on the ground like dead, and holds his breath. Thus as he seems to be all raw and swollen, the unwary birds have no doubt that he is dead. So as they alight to feed on him, he suddenly jumps up and snatches them, truly devouring these very birds he had deceived into feasting on him. The ancient schemer acts like this. For those seeking after carnal pleasures, he pretends to be dead, showing them what he has done as if he were baring his limbs on which they might feast. "Anyone can see the kind of behavior that belongs to the lower nature," as the Apostle says: "fornication, impurity, and indecency; avarice, idolatry, and sorcery; quarrels, a contentious temper, envy, fits of rage, selfish ambitions, dissensions, party intrigues, and jealousies; murder, drinking bouts, and orgies."[49] These clearly are the entrails of the wicked spirit, these are the daily food of the reprobate and of those who live by the flesh. While those to be damned hunger after these things, the evil spirit swallows them up as does the deceitful fox with the birds, and transforms them into his own body. The prophet says this of them: "They shall sink into the depths of the earth; they shall be given over to the sword; they shall be carrion for foxes."[50] Acting like this fox, Herod was characterized as such when the Lord said, "Go and tell that fox."[51] This fox lay hidden in the scribe, as in a ditch used as a snare, and he heard truth itself say, "Foxes have their holes."[52] The offspring of this fox are those, namely heretics, of whom it is said in the Song of Songs, "Catch for us the little foxes that spoil our vineyards."[53]

48. Cf. Isidore, *Etymologies* 12.2.29; *Physiol. lat.* Y 18.116.
49. Gal 5.19–21.
50. Ps 62.10–11.
51. Luke 13.32.
52. Matt 8.20; Luke 9.58.
53. Cant 2.15.

The Polyp

(20) Why should we marvel if the wily devil seems to have learned his cunning from the fox, since also among the fish we find an artfulness no less designing, so that while man has been set above all other living things, he should be advised to avoid danger from the very creatures over which he presides? Now the polyp[54] finds a rock in the shallows along the seashore, to which it attaches itself in a marvelous way, and then assumes its color and form. Drawing up its back to look like a rock, it catches many fish that glide up against it, not suspecting the deception. And as they take it to be just another rock, it catches them with its hidden snares. Deceived by these devices, the fish approaches freely and is caught, and while not afraid of any trickery, it is unable to avoid its ultimate fate. Now the rock is Christ, and the polyp is the crafty and wicked man, even a heretic. He attaches himself to the rock and deceitfully takes on its color because, like his master, he masquerades as an angel of light.[55] It is attached to the rock, because while he is enrolled in the Church—not by his deeds but at least by profession—he devours, as it were, unwary fish that he has caught, since he entangles weak and simple souls in the errors of his disbelief. And so the Apostle says, "Put up with it if a man exploits you and gets you in his clutches."[56] Nevertheless, in such animal wiles and deceits we can sometimes discover mysteries of allegory that will be to our profit.

The Hydra and the Crocodile[57]

(21) Now the hydra is an animal that lives in the swirling waters of rivers and is the fierce enemy of the crocodile. When it sees a crocodile sleeping with open mouth on the bank of a river, it covers itself with mud so that, with its body all slippery, it may more easily slide down the great beast's throat. It then

---

54. Cf. Pliny, *Naturalis historia* 9.46.85; Ambrose, *Hexameron* 5.8.21,156; Isidore, *Etymologies* 12.6.44.
55. Cf. 2 Cor 11.14.   56. 2 Cor 11.20.
57. Cf. Pliny, *Naturalis historia* 8.37.90; Isidore, *Etymologies* 12.6.20; *Physiol. lat. Y* 38.129.

quickly jumps into the mouth of the sleeping crocodile and the latter swallows it immediately. But the hydra tears all its enemy's entrails to pieces and then, when the crocodile is dead, it emerges alive and triumphant from its body. What is the crocodile if not the figure of death and of the nether regions? What can the hydra signify, if not the victory of our savior? For as the hydra covers itself with mud, so our redeemer put on the lowliness of human flesh. The former enters the stomach of the crocodile, just as the Lord descended into the depths of hell. The hydra destroys the internal organs, and the Lord subverted the power of death. By gnawing its way through the dead body, the former returns after its victory, while by his death our savior destroyed the power of hell as he rose in triumphant glory from the tomb. And so, in his victory he derides death in the words of the prophet: "O Death, where is your victory? O Death, where is your sting?"[58] And again: "O Death, I will be your death; O Hell, I will be your sting!"[59]

The Caladrius[60]

(22) We have no doubt that the caladrius is also a figure of our savior, if we will only marvel at its wonderful qualities. This bird is totally white, and not a single black spot is found on its feathers. When someone is sick, one cannot fail to tell by the appearance of this bird whether he will quickly recover, or whether death is near and he must die. For if the illness is fatal, the caladrius turns away as soon as it sees the sick person, and will no longer look at him. And so we have proof that from the disease he has contracted, the sick man is to die. But if, on the other hand, the sick man is to recover, the caladrius at once fixes his gaze upon his face and takes within himself all his illness. It then quickly flies toward the heat of the sun and burns up the sick man's infirmity by exposing itself to the sun and, by flying through the air, disperses it. Wonderful to behold, the sick man at once gets up and, after discharging all ill effects of his disease, he recovers.

58. 1 Cor 15.55.
59. Hos 13.14.
60. Cf. *Physiol. lat.* Y 5.105–106.

(23) Reason tells us without a doubt that this bird figuratively conforms to our redeemer. For like the caladrius, Christ is garbed in white, since no stain of reproach appears in him, in that "he committed no sin, he was convicted of no falsehood."[61] And of him the bride says in the Song of Songs, "My beloved is fair and ruddy"[62]—fair by reason of his virginity and innocence, ruddy with the blood of martyrdom. He came, indeed, to the sick people of Israel as a compassionate visitor, but turned his face from them because they were dying of the disease of infidelity and unbelief. But when he saw the gentile world, which was equally sick, he lovingly looked upon them with pity, took their sickness upon himself, and restored them to the health they had previously enjoyed. "For indeed," as was said by Isaiah, "he took upon himself our sufferings and himself bore our sins. We counted him to be a leper, smitten by God, struck down by misery; but he was pierced for our transgressions, tortured for our iniquities; the chastisement he bore is health for us, and by his scourging we are healed."[63] He dispersed illness by flying through the air, which means that by his strength he subdued all lofty powers. He ascended toward the heat of the sun and consumed the force of our sickness. That is, by returning to the Father, who is the sun of justice,[64] and by swallowing up death, "he ascended into the heights with captives in his train; he gave gifts to men."[65]

The Phoenix[66]

(24) Now the phoenix, a bird that lives in regions of India or Arabia, by its death and resurrection is also the figure of our redeemer. For he said, "I have the power to lay down my life, and I have the power to receive it back again."[67] When this bird is 500 years old, it enters the forests of Mount Lebanon

---

61. 1 Pet 2.22; Cf. Isa 53.9.
62. Cant 5.10.
63. Isa 53.4–5; cf. Sabatier 2.609.
64. Cf. 1 Pet 3.22.
65. Eph 4.8; cf. Ps 67.19.
66. Cf. Pliny, *Naturalis historia* 10.2.4; Isidore, *Etymologies* 12.7.22; *Physiol. lat. Y* 9.108–9.
67. John 10.18.

and loads both its wings with a variety of spices. By certain signs, a priest of the city of Heliopolis came to learn of this and at once gathered twigs and branches and heaped them all together. Then the phoenix, burdened with spices, landed on the pile of brush, set fire to the pyre, and died in the flames. The next day the priest came along and found that the wood he had gathered was completely consumed. After carefully inspecting the ashes, he discovered a very tiny worm, but one that gave off a fine sweet odor. Returning on the second day, he noted that the worm had taken the form of a small bird, bearing feathers and wings. Finally on the third day the priest saw a phoenix standing there, perfectly restored.

(25) Now the phoenix had its wings loaded with sweet-smelling spices, because our redeemer came down to us from heaven with the twofold fragrance of both Testaments, saying, "I did not come to abolish the Law, but to complete it."[68] And elsewhere he said, "When, therefore, a teacher of the Law has become a learner in the kingdom of heaven, he is like a householder who can produce from his store both the new and the old."[69] What was first discovered to be a worm was undoubtedly he who said, "But I am a worm, not a man."[70] It was he, I say, symbolized by the worm that, starting out at dawn, gnawed at the ivy that had grown up over Jonah's head and made it wither.[71] Then, rising like the morning sun of grace, that is the gospel, the Lord cut off the synagogue as if it were a barren ivy, using the teeth of his severe judgment, causing it to wither and become completely dry. The phoenix recovers its plumage and, supplied with wings, is lifted up in the air, as the Lord, the conqueror of death, is raised up to be seated at his Father's side, while all about him the heavenly powers rejoice. The psalmist says this: "He rode on the cherubim, he flew through the air, he swooped on the wings of the wind."[72] We too, in keeping with our capacity, are supplied with wings, namely, spiritual virtues, and if we put them to good use, we are carried aloft to

68. Matt 5.17.
69. Matt 13.52.
70. Ps 21.7.
71. Cf. Jonah 4.6–8.
72. Ps 17.11.

heavenly things. But if through sloth we put them aside, we will surely fall into the depths of vice that slowly creeps upon us.

The Sarra[73]

(26) Something like this is the sarra, a marine animal that has long wings. As soon as it sees a sailing ship, by using the wings with which it is equipped, it tries to sail in the wake of the ship. But after engaging in this great effort for some forty stadia,[74] it gives up and, thus exhausted, it lets down its wings amid dangerous seas. With the waves running high, it is forced to return to the place from which it began to sail. Clearly, the sailing vessel[75] signifies the Holy Church or any faithful soul. With the wood of the cross raised on high, it avoids the foaming crests of a wave-tossed world, and in the ship of virtue strives to reach the port of everlasting peace. But the cross was wanting to the sarra as it sailed along, since every soft and dissolute soul starts out eagerly, but tiring of the effort, it does not arrive at the shores of perfection it had determined to reach. There are also those who, while observing others progressing along the road of an upright life, are inspired by good intention to follow them. But when overcome by too much work or by the waves of any adversity that besets them, they give up trying and, like the sarra, return from where they had set sail. Of such this was truly written: "Woe to those who have given up the struggle."[76] And the wise man says, "He is your friend when he sits at your table, but is nowhere to be found in time of trouble."[77] By constant exhortation, pastors of churches must assist such as these and strengthen them with the powerful arm of their preaching, as they toss amid the dangers of a savage sea.

---

73. Cf. Isidore, *Etymologies* 12.6.16; *Physiol. lat. Y* 4.105, where it is called *serra*.
74. About four nautical miles.
75. Cf. C. Frugoni, "Letteratura didattica ed esegesi scritturale nel *De bono religiosi status* di S. Pier Damiani," *Rivista di storia della Chiesa in Italia* 34 (1980) 23f., where Damian's dependence on Augustine, *Contra Faustum* 12.14. 344 is noted.
76. Sir 2.16.   77. Sir 6.10.

They must keep them from shipwreck in waters that would engulf them, while encouraging them with unshakable constancy to have the strength to persevere.

The Sea Urchin[78]

(27) A short little fish, the sea urchin hints at the same thing, since it is able to stop great ships running under full sail. It is indeed marvelous how this tiny fish can so resolutely hold up the progress of a caravel of great displacement that it seems to be anchored in one place. Thus, as the sea urchin holds a ship immobile in the water, should not a pastor strengthen a soul floundering in the waves of temptation? This was said to one who once faltered as he began to sink in the sea,[79] but was worthy to receive a helping hand from his rescuer: "And once you have been converted, you must lend strength to your brothers."[80] Therefore, pastors who have the cure of souls must ingeniously be on their guard lest the plunderer again attack those they have once rescued from the snares of the world, and compel them to return to their own vomit.[81]

The Tigress[82]

(28) Again, the tigress is a figure of just this sort of thing. For as it is reported, upon finding her lair empty and her offspring carried away, she quickly takes up the scent of the thief. But the latter, even though he rides with the speed of a runaway horse, has little doubt that he will be outrun by this more agile beast that seems almost to fly. Seeing that there is no refuge anywhere about, he fraudulently devises an enclosure just as he finds the animal getting near him, and throws out before it a ball made of glass. But the tigress, seeing her own body in a mirror, as it were, is deceived into thinking that it is her cub. And so, she keeps on coming, hoping to fondle her offspring. But as the tigress finds herself frustrated by the empty image, she pours every effort into catching the rider. Just as the angry

---

78. Cf. Ambrose, *Hexameron* 5.9.24,158; Isidore, *Etymologies* 12.6.34.
79. Cf. Matt 14.30–31.   80. Luke 22.32.
81. Cf. 2 Pet 2.22.
82. Cf. Ambrose, *Hexameron* 6.4.21, 217; *De bestiis* 3.1 (PL 177.83 B–C).

beast gets near the fleeing thief, the latter throws out another ball for his pursuer to see, and the memory of the previous deceit in no way prevents the mother's zeal. For the tigress, just as if she were preparing to milk her cub, plays with the useless image. And so she lost her cub, and took no revenge on the hunter.

(29) But now to apply this narrative aptly to ecclesiastical use. Who but the preacher is the hunter in this tale? And so the prophet says, "I shall send for many hunters, and they shall hunt them out from every mountain and hill."[83] And what should be meant here by the tigress, if not the devil? We steal the tigress's cub when we challenge a person who has turned his back on the world, the lair of the devil, to embrace a life of sanctity. Thus, when we are aware of this figurative tigress pursuing us with the wiles of its temptations, we place a glass ball in its path as we show him weak men in whom he can see his image. To show him his own followers is to hide our own from his baleful eyes. In those who are his, the ancient enemy sees his own image, finding in them, indeed, the depravity of his own wickedness. It was of these men of glass who reflect his image that Revelations speaks: "Whoever worships the beast and its image and receives its mark on his forehead and hand," and so on.[84] We should, therefore, strive to keep from the tigress the cubs we have taken so that, snatched away from the wild breasts of the cruel beast, they will not fail to be fed with the daily milk of God's word so that, God forbid, we may not be reproached in the words he spoke to the Pharisees: "Alas for you who travel over sea and land to win one convert; when you have won him you make him twice as fit for hell as you are yourselves."[85] Might it rather be said of us what truth said of himself to his Father: "I have not lost one of those whom you gave me."[86] Of this John also speaks: "Since he had always loved his own, now he would show the full extent of his love."[87]

83. Jer 16.16.
84. Rev 14.9.
85. Matt 23.15.
86. John 18.9.
87. John 13.1.

The Pelican[88]

(30) Just how much he was to love his own, the pelican demonstrates by its natural instinct. As we are told by those who have spent much effort in exploring the nature of animals, this bird loves its young as no other, but the ungrateful offspring do not in turn repay this love. As soon as the chicks begin to grow, they engage together in attacking both parents. The latter strike back, but since they are unable to be moderate in their discipline, they seem to turn the rod of correction into a sword, killing their young by excessive punishment. On the third day, as the mother sits on the dead chicks, it pecks at its side with its beak and opens it, from which the mother's blood drips down on the dead birds and suddenly brings them safely back to life. This event seems to be not so much a symbol as actual gospel history. For through Isaiah the creator of men clearly stated, "I have sons whom I reared and brought up, but they have rebelled against me."[89] He was also struck by his equally ill-behaved children, just as the pelican was by its young, as another text of Scripture says: "Wicked men without mercy rose up against me; they sought to kill me. They did not refrain from spitting in my face, and with their lances they wounded me."[90]

(31) Yet as the pelican killed its chicks with repeated blows, God afflicted his wayward people with the severe scourge of captivity and war, as the prophet said to him, "You struck them down, but they took no heed; you pierced them to the heart, but they refused to learn."[91] But the pelican repaid the evil of her ungrateful offspring with good, when they were restored to life by their mother's blood. Now God's wisdom, the mother of all the living, opened his side as he hung on the cross and thus, by shedding his precious blood restored to life those who had been slain. And just as the young of this bird, as I have said, show themselves to be insensible and ungrateful children,

---

88. Cf. Isidore, *Etymologies* 12.7.26; *Physiol. lat. Y* 6.106–7.
89. Isa 1.2.
90. A conflation of Ps 26.12; Hos 1.6; John 8.37; Deut 25.9; and Job 16.14.
91. Jer 5.3.

so the hoopoe, on the other hand, expresses the symbol of love. For while a discerning person can find in the first case what he should avoid, so too, in the other, Christian charity discovers what it might imitate.

The Hoopoe[92]

(32) When these birds, the hoopoe, are afflicted with old age so that they can neither fly nor see, their young, with loving compassion for their parents, pluck out their aging feathers, warm their eyes with their own wings, stroke them in every part, softly patting and rubbing them until new feathers appear all over the body. Thus through the solicitude of their tender offspring, they recover their sight and the ability to fly, which they had when they were young.

The Eagle and the Coot

(33) But why do we marvel at the hoopoe that shows such loving care for its elders, since we can observe the coot extending maternal care also to the young of other species? For, as the naturalists tell us, the eagle, which is the queen of birds, exposes its young to the bright rays of the sun,[93] lovingly holding the eaglets suspended by its talons at great altitude. Whichever of the young is able to retain its formidably sharp eyesight unimpaired is judged fit by the mother to propagate the splendor of this royal breed. But should one of them, blinded by the sun, turn its eyes away, it is abandoned as though it were lowborn and unworthy of such high honor and, as one disinherited and bastardized, is not retained among the brood. And the young bird, which because of poor sight lost the status of nobility,[94] would not later receive its inheritance along with the wellborn offspring. But a common bird, namely, the coot, which in Greek is called the *fene,* adopts such an eaglet, lovingly feeding it like the dove as if it were its own. In this way, the

---

92. Cf. Isidore, *Etymologies* 12.7.66; *Physiol. lat. Y* 10.109.
93. Cf. Isidore, *Etymologies* 12.7.10–11.
94. Cf. Ambrose, *Hexameron* 5.18.60–61, 185ff.

little one that the eagle cruelly deprived of its fraternal lot is adopted by the latter with truly maternal instinct to share equally with its own young.[95]

The Vulture[96]

(34) We may borrow weapons for our spiritual encounter from these birds: just as we were astounded by the human, even Christian, compassion found in the coot, so may we also be more greatly astonished by the prolific virginity of the vulture. It is said that, unlike other birds, the vulture does not indulge in intercourse, but conceives without any participation of the male. If human example does not incite us to be chaste and pure, the modesty of the vulture at least should compel us to practice virginity. Nor does any fear of a short life span worry these birds, born in this unique fashion, for their life goes on for 100 years.

Bees[97]

(35) Since bees, too, do not practice intercourse, they are also not corrupted in giving birth. And because male and female do not come together to conceive, in bringing forth their young, virginal integrity is not violated. They do not give birth in the womb but in the mouth, so to speak, and thus remain completely unsullied and untouched by any stain of corruption. With their mouth they gather their young from the leaves, and thus let go a swarm of young bees to succeed them.

The Mustela

(36) But why should we speak of this marvel of prolific virginity among the birds, when we might be no less surprised by conception and birth found also in lowly reptiles? The mustela,[98] as naturalists report, conceives in the mouth but gives

---

95. Cf. Ambrose, *Hexameron* 5.18.61, 186–87.
96. Cf. Ambrose, *Hexameron* 5.20.64, 188.
97. Cf. Ambrose, *Hexameron* 5.21.67, 189f.; *De bestiis* 3.38 (PL 177.98B).
98. Cf. *Physiol. lat.* Y 34.127–28; Isidore, *Etymologies* 12.3.3, rejects this opinion.

birth through the ear. If in unclean and trifling matters we should consider it proper to compare human affairs to these animals, we might perhaps appropriately liken them to certain brothers who do not fast enough, but are otherwise humble and obedient. By conceiving in the mouth we might understand food, as truth itself says: "Whatever goes in by the mouth passes into the stomach and so is discharged into the drain."[99] Giving birth through the ear signifies obedience, as it is written: "A people I never knew have become my subjects; as soon as they heard tell of me, they obeyed me."[100] Now there are some brothers who can hardly fast, either for reasons of health, or because of weakness of will, but are eager to carry out whatever obedience commands them. The healthier they become from eating, the greater are the burdens of obedience that they undertake. They conceive, as it were, by enjoying food that enters the mouth like seed, and they produce fruit of this food by the effort of obedience, as if they were giving birth through the ear. The seed that enters the mouth emerges through the ear since, if I might put it so, whatever is conceived by food bears fruit through obedience, and he who takes pleasure in eating his food, as if he were conceiving, is worn out by the labor of obedience, as if he were giving birth.

The Asp[101]

(37) But the asp, on the other hand, because it closes its ears to incantations, symbolizes the disobedience of one possessed of an obstinate disposition. For as the snake charmer chants at the mouth of the cave, enticing it to come out, the asp promptly places one ear firmly on the ground, and into the other stuffs its tail as an impenetrable obstacle. And so, since the voice of the wizard is unable to enter its ears, the asp remains fast in its lair. Many wicked men imitate the example of this serpent, for while on the one hand they love the things of this world and

---

99. Matt 15.17.   100. Ps 17.45.
101. Cf. Isidore, *Etymologies* 12.4.12; *Physiol. lat. Y* 34.128; *De bestiis* 2.18 (PL 177.66 C–D).

on the other place their trust in a long life yet to come, they close their ears, as it were, by using the earth and their tail to block out the sound of preaching.

The Ostrich[102]

(38) But while the asp is the figure of those who fix their sights on earthly and temporal goals, the ostrich symbolizes those who place their hopes in heavenly objectives. It is indeed a winged animal, but it is unable to fly. By nature it is also forgetful and has lost all powers of memory, and therefore never lays its eggs until it has first looked to the stars and is aware that the Pleiades have reached their zenith. It therefore lays its eggs in the summertime, about the month of June and, trusting in the heat of the sun, hides its eggs in soil or in the sand. Since the mother has forgotten its young and cannot at all remember where she laid her eggs, the heat of the sun together with the mild climate warm the eggs, and the young emerge just as if they had been hatched by a mother's care. And so, with the sun functioning as midwife, the chicks are born as if they had been kept warm by their mother sitting on them. Now this bird, aware of its own forgetfulness and being uncertain of the time of birth, first looks to the skies to be sure that good weather will supply for its own maternal stupidity. We too should not hesitate to beg for the warmth of God's Spirit from above, that the seed of good works may sprout forth from us and, while our own folly deadens the heart, the Spirit may strengthen it to bear life-giving offspring.

The Halcyon[103]

(39) There is also a bird called the halcyon or kingfisher, which is truly remarkable as it produces its young. While the ostrich, as we have said, looks for the summer heat as it bears its chicks, the latter chooses the seacoast in winter time. It lays its eggs in sand along the beach when the weather is cold, as

102. Cf. Isidore, *Etymologies* 12.7.20; *Physiol. lat. B* 27.48f.
103. Cf. Ambrose, Hexameron 5.13.40,172; *De bestiis* 3.29 (PL 177.95 B–C).

strong winds force the sea to run high and waves violently dash against the shore. How wonderful is this miracle of divine providence! For just as the halcyon lays its eggs on the sandy beach, no matter the force of the waves or the raging tempest, the sea suddenly lets up and all is peaceful. The waves subside and the wild winds grow quiet and, so long as this bird provides warmth for its eggs, the sea lies still and mild. For seven days it sits until the eggs are hatched, and for seven days it feeds its young after they are born. During this very short space of time the chicks mature and begin to fly, using their untested wings. During these fourteen days time passes serenely, the seas are calm, and the high winds abate. Here we have the exact symbol of the Church, which fondles and nourishes its offspring, using the number seven, because those whom it begets to faith by baptism through the sevenfold grace of the Spirit,[104] it leads to a wealth of good works by the gifts of the same Spirit. But I shall spend no more time explaining how this bird gives birth, so that by so doing I may not appear to my readers to engage in bad taste. So I proceed without further remark, that my readers may recognize this as a miracle, if only they are aware of the hidden mystery by applying a spiritual interpretation.

The Dove[105]

(40) It is no ordinary wonder that nature shows us regarding the dove. Now there is a tree in the regions of India[106] that in Greek is called a *peredixion*,[107] whose fruit is very sweet and tasty. Doves take great delight in the charm of this tree, where they are fed by its fruit and protected by its shade. But a fierce dragon is always after them, with open jaws trying with dreadful savagery to swallow them and get them down its cruel throat. But while the dove is terrified of the dragon, the dragon too is afraid of the tree I have described. It especially fears its

---

104. Cf. H. Meyer, *Die Zahlenallegorese im MA*, Münstersche Mittelalter-Schriften 25 (1975) 133ff.
105. Cf. *Physiol. lat. Y* 19.116–17.
106. The Latin edition (Reindel, *Briefe* 2 [1988] 484, line 8) prefers the reading *Iudeae*. I have chosen to follow MS C2.
107. DuCange, s.v. *pereclixion*, describes this tree as a kind of oak, called the turkey oak.

shade, so that if the shade is on the right side of the tree, the dragon, even though far away, rushes to the left side. But if it sees the shade on the left, it goes to the right. Now so long as the doves stay within the shadow of this tree, the cruel beast can do them no harm; if, however, it should find them outside its protection, it attacks at once with absolutely nothing to fear. Obviously, we who are taught to be as simple as doves should take refuge in the tree of sacred Scripture if we would wish to avoid the fierce madness of the dragon within us.

On the Nature of the Ibis[108]

(41) Now the ibis has the same significance as the dragon. It is a ghastly, unclean bird, fouled by the obscene filth of ill-smelling squalor. For it feeds on carrion and lives along the banks of the ocean, or of pools and rivers. In satisfying its hunger it searches for some foul or rotting dead body that has been thrown ashore by the water, for it fears going into the waves. Since it is unable to swim, it will never dare to enter the water, and is content to satisfy its ravenous appetite on anything unclean cast up by the wash. But who is signified by this bird that hunts along the banks of rivers to satisfy its hunger, if not the one of whom Peter says, "For our enemy the devil, like a roaring lion, prowls around looking for someone to devour"?[109] And what is meant by the dead fish rejected by the waters, if not the putrid and decaying hearts of reprobates who live according to the flesh? Of these the Apostle says that "they are lost souls, shipwrecked in matters of faith."[110] The sea indeed provides a home for living bodies, but casts off the dead; likewise, those who live for God can continue to stay in the rivers of Scripture. But anyone who is dead to faith or good works must be spewed forth as something corrupt and fetid from the body of Christ, which is the Church, as Scripture says: "Because you are lukewarm, I will spit you out of my mouth."[111]

108. Cf. *Physiol. lat.* Y 17.115.
109. 1 Pet 5.8; for the variant, cf. Sabatier 3.955.
110. 2 Tim 3.8.
111. Rev 3.16.

The Hyena[112]

(42) Now he who grows lukewarm about the position he had previously taken, from the man he was before, turns himself, as it were, into a woman. He is thus rightly compared to the hyena that changes at times from male to female, at times from female to male, and is therefore called an unclean animal that humans are forbidden to eat. In Jeremiah this is said of this animal: "This land of mine has become for me a hyena's lair."[113]

The Panther[114]

(43) Because of the diversity of its nature, the panther seems to be quite unlike the hyena. This animal of various colors, yet beautiful and mild because of its ingenuous qualities, is known to have only the dragon as its enemy. Shortly after the panther has eaten the various kinds of food it has hunted, it goes into its lair to sleep. Refreshed after three days of rest, it gets up and gives out a mighty roar. With this roar comes forth a scent of such sweet fragrance that it seems to surpass every other spice or aroma. When this odor reaches all the other animals in the forest, they at once run toward it and are delighted by its rich bouquet. Only the dragon upon hearing this sound is seized with great terror and hides in its underground cavern. Unable to bear the overwhelming odor, it becomes rigid with fright and lies there like dead, absolutely lifeless and deprived of all its strength. But the other animals, because they enjoy the pleasantly sweet smell, never leave off following the scented panther wherever he might go.

(44) What an abundance of flowery exposition this material might provide for one who is able to devote himself to sacred Scripture! But I will avail myself of this opportunity as expeditiously as possible, for I must move on to other things. Obviously, the word "panther" may be interpreted as 'something that catches all things,' which, I have no doubt, applies to him who said, "And I shall draw all men to myself, when I am lifted

---

112. Cf. *Physiol. lat. Y* 37.129.
113. Jer 12.8; for this variant, see Sabatier 2.667.
114. Cf. *Physiol. lat. Y* 29.124; *Physiol. lat. B* 23.40–43.

up from the earth."[115] It is multi-colored, and Christ is clothed with a variety of all nations. And since the panther is a beautiful animal, it does not differ from him of whom this was written: "You surpass all mankind in beauty, your lips are molded in grace."[116] And in the Song of Songs the bride says, "How beautiful you are, my dearest, O how beautiful!"[117] That it is a mild-mannered animal was also said of Christ by Isaiah: "Rejoice, rejoice, daughter of Zion, shout aloud, daughter of Jerusalem; for see, your king is coming to you, gentle and providing you with salvation."[118] And when he said, "I have food to eat of which you know nothing,"[119] it was just as if in his hunting he were satisfied with the firstfruits of the elect. He too slept in death for three days. Afterwards he gave forth a roar of apostolic preaching, and throughout the forests of all nations sent forth the fragrance of his spiritual scent. "Their sound goes out through all the earth, their words reach to the end of the world."[120] These men also say, "But thanks be to God, who continually leads us about, captives in Christ Jesus' triumphal procession, and uses us to reveal and spread abroad the fragrance of the knowledge of himself! We are indeed the incense offered by Christ to God, both for those who are on the way to salvation, and for those who are on the way to perdition: to the latter it is a deadly fume that kills, to the former a vital fragrance that brings life."[121] This then is the spiritual scent of grace, the fragrance of man's salvation given off by this heavenly panther that he might draw to himself the wild beasts of the forest, that is, the masses from all nations. But only the dragon rushes into the depths of its underground lair, since the ancient enemy that, according to John, is called devil and Satan[122] was cast out of heaven into the abyss, there to be bound with the chains of God's judgment.

---

115. John 12.32.
116. Ps 44.3.
117. Cant 1.15.
118. Despite Damian's attribution of this text to Isaiah, it seems rather to echo Zech 9.9 and Matt 21.5.
119. John 4.32.
120. Ps 18.5.
121. 2 Cor 2.14–16.
122. Cf. Rev 20.2–3.

The Salamander[123]

(45) The salamander also, even though it is very small, is said to possess a marvelous nature. If ever it is accidentally thrown into the fire, the blaze is suddenly extinguished as if drenched by a flood of water. And that it might become evident what is here symbolized, humble patience restrains a firebrand from exacting dire vengeance.

The Gazelle[124]

(46) The gazelle, which in Latin is called the wild goat, exhibits qualities that are not without application to our life. This animal that lives at great heights in the mountains not only has the power to see sharply, but also to distinguish wonderfully one object from another. Thus it can see men at a great distance in very remote regions, and can quickly tell whether they are hunters or travellers. We too, after deserting earthly things, if we could reach the heights of our mental power and be able to distinguish spirits to see whether they are from God, would be sustained by the divine grace of discernment. By it we can determine whether these spirits are directing us as travellers to our heavenly home, or whether, like hunters, they are driving us toward the hidden snares of their temptations, toward the treacherous nets they have placed in our way.

The Lynx[125]

(47) The lynx, too, possesses such incomparable sharpness of vision that it can see not only through any solid object, but even through stone walls. This can be demonstrated: if a lynx is on one side of the wall and meat is placed on the other, it at once begins to gape and drool as if nothing stood in between, and begs and pants until someone brings it to him. Now if a dumb animal has such acute sight, how much more deeply can

---

123. Cf. Isidore, *Etymologies* 12.4.36; *Physiol. lat. Y* 45.132.
124. Cf. Isidore, *Etymologies* 12.1.15; *Physiol. lat. Y* 21.119–20.
125. No reference to the lynx is found in the printed editions of the *Physiologus*. But see Ovid, *Metamorphoses* 5.660 and Boethius, *Philosophiae consolatio* 3.8.10, ed. L. Bieler, CC 94 (1957) 48.

almighty God peer into the secrets of the human heart? "For the word of God is alive and active. It cuts more keenly than any two-edged sword, piercing as far as the place where life and spirit, joints and marrow, divide. It sifts the purposes and thoughts of the heart. There is nothing in creation that can hide from him, everything lies naked and exposed to his eyes."[126]

On the Nature of Serpents[127]

(48) There are also certain indications of natural astuteness in serpents that provide useful examples for our lives. When the snake reaches old age and becomes blind, it fasts for a period of forty days and forty nights, and it grows thin by this constant abstinence. The more its body shrivels and becomes lean and dry, the looser is its scaly skin. As it loses weight, its old skin seems to expand. Then it searches for either an opening in the hard earth or for a cleft in the rocks and, supporting itself against the sides, it passes through this narrow area, thus sloughing off its skin together with its advanced age. And so it again becomes young and its strength and vision return.

(49) We too, if at times we lose our youthful fervor for sanctity and grow blind and feeble because of a dissolute life, must follow the narrow path of penance, so that, by sloughing off the old skin of bodily concupiscence, we may recover the youth of the inner man we once enjoyed.

(50) The serpent has yet another quality, namely, that when it wants to drink, it first ejects its poison. After it has drunk water enough, it returns to the place where it had vomited and consumes what it had spit out. A certain priest told the story that before his very eyes a snake had vomited against a rock and then quickly crawled to a spring to drink. While it was drinking, the priest turned over the rock. When the snake returned to the rock and could not find the poison it wanted to recover, it searched everywhere and suddenly died. When we too wish to drink from the spring of God's word, we must spit

126. Heb 4.12–13.
127. Cf. *Physiol. lat. Y* 13.110–12.

up all the poison of our vices and sins by making a good confession. But God forbid that we should return to our vomit, since we are taught not to crawl along the ground like serpents, but to hurry on our way to join the angels.[128]

(51) This further quality is said to be native to the serpent, and something quite noble: it flees from a naked man but will attempt to bite one who is clothed, as if, like a brave warrior, it will attack an armed man but fears one who is unarmed. Do you wish to lose all fear of the devil? Then put off your clothes of earthly concern. But if you are so clothed, beware of the serpent that circles about you. Do you wish, like the serpent, to grow young again and replace the old age of a tired soul with the beauty you had in your youth? Then fast like the serpent for a period of forty days, that is, abstain during your whole life from carnal desires. Now this very serpent demonstrates what power there is in fasting, for as soon as it tastes the spittle of a person who is fasting, it dies on the spot.[129] Therefore, servant of God, you should not be irked by fasting, so that you may be the death of him who, seeing you stuffed with food, tries to swallow you alive. The serpent, moreover, will expose its whole body to the blows of one who strikes at it, hiding only its head. You also, when you are forced to suffer persecution, treasure Christ in the recesses of your mind, but if necessary, hand over your body to those who attack you.

(52) There is also thought to be another species of snake that, if it bites a man, turns his whole body into poison. It is also reported that there is a certain type of serpent whose poison is so pungent that, if a bird tries to fly over these snakes, it will suddenly fall dead to the ground because of their foul-smelling breath.[130] This species is also naturally endowed with this manner of intercourse or of giving birth:[131] the male thrusts its head into the mouth of the female. Impatient in her lovemaking, she bites off the head and swallows it. From the eyes in this head two young snakes are produced, which at the time of

128. Cf. Col 3.2.
129. This interesting legend is not found in any version of the *Physiol. lat.*; but see *De bestiis* 3.53 (PL 177.103B).
130. Cf. Isidore, *Etymologies* 12.4.6; *De bestiis* 3.41 (PL 177.100 C–D).
131. Cf. Isidore, *Etymologies* 4.10–11; *Physiol. lat. Y* 12.110.

birth gnaw through both sides of the mother and thus emerge from each side, simultaneously killing and being born. And so they were parricides before they were offspring, and therefore never more than two can be found that are born of this species.

(53) According to reports, there is also another kind of snake that is called the darter,[132] which suddenly flies at a man and pierces him. It passes right through as if there were no obstacle in its way. And thus, the loving creator gave various powers and adroitness to dumb animals, so as to instruct human beings that also from our investigation of animal shrewdness we should not disdain imitating their example in our own actions.

The Wild Ass[133]

(54) Now who taught the wild ass that when we have reached the vertical line of the equinox in the month of March, it brays twelve times during the twelve hours of the day and of the night, and like a natural clock counts off the hours? It brays once each hour, day and night, and thus tells us that we have arrived at the time when day and night are equal.

The Elephant[134]

(55) Who instructed the elephant to love perpetual chastity? When forced by its natural instinct to copulate, it turns its head away as if it were unwilling and disgusted, and once the female has conceived, it never again has intercourse. Since she is terrified by the dragon which tries to kill her, she bears her young in the water which reaches up to her chest. For if she gave birth away from the water, the dragon would suddenly attack the young, hoping to devour them.

The Unicorn[135]

(56) Who gave the unicorn the natural quality that helps it resist capture by men, but endows it with a kind of humility that allows it to be easily overcome? For it is never taken by hunters unless it first lies in the lap of a virgin.

---

132. Cf. Isidore, *Etymologies* 12.4.29; *De bestiis* 3.46 (PL 177.101C).
133. Cf. *Physiol. lat.* Y 11.109.
134. Cf. Pliny, *Naturalis historia* 8.5.12; *Physiol. lat.* Y 20.117–19.
135. Cf. *Physiol. lat.* Y 35.128; Jürgen W. Einhorn, *Spiritalis unicornis* . . . , Münstersche Mittelalter-Schriften 13 (1976) 53ff.

The Eagle[136]

(57) Who gave the eagle this sort of healing power that, when it grows old, as its wings begin to grow heavy and its eyes become blind, it searches for a fountain of water? When it is near the spring, it flies up to the region of the sun, and poised there in the pure reaches of the air, it sets fire to its wings in the sun's intense heat and completely burns out the blindness from its eyes. It then plunges three times into the water and thus restores the strength of its wings and the sharpness of its vision to a state surpassing anything it enjoyed when it was young.

The Ant[137]

(58) Who, I ask, taught the ant to thresh in such a way that it can distinguish between the kernels of grain, ignoring those of inferior quality and selecting the more elegant product? It carefully inspects a pile of grain and rejects the barley, disregarding it as fodder for horses. But where it finds wheat, the ant gladly gathers it. This insect can also detect certain indicators of good weather. When it finds that its underground store rooms are becoming moist, it carries out on its back the grain that was stored for food, and thus averting damage for its household, dries the kernels in the heat of the sun. And as if this were not enough, it cuts each grain in two with its mouth, so that they will not grow damp during the winter rains and, contrary to expectations, begin to germinate.

The Viper[138]

(59) Who, moreover, instructed the viper, that when urged to have intercourse it immediately crawls to the seashore and there copulates with the marine *murena*? When the viper indicates its presence by its hissing, the *murena* at once approaches, and the qualities of another strain are bred into the offspring of this venomous beast.

---

136. Cf. *Physiol. lat. Y* 8.107–8.
137. Cf. Isidore, *Etymologies* 12.3.9; *Physiol. lat. Y* 14.112–13.
138. Cf. Isidore, *Etymologies* 12.6.43; *De bestiis* 3.55 (PL 177.108C).

The Hawk[139]

(60) Who prescribed regulations for hawks that they never engage in plunder in a wide area around their nesting place? And while everywhere else they live by war, a general peace is maintained where as victors they bring back their spoil. But when they become aware that their young have grown feathers and are able to fly, they force them from the nest with feet and beak and drive them far from their habitat, as if they were now freed from all legal restraint. This is done so that even as young birds they are already prepared to hunt; nor do they spend their time in inactivity, hoping to be fed by their parents, but are accustomed from the very first moment of flight to the repeated violence that accompanies their plundering.

The Bear[140]

(61) Where, again, did the bear learn to lick its cubs, which are born as shapeless creatures, and fashion the various parts of their bodies with its tongue, forming them into the likeness of their natural species like the potter? What is more, who taught it the art of medicine, who told it about the power of herbs and various curing poultices? For if it is injured by savage blows, or even pierced so as to suffer gaping wounds, it applies herbs called mullein, known in Greek as *flomus*. And once these have touched the sore spot, all pain disappears and the bear recovers its former good health.

The Serpent[141]

(62) I forgot to mention above that if the serpent becomes blind, its previous sight is restored by eating fennel. So as soon as it notices that its eyes are becoming clouded, it at once searches for this remedy, and its hope for good results is not frustrated.

---

139. Cf. Ambrose, *Hexameron* 5.18.58,185 and 5.14.46–47,176; Isidore, *Etymologies* 12.7.56.
140. Cf. *De bestiis* 3.6 (PL 177.85 A–B); Ambrose, *Hexameron* 7.4.18–19,214.
141. Pliny, *Naturalis historia* 8.41.99; *De bestiis* 3.52 (PL 177.103A).

The Turtle[142]

(63) When the turtle has eaten the flesh of a serpent and is aware that its poison is spreading through its entrails, it wastes no time in using origanum as a remedy.

On Various Animal Medicines

(64) When the fox is sick and senses that death is at hand, it treats itself with resin secreted by the pine tree, and by this remedy its life is prolonged.[143] Indeed, animals that use medicines obtained from sources outside themselves show that within their bodies also they have the means of recovering health.[144] For from the flesh of the serpent, which is called the *tyrus*, we can produce not only theriaca, but also various other medical remedies.[145] Pieces of ivory are used in various cures. The bile of a hyena restores sight to the eyes, and its dung is likewise known to cure the wounds of dogs. Moreover, every sick animal in the wild that drinks the blood of a dog is restored to good health. Galen[146] also describes the many uses of human excrement in preparing medicine. How the ostrich, how frogs, chameleons, cranes and storks, the bile of an eagle, the blood of a hawk, and the dung and flesh of a swallow provide medicine for certain diseases, this is for him who would discuss bodily cures to explain.[147]

(65) Naturalists tell us that if the skin of a snake, which it has just sloughed off, is cooked in boiling oil, it works wonders in treating earache. To those who are unaware, bugs seem to be useless. But if a leech takes one in its mouth, when it gets a whiff of its fumes, the bug is at once spit out. Likewise, difficulty in urinating is eased by the application of the bug. Moreover, physicians are not unaware of the medicinal properties contained in the fat of pigs, geese, chickens, and pheasants.

---

142. Pliny, *Naturalis historia* 8.41.98; *De bestiis* 3.52 (PL 177.103B).
143. Papias, *Vocabularium latinum* 379.
144. Cf. Jerome, *Adversus Iovinianum* 2.6 (PL 23.292A).
145. Cf. Isidore, *Etymologies* 4.9.8.
146. Cf. Jerome, *Adversus Iovinianum* 2.6 (PL 23.292 A–B).
147. Cf. Jerome, *Adversus Iovinianum* 2.6 (PL 23.292 A–B).

The dung of the peacock is known to lessen the inflammation of gout.[148] And if a sick lion devours a monkey, it at once gets well. If a leopard tastes the blood of a wild goat, it avoids becoming ill. A sick bear eats ants,[149] while a sick deer hunts for tender olive branches.[150]

(66) But why did the almighty creator of all things endow animals with these qualities, if not to provide human life with a variety of benefits? He did this so that, as creatures who are subject to man support one another, all things might be found useful for man who is superior to all animals. And while man marvels at the goodness of his maker in all his undertakings, he should not be attached to created things, but yearn for the sight of his creator. If one makes the effort and is expert in investigating all these qualities in animals, he will find it useful to apply them as examples for human behavior. Thus, even he who is unlettered might learn from the nature of animals how man should live. For as the Apostle says, "Are not oxen God's concern?"[151] But when man observes something significant in dumb animals, no matter what it might be, he is well advised to apply it to his own use.

The Wolf[152]

(67) How is it that if a wolf is prevented from seeing you, he is unable to escape; but if he sees you first, you will surely stand there speechless? And what is still more wonderful, if you remain silent and take off your coat, you at once recover your speech. But if the wolf should suddenly attack you, pick up a rock and he will promptly run away. What does this rock of yours mean if not Christ?[153] If indeed, as is proper, you take this rock in hand, you will put to flight the wolf of spiritual iniquity that pursues you. And that I may hurry on to other things, take off your coat by confessing your sins, so that you

---

148. Cf. Jerome, *Adversus Iovinianum* 2.6 (PL 23.292 A–B).
149. Cf. Ambrose, *Hexameron* 6.4.26,222.
150. Cf. Ambrose, *Hexameron* 6.4.24,222.
151. 1 Cor 9.9.
152. Cf. *De bestiis* 2.20 (PL 177.67B–68D).
153. Cf. 1 Cor 10.4.

will not be speechless but eloquent, possessed of the freedom to preach the word of God, as Scripture observes: "First set forth your sins," it says, "that you might be justified."[154]

The Sheep[155]

(68) Who, I ask, taught the sheep to fear the scarcity of winter, so that in the fall it ravenously grazes as if it can never get enough? For then, as is its custom, it greedily crops its food, not aware that grass will later not be there and, while it can, stuffs itself as if it were preparing for future scarcity, hoarding its food before the grass dies off. Nor is this without good reason that the elephant, such a terror to bulls, is terrified by a mouse.[156] The lion, the king of beasts, is afraid of the tiny scorpion,[157] for the lion can be killed by a serpent's venom and by the sting of a scorpion. Who will not marvel that the lion, which shakes hairy bulls by the neck and, puffing out its chest, proudly bears its terrible fangs at other wild animals, should fear the sting of a poor little scorpion? Who also will consider it unworthy of our attention that the elephant that can carry defensive turrets filled with armed men should go down from the blow of a single tree? For though it will not fall under the weight of thirty-two or more armed men, it will be brought down by one falling tree against which it often leans or rubs its sides, or relaxes when taking its rest. Some will set snares for him because of his ivory, so that they cut through the tree against which the elephant often rests, severing it on the other side just about to the middle, and thus the tree will fall under the weight of his enormous body.[158]

(69) My brothers, while I have been busy enumerating the qualities of certain animals for your edification, I must not forget that I have undertaken to write a letter and not a book. For this reason I must restrain my freedom of style and curb my will, so that charity may so serve edification that I do not breach the moderation that epistolary brevity dictates.

---

154. Isa 43.26; see Sabatier 2.589.
155. Cf. *De bestiis* 3.13 (PL 177.88f.).
156. Cf. Ambrose, *Hexameron* 6.6.37,228; *De bestiis* 2.26 (PL 177.73C).
157. Cf. Ambrose, *Hexameron* 6.6.37,228; *De bestiis* 2.26 (PL 177.73C).
158. Pliny, *Naturalis historia* 8.8.24; *Physiol. lat.* Y 20.117ff.

(70) And so, my dear friends, your monastery is a kind of paradise in which the omnipotent creator, while establishing various human customs, created as it were three types of animal, those that live on land, in the sea, and in the air. Here, then, we find the ancient, mystically significant Ark, containing all species of animal. And finally, it is the device that Peter saw, slung by the four corners and lowered to the ground, in which there were all sorts of quadrupeds, land serpents, and birds of the sky. But as it was then said, "Up, Peter, kill and eat,"[159] we believe through Christ's mercy that you, who are these animals, have been cut away from this world by the sword of God's word, and have been assumed into the body of your redeemer by the ardor of perfect love.

(71) But you must be very careful that, since you are not yet safely ashore but still at work fighting the wind and the waves, you do not allow the breeze of a boastful spirit to blow from your mouth and extinguish the flames of this fire. For a breath will sometimes bring forth flames, while on occasion it will snuff them out. For, if I might put it so, a man seems to blow when preaching the mysteries of sacred doctrine, and he also blows when engaged in idle conversation. But since by uplifting words the heart of the hearer is enkindled with the love of God, it so happens that by idle words it grows cold and turns away from heavenly desires. But speaking so of this breath might seem ridiculous, were it not referred to approvingly in the pages of sacred Scripture. So listen to what the Lord says of this salutary breath, using the words of Isaiah: "I will not be always accusing, I will not continually nurse my wrath. For a breath will go forth from my mouth, and I will make a creature that breathes."[160] Listen to what Paul says in other words of the evil breath: "Avoid empty and worldly chatter; those who indulge in it will stray further and further into godless courses, and their teaching will spread like cancer."[161] Listen further to God breathing through Isaiah: "It was I who created the smith to blow the coals into flame and forge weapons, each for its

---

159. Acts 10.13; cf. Sabatier 3.534.
160. Isa 57.16.
161. 2 Tim 2.16–17.

purpose."[162] And then he spoke of useless weapons, which by idle words are fashioned for our undoing: "And I have created the destroyer to lay waste; but now no weapon made to harm you shall prevail."[163] But from what immediately follows we learn the meaning of this weapon that the destroyer smashes: "You shall rebut every charge brought against you."[164] The meaning of these words of Isaiah: "You shall rebut every charge brought against you," is the same as what Truth itself stated in the gospel: "There is not a thoughtless word that comes from men's lips but they will have to account for it on the day of judgment."[165]

(72) Let me say, my brothers, that hardly anything else that goes on in the monastery causes me more worry about the terrible judgment of God that awaits the monks. For with every breath they take, their tongue keeps on going like a torrent rushing down rutted slopes and, when the bell sounds, it is as if someone suddenly hit them over the head. But here I am speaking only of some and not, God forbid, of all. Now the *Rule* requires that from Easter to the first of October they shall go to work from seven to ten o'clock, doing what is to be done; but from ten o'clock to about twelve they shall spend their time reading.[166] But there are some who disregard working and reading during these hours, and waste their time in conversation. While they should have been working and reading, they were busy with idle chatter. Now the holy man who established the *Rule* would never change these times unless there were a need to continue working, nor would he have said ten o'clock instead of nine o'clock unless he had seen that it was necessary to work.

(73) Such men, indeed, are unjust workers who use "the hands of their tongue" in idle conversation. Who will say that the tongue does not have a hand, since Scripture states that "life and death reside in the hand of the tongue"?[167] And how wrong it is that a man most frequently offends against a provident God by using the very gift by which man is placed over

---

162. Isa 54.16.
163. Isa 54.17.
164. Isa 54.17.
165. Matt 12.36.
166. *Benedicti regula* 48.3 and 4.126.
167. Prov 18.21.

all other creatures. And since man is in command over all nature, controlling it by his laws, what a shameful thing it is that he cannot subdue that little piece of flesh he has in his mouth. And so James says, "Beasts and birds of every kind, and creatures that crawl on the ground can be subdued and have been subdued by mankind; but no man can subdue the tongue."[168] Indeed, no teacher can curb the tongue of one who is unwilling to be restrained, otherwise he would urge and insist, and whatever he wishes would undoubtedly be carried out. Moreover, God's voice, speaking to Noah, bears witness that all creatures obey man's command when he says, "The fear and dread of you shall fall upon all wild animals on earth, on all birds of heaven, and all fish in the sea; they are given into your hands."[169]

(74) Now that we might more readily stand in awe at how serpents also can be tamed by man, Pliny reports[170] that an enormous viper was trained by a certain householder in Egypt, so that daily it used to leave its cave and come to eat at his table. The Count Marcellinus also writes of a tame tiger sent from India to the emperor Anastasius.[171] And so the Apostle aptly gives this warning: "All sorts of wild beasts are found in the tongue."[172] There, indeed, we find the mobility of birds, the ferocity of beasts, and the poisonous deceit of serpents.[173] They are birds who lift their voice to heaven and whose every word is false, mobile as the birds. Those who "sharpen their tongues like swords"[174] are ferocious beasts. Finally, they are serpents, of whom it is said that "the venom of vipers is upon their lips."[175] And so, where people engage in useless and foolish trifles as if they were at a banquet engaged in idle chatter, it does not sound like human speech to someone hearing this babble, but rather like a noisy gathering of animals. This observer is he of whom it is said in the Song of Songs, "My beloved

---

168. Jas 3.7–8. 169. Gen 9.2.
170. Cf. Pliny, *Naturalis historia* 8.22.61.
171. Marcellinus Comes, *Chronicon*, ed. Th. Mommsen, MGH Auct.ant. 11 (1894) 94.
172. Undoubtedly a play on words in Jas 3.5–8.
173. Cf. Ps 72.9, 143.8. 174. Ps 63.4.
175. Ps 13.3.

is peeping in at the window, glancing through the lattice."[176] And with the prophet he states, "I have listened to them and heard: not one of them said anything worthwhile."[177]

(75) So that my discussion may not digress from the topic at hand, let me continue with examples of the vices of human speech compared with those of dumb animals. The hydra never enters the mouth of its enemy except when it finds the crocodile yawning. For if the latter keeps its mouth shut, it has no fear of attack. When the antelope cries out, it unwittingly occasions its own death at the hunter's sword. But so long as it remains quiet, it makes sport of the hunter's efforts because of its fabulous speed. And I might also mention that what the crab does to the oyster, the devil frequently achieves with a monk.

The Crab and the Oyster[178]

(76) Now since the crab loves to feed on oysters and considers their meat a delicacy, it is worth hearing about the tricks it plays on them. Even though the crab is eager to eat them, it is acutely aware of the danger. The hunt is difficult, and it is also perilous. It is difficult, because the edible meat is enclosed by most powerful shells; dangerous, since if the crab reaches in with its claws, the double shell suddenly closes and the crab is unable to get away. So what will the crab do to get what it is after? How can it satisfy its urge without turning to exquisite types of fraud? Hence it carefully watches until the oyster finds a spot completely sheltered from the wind, where it can open its shells to the rays of the sun. Then the attacker stealthily inserts a small stone that keeps the oyster from closing its valves. Thus, finding the shells apart, the crab safely inserts its claws and snatches the body of the oyster that lies within.

(77) To what may we more aptly compare the oyster than to the monk? For the latter is alive so long as he is shrouded in a mantle of silence, but he perishes when he opens himself to unbridled speech. Like the oyster, if he does not open his

---

176. Cant 2.9. 177. Jer 8.6.
178. Cf. Ambrose, *Hexameron* 5.8.21–23, 156–57.

mouth, he maintains the health of his soul. But let him give rein to his tongue, and all life signs disappear. What is signified by the small stone inserted into the oyster so that it cannot close its valves, if not the habitual obduracy by which one hardens his attitude toward penance? For this pebble of bad habit is the obstruction, as it were, that keeps one who wastes his time in idle chatter from shutting himself off from his purposeless ways. And what is meant by the symbol of the crab, which naturally walks backward, but the apostate spirit, which never ceases to relapse into its former sins when it has abandoned its creator? Thus the word "devil" has the meaning of 'flowing downward.'[179] For, as it was said of the sacred animals, that their feet were straight,[180] so with the devil and his followers, the feet are always turned backward.

The Monkey

(78) And, since we have been talking about feet, the diabolically clever trapper often ensnares the soul just as the hunter did the monkey.[181] What follows, I have not seen in writing, but heard from the lips of the hunter himself. Whoever wants to catch a live monkey must first sew a pair of red shoes with soles made of lead. When the hunter sees the monkey observing him some distance away, he puts the shoes on his feet, tying them with laces that are also red, and thus like a teacher shows the monkey what it should do. After this, the wily hunter covertly takes off the shoes, leaves them there, and hides nearby. Thinking that the hunter has gone, the monkey imitates what it had seen the man doing, puts the abandoned shoes on its feet, and ties them good and tight. But then the hunter suddenly leaps from his hiding place and captures his student, caught in his own snare.

(79) Thus the evil spirit often teaches his proxy, that is, any wicked and depraved individual, to catch innocent men in the toils of sin, so that, like his leader and teacher, he might lure

---

179. Jerome, *Nom.hebr.* 80.16 (CC 72.160).
180. Cf. Ezek 1.7.
181. Cf. Pliny, *Naturalis historia* 8.80.215.

them to embrace the evil that he holds before their eyes. And by imitating this bad example, the man is caught in the devil's trap.

The Maimo

(80) Now what follows is something I heard from the lord Pope Alexander[182] less than a month ago. He told me that recently Count William,[183] who lives in the district of Liguria, had a male monkey, called a *maimo* in the vernacular. He and his wife, a completely lewd and wanton woman, used to play in shameless fashion with him. I myself have met his two sons whom this vile woman, who deserves a beating, had borne of a certain bishop whose name I will omit, because I do not enjoy defaming anyone. She often used to play with the lecherous animal, taking it in her arms and fondling it, and the monkey in the meantime gave signs of being aroused and tried with obvious effort to come close to her nude body. Her chambermaid said to her, "Why don't you let him have his way so we can see what he is after?" What more should I say! She submitted to the animal, and, what a shameful thing to report, it mated with the woman. This thing became habitual, and she frequently repeated the unheard of crime.

(81) One day when the count was in bed with his wife, aroused by jealousy the *maimo* suddenly jumped on both of them, tore at the man with his arms and sharp claws as if he were his rival, got him by the teeth and wounded him beyond all recovery. And so the count died. Thus as the innocent man was faithful to his wife and fed his animal at his own expense, he suspected no evil from either of them because he showed them only kindness. But what a heinous crime! The wife shamefully violated his marriage right, and the beast sank his teeth in his master's throat.

---

182. On Damian's close relationship with Pope Alexander II, see Schmidt, "Alexander II" 179ff.
183. Cf. Mittarelli-Costadoni, *Annales Camaldulenses* 2.276f.

The Boy Who Looked Like a Maimo

(82) It was also reported to the same pope while I was with him that a certain boy, who seemed big for his age, even though, as it was said, he was already twenty years old, was still completely unable to speak. Besides, he had the appearance of a *maimo*, and that was also what they called him. And so the unfortunate suspicion arose that something like a monster, I will not say a wild animal, was being brought up in its father's house.

The Whale[184]

(83) But while I was speaking of that woman's shameful infidelity, I was reminded of the whale that lives in the ocean. Its enormous body is covered with sand and, when it raises its back above the waves, it extends from the water like an island. Thinking it to be an island, sailors without another thought row in its direction, drive stakes into it, moor their ship, and start a fire. But as soon as the beast feels the heat, it suddenly plunges into the deep and swallows up both ship and seamen in a fatal shipwreck.

(84) One of my monks, named Gerard, reported that he saw a mighty whale captured on the sea coast of Normandy. It was so large that it took fourteen pack animals, fully laden, to carry the meat from its tongue. But to get back to what I was saying. Why should we marvel at a sailor not being able to trust a whale, since the husband found that his own wife was not faithful? Why should we wonder at a dumb animal pretending to be an island and diving into the depths of the sea, when a woman in violating her marriage vows gave herself to the embraces of an animal? For what is there that we can truly call our own in this world and not be suspicious about in changing times?

Of the Boy Drowned by the Conger Eel

(85) Indeed, what I now relate happened in our own day. There was a certain fisherman who placed his son in the prow of his boat and, rowing out into deep water, caught a great

---

184. Cf. *Physiol. lat. Y* 30.125.

conger eel. Happy with his catch, he heaved it into the boat so that its head was toward the boy who sat at the far end of the boat. But while the fisherman, busy with his rowing, was turning about to go home and, in high spirits over his good luck, had no worry in the world, the boy was terrified at the fish and began to cry out: "Look at the way the beast is eyeing me, it wants to swallow me!" But the father replied jokingly, "Don't worry," he said, "you will devour him, and not he you." But when the boy repeated what he had said, and his father thought he was talking nonsense, the fish suddenly leapt into the air, violently attacked the boy, and then, quickly taking hold of him, it sprang into the water with its prey, and neither was seen again.

Conclusion

(86) So there you have it, my brothers. What in the world is so securely our own that we can safely trust it? Which of our possessions is so unassailable that we must not think of it as a wheel of fortune? Solomon teaches us to beware of this wheel and always be reminded of our creator. For when he said, "Remember your creator in the days of your youth, before the time of trouble comes,"[185] he added quickly thereafter, "before the wheel is broken at the well, before the dust returns to the earth from which it sprang."[186] So never put your trust in any risky possessions or, like the unwary seamen, row toward the sands of a specious island. We should go to Christ, the sailor's surest harbor, the safest and most quiet refuge for those delivered from the dangers of the sea. Let the voice of those endowed with speech call out to him alone who disposes and decrees the natural qualities of dumb animals, that in all his creatures we may proclaim only the power and majesty of the creator.

185. Eccl 12.1.   186. Eccl 12.6–7.

LETTER 87

Peter Damian to Oldericus, bishop of Fermo. Written in his cell at Fonte Avellana, this letter reflects on the evil days brought on by the schismatic crisis caused by Cadalus, bishop of Parma, the antipope Honorius II. These bad times remind him that the world, in its corruption, is nearing its end. But he raises this question: In view of the current depredation of ecclesiastical property, are bishops and abbots permitted to take up arms in defense of their temporalities? Damian thinks not, claiming only the spiritual sword for the *sacerdotium,* and he takes occasion to criticize the late Pope Leo IX for having fought Robert Guiscard. The example of an abbot in Gaul, arraying his monks armed only with cowls about their heads against his foe, was more to his liking, especially since, by the grace of God, the tactic was successful.

(Early months of 1062)[1]

O SIR OLDERICUS, the bishop of Fermo,[2] the monk Peter the sinner sends his inexhaustible love and devotion.

(2) My long stay here is proof of the heartfelt eagerness with which I received the charming letter sent by your holiness. Indeed, I keep it always with me in my cell, I often converse with it, and in it I clearly behold the very likeness of your face and the image of your inner self. Yet there is something in it that disturbs me, for I find myself not so much honored as burdened by the praise of such an esteemed man as you. In this, truly, my misfortune is all the more deplorable: not only are my sins an impediment to me, but also, unfortunately, it seems to me that holy men are at fault. God forbid that I should say that such a man is lying by praising me so but, since you are human, it is possible that you are deceived by friendship. For,

---

1. The dating follows Lucchesi, *Vita* no. 164.
2. On Oldericus, bishop of Fermo 1057–1074, see Schwartz, *Bistümer* 223f. See also Prete, *S. Pier Damiani* 125; Prete, "Fermo," DHGE 16 (1967) 1084–91, esp. 1087; Lucchesi, *Vita* no. 39.

since lying is to say the opposite of what one thinks, it sometimes happens that something is subjectively true, but objectively is a lie. I admit to my lord that it has often occurred to me that when someone praises me to my face, he is undoubtedly accusing me of desiring such flattery. As my conscience assails me, I at once say, "Since this person wishes to speak with me, I should respect his desire and be friendly; he would never address me with such smooth and captivating words if he did not hope to please me by the favor of his esteem." So, when someone praises me, I am disturbed, and while seeming to be honored, I begin to blush. His very benevolence rebukes me, because he who appears to praise me thinks that I am seeking his praise.

(3) To this I may add that if any human mind, supported by sound advice, examines itself carefully and in great detail, it can scarcely find within itself anything for which it can justly expect to be commended. For of what is our mortal estate aware, in all things so constrained and restricted, for which someone might congratulate it? Indeed, who knows what happened in eternity before God created the world? But since he is ignorant of what happened before the world began, perhaps he knows what will take place after it comes to an end. For example, will the stars continue to be useful in attending to its orbit, or, on the contrary, will other elements take the place of those things which now exist? And thus, each of the seraphim, which the prophet Isaiah saw attending the Lord, were said to have six wings: "One pair covered his face and one pair his feet, and one pair was spread in flight."[3] It was not their face and feet that were covered, but God's. And what should we understand by God's face, if not the beginning of the world? What by his feet, if not the world's end? And so, the seraphim had many wings that were used for covers but few to fly; from God's exalted works only a minimal number have been allowed to come to our attention, the most by far are kept hidden in the treasury of his heavenly secrets. Isaiah, too, agrees that we are

---

3. Isa 6.2. Damian's variant from the Vulgate is found also in Jerome, *Epistula* 18A, c. 6, 1.80. The interpretation of "God's face" as the beginning of the world is also in Jerome, *Epistula* 18A, c. 7, 1.82f.

totally ignorant of what went on before the world began, and of what will happen after the world comes to an end: "Tell me the meaning of past events," he said, "and what will happen hereafter, and I will say that you are gods."[4] Of that which happens in between, however, we know a few things that have been disclosed to us by the evidence of Scripture. Yet even in these, how little we know. For even Solomon, who was a bit shrewder than other men, was not ashamed to admit: "There are upright and wise men, and all their doings are under God's control, yet no man knows whether he is deserving of love or hatred, since all things in the future remain uncertain."[5] Here we should note that, although he is speaking of upright and wise men who should be keenly aware of hidden things, he states that they too are ignorant of the future.

(4) Now since you have praised me, not only for my wisdom but also for the apparent holiness of my life—not that you in your holy prudence are convinced of this, but perhaps for the purpose of sharply inciting me to engage in spiritual combat—how can I be sure even here in giving my unqualified consent? Indeed, one must render an account for every idle word; just for calling a man a fool, one feels the threat of punishment in hell[6] since not a letter, not a stroke will disappear from God's Law;[7] or merely looking on a woman with a lustful eye makes one liable for the crime of adultery.[8]

(5) Whoever pays close attention to these and similar matters, venerable father, can indeed count on God's mercy. But I know not whether he can sleep with the assurance that he has amassed any merits at all, especially since everywhere the world is in uproar, everywhere, like the open sea, it throws up its angry waves. It heaps such burdens on us religious superiors, whoever we might be, that for the most part it compels us to engage in worldly affairs rather than in the service of God or in aspiring toward cleanness of heart. Surely the evil spirit, as is typical of him, now wildly dashes the human race onto all

---

4. Isa 41.22–23; for variant from the Vulgate, cf. Sabatier 2.584, where Damian's citation is again found in Jerome, *Epistula* 18A, c. 7.
5. Eccl 9.102.
6. Cf. Matt 5.22.
7. Cf. Matt 5.18.
8. Cf. Matt 5.28.

the rocks of vice, and savagely throws all into confusion by the malice of his hatred and jealousy. Daily there are many wars being waged, armed bands are rushing forth to battle, hostile attacks occur, armies are dying by the sword rather than ending their days in an illness that besets the body as they peacefully rest in their beds; indeed, this world seems almost to gratify the brave. For just as when the wind picks up, lightly disturbing the sea, causing the heat to be excessive near the shore, so now at the end of the world,[9] as though we were near the sea coast with the waves of discord and dissension crashing about us, the hearts of men are disturbed and dashed to bits as by the pounding of wave after wave. For the insatiable murderer searches everywhere, wanders through all the places of the world as if it were a single field, lest anything unproductive escape his planting the fires of discontent.

(6) Thus it is that with danger everywhere threatening the state of the Church, the *sacerdotium* and the *imperium* recoil from one another and, to the prejudice of almighty God, now that one pope is seated on the apostolic throne, another is considered to have been elected by the lands to the north.[10] But it was he undoubtedly who improperly added another pope to the pope we already have who first declined the name of almighty God in the plural: "You will be like gods, knowing both good and evil."[11] Indeed, over this matter I am forced to weep rather than find pleasure in expressing myself at length. And so, in tears, a few days ago I wrote the following lines of verse:

> Alas, the Apostolic See
>   once gloried in hegemony,
> but scoffing men now note with glee
>   your forge transformed to simony.
> Hammers on the anvil pound
>   and hellish coins there now abound;
> by God's just judgment this is so,

---

9. Cf. Miccoli, *Chiesa Gregoriana* 301–3.
10. On 30 September 1061 Alexander II was elected, and on 28 October 1061 Bishop Cadalus of Parma was selected as pope at a session of the Royal Court in Basel. See Schmidt, "Alexander II" 104ff., 126f.
11. Gen 3.5.

> that at your hand weal turns to woe.
> And yet should one attempt to buy
> the See of Peter raised on high,
> he could not ransom such high station
> until he dies to reap damnation.[12]

Having written this, I was overcome by grief and refrained from saying more.

(7) But since amid such evils that insolently occur in our day, with violent men seizing our very churches and invading the lands and other properties dedicated to sacred use, some raise the question whether spiritual leaders should not seek revenge and, like laymen, repay evil for evil. For there are many who, as soon as violence is used against them, at once rush out and declare war, gather their armed men, and thus punish their enemies more severely, perhaps, than they themselves were injured. But to me this seems to be quite absurd, that the very priests of the Lord should attempt to carry out the very thing they forbid their people to do, and to assert in deed what they attack in word. For what is more certainly contrary to Christian Law than repaying injury with injury? Where, I ask, are all the proclamations of Scripture? Where are the Lord's own words: "When a man takes what is yours, do not demand it back"?[13] And if we are not allowed to take back the very things that were stolen from us, how is it permissible in their regard to seek revenge and to inflict wounds in retribution? There is also this in Scripture: "If someone slaps you on the right cheek, turn and offer him your left. If he makes you go one mile, go with him two. If he takes away your shirt, let him have your coat as well."[14]

(8) But perhaps someone will object that these rules are for laymen and not for bishops, that is, that the heads of churches must preach such things, but not observe them. Yet even a fool would have such ideas, since the Lord says, "If a man sets aside even the least of the Law's demands, and teaches others to do

---

12. Damian, *Rhythmus* 50 (Lokrantz, *L'opera* 134). Only the first two strophes appear in this letter. For the complete poem, see *Letter* 88.
13. Luke 6.30, with wide variation from the Vulgate.
14. Matt 5.39–41; again, Damian is quoting loosely.

the same, he will have the lowest place in the kingdom of heaven, whereas anyone who keeps the Law, and teaches others so, will stand high in the kingdom of Heaven."[15] Therefore, a bishop who would attain a high position in the kingdom of heaven should lead the way for his people, so that what he prescribes in word for those who follow him, he should first fulfill in living deeds. And so, to avoid every occasion for misunderstanding, as the first among all the Church's priests he should not say, "Lord, how often should a brother forgive a brother if he goes on wronging him?" But rather, speaking as one who has assumed the burden of all other priests, he should say, "Lord, how often am I to forgive my brother if he goes on wronging me?"[16] And when the reply comes back that he should forgive "seventy times seven times," there can be no doubt that this universal command must also be observed by bishops. On the evidence of Luke the evangelist we learn that, when the Lord was on his way to Jerusalem, the disciples set out and went into a Samaritan village to make arrangements for him.[17] But when the Samaritans would not have them, James and John were angry and, letting human nature have its way, they said, "Lord, may we call down fire from heaven to burn them up, as Elijah did?"[18] But he turned and rebuked them: "You do not know," he said, "to what spirit you belong; for the Son of Man did not come to destroy men's lives but to save them."[19] And then he continued thus: "And they went on to another village," as if he were saying, not in so many words, but by his actions, "Do not seek revenge";[20] or rather, what he himself said, "When you are persecuted in one town, take refuge in another."[21]

(9) Evidently, our savior's earthly life, no less than his preaching, is for us the gospel and his proposal for the direction in which our life should progress. And so, just as he overcame all obstacles of a world gone mad, not by threats of dire punish-

---

15. Matt 5.19, also with some divergence from the Vulgate.
16. Matt 18.21–22.   17. Cf. Luke 9.52.
18. Luke 9.54; cf. 2 Kgs 1.10–12; see also Sabatier 3.308.
19. Luke 9.55–56.   20. Rom 12.19.
21. Matt 10.23; cf. also Sabatier 3.58.

ment but by the insuperable majesty of his resolute patience, he taught us in this way to bear quietly this rabid world, rather than to take up arms or to answer him who harms us with injuries. This is especially so, since within the *imperium* and the *sacerdotium* we must distinguish functions that are proper to each, so that the king may employ secular arms, while the bishop should buckle on the sword of the spirit, which is the word of God.[22] For Paul says of the secular prince, "It is not for nothing that he holds the power of the sword, for he is God's agent of punishment, for retribution on the offender."[23] Because King Uzziah usurped the priestly office he was afflicted with leprosy,[24] and what price will a bishop pay if he takes up arms, which is a function that belongs to laymen?[25] Indeed, we may say that even before the preaching of the gospel, David lived according to evangelical principles, since we find him sparing not only Shimei and Saul,[26] but many other enemies. To this I might add further examples from the other holy Fathers, if I were not certain that these and other cases are much better known to you than they are to me.

(10) Clearly, who is not aware how indecently confusing it would be for the Church brazenly to do the very thing against which it inveighs and, while preaching patience to others, to react against those who do her harm with unbridled anger? Anyone so doing can expect the fulfillment of the Apostle's words: "For fear that after preaching to others I should find myself rejected."[27] Or better still, perhaps that which he said to the Romans, "You, then, who teach your fellow man, do you fail to teach yourself? You proclaim, 'Do not steal,' but are you yourself a thief? You say, 'Do not commit adultery,' but are you

22. Cf. Eph 6.17. 23. Rom 13.4.
24. Cf. 2 Chr 26.19.
25. On this reference to the relationship between the *sacerdotium* and the *imperium*, and Damian's adherence to the Gelasian tradition, see Ryan, *Sources* 81ff., no. 150; Gelasius I, *Tractatus* IV.11, ed. A. Thiel, *Epistolae Romanorum pontificum genuinae* 1 (1867–1868) 567f.; JK 701; Nicholas I, *Epistola ad Michaelem imperatorem*, in Gratian, *Decretum* D 96.6; JE 2796; A. K. Ziegler, "Pope Gelasius I and His Teaching on the Relation of Church and State," *Catholic Historical Review* 27 (1942) 412–437.
26. Cf. 1 Sam 26.7–12; 2 Sam 19.18–23.
27. 1 Cor 9.27.

an adulterer? You abominate false gods, but do you offer sacrifice to them?"[28] And the words that follow seem most aptly to apply to a bishop: "While you take pride in the Law, you dishonor God by breaking it."[29] A priest of God whose ministerial function it is to proclaim the commands of the Law may justly take pride in God's Law, but by breaking it he is guilty of dishonoring God, since he has no fear of transgressing his decrees. And while doing one thing and teaching another, he does everything in his power to dissuade all others from observing the Law, as the Lord says of the scribes and pharisees: "Alas for you! You have taken away the keys of wisdom and knowledge. You did not go in yourselves, and those who were on their way in, you stopped."[30] And indeed, how dare a bishop exert himself in league with those who are at variance with the Law, by himself not forgiving those who hate him, and implacably seeking revenge?

(11) Among all the gems of virtue that our Savior bestowed on us by coming down from heaven, there were especially two, namely, charity and patience, which in all their splendor he showed us, and which he first practiced and then taught, that they might also be set in us. And of charity, the Apostle says, "Because of the great love he bore the world, God sent his own Son."[31] Of patience he said, "For all the ancient Scriptures were written for our own instruction, in order that through patience and the encouragement that they give us we may maintain our hope."[32] It was out of love that the Son of God came down from heaven, but by patience he overcame the devil. Armed with these virtues, the founding apostles built Holy Church and with their help, its champions, the holy martyrs, triumphantly suffered various kinds of death. If, therefore, it is never permitted to take up arms in defense of the faith by which the universal Church lives, how may armored hosts revel in bloodshed for the sake of earthly and transitory possessions of the Church? Moreover, if when holy men prevailed, they never killed heretics and idolators, but instead refused to flee death

28. Rom 2.21–22. 29. Rom 2.23.
30. Luke 11.52, with variants from the Vulgate.
31. Eph 2.4; Gal 4.4. 32. Rom 15.4.

at their hands for the sake of the Catholic faith, how can a Christian wage war against a Christian over the loss of trivial things, since he is not unaware that the other was also redeemed by the blood of Christ?[33]

(12) The event that I now relate came to my attention as having happened in Gaul. A grave dispute over lands occurred between an abbot and a certain most powerful secular lord. After the supporters of each had engaged in protracted quarrels and threats, both sides at length decided to fight it out. The secular prince, indeed, after gathering his troops, entered the field of battle, drew up his lines, and arranged his forces. With a vigorous harangue he fired up his men to fight bravely. The place was dense with swords and red with shields, and the clamor of shouting men grew more intense. The threatening clash of armed men was frightening as they unsheathed their weapons, and only the attack by the opposing side was awaited by excited men prepared to engage. But the abbot, placing his hope not in earthly weapons but in him who had won man's salvation, forbade all those who had come to fight for him to enter the fray. Advancing, with only his monks mounted on horses, he ordered them to cover their heads with their cowls and so, under the banner of the cross, came to the site of battle with his monks covered and corseted with the arms of faith. When his opponent, as he had hoped, saw nothing of weapons but beheld something like a heavenly and angelic array approaching, such a dreadful fear of God gripped him and all his men that, dismounting from their horses, they at once threw down their arms, prostrated themselves humbly on the ground, and begged to be forgiven. It was thus that the abbot gained victory and fame, not by trusting in neighing horses and flashing swords, but only by virtue of the power of God.

(13) Now if someone should object to my arguments by stating that Pope Leo[34] often became involved in acts of war, even

---

33. Cf. Ryan, *Sources* 83 no. 151. Damian's intention here is the condemnation of a recourse to arms by clerics. But in translating *sancti viri* as 'holy men,' rather than bishops, as I have done, others have noted Damian's opposition to capital punishment for heretics.

34. On Leo IX's involvement in military affairs in his early career and as

though he was holy, I will tell you what I think. Peter did not obtain the apostolic primacy because he denied the Lord,[35] nor was David found worthy of the gift of prophecy because he violated another man's marriage rights,[36] since good and evil are not weighed on the basis of someone's merit, but must be judged on their own quality. Have you not read what Gregory did or taught in his writings, a man who had to suffer so many raids and so much violence from the wild Lombards?[37] And did Ambrose take up arms against the Arians who so savagely attacked both him and his diocese?[38] Do we ever hear of any of the saints who had recourse to war? Therefore, let secular law or the decisions of episcopal councils decide ecclesiastical cases, so that what should be handled by judicial tribunals or judged by the decision of the bishops, to our shame, not be adjudicated in trial by battle.

(14) But now, while extending my remarks out of my great desire to speak with you, I have exceeded, as I see, the measure of epistolary brevity. May almighty God keep you well, venerable father, to direct the affairs of your diocese, and may you be so kind as to remember me in your holy prayers.

---

pope against Robert Guiscard and the Normans, see Dressler, *Petrus Damiani* 105f. and 158; I. S. Robinson, *Authority and Resistance in the Investiture Contest* (Manchester, 1978) 98f. and 103.

35. Cf. Mark 14.66–72.   36. Cf. 2 Sam 11.4–5.
37. Cf. Gregory I, *Registrum epistolarum* (MGH Epp. 1–2 [1891–1899]) passim.
38. Cf. M. R. P. McGuire, "Ambrose, St.," NCE 1 (1967) 372–75.

LETTER 88

Peter Damian to Cadalus, bishop of Parma, the antipope Honorius II. Shortly after the election of Pope Alexander II, Cadalus, the bishop of Parma, was chosen on 28 October 1061 as antipope Honorius II by bishops partial to the German court. Damian warns him of his irregularity in view of the Election Decree of 1059, and highlights the purpose of his action as the accumulation of ecclesiastical resources to be used for his own designs. Damian contests Cadalus's record, thrice condemned by synods in Pavia, Mantua, and Florence, and predicts his early death if he does not repent. This letter was written before the antipope engaged in battle with papal forces on 14 April 1062.

(March to 14 April 1062)[1]

TO THE SO-CALLED Bishop Cadalus,[2] the monk Peter the sinner sends a message that he justly deserves.

(2) If one does not correct a boy who is stealing eggs, he will later have to bear with a major thief who breaks into his stables. If an eminent matron should neglect to keep a lecherous character away from her personal maids, who will be surprised if later he directs his wanton intentions also in her direction? And to cite several examples from Scripture: Because King David failed to punish Absalom for killing his brother,[3] he later lost his throne after Absalom had forced him into exile. When Adonijah, son of Haggith,[4] impudently showed his colors, and as his father let him go uncensured, he provided himself with horses and chariots and announced that he was taking the throne. He finally went so far as to ask for Abishag the Shunammite as his wife, and sought to dishonor his father's marriage.

(3) In many ways, my brother, the Roman Church has dealt

---

1. The dating follows Lucchesi, *Vita* no. 163.
2. On Cadalus, see F. Baix, "Cadalus," DHGE 11 (1949) 53–99.
3. Cf. 2 Sam 13.28–29.   4. Cf. 1 Kgs 1–2.

lightly with you, and often shielded you from the rigorous chastisement you deserved. Thus, as those who claimed to have been present have asserted, a clear sentence of condemnation was handed down against you at the three synods that were held in Pavia, Mantua, and Florence.[5] But in all cases, the Church compassionately forgave you with maternal love and apostolic affection. But while she made every effort to restrain the vigor of the canons in your case, you did not fear to repay her with tyrannical attack. Moreover, if we carefully note the Scriptural accounts, we will find that David was three times anointed king.[6] He was first anointed by Samuel in Bethlehem; then by the men of Judah in Hebron; and for a third time in the presence of all the tribes of Israel, again in Hebron. And I will relate something similar for you about our fisherman, whom you so much wish to succeed, namely, that Peter had three sees, which he exalted by various prerogatives of his episcopal dignity. There was Antioch where, after establishing himself as the foundation of the faith, he soon consecrated Ignatius to be bishop in his stead.[7] Also Alexandria, where St. Mark the evangelist, after spreading the seed of the new faith, faithfully established this see to the glorious name of blessed Peter, his teacher.[8] And finally, he presided over the city of Rome for twenty-five years, which, together with his fellow apostle Paul, he also triumphantly purpled with the precious blood of victory.[9]

(4) But why in this debate do I make a point of the former's threefold anointing and of the latter's triple tenure of episcopal office? Only to bring you to consider that you were deposed the same number of times, if not by the judgment of the bishops, at least by the authority of the canons, and consequently to note how far removed you are from these holy men. For even

---

5. Other than Damian's statement, we can find no other evidence for these condemnations. But see Davidsohn, *Geschichte* 200f.; Lucchesi, *Vita* no. 163.
6. Cf. 1 Sam 16; 2 Sam 2; 2 Sam 5.
7. On Peter's presence in Antioch, see Gal 2.11ff.; on his role as bishop there, see Jerome, *De viris illustribus*, ed. E. C. Richardson, TU 14.1 (1896) 1.6.
8. See Jerome, *De viris illustribus* 8.11; on Mark's relationship to Peter, see 1 Pet 5.13.
9. See Jerome, *De viris illustribus* 1.6; *Liber pontificalis* 1.1.118.

though for each of them their threefold promotion, just as if it were only one preferment, produced no increase in authority or episcopal dignity, still in a certain sense it was a sign of their more abounding holiness. Just as David transcended other kings in piety and justice, so also Peter surpassed all other bishops by his preeminence. And thus, while we bestow this honor on no other saint, we celebrate in the liturgy only the feast of the chair of blessed Peter.[10]

(5) Now that your episcopal tenure is held in such ill repute, how dare you presume, or, to put it more mildly, how can you acquiesce without the knowledge of the Roman Church in being elected bishop of Rome? Meanwhile, I will say nothing of the subsidiary cardinals,[11] of the lower orders of the clergy, or of the people. And what are your thoughts about the cardinal bishops, whose privilege it is to elect the Roman pontiff,[12] and who, by reason of certain other prerogatives, surpass the rights, not only of all other bishops, but also of patriarchs and metropolitans?[13] Without wishing to violate the mystery of the universal Church, they are the eyes of this one stone, that is, of the Roman Church, of which Zechariah says, "Here is the stone that I set before Jesus. In this one stone are seven eyes."[14] They are the lamps on the one lampstand, of which he later spoke when he said, "I saw, and behold there was a lampstand all of gold, and a bowl on top of it holding seven lamps."[15] They are the lamps among which, according to the words of blessed John, Jesus moved,[16] and the statement that he then makes, he seems to be directing especially to you: "Think," he said, "from what a height you have fallen, and do penance."[17]

(6) Certainly, if one is rightly compelled to do penance for

10. On 22 February.
11. Scheffer-Boichorst, *Disceptatio synodalis*, 63 n. 3 and Michel, *Papstwahl* 82, 98 think of the Latin word *senatus*, used here, as the lesser members of the college of cardinals; but Krause, "Papstwahldekret" 79 n. 25 proposes that a fourth group of electors is here intended.
12. *Das Papstwahldekret*, ed. D. Jasper, *Beiträge zur Geschichte und Quellenkunde der MA* 12 (1986) 101f. See also Ryan, *Sources* 76f. no. 142.
13. See H. Fuhrmann, "Studien zur Geschichte ma. Patriarchate," ZRG Kan. 39 (1953), 112–76, esp. 41 (1955), 132 n. 117.
14. Zech 3.9.   15. Zech 4.2.
16. Rev 1.13.   17. Rev 2.5.

having injured just any bishop, what sort of sentence should be passed on you who have caused damage to those bishops by whose counsel and judgment the public rights and discipline of the whole Catholic Church must be directed? And since canonical authority decrees that the clergy of even the humblest of dioceses is allowed freely to exercise their judgment on one who is to preside over them as bishop,[18] with what arrogant audacity can you presume to obtrude with violence upon the rights of those who, beyond the common practice of the Church, are empowered to pass authoritative judgment on the supreme pontiffs themselves?[19] Why, out of your ambition to acquire this high and inaccessible dignity, have you aroused almost the whole world to rise up in condemning you? At the top of their voices they seem to shout the saying of the prophet Jeremiah: "O land, land, land, hear the words of the Lord: Write this man down as stripped of all honor, one who in his own life shall not prosper."[20] And you, on the other hand, might well respond in the words of that same prophet: "Alas, alas, my mother, that you ever gave me birth! A man doomed to strife, with the whole world against me! I have borrowed from no one, I have lent to no one, yet all men abuse me."[21] Or again, you might use that equally prophetic statement: "A curse on the day when I was born! Be it forever unblessed, the day when my mother bore me!"[22] And then he goes on saying, "A curse on the man who brought word to my father, 'A child is born to you, a son,' and gladdened his heart! That man shall fare like the cities that the Lord overthrew without mercy, because he did not kill me before birth so that my mother might become my grave, her womb great with me forever."[23] It is not that he curses the day on which a man was born, but condemns rather the good fortune he enjoys for having fallen into sin. You would, as it were, have died in the womb on that very day, if you had retreated from the evil that you started, in which, indeed, you were accursedly born.

18. See Ryan, *Sources* 77 no. 143.
19. See Jasper, *Papstwahldekret* 104; Ryan, *Sources* 77 no. 144.
20. Jer 22.29–30.
21. Jer 15.10.
22. Jer 20.14.
23. Jer 20.15–17.

(7) Now since it was foreigners and not sons of the Apostolic See who chose you, they should have deprived you of the see you now hold, rather than promote you to another amid wild confusion and not with good judgment, as thus it is written: "You cast them down as they were being raised on high."[24] We keep laymen from entering the Church if after abandoning their wives they are married to others; how much meaner is his adultery who, without synodal approval, like a plunderer, invades a church of another's jurisdiction after abandoning his own? The prophet deplores this adultery when he says, "Deep within me my heart is broken. There is no strength in my bones; because of the Lord, because of his dread works, I have become like a drunken man, like a man overcome with wine."[25]

(8) He soon discloses why he has been consumed with such wearisome sorrow when he adds, "For the land is full of adulterers, and because of its curse the earth is in mourning, the desert pastures have dried up."[26] He explains that the human race had committed this adultery for which the earth was in mourning, and men's hearts, like an oasis in the desert, dried up for lack of the generous rains of preaching: "For prophet and priest alike are godless; I have come upon the evil they are doing even in my own house, says the Lord."[27] But in the words that follow he makes clear what is in store for these adulterous priests and prophets: "Therefore the path shall turn slippery beneath their feet; they shall be dispersed in the dark and shall fall there. For I will bring disaster upon them when their day of reckoning comes. They prophesied in Baal's name and led my people Israel astray. In the prophets of Jerusalem I see the likeness of adulterers and the way of deceit."[28]

(9) Do you hear these words: "the likeness of adulterers and the way of deceit"? For the one depends on the other. One strays indeed from the path of truth, if by following the road of lust and passion he besmirches the luster of ecclesiastical chastity. Unfortunately, we now lament the Church defiled from top to bottom that Jeremiah had once observed happen-

---

24. Ps 72.18.
25. Jer 23.9.
26. Jer 23.10.
27. Jer 23.11.
28. Jer 23.12–14.

ing to Jerusalem: "Men of Memphis and Daphne have despoiled you to the very limit."²⁹ Now Jerusalem is defiled from top to bottom, when venal lust reaches from the smallest church right up to the Apostolic See, which is the head of all the churches. But then the voice of God promptly tells us of the bitterness that will follow upon the sweetness of this adultery: "See," he said, "I will give them wormwood to eat and a bitter poison to drink."³⁰

(10) Therefore, my brother, act in accord with the words of the prophet when he says, "Consider this well, you rebels."³¹ Examine your conscience, I beg you, and discreetly explore how quiet and peaceful it was after you plunged into this dangerous business, like entering the whirlpool at the foot of the rock of Scylla!³² The money for which you lusted was squandered, the bags that swelled with coins of various kinds are empty, and the goods of the Church that should have gone to supporting the poor are lavished on hosts of knights. That you might surpass all others in dignity, you must now obey them all as their subject, and your ambition to rule now delivers you up to slavery.

(11) Let one thing be clear: Whoever once steals into the Church by venality will never cease paying the price for trying to reach the top. The just judgment of God is here at work, decreeing that whoever attacks the administration of the Church by attempting to buy or sell it will not gain by his trafficking the benefits of easy wealth for which he had hoped. Taking his seat among the scornful,³³ he must always ply his busy hammers, so that as the stream of his mercenary preferment flows its sordid and tortuous way, it may always conform to the source from which it so dismally began. For since any religious man fears to assume the burdens of such a strenuous see—and to be there installed will resist almost any amount of human pressure—why is it that you not only do not prepare to flee this "burden of all burdens," as the saintly Pope Leo³⁴ called it, but

29. Jer 2.16. 30. Jer 23.15.
31. Isa 46.8.
32. Cf. Isidore, *Etymologies* 11.3.38; 14.6.32.
33. Cf. Ps 1.1.
34. Cf. Leo I, *Sermo* 5.2 (PL 54.153D).

even actually try to force yourself upon it by soliciting it and offering to pay its price? It seems obvious that the sentence that God's word passed on Jerusalem through Ezekiel applies to you: "Every prostitute takes her fee," he said, "but you give presents to all your lovers. But because you give a fee and do not receive it, you are the very opposite."[35]

(12) Moreover, since the sacred canons label those who are not in accord with the Roman Church as heretics,[36] of what sentence do you deem yourself worthy, since not as a shepherd but as a tyrant you inflict yourself upon her by your resistance and most obstinate opposition? As an upstart warrior along with your satanic followers, you subvert her whom Peter established upon the rock of faith by his preaching, and by unworthily assuming the title of shepherd you dare to destroy and tear up the very pasture with its flocks. But listen to what the Lord has to say to you and to others like you as he speaks through the prophet: "Woe to the shepherds who let the sheep of my flock scatter and be lost, says the Lord. Therefore these are the words of the Lord the God of Israel about the shepherds who tend my people: You have scattered and dispersed my flock. You have not watched over them; therefore I will punish you for your evil deeds."[37] But that which you have now set in motion is not to watch over the Lord's flock, but rather, like a robber and a thief, to destroy and kill, as the Lord says in the gospel: "The thief comes only to steal, to kill, to destroy."[38]

(13) Was it not for this that you were born, that you should

---

35. Ezek 16.33–34.
36. According to Ryan, *Sources* 78ff. no. 145, Damian depended on Anastasius Bibliothecarius, *Interpretatio synodi VIII (Concilium CPL IV, 869) Actio I, Libellus fidei* (PL 129.35f.). But since Damian is not the author of *Opusc.* 28 (PL 145.511C–518A), where an eighth council is spoken of, and in *Letter* 65 had the Milanese swear on the doctrines of "the seven holy councils," he was probably unacquainted with the work of Anastasius Bibliothecarius. A better source for Damian's knowledge of the heretical label here alluded to is the *Collectio Avellana* (CSEL 35), the best MS of which was in the library of Fonte Avellana. On which, see Blum, *St. Peter Damian* 60 n. 75. For further discussion of Damian's dependence on Ambrose and Gregory VII in this matter, see Reindel, *Briefe* 2 (1988) 521f. n. 16.
37. Jer 23.1–2.   38. John 10.10.

incite the world to war, to destroy the efforts and achievements of the apostles, and to disturb the entire Church of Christ by your selfish ambition? And perhaps this disorder was purposely predicted by your name. For you are called Cadalus.[39] Indeed, the first part of your name obviously means a 'fall,' and the second, the 'people'; in Greek, the word λαός means the 'people.' And what else is expressed by this name but what was said in Scripture, namely, that bad priests are the ruin of the people?[40] In this way, therefore, you who were formerly a son of Holy Church have become a sword opposing her. And perhaps you are that sword of which the prophet Ezekiel spoke: "A sword, a sword is sharpened and burnished."[41] But why this sword should have these two qualities, that is, that it is burnished and sharp, is explained by what follows: "It is sharpened to kill its victims, and burnished to flash like lightning."[42]

(14) These qualities seem to fit you who alone strive to be brilliant in your dignity, but work to involve the whole empire in war as if you were gathering victims for the slaughter. But listen to what immediately follows: "You who wield the scepter of my son have cut down every tree; you have given the sword to be brandished, ready for the hand to grasp."[43] And then we read: "The sword—it is sharpened, it is burnished, ready to be put into the slayer's hand."[44] It is indeed you; you are that sword who wields the scepter of the Son of God, that is, you who disturb the people in the kingdom where he rules and commands. The scepter of the Son of God is the Catholic Church, she is the kingdom, she is the empire of our redeemer, which you deservedly are said to disturb as you strive to harass and molest her. It is not my purpose to explain the words of the prophet like a commentator, so that I am called upon also

---

39. On the interpretation of the name Cadalus, see Peter Damian, *Cadaloo non pastori sed antiquo draconi*, Lokrantz, *L'opera* 58f.; his *Triste tristichon Cadaloo*, Lokrantz, *L'opera* 59; and also *Letter* 89.
40. Cf. Ezek 7.26.
41. Ezek 21.9.
42. Ezek 21.10.
43. Ezek 21.10–11.
44. Ezek 21.11.

to discuss the wood[45] of which the Church is built, after the model of Noah's Ark. It will suffice merely to touch on those things that appear applicable to your madness.

(15) Moreover, since your undertaking will never be successful, but will end in your unfortunate death, you who proudly attack the exalted dignity of Rome will return in disgrace to your own estate. So listen to what follows. For after the voice of God said, "You are a sword, a sword drawn for slaughter, burnished for destruction, to flash like lightning,"[46] it then continued, "Sheathe it again. I will judge you in the place where you were born, the land of your origin. I will pour out my rage upon you; I will breathe out my blazing wrath over you."[47]

(16) Perhaps you now have the mitre and, after the fashion of the Roman pontiff, are possessed of the red mantle.[48] Beware that God's word does not use it in sentencing you as he speaks by the lips of the same prophet: "You, too, you impious and wicked prince of Israel, your fate has come upon you in the hour of final punishment. These are the words of the Lord God: Put off your diadem, lay aside your crown. Is it not this that has raised up the lowly and brought down the high?"[49] It is as if he were putting it very clearly, that anyone who arrogantly strives for this diadem or priestly crown will justly be suppressed, but he who declines and proclaims himself unworthy will deservedly receive high position.

(17) A glad occasion it was when such bishops as those of Piacenza and Vercelli elected you,[50] wanton fellows who had lured many women, and because they could ably hold forth on feminine beauty, were just the men who would be sharp judges in electing a bishop! Here again we have those two old men of whom the Lord spoke: "Wickedness came forth from Babylon

---

45. Cf. Gen 6.14.   46. Ezek 21.28.
47. Ezek 21.30–31.
48. For commentary on the papal vestments here referred to, see Reindel, *Briefe* 2 (1988) 523–24 nn. 21–22.
49. Ezek 21.25–26.
50. On the election of Cadalus, see Reindel, *Briefe* 2 (1988) 524 nn. 23–25. The two electors were Dionysius of Piacenza and Gregorius of Vercelli.

from elders who were judges and were supposed to govern my people."[51] Here again was Susanna accused and brought to trial; here was an innocent person falsely charged with crime, and blood without blame is condemned. But was Daniel not there as her spirit was suddenly revived and the wickedness of false witnesses was avenged? He was indeed present, this man of desires,[52] of whom the prophet said, "One more thing: the one expected by all nations shall come hither."[53] A stronger one than Daniel was here, I say, convicting those impious men of false judgment and clearing our Susanna from unjust condemnation. Of his lightning-quick judgment another prophet said, "See what a scorching wind has gone out from the Lord, a furious whirlwind; it whirls around the heads of the wicked. The Lord's anger is not to be turned aside, until he has accomplished and fulfilled his deep designs."[54]

(18) With all due reverence to our rulers, who by reason of the weakness of their sex or of their years could have their right stolen from them,[55] whoever, besides them, urged you on to commit this disgraceful deed must be called sons of Caiaphas, the firstborn of Satan, aides to the antichrist, and opponents of truth. Therefore, I am compelled to cry out, "O heaven and earth, along with which all the elements will be disturbed![56] What a tragedy, unheard of in all the ages that preceded us, that a foreign bishop who despised his own see should be set over the Roman Church—unknown to God, unknown to Peter, unknown to the Roman Church! And what no other church of the lowest rank must suffer, that church which is the mother and mistress of all Christian religion is forced to endure!"[57]

(19) But perhaps someone may object that some Roman had taken part in this irregular election. Of these words such a

51. Dan 13.5; cf. also Dan 13.41–62.
52. Cf. Dan 10.11. 53. Hag 2.8.
54. Jer 23.19–20.
55. This is the so-called "King's paragraph" in the *Papstwahldekret 1059* 101f.; for further literature, see Jasper, *Papstwahldekret* 5f. n. 16; Ryan, *Sources* 80 no. 146.
56. The "anathema formula" in the same decree; cf. Ryan, *Sources* 81 no. 147.
57. See Ryan, *Sources* 77 no. 143.

frantic tongue should be ashamed, and if unable to be eloquent, it should at least learn to be silent. If it can say nothing useful, it will at least not inflict injury by failing to speak. This is especially so since this election should in the first instance have been the decision of the cardinal bishops; in the second place, the clergy should by right have given its assent; in the third place, popular approval should have raised its voice in applause; and then the election should have been suspended until the authority of his royal highness had been consulted, unless, as recently happened, some imminent danger should occur which compelled the election to be expedited as soon as possible.[58]

(20) Moreover, since it was the devil who applied the plural form to God's name, when he said to the woman, "You will be like gods knowing both good and evil,"[59] you too added something new to the rules of the grammarians, so that in declining the word "pope," youths could now say "the popes, of the popes." Therefore, it was through you that this old world of ours learned something that it previously had not known. And as Paul said, once a year the high priest entered the holy place with the blood he offered for others,[60] so now you too slaughter miserable men like pigs and shed their blood, that by your cruelty you may enter the sanctuary of blessed Peter. Beware, brother, beware that you do not too readily take up arms against Peter like an enemy. For as you know, Peter cut down Ananias and his wife with the sword of his words, and hurled Simon, arrogantly reaching for the stars, into the depths of hell.[61]

(21) Let me tell you what I heard from certain men older than me. The Apostolic See used to have a piece of property in the region of Babylon,[62] from which it annually received such a return in balsam that it sufficed to keep a lamp always burning before the altar of the blessed prince of the Apostles.

---

58. Ryan, *Sources* 81 no. 149.
59. Gen 3.5. 60. Cf. Heb 9.7.
61. Cf. Acts 5.1–10; Acts 8.20.
62. For the medieval use of Babylon as a substitute for Cairo, see D. Kaufmann, *Zeitschrift der deutschen morgenländischen Gesellschaft* 51 (1897) 437f. n. 6.

The pope sold this property for a certain amount of money, and lost the payment of aromatic oil that was customarily received. Some time later, as the same pope knelt and prayed before that same holy altar, suddenly a terrifying old man, whose face was shaved, raised his arm and gave the pope a violent blow, and said, "You have put out the lamp that burns in my presence, and I shall extinguish your lamp in the presence of God." And then he disappeared. With that, the pope collapsed and died shortly after. Just so will he deserve to be struck down who is an enemy of him who, as the chief pastor, was given primacy over heaven and earth.

(22) Which of the two popes, I ask, seems in your opinion to deserve the greater penalty? Was it he who dared to extinguish the lamp before the sacred altar, or you who attempt to darken the whole Church by undertaking your clandestine promotion? For according to the words of truth itself, he who enters by the door is the shepherd, but he who climbs in by another way is a thief or a robber.[63] But since he who now presides came in by the shepherd's gate and enlightened the house, so by your fraudulent entry you brought nothing but smoke and gloom, chaos and horrible darkness. To this I may add that while one is in a lowly station, his vices somehow lie hidden; but when he reaches a position of importance, they promptly come to the surface. What hitherto was unheard of is now made public, spread by the oral report of a rumor-mongering people. How many thousands of men now recount your deeds, men who until today knew nothing of them? For your damnable trafficking in the benefices of your diocese or of other dioceses, and other much more shameful affairs which I blush to speak about, were discussed until now only in your small town. But now everywhere in the empire one tells the other: merchants chatting in the market, diggers in the field; boys who are studying rhetoric in the schools; citizens who come together to gossip over trivia; almost all of them abuse you and pass judgment on you. We can be sure that the same thing happened to you as that which Jeremiah reported of a certain sinner: "For your many sins

---

63. Cf. John 10.1–2.

your skirts are torn off you, your limbs uncovered."[64] And then he goes on to say, "This is your lot, the portion of the rebel, measured out by me, says the Lord, because you have forsaken me and trusted in false gods. So I myself have stripped off your skirts and laid bare your shame. Your adulteries, your lustful neighing, your wanton lewdness, are an offense to me."[65]

(23) Indeed, if I were to decide to meet with you, I would use these words in rebuking you to your face. Did you not sell those things which in the Church were to be given freely? Did you not commit these and other acts with heaven and earth as witnesses? And if I were to say such things to you, I have no doubt that with all the world on the stand against you, it would be impossible for you to deny them, and you would plead for the opportunity to amend your ways in the future. For every charlatan whose conscience accuses him as he is rebuked for his past life may promise himself to mend his ways in the days that follow. But since reaching the top is an occasion for sin, how will he avoid stumbling on the rocky paths in the mountains if he loses his balance when walking on level ground? I would be able to answer in the words of the prophet that the Lord addressed to you and to others like you: "Can the Nubian change his skin, or the leopard its spots? And you? Can you do good, you who are schooled in evil?"[66] And of this difference in color he said elsewhere, "Is this bird of another color to be my inheritance? Is it not a bird dyed through and through?"[67] But for this fault of being different, he at once issues the sentence of condemnation: "Come, you wild beasts; come, all of you, flock to the feast."[68] And for those threatened with the danger of being devoured, he at once announces, as he continues, "Many shepherds have ravaged my vineyard and trampled down my field, they have made my pleasant field a desolate wilderness, and made it a wasteland."[69]

(24) All of this signifies nothing else but the Church ravaged by evil pastors. But I will not explain it since I believe that it is

64. Jer 13.22.
65. Jer 13.25–27.
67. Jer 12.9.
69. Jer 12.10–11.

66. Jer 13.23.
68. Jer 12.9.

well known to you and would require me to go on at length. Only I will not allow this to escape your notice, that both you and all others like you, ambitious to attain the highest position in the Church, by undoubtedly ignoring God, you tear the Church to pieces. And so the same prophet says, "For these shepherds have acted like fools; they never consult the Lord, and so they never understand, and all their flocks are scattered."[70] So now you swear to mend your ways that you might reach the dignity you yearn for. You speak like a humble man, so that you may be promoted to high office. But this humility, since it springs from the root of pride, does not appear likely to satisfy.

(25) In the meantime, I am reminded of the account found in the narrative of the book of Genesis, that "when Shechem, son of Hamor the Hivite, the local prince, saw Dinah, the daughter of Leah, he took her, lay with her, and dishonored her. He remained true to the girl and comforted her."[71] He was so restless in his love for her that he had himself and all the males of the city circumcised, only that he might obtain consent to his marriage. But this agreement was not pleasing to God and did not placate her brothers, since it was not made out of religious motives, but to gain carnal pleasure. For then her brothers, who were enraged over the rape, put to the sword all those who had been circumcised.

(26) And so it is with you. You are the new Shechem, the seducer of Dinah, the profaner of the Church. You circumcise your flesh that you might fulfill the desires of the flesh. You promise to cut off your evil practices so that afterwards you might persist, without risk of punishment, in your depravity. You should note that Simeon and Levi attacked with their swords, that is, both the Old Testament and the New Testament, as they condemn you by their statements, cut you down like two brothers armed with swords. But, to speak of avengers closer to our time, Peter and Paul, who are the world's judges, will also require retribution for your offense. "For you have done a foul deed in Israel."[72]

70. Jer 10.21.　　　　　　　　71. Gen 34.1–3.
72. Gen 34.7.

(27) But lest anyone should perhaps object that Simeon and Levi, the murderers of Shechem, deserved to be cursed as the patriarch Jacob lay dying,[73] let him know that here the prophetic spirit is looking forward to the future death of the savior rather than properly condemning the previous slaughter of a passionate man. For the Jewish scribes are descendants of Simeon, while the high priests stem from the tribe of Levi. And of them it was written that they "conferred together on a scheme to have Jesus arrested by some trick and put to death."[74] Of this conference this was said: "My soul shall not enter their council, and my heart shall not join their company, for in their anger they killed a man," he said, "and with their consent they undermined the wall,"[75] namely, that man of whom Isaiah said, "Let us overwhelm this just man, for he is a hindrance to us at every turn."[76] They undermined the wall, that is, the powerful, spiritual fortress that stands as a bastion for Israel.

(28) Leaving the rest to the interpreters of Scripture, let it suffice to say that here we do not observe vengeance for rape, but the condemnation of the sacrilegious killers of Christ. Judith also taught that the latter vengeance was pleasing to God when she said, "O Lord, God of my forefather Simeon, you put a sword in his hand to take vengeance on those foreigners who had stripped off a virgin's veil to defile her, uncovered her thighs to shame her; you gave their wives as booty, and their daughters as captives, and all their spoils to be divided among your servants who were aflame with zeal for your cause."[77]

(29) You are not satisfied, moreover, to be an ordinary man, but wish to be thought of as a mountain to the human race and, like a proud mountain ridge, you exalt yourself to the most lofty dignities. You wish to hear nothing of valleys, of which it was said, "The valleys abound in grain."[78] But listen to what the Lord tells you through the prophet: "I am against you, O destroying mountain, you who destroy the whole earth, says the Lord, and I will stretch out my hand against you and send you

73. Cf. Gen 49.5–7.
74. Matt 26.4.
75. Gen 49.6.
76. Not Isaiah, but Wis 2.12.
77. Jdt 9.2–3.
78. Ps 64.14.

tumbling from your terraces and make you a burned mountain. No stone of yours shall be used as a cornerstone, no stone for a foundation, but you shall be desolate, forever waste."[79] And again, "I am against you, insolent one, says the Lord, for your time has come, your day of reckoning. The proud man shall stumble and fall and no one shall lift him up."[80]

(30) Has the fire of damnation seethed enough within you? Has your contemptuous pride and ambition for preferment brought you to this, that you would defile the queen of churches or, to put it so, the imperial authority over all kingdoms? But "the virgin daughter of Zion has disdained you, she has laughed you to scorn; the daughter of Jerusalem tosses her head as you retreat. Whom have you taunted and blasphemed? Against whom have you clamored, casting haughty glances at the holy one of Israel? With my countless chariots," you say, "I have gone up high in the mountains, into the recesses of Lebanon,"[81] into the Roman Church, built on the summit of all the world, resplendent with the brilliance of virginal chastity. But hear what the voice of God says to you through the same prophet: "I know your dwelling, your going out and your coming in and your madness against me; when you rage against me your arrogance comes to my ears." And then he brings the sentence to its conclusion: "I have put a ring in your nose and a bit in your mouth, and I will take you back by the road on which you have come."[82]

(31) But now, as I dictate this letter, there is still much more that I wish to say, but already I have exceeded epistolary brevity. I must at least, therefore, ask almighty God to call you back to the spirit of humility and, having laid to rest the wrongdoing and strife in his Church, may he establish the foundation of peace and harmony that you have torn asunder. In closing, I would like to sing the following lament:

> Alas, the Apostolic See
> once gloried in hegemony,
> but scoffing men now note with glee

79. Jer 51.25–26.
80. Jer 50.31.32.
81. Isa 37.22–24.
82. Isa 37.28–29.

LETTER 88

> your forge transformed to simony.
> Hammers on the anvil pound
> and hellish coins there now abound;
> by God's just judgment this is so,
> that at your hand weal turns to woe.
> And yet should one attempt to buy
> the See of Peter raised on high,
> he could not ransom such high station
> until he dies to reap damnation.
> Now he fills like priests of old,
> killers of Christ, as we are told,
> the seat on which the scornful nod,[83]
> struck down by the curse of God.
> Iron be the earth beneath his feet,
> a brazen throne the heavens mete.[84]

Therefore, give careful attention to what I have to say:

> Life, that like smoke disappears, unforeseen is the death that awaits you.
> Swiftly the end of your days, of an age run its course, is approaching.
> Nor do I bluff when I warn, In the spring, time for you will have ended.[85]

---

83. Cf. Ps 1.1.
84. Cf. Deut 28.23. See Damian, *Rhythmus* (ed. Lokrantz, *L'opera* 134). The first six verses appear also in *Letter* 87.
85. Since Cadalus did not die as Damian had predicted, he tried to justify his prophecy in *Letter* 112.

LETTER 89

Peter Damian to Cadalus, bishop of Parma, the antipope Honorius II. Written somewhat after the first letter to Cadalus (*Letter* 88), the present piece drops all pretense of leniency, and savagely attacks the antipope with every weapon in Damian's verbal arsenal. He has now been made aware of the massacre of 14 April 1062, and this accounts for the change in his tactics. This letter is noteworthy for its use of historical precedent in comparing and contrasting the actions and intentions of Cadalus, to whose greed Damian attributes most of his ambition. A previously unrecognized importance attaches to this letter, since it now contains the legal debate, the *Disceptatio synodalis*, which once stood as a separate work. It was written to influence the coming synod held in Augsburg in October 1062, where the schism between Pope Alexander II, Anselm of Lucca, and antipope Honorius II, Cadalus of Parma, would hopefully be resolved. This procès-verbal between the fictitious Imperial Counsel and the Attorney for the Roman Church allows Damian to explore in depth the significance of the Papal Election Decree of 1059, and to explain his own position on the relationship between Church and State in this period. In the rebuttal, both lawyers surprisingly conclude with a plea for harmony and for a peaceful solution.

(Between 14 April and 1 October 1062)[1]

THE MONK PETER the sinner sends to the pseudo-bishop, Cadalus, what he deserves.

(2) If after Jonah had preached at Nineveh,[2] that city had continued to reform its evil ways and, turning its back on vice, had not again defiled itself with sin, the prophet Nahum would never have levied this charge against her, at the very

---

1. The dating follows Lucchesi, *Vita* no. 163. In earlier editions this letter, known as *Epist.* 1.21, was separated from *Opusc.* 4 entitled the *Disceptatio synodalis*, referred to above in the *analyse*. That they belong together as one "open letter," is borne out by the best MSS, especially V1. Baronius in his *Annales ecclesiastici* 11 (1608) 299–303 and 305–17 recognized that they form one literary piece and published them in succession. But Gaetani chose to separate them. Now they appear together as *Letter* 89.
2. Jonah 3–4.

beginning of his book where he gave vent to these words: "The Lord is a jealous God, a God of vengeance, filled with fury. The Lord takes vengeance on his adversaries, against his enemies he directs his wrath."³

(3) Before your attack on Rome with the aid of the followers of Satan, I recently wrote to you, enjoining and earnestly admonishing you to refrain from such a bloody undertaking, to hold yourself in restraint with every means at your disposal, and not to excite God's fury against you, nor provoke the world into disastrous war against the Church. But belching hellish flames like Vesuvius,⁴ you never remain quiet; you scatter, so to speak, the fiery embers of money among the people and, by heating up their cupidity, corrupt the hearts of miserable men. You ruin your own diocese for the sake of obtaining another. In some quarters gold and silver are put on the scale; in others bargaining, tax assessments, and loans go forward; church buildings are mortgaged, and thus the property of a collapsing church is dissipated. You have fortified towns behind you, armed with gold rather than with steel, and thus money pours forth from your purses like swords drawn from their scabbards. Clearly, it is not the blare of trumpets, horns, or other brass that arouses the ranks that follow your banners, but the source of glittering metal that allures them. For with a golden fist, the farmers say, you can break through a wall of iron.⁵ "Wealth that is hoarded," Solomon writes, "will produce evil to its owner."⁶

(4) What good was gold to Ptolemy, the king of Egypt,⁷ who, after the naval engagement he had so treacherously and arrogantly fought with Julius Caesar, was killed on the sea, lay abandoned and despised on the shore with no one standing watch, and could be recognized among the other dead only because he wore a gold cuirass? It would have been better for him to live in woolen attire than to perish in purple and gold.

3. Nah 1.2.
4. For Vesuvius as the entrance to hell, see *Letter* 72 n. 76.
5. No direct source for this popular proverb has been found. But see Reindel, *Briefe* 2 (1988) 533 n. 5.
6. Eccl 5.12.
7. Cf. Eutropius, *Breviarium* 6.22 (MGH Auct.ant. 2.108).

(5) As history relates, the emperor Nero went fishing with golden nets, and hauled them out of the water with purple ropes; but neither his wealth nor his luxury could save him from the death that awaited him. For when the Romans sought his death because of his incomparable excesses, he fled in terror from the palace and killed himself in the outskirts of the city.[8]

(6) The emperor Justin had such an abundance of treasure that his wife built iron vaults for its safekeeping; but later as he lay dying, afflicted with a mental disease, he lost all his possessions together with the royal scepter.[9] And so the prophet put it well: "They shall fling their silver into the streets and cast aside their gold like filth; their silver and their gold will be powerless to save them on the day of the Lord's fury. Their hunger will not be satisfied nor their bellies filled, for their iniquity will be the cause of their downfall; they have fed their pride on their beautiful jewels."[10]

(7) As authentic history tells us, while Alaric, the leader of the Goths, boasted of the unexpected wealth that came to him, he suddenly died in the region of Cozenza. The Goths promptly diverted the Busento River from its bed into another channel, using captive labor, and then buried Alaric with much of his wealth in the riverbed. Later they turned the stream back into its accustomed course. And that no one would discover the site, they killed all the captives who took part in the burial.[11]

(8) Oh, that your army would also bury your money so that you should not be able to ruin the estate of the Church, a course you have already begun! Would that, as we read, these words spoken to your master were also rightly addressed to you: "Your money go with you to damnation."[12] Moreover, as we find in the book of Judges, the mother of Micah had collected silver coins from which an idol was carved,[13] but God forbid

---

8. Cf. Eutropius, *Breviarium* 7.14–15 (MGH Auct.ant. 2.124–26).
9. Cf. Paulus Diaconus, *Historia Langobardorum* 3.12 (MGH SS rer. Lang. [1878] 97–98).
10. Ezek 7.19–20.
11. Iordanes, *Romana et Getica* 30 (MGH Auct.ant. 5.1 [1882] 99).
12. Acts 8.20.   13. Judg 17.1–5.

that such a sacrilegious thing should happen to your money as happened to hers. Because of her hoarded money this scandal occurred in only one tribe of Israel, but your money serves to destroy the foundation of the Christian faith and of the Holy Church entirely.

(9) What an unheard-of crime! The soldiers of Pilate did not dare to rend the seamless tunic of the Lord,[14] and do you presume to divide the Catholic Church between two popes? The former did not break the bones of the savior as he hung on the cross, and do you, after cutting off the members of the Church which are indeed his body, dare to profane this sacrament of unity? The princes of the Philistines were not rash enough to desecrate the ark of the God of Israel, which they had taken in battle, but kept it closed and altogether unharmed.[15] Do you, then, with the aid of wild, armed men, dare to abuse and destroy the hidden secret of Christian devotion—not the tables of stone, but the heavenly mystery of the word of the living and everlasting God? If Uzzah died because he had used his shoulder to keep the ark of the Lord from falling,[16] what will deservedly happen to him who sets himself above the Church of Christ, there to be seen presiding on high among its ruins? Listen to what the voice of God says to you in the words of Obadiah: "Your proud, insolent heart has led you astray; you who haunt the crannies among the rocks, making your home on the heights, you say to yourself, 'Who can bring me to the ground?'"[17] And then he continues, "Though you soar as high as an eagle and your nest is set among the stars, still I will bring you down from there, says the Lord."[18]

(10) It is as clear as day that David was anointed king by Samuel,[19] but that Saul was rejected by the judgment of God. Now, so long as Saul lived, David did not once dare to usurp even the smallest part of his kingdom. But in saying that while Saul was still alive, David did not reach for the high honors of royal authority, it must also be noted that after he had died, he did not at once try to grasp the royal scepter, but humbly asked

14. Cf. John 19.23.
15. Cf. 1 Sam 5.1–12.
16. Cf. 2 Sam 6.6–7.
17. Obad 3.
18. Obad 4.
19. 1 Sam 16.13.

whether he at least might be allowed to live in some town of the realm, saying, "Shall I go into one of the cities of Judah?" And when God replied, "Go,"[20] he did not even then trust going to the town that seemed best for him, but repeated the question that he might be certain. He again asked where specifically he should go, so that, God forbid, he would not give offense by personally making a decision in even the slightest detail: "To which city?" he asked, and the Lord said, "To Hebron."[21] Thus it was that David never presumed, not only to reign in the kingdom given him by God, but even to reside there, until God had repeated his command. And we who are called bishops, like thieves and robbers, invade the dioceses of others and, as all the world stands there in astonishment, rush in to purchase them, contrary to the prohibition of God, the commands of the Law, and the decision of the canons.[22] While speaking of adulterers, Jeremiah says, "I gave them all they needed, yet they preferred adultery, and haunted the brothels; each neighs after another man's wife."[23] And then he continues, "Shall I not punish them for this, the Lord asks? Shall I not take vengeance on such a people?"[24]

(11) Thus, as by intensification we say "the Holy of Holies" and "the Song of Songs," so the attempt to sell the Roman Church is truly the sin of sins. Whoever buys another church is a simonist; but whoever sets a monetary price on the Roman Church thereby seeks to acquire all the churches in the world through purchase, since she is the head. Truly, just as Judas Iscariot sold the Lord for thirty pieces of silver,[25] so he was thirty times cursed in the psalm the prophet wrote against him. These curses begin with the verse that states, "Put up some rascal to denounce him,"[26] and end where it says, "Wrapped in their shame as in a cloak."[27]

(12) Therefore, if curses and damnation are measured ac-

20. 2 Sam 2.1. 21. 2 Sam 2.1.
22. Cf. Ryan, *Sources* 83 no. 152, citing the *Collectio Dionysio-Hadriana* c. 14 (PL 67.143); Burchard, *Decretorum libri* 1.75 (PL 140.565).
23. Jer 5.7. 24. Jer 5.9.
25. Cf. Matt 26.15. 26. Ps 108.6.
27. Ps 108.29.

cording to the quantity of the sin, of how much perdition will the seller of the Roman Church be liable since, while trafficking in one, he is found guilty of acquiring all other churches together with her? Wherefore, have no doubt that the sentence the Lord handed down by Ezekiel also refers to you: "The time is coming, the day of execution is near, not the day of glory in the mountains. Now, in an instant, I will vent my rage upon you and let my rage spend itself. I will call you to account for your doings and bring your abominations upon your own head. I will neither pity nor spare; I will make you suffer for your doings and the abominations that continue in your midst. So you shall know that it is I, the Lord, who strikes the blow."[28]

(13) When Caesar Augustus died, during whose reign the savior of the world deigned to be born,[29] in their grief the Roman people sadly cried out, "Would that he had either not been born, or had not died."[30] But of you, Cadalus, we say with good reason, "Would that you had either not been born, or had immediately died." Thus, according to Scripture, "Would that you had remained in the womb forever,"[31] that your mother had aborted, had never borne you, and that she had had a miscarriage rather than given birth to a child!

(14) Eutropius relates that shortly before the people of Sagunto, dying of starvation, were captured by Hannibal and put to the sword, one of the women was in childbirth, and the baby went back into the womb, portending the destruction of the city.[32] We might also have hoped that you too, returning to your mother's womb, would only have been a sorry omen of a city's fate, rather than grow to maturity to destroy the entire Catholic Church, not only figuratively but in actual deed. It was not your insane desire to reach the top, but your furious lust for power that propelled you. Not content with ruling one diocese, you strive for complete authority over the universal

---

28. Ezek 7.7–9.
29. Cf. *Martyrologium Romanum* for 25 December 317f.
30. Cf. Paulus Diaconus, *Historia Romana* 7.10 (MGH Auct.ant. 2.121.19 and 104.15).
31. Jer 20.17, a variant of the Vulgate text.
32. Cf. Eutropius and Paulus Diaconus, *Breviarium* 3.7.42, 50.

Church, and that you alone should be preeminent, you have no fear of dashing the whole world to its destruction.

(15) The emperor Diocletian himself, as ancient history reports, retired from his imperial title, and for nine years, until his death, lived as a private citizen not far from Salona, engaged in the pleasant task of caring for his garden. When harried by requests from Herculius and Galerius that he again rule over the empire, as if dreading some sort of disease, he was reported to have given this reply: "If only you could come to Salona and see the vegetables planted by my own hand, you would surely not try to place this burden on my shoulders once again."[33]

(16) When Constantius, the father of the great Constantine, and Galerius were created emperor, the Roman world was divided between them, so that Gaul, Italy, and Africa went to Constantius, while Galerius obtained Illyricum, Asia, and the East. Constantius, however, satisfied only with the imperial title, refused to assume the burden of administering Italy and Africa. Now this celebrated man, a person of outstanding affability, while promoting private and provincial wealth, did not much try to enhance imperial holdings, judging that it was far better that public goods be in private hands then held in the grasp of the treasury.[34]

(17) And so, while pagan rulers turned their backs on expanding imperial rule and fled from high imperial dignity because of the vexation of their mounting duties, God's bishops (whose special obligation it is to preach) assert themselves in their pride and yearn to grasp, not sacerdotal, but royal and even tyrannical authority over the human race. The former lay down the arms proper to their rank, that they may enjoy quiet leisure; the latter, however, surrounded by hosts of armies, attack the churches of Christ as if they were enemy strongholds, feasting on the blood of those who died by the sword as if they were feeding on the fat of wild animals. Even though the vicious screech-owl sucks the blood of strangers, it nevertheless

---

33. Eutropius and Paulus Diaconus, *Breviarium* 9.28 (MGH Auct.ant 2.168.1).
34. Cf. Eutropius, *Breviarium* 10.1-2 (MGH Auct.ant. 2.168).

spares its own children.³⁵ When Saturn tried to devour his own son, he was surprised to find a meteorite between his teeth.³⁶ Certainly, you claim the Romans as your children; but you have decided to put them to the sword, not like a father, but rather like a cruel stepfather. With the brave, you encountered stony resistance; but over the weak and wretched you rejoiced to claim victory.

(18) Indeed, in this engagement you will be judged as exceeding the barbarity of King Totila, and your troops as surpassing the Goths in cruelty. For when this king, as we know from his history,³⁷ was besieging Rome by surrounding it with his troops, and the people in the city were at the point of starvation, so that mothers were about to eat the flesh of their children, he finally entered the city by the Ostian gate. Wishing to spare the Roman citizens, he had trumpets sounded throughout the night. From the continuous blare of the horns they would know that the enemy had broken into the city, and could seek any shelter they could find to escape the swords of the Goths. But you and your army subjected this helpless and inexperienced people to such a slaughter that no one knows the number of those who were slain.

(19) It is another acknowledged fact that, when Pompey was fighting his civil war with Caesar and was exhorting his troops, he nevertheless said to them, "Spare the lives of the inhabitants." But Caesar, on the other hand, while speaking to his soldiers, said, "Men, kill on sight."³⁸ And you, impelled by Caesar's cruelty as you fired up the warlike spirits of your followers, gathered the spoils from the bodies of the dead, so that this could also be said of you: "And the story of Judas' battles was told in every nation."³⁹ In all of this, you had no other purpose but to expel the head of the Apostolic See, so that like a foreign

---

35. Cf. Ovid, *Fasti* 6.131–40; Pliny, *Naturalis historia* 11, 39, 95, 232.
36. Cf. Priscian 2.6; DuCange 1.7. Damian uses the word *abbaddir*, the stone that Rhea, the mother of Zeus, gave Saturn to swallow.
37. Cf. Paulus Diaconus, *Historia Romana* 16.22 (MGH Auct.ant. 2.224).
38. Cf. Paulus Diaconus, *Historia Romana* 16.21 (MGH Auct.ant. 2.106.14); Orosius, *Adversus paganos* 6.15.26.192; Florus, *Epitome de Tito Livio bellorum omnium DCC* 2.13.
39. 1 Macc 3.26.

invader you might occupy the chair of Peter that was not vacant. But that you can know that this effort of yours will never succeed, I will cite an example from an area that borders on yours.

(20) Piacenza, indeed, lies in your vicinity, and not long before our own time its bishop,[40] a sly and underhanded man who, like you, burned with ambition for glory and high estate, at first succeeded in having a silver cross carried before him, just as you are said to be doing today. It was also reported that he was having a shameful affair with the empress of that period and then, gradually attempting still greater deeds, like you, with the aid of money, he finally violently invaded the Apostolic See. After Gregory, a relative of the emperor Otto, was forced from office, the bishop of Piacenza gained control of the episcopal honors of the Roman Church, not as supreme pontiff, but as a thief and a tyrant. But shortly thereafter, as the Roman civil population came to its senses, they rose and attacked him, tore out his eyes and cut off his ears and nose. And so he experienced what the Lord had threatened in the words of the prophet Ezekiel, first in his case, and now in yours: "They will come against you with chariots, with a host drawn from the nations, armed with shield, buckler, and helmet; they will beset you on every side. I will give them authority to judge, and they will use that authority to judge you. I will turn my jealous wrath loose on you, and they will make you feel their fury. They will cut off your nose and your ears, and in the end they will kill you with the sword."[41]

(21) But now let me bring this narrative, worthy of your consideration, to its conclusion. After the Romans had thus reacted to this pontiff, as I have related, they sat this glorious knight backwards on a donkey and, as he held the beast's tail in his hand, they drove him down all the streets of the city, forcing

---

40. John Philagathos, abbot of Nonantula, later bishop of Piacenza (cf. Schwartz, *Bistümer* 189), and from April/May 997 to May 998, antipope John XVI. With the help of Crescentius II he replaced Pope Gregory V, a relative of Emperor Otto III. For commentary on these events, see Reindel, *Briefe* 2 (1988) 539 nn. 23–24.

41. Ezek 23.24–25.

him to sing, "This is the punishment one must endure who tries to oust a Roman pope from his see."[42]

(22) Therefore, let every defiler of the Church be aware of this story. Let that same person today be terrified by the judgment of divine severity that awaits him. Let him attend to the message that God has for him in the words of the same prophet, "In the end you will be burned. They will strip you of your clothes and take away all your finery. So I will put a stop to your crimes and to the whoring you practiced in Egypt. For this is the word of the Lord: I am handing you over to those whom you hate, those who have filled you with revulsion, and they will make you feel their hatred. They will take all you have earned and leave you naked and exposed, and the shame of your whoring will be revealed. It is your lewdness and your fornication that have brought this upon you."[43]

(23) Surely, to abandon one's own diocese and to profane the see of another with simoniacal filth is recognized as the worst kind of fornication. Moreover, if God should fail to provide for the world, and you were at the helm of the Apostolic See, all reprobates would burst into exultant song and all the enemies of the Christian religion would dance with joy. But, on the other hand, those who thirst for justice, who yearn to look upon deeds of piety, will be convinced that your promotion to this highest office would mean the total destruction of the Church.

---

42. For these events, cf. *Liber pontificalis* 2.261f.; Rodulfus Glaber, *Historiarum libri quinque* 1.4.12; and Reindel, *Briefe* 2 (1988) 540 n. 25. But Damian's account, almost contemporary with these narratives, is more detailed and could well be original. Telling of Roman affairs some 64 years before this letter, Damian was in a position to have learned of these events from Roman eyewitnesses.

43. Ezek 23.25–30.

336   PETER DAMIAN

The Synodal Procès-Verbal between the Imperial Counsel and the Defense Attorney for the Roman Church.[44]

(24) But in response to this, you boastfully declare, "The king and his mother, the empress, have elected me,[45] his royal highness has promoted me to this exalted position." Yet since, on the one side, the royal court supports the candidate it has elected and, on the other, the Roman Church defends its own bishop already enthroned,[46] it is proper that this large gathering of holy and prudent bishops should assemble and, after discussing this matter, should come to a decision under the authority of canon law.[47] And since on this account, as is our expectation, the council of Augsburg will soon take place,[48] let us then here produce a dress rehearsal, something like a preview of this council. And so, as in the vision of Daniel,[49] let the chairs be put in place to seat the court, let the books be opened, and let the disputed matter we hope to solve be brought before us. On the one side, the attorney for the Roman Church will make his opening statement; on the other, the imperial counsel will present the arguments for his client. Parma and its heresiarch

---

44. Heinemann, MGH Ldl 1 (1891) 76–77, Lucchesi, *Vita* 2.157, and O. Capitani, "Problematica della *Disceptatio synodalis,*" *Studi Gregoriani* 10 (1975) 143–44 n. 1, recognized that the *Disceptatio* belonged to *Letter* 89, but until now it has not been edited as such. The situation is identical with that of *Opusc.* 2–3 (PL 145.41–68), now edited as *Letter* 1 (cf. O. J. Blum, *The Letters of Peter Damian* 1 [1989] 37–83), since *Opusc.* 3 is a dialogue that completes *Opusc.* 2. Here, the opening of the *Disceptatio* is clearly in response to the last paragraph of *Letter* 89. Its conclusion, in verse, speaks directly to Cadalus, indicating that all that went before was also addressed to him. Gaetani was responsible for separating the two, even though the MSS he used, especially V1, clearly associated them.

45. The empress Agnes and her twelve year old son, King Henry IV. On the promotion of Cadalus in Basel on 28 October 1061, cf. Schmidt, "Alexander II" 104ff. and 80–83.

46. See Schmidt, "Alexander II" 80ff.

47. Ryan, *Sources* 84 no. 153 here cites S. Kuttner, *Studi Gregoriani* 2 (1947) 398 n. 57 and Michel, *Papstwahl* 186.

48. The council of Augsburg was held on 27 October 1062. This is known only from *Letter* 112. On the council, see Hefele-Leclercq, *Histoire* 4.2.1228; F. Baix in DHGE 11 (1952) 77–78; Palazzini, *Dizionario dei concili* 1 (1963) 109. The acts of this council have not survived and, contrary to Damian's optimistic statement in *Letter* 112, the council did not reach a decision.

49. Cf. Dan 7.9–10.

must now be silent, permitting only the imperial lawyers and the Roman Church to address one another. The holy bishops should pay close attention, so that they might compare what both will say and reach a just decision in the case argued before them. So let us get on. The attorney for the Apostolic See will begin, and then the imperial counsel will present his brief as he sees fit.

(25) *Attorney for the Roman Church:* Venerable Fathers, since your holiness is examining the estate of the Apostolic See, you are not unaware that the matter in hand touches all other churches. If the former stands firm, the others will stand along with her. But if she, who is the foundation of all others, should be overthrown, it follows that the condition of the rest will disintegrate. All patriarchal honors, metropolitan primacy, episcopal privilege, and the dignity of churches of every rank were established by some king or emperor, or some mere man of whatever station; as he saw fit or found it in his power, he prescribed the rights of their special prerogative. But only he who granted to the blessed custodian of the keys of eternal life the powers of earthly and heavenly dominion, founded the Roman Church and built it on the rock of faith[50] that would soon emerge. It was no ordinary earthly utterance, but the Word by whom heaven and earth were made, and through whom finally the elements of all things were structured, who founded the Roman Church. Clearly, it enjoys his privilege and is supported by his authority.

(26) And thus, without doubt, whoever deprives any church of its rights commits an injustice; but if one should attempt to deny the Roman Church the privilege granted it by the head of all the churches himself, he doubtless falls into heresy; and while the former may be called an unjust man, the latter must surely be labelled as a heretic. He who acts contrary to her who is the mother of faith certainly does violence to the faith, and obstinately opposes him who is known to have preferred her to all other churches.[51] Consequently, since all of this is un-

---

50. Cf. Matt 16.18–19.
51. Cf. Ryan, *Sources* 84 no. 154, where he refers to *Letter* 65 n. 15 (formerly *Opusc.* 5), citing the exact words of the last two paragraphs of this letter.

doubtedly known to your holiness, you who are not just ordinary sons of the Roman Church, but her more noble and outstanding offspring, must demonstrate love and compassion for your mother, and decide whether she should be destroyed for having chosen her own pontiff. We must certainly marvel if what the vigor of all the canons has allowed to lesser churches should not be permitted to her alone, who is the head of all.[52]

(27) *Imperial Counsel:* This verbose exercise in oratory has produced attentiveness, good will, and docility according to the manner of a civil court rather than the norms of a synodal council where, indeed, we ought not highly regard polished and elaborate style, but rather the purity of the living word. Therefore, in placing our complaint before these holy bishops, it suffices for us to say that you have enthroned a pope without the consent of our emperor, an act injurious to and in contempt of his royal majesty.

(28) *Attorney for the Roman Church:* We cannot, nor must we, disavow the installation of the pope, but in every way possible we reject the charge of injuring the emperor. But first of all, if we may, let us see whether a pope may be inducted without the emperor, and then later let us argue the matter of injury to his majesty.

(29) *Imperial Counsel:* Certainly we know that when a pontiff is installed, canonical authority determines that those whose duty it is to elect him must obey him after he has been inducted. But not only the Roman people but also the Roman emperor, who is the people's head, owe obedience to the pope because he is the universal pontiff. Are we, therefore, to judge that the people without their head should elect the pope, and that the emperor should obey him whom he did not elect?[53] Therefore we must conclude that unless the emperor of the Romans has

---

52. Cf. Ryan, *Sources* 84f. no. 154, with reference to the *Collectio Dionysio-Hadriana* (PL 67.276D–277A); JK 369.
53. Ryan, *Sources* 85 no. 155 cites the decree of Anastasius II in the *Collectio Dionysio-Hadriana* (PL 67.313) and the same text in Burchard, *Decretorum libri* 15.15 (PL 140.897 B–D); JK 744; Michel, *Papstwahl* 186.

granted his assent, the election of the Roman pontiff will not be complete.[54]

(30) *Attorney for the Roman Church:* It must therefore be asserted, according to the point you have just made in your response, that neither Stephen, nor Sixtus, nor Cornelius, and finally, neither Clement, nor Sylvester, nor even the blessed apostle Peter are worthy to be called popes, because they were not elected by the emperors of their day.[55]

(31) *Imperial Counsel:* Pagan kings are not to be used in arguing the matter of the election before us, for since they were ignorant of the Christian faith, they could not induct a Christian pontiff. Otherwise, Christian princes have always elected the Roman pontiffs.

(32) *Attorney for the Roman Church:* He who prevaricates in ordinary speech is called a liar; but he who speaks an untruth in the presence of venerable bishops undoubtedly commits the crime of sacrilege. You have said that Christian princes always chose the Roman pontiffs. Let us run through the ancient history of the Church, and carefully examine the list of the Roman popes. There you will find that in very few cases was there royal assent to their election, so admit that you have told an obvious lie.[56] Which emperor elected the Spaniard Damasus, the son of Antonius, or Innocent, an Alban, the son of Innocent, or finally Zosimus, a Greek, the son of Abramius? Which emperor, moreover, elected Leo, by nationality a Tuscan, son of Quintianus, or Hilary, son of Crispinus, by nationality a Sar-

---

54. Cf. *Liber diurnus Romanorum pontificum* 60, ed. Th. von Sickel (1889, reprint 1966) 188. Cf. also Ryan, *Sources* 86 no. 156.
55. Damian here, and in the next long response of the attorney for the Roman Church, depends on the *Liber pontificalis* 1.220ff. for further identification of individual papal elections.
56. The popes listed here by Damian are the following: Damasus I (366–384), Innocent I (402–417), Zosimus (417–418), Leo I (440–461), Hilary (461–468), Celestine I (422–432), Boniface I (418–422), Anastasius I (399–402 or Anastasius II (496–498), Simplicius (468–483), Felix I (268/9–273/4) or Felix II (483–492), Gelasius I (468–496), Symmachus (498–514), Hormisdas (514–523), John I (523–526), Felix III (526–530), Boniface II (530–532), Mercurius = John II (533–535), and Agapite I (535–536).

dinian? Who chose Celestine, son of Priscus, a Roman citizen, or Boniface, or Anastasius, both of whom were Romans? And thus, I could add many more if it would not become boring.

(33) But that you do not think that I am unable to continue this count because there are no others to name, which emperor elected Simplicius, Tibertinus, Felix, by nationality a Roman, or Gelasius of the province of Africa, the son of Valerius, or Symmachus of the province of Sardinia, the son of Fortunatus? Who chose Hormisdas, son of Justus, a Campanian, John, by nationality a Tuscan, Felix, a Samnite, Boniface, the son of Sigibaldus, Mercurius, son of Projectus, Agapite, son of Gordian, all Romans by birth? Of which emperor do we read that he ever gave his assent to the election of any of these, since at their time we know that Christian princes presided over the Roman state? There were Valentinian the Elder, his brother Valens, who was killed in battle with the Goths near Adrianople; Gratian, who was killed by the tyrant Maximus; the younger Valentinian, murdered by his count at Vienne; following these were Arcadius, Honorius, Theodosius; John, who was killed at Ravenna; Valentinian the third, who was killed in the Campus Martius; Marcian, Leo, Majorianus, Severus, Anthemius, Olibrius, Glycerius, Zeno; Nepos, who was killed in his villa near Salona; Augustulus, Anastasius, Justin, and all the other Roman emperors whom I pass over to avoid becoming excessively wordy in my style.

(34) Now then, show me someone of those I have enumerated who either sought to install a pope or gave his imperial consent to an election, and I will congratulate you and declare you worthy to be crowned with the laurel of victory. But if you are unable to produce such a name, you must admit that in all this you have been routed. Indeed we read of blessed Gregory, however, that he received an imperial assent from the Emperor Maurice, and that a very few other emperors promoted still others, but this was necessitated by the turbulent times and by a horrible period of war.[57]

57. Cf. Ryan, *Sources* 86 no. 157; Gregory of Tours, *Historia Francorum* 10.1 (MGH SS rer. Mer. 1.407); John the Deacon, *S. Gregorii magni vita* 1.40 (PL 75.79 B–C).

(35) *Imperial Counsel:* If lying is to speak contrary to what one thinks, it is rash and impudent to accuse me of lying, since I was of the opinion that I spoke the truth and not something false. But I agree with you, and still do not admit that I was here defeated.

(36) *Attorney for the Roman Church:* But, that this matter may be still more evident, and that I might more clearly show that you have lost this debate, read the decree of the Emperor Constantine, where he established the primacy of the Apostolic See over all the churches in the world. For after founding the basilica over the body of blessed Peter, and after constructing the palace of the Lateran in honor of the blessed savior, he at once defined the preeminence of the Roman Church by the terms of his imperial rescript. Here he bequeathed to blessed Sylvester and to his successors that they might wear on their head a golden crown in royal fashion, and might employ other ornaments of royal honor. Blessed Sylvester, however, assumed for his own use only those adornments that he thought to be in keeping with the episcopal office, but disregarded the crown and other items that appeared to be ostentatious rather than symbolic. Constantine also granted him a perpetual right to the palace of the Lateran, which had up to that time been the royal court, and the right to jurisdiction over the kingdom of Italy. For these are this emperor's very words: "Wherefore we have thought it proper," he said, "that our empire and the royal power be transferred and shifted to the East, and that in the province of Byzantium, on a most suitable site, a city be built that bears our name, and there establish our rule; for where the chief bishop and head of the Christian religion was stationed by the celestial emperor, it is not proper for the earthly emperor there to have power."[58]

(37) Did you not just hear that the earthly emperor has no power over the Roman Church? How is it unlawful, therefore, to elect a bishop without his consent, since there he has no authority? So Constantine departed for Constantinople, as to a

---

58. *Constitutum Constantini* c. 18. 94f., ed. H. Fuhrmann (MGH Fontes iuris 10 [1968]) 12.f. and 22.

second Rome, to rule there in perpetuity. Many years later, the emperor Theodosius began the building of the basilica of St. Paul.[59] After his death his son, Honorius, completed the same basilica. Both also confirmed the privilege of the Roman Church. How, therefore, could they have left behind them their prerogative over the election of the Roman Pontiff, since they never sought to subdue the Roman Church, but wished rather to make it preeminent, not to direct it, but to be in submission to it, not to be its superior, but its subject?

(38) *Imperial Counsel:* I obviously admit and confirm what you say. Granted further, that in our day his royal highness cannot claim this right from the custom of ancient emperors.[60] But this you are unable to deny, that the emperor Henry, the father of my lord, the emperor, was created Patrician of the Romans, from whom also he received at the election the privilege of always inducting the pope.[61] To this I may add, and this is much more important, that Pope Nicholas granted my lord, the emperor, this privilege which had come to him from the right of his father,[62] and again confirmed it in the document of the synodal decree.[63] Therefore, since no private person is required to forfeit his right until the matter has been heard and a sentence pronounced against him, how has his royal majesty lost this privilege that belonged to him by the right he had received from the generosity of the Apostolic See, and to which he had succeeded by reason of the imperial rights of his father? How without trial, I say, did he lose the position of dignity he had acquired in the Roman Church, since he had not given offense to the Roman Church?

(39) *Attorney for the Roman Church:* I also defend the privilege

59. Cf. *It.Pont.* 1.164–69.
60. Cf. *Liber pontificalis* 81.1.354 as Damian's source for this statement.
61. Here he refers to the council held in Rome in December 1046, at which Damian was present for the coronation of Henry III and all associated events; see *Letter* 70 n. 20.
62. Cf. Ryan, *Sources* 87 no. 160.
63. For the interpretation of the decree at this point, see Reindel, *Briefe* (1988) 548 nn. 64–65.

granted to our invincible emperor himself, and hope with all my heart that he will always be in full and undiminished possession thereof. But the Roman Church, in a much more noble and sublime way than any natural mother, is the mother of the emperor. The latter, indeed, gave him birth, that by his descent from her he might return to dust; the former, however, bore him that he might become a coheir of Christ to rule forever. And all of us surely know that the emperor, even though of impeccable stock, is still only a boy. Therefore, what evil has the Roman Church committed if, since he is still not of age but rather in need of a tutor, she took her son's place by reason of her tutorial duty, and exercised the right that belongs to him? For who is unaware that a boy does not know how to elect a bishop? Often a mother will intrude upon a judge's tribunal, receive witnesses, call together the clerks for consultation, and thus by the testimony given and confirmed, together with the written evidence, guarantee to her son all the rights to his property. In the meantime, however, until he has reached his majority and is capable of handling his own affairs, she controls and manages everything, and thus disposes as she sees fit of that which belongs to another through inheritance. Can such a mother on this account be said to withhold those things that have been granted to her son? It is rather more true to say, I think, that she is fulfilling her maternal duty, because what her inexperienced son might otherwise destroy or squander, she preserves, in that his goods were properly handed over to her for safekeeping and reasonable management. Thus as a natural mother assists her son in earthly matters, should mother Church not render help to her son, the emperor, in the matter of his spiritual gifts?

(40) Therefore, let this cunning deceit that deserves to be punished hold its peace, because it condemns an action that should properly by praised. It tries to accuse her of crime when, because of benefits rendered, she should rightly be found worthy of honor. To this may be added that occasionally, because of the changing times, the order of events must often be altered. For on the day the Roman Church appointed her

pontiff,[64] such fiery hostility and seditious action broke out among the inhabitants of the city, such ill will and hatred aroused the feelings of the tumultuous crowd, that it was impossible for us to await a decision from our gracious emperor who was so far away. For, unless the pope were immediately inducted, the people would have savagely wounded one another with their swords, and no small slaughter of Roman citizens would have occurred.

(41) *Imperial Counsel:* Give any excuse you wish, and argue as you like, so long as it remains clear that in no way can we alter what the pope granted, what he established by his decree, and what he confirmed in writing.[65]

(42) *Attorney for the Roman Church:* Why need we wonder that the statutes of men, still encumbered by weakness of the flesh, should be changed, when even almighty God, who knows all things that will come to pass, also changes things that were established by him? For at times he alters a thing he has promised, at times diminishes something or even totally withdraws it, and at times threatens evil and then does not inflict it.

(43) *Imperial Counsel:* Let us have examples from Scripture for the statements you have just made. What has God ever promised that he later altered?

(44) *Attorney for the Roman Church:* If it has not been forgotten, you will be able to recall that the Lord said to Noah, "My spirit shall not remain in man forever; he for his part is mortal flesh; he shall live for 120 years."[66] But since Scripture states that Noah was then 500 years old when the Lord said these things to him, but was already 600 years old when all the springs of the great abyss broke through, it is clear that twenty years were subtracted from the number he referred to before. And so God diminished the life span that he had promised to

---

64. On the election and enthroning of Alexander II, done simultaneously on 30 September 1061, see Schmidt, "Alexander II" 83ff.
65. For the *Privilegium* of Nicholas II, granted to Henry IV before the *Papal election decree* of April 1059, cf. Ryan, *Sources* 88 no. 162.
66. Gen 6.3.

the human race. The Holy Spirit also, in the words of the patriarch Jacob, made this promise to Judah when he said, "The scepter shall not pass from Judah, nor the leader from his descendants, until he arrives who will be sent."[67] And still, we do not read that at the time of the Judges, men of the tribe of Judah ruled over Israel, nor do we find kings from that same tribe holding power down to the coming of Christ. It is obvious, therefore, that almighty God often lessened what he had promised to man, because man had not fulfilled his duty to God.

(45) *Imperial Counsel:* Tell us also about situations in which God had promised something good, and did not effectively carry out his plan.

(46) *Attorney for the Roman Church:* Call to mind what the Lord said to Josiah, the king of Judah: "Because you read what was in the book," he said, "and your heart was filled with terror, and you humbled yourself before the Lord when you heard me say that I would bring disaster on this place and its inhabitants, and rent your clothes and wept before me, therefore, I will gather you to your forefathers, and you will be gathered to your grave in peace."[68] And yet, a bit farther on, Scripture says, "It was in his reign that Pharaoh Necho, king of Egypt, set out for the river Euphrates to help the king of Assyria. Josiah went out to meet him; when they met at Megiddo, Pharaoh Necho slew him."[69] Through Jeremiah it was also said to Zedekiah, the king of Judah: "Listen to the Lord's word, Zedekiah, king of Judah. This is the Lord's word to you: You shall not die by the sword; you will die a peaceful death, and they will kindle fires in your honor like the fires kindled in former times for the kings, your ancestors, who preceded you. 'Alas, my lord!' they will say as they mourn for you. This I have spoken. This is the very word of the Lord."[70] But whoever searches the historical record will never be able to find all this taking place. For after he was captured by the Babylonian king and carried off to Babylon, we never again hear that he was freed

67. Gen 49.10.
68. 2 Kgs 22.18–20.
69. 2 Kgs 23.29.
70. Jer 34.4–5.

from his chains. And thus, in his just judgment God at times withdraws the good things he has promised when rebellious man refuses to obey his commands.

(47) *Imperial Counsel:* Please go on. How was it that God did not inflict the evil that he had threatened?

(48) *Attorney for the Roman Church:* No one who belongs to the Church will be unaware that Jonah, who was sent by the Lord to Nineveh, proclaimed, "In forty days Nineveh shall be overthrown."[71] But because that city had totally converted to God, it was not conquered and destroyed as the Lord had threatened. Therefore, since almighty God is not only truthful but is truth itself, while his decision remains inviolate, he often changes the course of a decision that lies outside himself, in keeping with the quality of what man deserves, whether for good or for evil. Thus, if man abandons his wicked behavior, he will escape from what God in his justice has threatened; and if he falls into sin, he will not receive the good things he has promised. And so he spoke through the prophet Jeremiah: "If you now mend your ways and your doings and obey the Lord your God, then he may relent and revoke the disaster with which he threatened you."[72] Thus too did the Lord speak to Eli in the words of the man of God: "The Lord's word was, 'I promise that your house and your father's house shall serve before me for all time.' But now the Lord says, 'I will have no such thing; I will honor those who honor me, and those who despise me shall meet with contempt.'"[73]

(49) *Imperial Counsel:* You have very properly provided evidence from Scripture for everything that you previously stated. But now let us go back a bit to what was said before and, as you promised, account for the damage that was done to my lord, the emperor.

(50) *Attorney for the Roman Church:* God forbid that as we elected the pope, we should inflict an injury on our glorious

---

71. Jonah 3.4. 72. Jer 26.13.
73. 1 Sam 2.30.

emperor, since, as was said above, it was necessity that persuaded us to this action, and not spoliation. It was the imminent danger of civil war that prompted us, unwilling as we were, to take this course, and not a malicious desire to harm or diminish his power.

(51) *Imperial Counsel:* You propose civil war and allege imminent danger in your defense; you might as well say that the heavens would come crashing down and the earth be torn to pieces. Going still further, why do you not say that the oceans would dry up and the earth would be overwhelmed by the flood? All of this concerns me not at all, so long as it is certain that, whatever happens, you will not be allowed to contravene the decision of his holiness, the pope,[74] and in no way be permitted to violate the sacredness of the synodal decree.[75] For, as it is written, "It is better that scandal should occur than that the truth be abandoned."[76] Surely, if the blessed martyrs had feared this kind of war, without doubt they would have deserted from the army of Christ.

(52) *Attorney for the Roman Church:* You are not ignorant of the fact that among all the holy martyrs, Peter and Paul hold the primacy at the summit of the apostolic senate.

(53) *Imperial Counsel:* Just as it is a sacrilege to deny this fact, so too would it be superfluous to affirm it.

(54) *Attorney for the Roman Church:* For us it is an obligation to follow in their footsteps, to place their mark upon our actions, and to live under the discipline they have taught us.

(55) *Imperial Counsel:* The point you make is clear and obvious. But I fail to see what sort of portent or prestige you might support by this line of reasoning.

(56) *Attorney for the Roman Church:* Forget about prestige, and try to understand the truth! If you are afraid that I am setting

---

74. Cf. Ryan, *Sources* 88 no. 164, where he again cites the *Privilegium* conceded to Henry IV. Cf. *supra*, n. 65.
75. Cf. Ryan, *Sources* 88 no. 161.
76. Gregory I, *Hom. in Hiezechihelem* 1.7.5 (CC 142.85).

snares for you, listen to Paul who was telling the truth about his fellow apostle Peter: "For until certain persons came from James," he said, "he was taking his meals with gentile Christians; but when they came he drew back and began to hold aloof, because he was afraid of the advocates of circumcision."[77] And so, here we have Peter acting with discretion. Indeed, he feared that the Jews, because of the gentile Christians, might abandon the Christian faith, and so, that he might not lose the flock entrusted to him, he followed the example of the good shepherd. With the Jews he acted like a Jew[78] that he might win over the Jews. For Christ came into the world endowed with sinful human nature that he might free man from sin, and he did not hesitate to abolish the Law of Moses. But he kept in mind that the brethren were still weak and improperly instructed, and so retained for a time the shadow of the Law that he might finally bring them to a perfect understanding of the full truth. In this case also, blessed Peter laid before us the norms of discretion, so that now and then, when it would not be harmful, we might deviate somewhat from the narrow path so as to be able to care for our weaker brothers.

(57) *Imperial Counsel:* While saying that Peter for a time upheld the Judaic Law, why do you not also tell us that in the same epistle we read that Paul opposed him to his face? "I opposed him to his face," he said, "because he was clearly in the wrong."[79] And then he said to him, "If you, a Jew born and bred, live like a gentile, and not like a Jew, how can you insist that gentiles must live like Jews?"[80] So, why did you mention the one situation and remain silent about the other?

(58) *Attorney for the Roman Church:* What Peter did out of mercy and compassion, Paul here asserted for the sake of teaching us how we should act. The former acted by way of dispensation, that he might not be a stumbling block to the weak; but the latter reproved him so that someone indiscreet might not heedlessly follow him as an example. From Peter we

77. Gal 2.12.
79. Gal 2.11.
78. Cf. 1 Cor 9.20.
80. Gal 2.14.

should learn that in dangerous situations we should be on our guard; from Paul's words we should be advised that in sober matters our life should be devoted to nothing but upright behavior.

(59) *Imperial Counsel:* I have only praise for the explanations you offer, but while proposing the two apostles as our teachers, you cause me to marvel that, in bypassing Paul, you hold up only Peter as a model.

(60) *Attorney for the Roman Church:* Don't act like a child, my brother. Not so fast, but take one step at a time. Because of the gravity of the matter before us we must speak with moderation. Listen carefully as we now come to Paul who also shows us how to act with golden discretion, and is himself a model of compassionate dispensation. As the historical narrative found in the Acts of the Apostles relates, "Paul started on his journey and travelled through Syria and Cilicia, bringing new strength to the congregations. He went on to Derbe and to Lystra, and there he found a disciple named Timothy, the son of a Jewish Christian, his widowed mother, and a gentile father."[81] To shorten this account, the Apostle therefore circumcised him because he especially feared the Jewish Christians who lived in those areas. Why, therefore, did he circumcise a Christian who was not a Jew, who indeed had been uncircumcised because he was a gentile, except to practice discretion, so that Christian Jews would not be scandalized and apostatize from the faith? I also now recall that for a while, according to the rite of the Nazirites, Paul vowed to let his hair grow long;[82] after sailing for Syria, he had his hair cut off at Cenchreae according to the prescript of the Law. Luke, the author of this sacred history, also reports this: "When we reached Jerusalem," he said, "the brotherhood welcomed us gladly," and the next day James and all the elders who were with him, after approving his ministry, said to him, "You see, brother, how many thousands of converts we have among the Jews, all of them staunch upholders of the

---

81. Acts 15.41; 16.1. Here Damian strays from the Vulgate; cf. Weber, *Biblia sacra* 2.1725.
82. Cf. Acts 18.18; Num 6.5.

Law. Now they have been given certain information about you: it is said that you teach all the Jews in the gentile world to turn their backs on Moses, telling them to give up circumcising their children and following our way of life. What is the position, then? A crowd is likely to gather, for they are sure to have heard that you have arrived. You must therefore do as we tell you. We have four men here who are under vow; take them with you and go through the ritual of purification with them, paying their expenses, after which they may shave their heads. Then everyone will know that there is nothing in the stories they were told about you, but that you are a practicing Jew and keep the Law yourself. So Paul took the men, and on the next day, after going through the ritual of purification with them, he went into the temple to give notice of the date when the period of purification would end and the offering be made for each one of them."[83]

(61) But why did Paul, in accord with the ceremonies of the Jews, shave his head, go barefoot, offer sacrifice, and, while destroying the Law, observe the precepts of the Law? Why, I ask, did he conform to all this, if not to avoid giving scandal to those who were converts from Judaism? He took on the appearance of one who was sick, that he might remove disease from those who were truly sick. He observed the ritual of the Law, of which he had said in his letter, "What formerly I considered assets, I now count as sheer loss, and because of Christ count as so much dung."[84] He circumcised a man, but still uttered this terrible statement: "I say to you that if you receive circumcision, Christ will do you no good at all."[85] I ask you, what can be a greater sin than to abandon Christ, to violate the norms of the Christian religion, to introduce the rites of the Jewish Law, and to impugn the new grace that proceeds from the gospel? And yet we see the apostle Paul doing all these things superficially, so that he might not scandalize those who were still immature in understanding the rudiments of the new faith. And, if we look only to externals, we find that Cerinthus

83. Acts 21.17–26.
84. Cf. Phil 3.7–8.
85. Gal 5.2.

and Ebion[86] had done nothing worse than what Paul had done. For, while believing in Christ, they were anathematized by their parents only because they had blended the ceremonies of the Law with the gospel of Christ, and professed to believe the new so as not to alter the old. But notice that while saying that James and all the elders had given Paul their advice, the text means that all the disciples likewise carried out what Paul had done. One thing, at least, is to their credit: they were in harmony—both he who did this thing, and those who had advised that it be done.

(62) Therefore, if these rulers of the world, whose laws are obeyed not only by earthly kingdoms but by all the highest heavens, did not hesitate to condescend to only a few men of their time in this perilous situation, why are we, truly insignificant men, who centuries later follow in their footsteps, not permitted to come to the assistance of countless numbers of men in the city of Rome? But why do we speak of the apostles and their solicitude not to scandalize the weak and the recent converts, when their Lord and Master himself, to whose rule all the ages are subject, avoided giving scandal to the Jews as an example for our imitation? "What do you think of this, Simon?" he asked. "From whom do earthly monarchs collect tax? From their own people, or from aliens?" When he answered, "From aliens," he promptly continued, "Why, then, their own people are exempt! But as we do not wish to scandalize them, go and cast a line in the lake; take the first fish that comes to the hook, open its mouth, and you will find a silver coin; take that and pay it in; it will meet the tax for us both."[87] And so, if Peter does not satisfy as a model for your action, then consider Paul if you would learn how rigid morality is to be softened and the virtue of discretion should be practiced. But if neither suffices for your bold obstinacy, be ashamed of yourself for trying to be holier than Jesus as you engage in your absurd

---

86. Judeo-Christian heretics, putative leaders of first-century sects; cf. G. Bardy, "Cérinthe," DHGE 12 (1953) 169f. and H. J. Schoeps, "Ébionites," DHGE 14 (1960) 1314–19.
87. Matt 17.24–26.

chatter: "For Christ is the end of the Law as a way to justice for every one who has faith."[88]

(63) *Imperial Counsel:* We cannot overrule the virtue of discretion, approved by such an array of scriptural evidence. But God forbid that any virtue should be so sublime or preeminent, that attempting to practice it should force us to fall into the abyss of anathema. For since everything prescribed for us in the Law of God undoubtedly has the purpose of associating us in eternal company with our creator, if, God forbid, we should happen to be cut off from him by the sentence of damnation, what virtue, what amount of discretion, or, as it is said, what compassionate love can compensate for such an indescribable loss? Surely, if we practice virtue only that we might be associated with almighty God, how can that be called a virtue that drives us away from enjoying God's presence?

(64) *Attorney for the Roman Church:* Please be a bit more explicit in explaining the point you make, since it is somewhat obscure.

(65) *Imperial Counsel:* The text of the synodal decree, which the pope ordained with the consent of the whole council, to which he affixed his signature, and which so many venerable and outstanding bishops approved as they signed, could not, according to custom, fail to have a formula of anathema attached to it.[89] Therefore, out of compassion or condescension for a raging crowd—I know not which motive you might have—you should never implicate yourself in the toils of such an inextricable condemnation. It is surely ridiculous to haul a drowning man from the furious sea in such a way that his rescuer himself should go down in the surging waves.

(66) *Attorney for the Roman Church:* In speaking so indiscreetly, you are fighting with me like those blindfolded gladiators[90] who, because they always engaged in combat with their eyes obstructed, were able, indeed, to wound others, but could not

---

88. Rom 10.4.
89. See Ryan, *Sources* 89 no. 167.
90. See Jerome, *Adversus Iovinianum* 1.36 (PL 23. 260A).

avoid being wounded themselves. You say that we must by no stretch of the imagination fall under the ban of excommunication, even though we might by this come to the aid of our weaker brothers. Here you are swinging your sword and trying to wound me, but you are unable to see where you should place your shield to protect yourself. Has what I cited above, namely, what Paul said in his epistle, "If you receive circumcision, Christ will do you no good at all," already escaped your memory?[91] And still, what he so strictly forbade, he himself did out of love for his weak brothers so that they would not be scandalized. What greater or more severe anathema could one suffer than to be told that Christ will do him no good in avoiding damnation for his sins? For he whom Christ does not benefit is undoubtedly under anathema, and no other anathema will he incur than that he be expelled from the company of Christ in whom all the nations are blessed. If Paul, therefore, had no fear of undergoing this anathema out of love for his brothers, in fact, utterly escaped it when he circumcised not just some ordinary person, but his own disciple who was a Christian, do you, I ask, you who have lost your inner vision, do you state that what the Apostle did should not be done by others? Indeed, he himself said, "All the Scriptures were written for our own instruction."[92]

(67) *Imperial Counsel:* It is very likely that when Paul upbraided his fellow apostle Peter for taking part in a revived Judaizing, after circumcising his own disciple, he probably pointed an accusing finger also at himself. And I will not be otherwise dissuaded from this thinking unless, perhaps, something to the contrary can be found in his writings.

(68) *Attorney for the Roman Church:* So that no blemish of ambiguity linger in your thinking, and that no further darkness obstruct your mind in this matter, listen to what the same Paul said to the Romans: "I am speaking the truth as a Christian, and my own conscience, enlightened by the Holy Spirit, assures me it is no lie; in my heart there is great grief and unceasing

---

91. Gal 5.2.   92. Rom 15.4.

sorrow. For I could even pray to be outcast from Christ myself for the sake of my brothers, my natural kinsfolk, who are Israelites."[93] So there you have Paul, not like us compelled by necessity, but of his own accord and willingly wishing to be anathema for the sake of his brothers; do you propose that I fear to suffer anathema, when you see that I was totally and inevitably bound by necessity, and under an obligation of charity to protect this large group of the brothers from suffering disaster? Listen also to what Moses said, as he asked God to help the people of Israel: "Hear me, O Lord, for this people has committed a great sin; they have made for themselves gods of gold. If you will forgive them, forgive. But if not, blot out my name, I pray, from the book that you have written."[94] Such a thing will be fulfilled when at the Last Judgment he will say to the reprobate, "The curse is upon you; go from my sight to the eternal fire."[95] Note that, on the one hand, Paul chose to be rejected for the welfare of his brothers and, on the other, Moses begged to be blotted out from God's book out of love for the people he led. Should only the Roman Church, whose principal and special function it is to promote love and compassion throughout the world, not dare to shield her children whom she daily begets through the sacrament of holy baptism from the threatening swords everywhere unsheathed against them? It was Saul who said, "A curse be on the man who eats any food before nightfall until I have taken vengeance on my enemies."[96] Jonathan fell under this curse, as we read, but the love with which he manfully fought for the people freed him from the sentence of death that threatened him.[97] Would you also like to hear what the same apostle says of Jesus himself, the author of all blessings? "Christ," he states, "bought us freedom from the curse of the Law by becoming for our sake an accursed thing."[98]

(69) Therefore, the very author of eternal blessing did not find it beneath his dignity to be under a curse that he might

93. Rom 9.1–4.
94. Exod 32.31–32; for variant, cf. Sabatier 1.201.
95. Matt 25.41.
96. 1 Sam 14.24.
97. Cf. 1 Sam 14.45.
98. Gal 3.13.

free us from the bondage of this curse. So too all the holy men of both the Old Testament and the New Testament, in following the example of their head, wished to aid their weak brothers when they were in danger, and were never afraid to undergo the sentence of anathema. So why do you attempt to accuse me of this sin and fail to see the love that prompts me to this action, a love that cancels innumerable sins?[99] For how can I be bound by the sentence of any man, when I am set free by love, which is God himself?[100] Let him, therefore, who thinks so highly of human curses be ashamed, since through the gift of charity the dispenser of everlasting blessing is on my side.

(70) *Imperial Counsel:* Should truth itself desert one who is engaged in debate, it would be useless to persist in depending on evasive tricks. And so, it is ridiculous to protract this discussion. You have so completely escaped from the bonds of excommunication, by which up until now I thought you were held, that I can no longer object, and in this matter I cannot rationally continue to oppose you. But I see that there is still more than enough remaining with which, as your opponent, I can properly charge you. You state that because you were constrained by necessity and, as it were, under pressure because of the brief time at your disposal, you were quite unable to wait for his royal majesty's consent to the election of the pope. That this is a frivolous objection is obvious. For it is clear that more or less three months had passed since the death of Pope Nicholas of blessed memory,[101] and it was not until the first of October that the latter[102] succeeded. Let us see, therefore, whether over such a long period of time, namely three months, it was not possible for a copy of the confirming document from the royal court to have reached you.[103]

(71) *Attorney for the Roman Church:* Now you compel me to

---

99. Cf. 1 Pet 4.8.   100. Cf. 1 John 4.18.
101. Nicholas II died 27 July 1061.
102. See Schmidt, "Alexander II" 83ff. n. 66.
103. For this translation of *apoca pragmaticae sanctionis*, cf. DuCange 4.476; *Mittellateinisches Wörterbuch* 1 (1967) 750.

divulge something about which I had decided to remain silent out of reverence for the imperial court. But because of the vehemence of your demands, let your distinguished deed be brought into the open, something unheard of throughout the ages. For the officials of the royal court, together with certain holy bishops of the kingdom of Germany, conspiring, I might say, against the Roman Church, assembled a council[104] in which you condemned the pope in some sort of synodal decree, and with absolutely incredible audacity, presumed to quash all the decrees that he had passed. Certainly, in this—I will not call it a judgment, but a preconceived sentence—you nullified, if I may so speak, that very privilege the previous pope had granted to the emperor. And, since what he had ordained was destroyed by your intervening sentence, it follows also that what had been conceded by him to the emperor was terminated.[105] But far be it from us that, because of any man's arrogance, the emperor, who was not involved, should on our account lose any of his rights. And he whom, God willing, we thoroughly hope to see promoted to the imperial office, we will not permit, because of another's fault, to suffer damage to his royal dignity.

(72) And now, let me review the entire history of this unheard-of calamity of ours. Stephen, a cardinal priest of the Apostolic See, a man renowned for his serious and upright character and, as is well known, outstanding by reason of his many virtues, was sent to the royal court bearing letters from the pope, but failed to be received by the royal officials. He was forced to wait outside the court for almost five days, an action that was an affront to blessed Peter and to the Apostolic See. As a man of dignity and patience, he calmly bore this insult, but as a result was unable to carry out the mission entrusted

---

104. Ryan, *Sources* 89 no. 168, suggests 1060 for the date of the *Concilium Germanicum*. But see Reindel, *Briefe* 2 (1988) 560 n. 89, where the date 1061 is proposed.

105. See Ryan, *Sources* 89 no. 169, where he presumes that the privilege in question is that which Pope Nicholas II had granted to Henry IV before the *Papal election decree* was issued. See also Reindel, *Briefe* 2 (1988) 560–561, nn. 90–93.

to him.[106] He brought back the confidential instructions signed by the principals unopened; he was the bearer because the blameworthy indiscretion of the court did not permit them to be presented to the emperor. Indeed, in this unexpected audacity there is so much room for debate that it might well tax the eloquence of Demosthenes and exceed the vast ability of Cicero. Wherefore, if we should wish to be most precise in pursuing the matter of the injury we suffered, we might rightly allege that you have deprived yourselves of the privilege over the Roman Church,[107] since, as a result of your indiscretion, you have done her harm. He indeed violates the bonds of friendship who gratuitously attacks his friend and causes him harm. For the Lord himself said to the Jews in the words of Jeremiah, "And I will make a new covenant with Israel and Judah. It will not be like the covenant I made with their forefathers, a covenant they broke."[108] Therefore, he who is first to violate his oath of friendship renders null and void the agreement by which a grant was bestowed. Nevertheless, the Roman Church does not wish to exaggerate what it has had to bear, but desires that what it liberally granted to his royal highness should continue to function.

(73) *Imperial Counsel:* In maintaining that our lord the emperor is not guilty, you are acting properly. But that, on the other hand, you charge the officials of the court with wrongdoing seems to be unjust. For whatever was done in your regard in these matters, we did under orders from the emperor's mother,[109] and not of our own free decision.

(74) *Attorney for the Roman Church:* And I will answer you in line with your obduracy. For I must tell you that at times it is even sinful to obey the words of almighty God.

---

106. Cf. Heinemann (MGH Ldl 1.88 n. 1). Stephen's legation took place before Nicholas II's condemnation, after Stephen's return to Rome from France in early 1060.
107. The privilege of the Roman patricianship, granted to Henry III. Even were it not a merely personal prerogative, it was now abrogated by the court's presumptuous action.
108. Jer 31.31.
109. The dowager empress, Agnes.

(75) *Imperial Counsel:* The human heart is terrified by what you have just asserted, and one's Christian feelings cannot bear to hear such a thing.

(76) *Attorney for the Roman Church:* Because you are so astonished at this, I hasten to add that because someone promptly obeyed God he was lost, but that another, for refusing to obey, rose to a higher level of grace.

(77) *Imperial Counsel:* What you say is totally incredible. Nevertheless, if you are able to prove this statement by examples, tell us: Who has ever obeyed God and has gone to hell for that reason?

(78) *Attorney for the Roman Church:* You certainly know that the Lord said to Judas Iscariot, who had already agreed to betray him, "Do quickly what you have to do."[110] And later, when Judas dared to come forward to kiss him, he added, "Friend, what you are here for,"[111]—and understood—"carry it out." And because this miserable man put these words into action, he perished irrevocably.

(79) *Imperial Counsel:* After clearing up the first part of your statement, please explain the other. Who has ever refused obedience to almighty God and, because of that, merited an increase of grace?

(80) *Attorney for the Roman Church:* If you will, recall what the Lord said to Jeremiah: "Go and speak to the Rechabites, bring them to one of the rooms of the treasures in the house of the Lord, and offer them wine to drink."[112] And a little farther on the prophet continued, "I set bowls full of wine and drinking cups before the Rechabites and invited them to drink wine. But they said, 'We will not drink wine, for our forefather Jonadab laid this command on us: "You shall never drink wine, neither you nor your children."[113] And so, after that Jeremiah said to them, "These are the words of the Lord God of Hosts: Jonadab son of Rechab shall not want a descendant to stand before me

---

110. John 13.27.
112. Jer 35.2.
111. Matt 26.50.
113. Jer 35.5–6.

for all time."[114] Here you have a man, diabolically obeying and carrying out his charge, who rushed to his ruin, and others who fortunately disobeyed, and were found worthy of forever seeing their creator face to face. This also applies to the matter we were discussing. Because we elected the pope without the consent of the emperor, you are not at once to judge the external act, but you must rather carefully note the spirit and the intention with which it was done.

(81) *Imperial Counsel:* Such arguments are familiar to us, and are never wanting because they are always in good supply. We may often sin in performing an evil deed but, because it is secret, we can take refuge in the purity of our intentions.

(82) *Attorney for the Roman Church:* Do you think that a question must always be decided on the appearance of things and the literal meaning of words? According to the exact sound of the words, what is more incongruous than to say that God the Father, the Son, and the Holy Spirit "betrayed" the mediator between God and men? Thus Judas "betrayed" or "handed over" Christ, and God the Father also "handed him over." Does this not seem to be almost the same deed? Therefore, are not both Judas and God the Father "traitors"?

(83) *Imperial Counsel:* How do you prove that the Father, the Son, and the Holy Spirit "handed over" the savior?

(84) *Attorney for the Roman Church:* Listen to the Apostle when he says, "He did not spare his own Son, but gave him up for us all."[115] On this point also Solomon says, "You are just and order all things justly, yet you condemn a man who ought not to be punished."[116] That the Son gave himself up is also stated by the same Apostle: "Who loved me and gave himself up for me."[117] The book of Wisdom also related that the Holy Spirit handed over the Son when it says, "Wisdom is a spirit devoted to man's good, and she will not hold an accursed man blameless

---

114. Jer 35.19. 115. Rom 8.32.
116. Wis 12.15. But see Sabatier 2.408, where Damian's citation is found in a MS of St.-Germain.
117. Gal 2.20.

for his words."[118] Among the ancients, all those who were hanged on a gibbet were called "accursed." "For Christ," as the Apostle says, "bought us freedom from the curse by becoming an accursed thing for our sake."[119]

(85) Therefore, the Holy Spirit did not hold an accursed man blameless for his words, because he did not suppress what was said by the prophets about the passion of Christ, but allowed everything to be done to him without exception. Hence, according to you who are always prepared to judge by external appearance and not by a man's intention, if the Father handed over the Son, and the Son gave himself up, and the Holy Spirit did likewise, what was so evil in what Judas did? There was a surrender brought about by the Father, by the Son, by the Holy Spirit, and also by Judas. The same act was undertaken by many, but this same act must be seen differently in those who carried it out. For what almighty God effected out of love, Judas did out of greed for money. What God did to provide a remedy for our salvation, the latter performed to satisfy his insatiable avarice.

(86) You will thus observe that we must not so much note what a person does, but carefully examine the spirit and the intention with which he does it. For if we look only to externals, we find the Lord and savior himself saying something he had forbidden, and acting contrary to what he had commanded. "If anyone," he says, "calls his brother a fool, he will have to answer for it in the fires of hell."[120] And still, on the very day of his resurrection he said to the two disciples who were in doubt as they spoke to him, "How foolish you are and how slow to believe."[121] In the Sermon on the Mount he also said to his disciples, "If someone slaps you on the right cheek, turn and offer him your left."[122] And when undergoing the passion, not only did he not turn the other cheek to the servant of the high priest who had struck him in the face, but even said to him, "If I spoke amiss, reproach me; if I spoke well, why strike me?"[123]

118. Wis 1.6.
119. Gal 3.13.
120. Matt 5.22.
121. Luke 24.25.
122. Matt 5.39.
123. John 18.23; for variants, see Sabatier 3.476.

And how can it be true when Luke said of him that he was reporting "what Jesus did and taught from the beginning,"[124] if he did not carry out what he taught?

(87) Undoubtedly, however, we must understand that he commanded this to show his readiness of spirit, and not as a vain display of action. For how can one say that he was not prepared in spirit to be struck on the other cheek, since he had decided to offer his whole body on the cross for man's salvation? Also, when Paul was struck on orders from the high priest, he retorted, "God will strike you, you whitewashed wall."[125] To those who are not able to comprehend, this seemed to be a verbal insult, but in the prophetic sense it contained an oracular mystery. For a whitewashed wall has the meaning of hypocrisy,[126] representing the priestly dignity by this term, but hiding within it the unsightly filth of evil. But that his words referred to the man's meanness, he marvelously kept hidden. For when someone said to him, "Would you insult the high priest?" he answered, "My brothers, I had no idea he was the high priest; Scripture, I know, says, 'You must not abuse the ruler of your people.'"[127] Here we can clearly see with what serenity he spoke these words while appearing to act out of anger. By these citations from Scripture I wish only to show that we should not judge by mere words alone, but should be aware of the spirit and intention with which they were spoken.

(88) *Imperial Counsel:* The doubtful passages you proposed, you have now cleared up by the examples you have quoted. But please, let us now return to what we were previously discussing, so that you might explain why you have accused us of having disadvantaged you by obeying the emperor's command.

(89) *Attorney for the Roman Church:* It is surely proper after every objection on your part has been answered in an orderly fashion and to the point, not by rhetorical arguments, nor flowers of oratory, nor finally by dialectical syllogisms, but rather

---

124. Acts 1.1. 125. Acts 23.3.
126. See Augustine, *Epistulae CXXIV–CLXXXIV,* ed. A. Goldbacher (CSEL 44.139).
127. Acts 23.4–5.

purged of falsehood by recourse to reason drawn from the obvious truth that, on the other hand, we should rightly speak, if only briefly, of the excesses you have committed. For the condemnation of a pope is such a grave and inexcusable act that it is subject not only to human but to divine judgment. Our rulers, however, are exempt, both by lack of age and by weakness of sex. Guilt is obviously not to be imputed to them but, as they deserve, to their counselors.[128] Not to speak of other perversity, how could you presume to elect a wicked man to be the Roman pontiff while Rome was unaware of your action?

(90) *Imperial Counsel:* As is evident, we indeed had an election. But we were persuaded to this action because, long before, Count Gerard[129] and other citizens of Rome, as it was reported, had persistently urged it. Also, the abbot of the monastery called Clivus Scaurus[130] was involved. Therefore, it was not, as you assert, that the Roman pontiff was elected without the knowledge of the Romans, for they were present and requested it.

(91) *Attorney for the Roman Church:* In this you are on my side, in that you testify that Gerard, who was under ban of excommunication, had joined your party. For the moment I will remain silent about the abbot and about the others, but of Gerard at least it can be said that he was not a subject of the Church, and in no way belonged to the faithful of Christ. On his one head had fallen anathemas and excommunications from almost all the pontiffs who presided over the Roman Church in his day, and at last, shortly before he died, he was banned for having attacked and robbed the English duke and archbishop as they returned from visiting the tomb of St. Peter, and forced them to pay 1000 pounds to Pavia.[131] For his action he was ex-

---

128. On relations between Nicholas II and the German bishops, see J. Haller, *Papsttum* 2.336.f.

129. The count of Galeria; see Reindel, *Briefe* 2 (1988) 566 n. 103.

130. The monastery of SS. Andrew and Gregory on the Coelian Hill; see L. H. Cottineau, *Répertoire topo-bibliographique des abbayes et prieurés* 2.1 (1937) 2504.

131. Earl Tostig and Alfred, archbishop of York. The latter had come to Rome to receive the pallium from Nicholas II; cf. Florence of Worcester, *Chronicon*, ed. B. Thorpe 1 (1848, reprint 1964) 218.

communicated in the plenary synod at which Pope Nicholas presided and, as the candles were extinguished, he was placed under perpetual anathema.[132]

(92) This holy council must therefore consider whether the election by this man and his accomplices had the force of law, since in such a terrifying and irrevocable way he had been cut off from the body of the Church by the pruning knife of the gospel and of canon law, so that even in death he could not have his Christian rights restored to him. And was it proper that the Roman Church be disposed of by him who had always been her cruel enemy, and had always fought against her? How was it justifiable for him to choose a leader for the highest Church, when he was not permitted to cross the threshold of any church whatsoever? The Lord cried out to Israel, "You have an accursed one in your midst, O Israel; you cannot stand against your enemies until you rid yourselves of him who bears the blemish of this crime."[133] And why was this? Because Achan, son of Carmi, took from the forbidden things in Jericho only 200 shekels of silver, a bar of gold weighing fifty shekels, and a scarlet mantle; and because of this minor theft, the perpetrator of this crime was not only stoned to death, but was buried under a great pile of stones.[134]

(93) If Israel was unable to stand up to her enemies because of this man who had committed only one deceptive sacrilege, how will the Church survive if it is under the direction of a man involved in such a great number of crimes? This is especially so, since he was to elect such a person as Cadalus, in whom, as all the world knows, the dregs of every vice have come together—the pseudo-bishop, the apostle of antichrist, the enemy of Christ, an effeminate,[135] and a trader in churches. Therefore, which of these two on careful inquiry should seem preferable, he who was chosen by a man under the curse of

---

132. *Concilium Romanum*, April 1061; cf. Ryan, *Sources* 89 no. 170; Hefele-Leclercq, *Histoire* 4.1206; JL 4454.
133. Cf. Josh 7.13.   134. Cf. Josh 7.21–26.
135. All MSS here have *animam puellarum*, which earlier Latin editors have altered by using *amicum, amasium*, or *amatorem*. My translation attempts to interpret the original wording.

perpetual excommunication, or rather the other who was unanimously elected by the cardinal bishops,[136] chosen by the clergy, and requested by the people, not in a far-off land, but within the city of Rome and in the bosom of the Apostolic See itself?

(94) *Imperial Counsel:* We might perhaps give our consent in view of all the arguments you have proposed, were it deemed seemly for his royal majesty to change the position he had previously taken by choosing the man from Parma to be pope. For it would appear to sully his high honor with the taint of inconsistency were he to alter even slightly something of the decree he had published.

(95) *Attorney for the Roman Church:* Who is not aware that God is greater than the king, and yet he was not ashamed to say, "I repent of having made Saul king,"[137] and through Samuel he went back on his word when he said, "The Lord has rejected you as king over Israel."[138] If God, who knew everything that would happen in the future, could say that he regretted his action, why should a man be ashamed to change his opinion for something better, since he is unaware of what he also will be in the future? Saul, who had previously been good, became evil; but this man, namely Cadalus, who beforehand had certainly been evil, like the devil became daily more evil still.

(96) *Imperial Counsel:* What nonsense you now speak when you say that the devil can become still more degenerate, since he is certainly now so evil that it is impossible for him to become worse.

(97) *Attorney for the Roman Church:* I would be a liar were I unable to prove what I say with evidence from sacred Scripture. Now, according to Isaiah, at the beginning of the world the proud devil said, "I will rise above the clouds and make myself like the Most High."[139] But Paul says that when the end of the world shall come, "he shall rise in his pride against every

---

136. Cf. Krause, *Papstwahldekret* 80 n. 29.
137. 1 Sam 15.11.   138. 1 Sam 15.26.
139. Isa 14.14.

god, so called, every object of men's worship."[140] Therefore, he who formerly presumed to be like God, at the end of the world will become worse, since he will wish to be greater than God. From this we may readily gather that the devil can fall to still greater depths. And since the word "devil" may be understood to mean 'flowing downward,'[141] "Cadalus" taken from the Latin word meaning 'falling,' signifies 'the people's ruin,' both words aptly agreeing with one another.[142] Tell me, therefore, how such a person can be pope, since it was not the Roman people, but a single individual with his accomplices, not a Roman but someone from the suburbs,[143] and not a subject of the Church, but one cursed and excommunicated, who elected him? In your judgment, should he be pope who sold his own diocese that he might acquire the Church of Rome, who put Romans to the sword that he might become the Roman pontiff? You tell me that I am not allowed to elect the pontiff without the emperor's consent, and should not have paid so great a price to forestall the death of these people. Note, on the one hand, that blessed Augustine headed the Church of Hippo while Valerius was still alive and, on the other, that eight days after he had been baptized, Ambrose was consecrated bishop after receiving all the orders of the Church.[144]

(98) In both cases, to be sure, the order prescribed by canon law was set aside, and for no other reason than to serve the welfare of the people.[145] And do you tell me that for the welfare of the people I must not advise the emperor himself, that in giving his consent, honoring us with a single letter would be to his benefit? For how could he later be crowned Roman emperor, if now the Roman people were to be annihilated by fighting among themselves? Moreover, that the Roman Church did

---

140. 2 Thess 2.4.
141. Cf. Jerome, *Nom.hebr.* 80.16 (CC 72.160); Isidore, *Etymologies* 8.11.18.
142. Damian plays with the etymology of the word *Cadalus*, suggesting that it derives from *cadendo*, 'falling,' and λαός, 'people'; cf. also *Letter* 88 n. 39.
143. Gerard, the count of Galeria, a town located near Rome.
144. On the problem of Ambrose's consecration, see B. Fischer, *Kyriakon: Festschrift für Johannes Quasten*, ed. P. Granfield and J. A. Jungmann (1970) 527–31.
145. See Ryan, *Sources* 90 no. 172.

not cease to be friendly to the emperor in electing the pope is proven by the fact that, while there was an abundance of holy and learned men among its own clerical family, it did not choose any of them, but elected a man who had been at the royal court and was almost of the emperor's household.[146]

(99) *Imperial Counsel:* Whoever opposes the truth after it has clearly been made evident will rightly be judged an adversary of almighty God, provoking his unextinguishable anger against him if he persistently and arrogantly attacks the truth that is God himself.[147] But now let me conclude my remarks in this debate with you. As we discussed the question whether there could be an election of the Roman pontiff without the consent of the emperor, in reviewing the historical record you have assembled such a great number of Roman emperors and Roman pontiffs, and have confronted me with such a cloud of witnesses that I was unable, after seeing all this, to utter a single word[148] against you. Concerning the excommunication, however, which Pope Nicholas had ordained,[149] on which, as I must now admit as true, I had placed my entire hope of winning, you answered in your turn at debate with such invincible arguments from Scripture and with such clear evidence, both from the blessed apostles and from our Lord and savior himself, that you were able to teach us something we had previously not known, and forcibly to free yourself from the bonds of this declaration. Moreover, what I had called damaging to my lord, the king, and which I had so sharply proposed against you, was so briskly answered in your speech that it seems clearly proven that in electing the Roman pontiff the Roman people were of tremendous service to his royal majesty. Nor did this action, as was said above, deprive him of his privilege, but rather strengthened it, since it promoted to the honors of the Apos-

---

146. Anselm of Lucca (Alexander II), as papal legate, had visited the German court several times after 1056. He had not been a chaplain there; see T. Schmidt, "Alexander II" (1977) 30–34.
147. Cf. John 14.6.
148. The preferred MS reading here is *muttum*. Both Gaetani and Migne (PL 145.85D) have *nutum*; cf. Reindel, *Briefe* 2 (1988) 570 n. 118.
149. Cf. Ryan, *Sources* 90 no. 173.

tolic See a bishop who had not belonged to the Roman Church but to the royal court.

(100) Finally, what shall I say about the election of the bishop of Parma? Shall I speak or hold my peace?[150] But to quote from Scripture, "Who could hold his tongue any longer?"[151] And certainly, if one is able to see the naked truth, it is a shameful deed to indulge in deceitful fabrication. We were clearly aware that Gerard had been excommunicated, nor were we ignorant of the fact that it was chiefly on his initiative that this bishop was inveigled into this affair. Therefore, if I may put it so, a tree that grows from the poisonous root of excommunication must by all means be eradicated before it has time to bear deadly fruit, and that on the evidence of truth itself, who says, "When a tree does not yield good fruit, it should be cut down and thrown into the fire."[152]

(101) *Attorney for the Roman Church:* Your holiness, venerable Fathers, has now heard how he who looks into our hearts[153] has been on our side in this debate. For you see that we were not here engaged out of malice, but to be of service in discovering the truth. Therefore, he has seen fit to allay this quarrel to which we were partners, and to inspire us with his own harmony. He who is our peace and has made the two one,[154] has brought two persons to agreement. Let us thank him who at first allowed the bark of Peter[155] to be put in peril from the raging winds and the rolling swells, but then turned and stretched forth his hand, assisted Peter to rise, commanded the winds, and quieted the tossing waves.[156] At once the sea that had been running high fell calm, the storm abated, the high winds died down, and the skies were clothed in a golden glow.

(102) *Conclusion:* And so, my dear friends, you the counsellors of the royal court on my right, and my fellow servants of

---

150. Cf. Vergil, *Aeneid* 3.39.
152. Matt 7.19.
154. Cf. Eph 2.14.
151. Job 4.2.
153. Cf. Prov 24.12.

155. On the use of *sagena*, see Woody, *Damiani* 242ff. and his *Sagena piscatoris* 36ff.
156. Cf. Mark 4.

the Apostolic See on my left, let us conspire to work together that the highest seat of the priesthood and the Roman Empire may be joined in harmony, so that the human race, which under both aspects of its nature is ruled by these two powers, should never again, God forbid, be torn apart, as was recently achieved by Cadalus. Thus let the summits of government in the world come together in a union of everlasting love, that the lesser orders may not be repelled by their dissension.[157] Thus, as these two, the empire and the priesthood, by divine dispensation are united in the one mediator between God and men, so may these two exalted persons be joined together in such harmony that, by a certain bond of mutual love, we may behold the emperor in the Roman pontiff and the Roman pontiff in the emperor, reserving to the pope, however, the dignity no other may possess.[158] Likewise, should the situation arise, the pope should be able to use civil law to control offenders, and the emperor with his bishops should be permitted to adjudicate matters where the welfare of souls is involved, but under the authority of the sacred canons. The former, as a father, should always enjoy paramount dignity by reason of his paternal rights; the latter, as his unique and special son, should rest securely in his loving embrace.

(103) As we know, Attalus, the king of Asia, and Nicomedes, the king of Bithynia, had such love for the Roman republic that at their death, both made the Roman people their heir.[159] The great men of Christendom, therefore, must work together in a closer bond of love, since to them especially was enjoined the duty of promoting good relations within the Christian people. Thus, from the harmony that should emerge from their filial devotion, the holy and universal Church may be gladdened, and by their joint effort right order in the Christian Church may be restored. Indeed, as we extricate the boat of our fisherman from the mouth of the whirlpool Scylla, as we bring the successor of Peter, engulfed by diminishing evidence of the

---

157. See Ryan, *Sources* 90f. no. 174, with Damian's strong appeal to Pope Gelasius I; JK 632 and JK 761.
158. See Ryan, *Sources* 91f. no. 175; cf. Gelasius I, JK 701.
159. Cf. Eutropius, *Breviarium* 4.18; 6.6 (MGH Auct.ant. 2.78.94).

faith, to the quiet of the shore, let us sing this pious cadenza to him who rescued us:

> Praise to our God let us sing, the Lord be
> acclaimed for his glory.
> Vengeance divine, Cadalus, people's ruin—
> this name well becomes you,
> God's powerful bolt from on high is your fate,
> it will surely transfix you.
> Seeking to scale Simon's heights, like Simon
> you reach for the heavens.[160]
> Hell's yawning pit lies in wait, its fires
> now burn to engulf you.[161]

160. A reference to the legend that Simon the Magician attempted to fly in a Roman amphitheater, and that St. Peter caused him to fall; cf. N. Adler, LThK 9.768–69.
161. See Lokrantz, *L'opera* 74 no. 102.

LETTER 90

Peter Damian to Desiderius,[1] the abbot of Monte Cassino. This fragmentary letter, reconstructed from the *Liber testimoniorum veteris et novi testamenti* of John of Lodi, lacks any personal references to the abbot. It was used by the editor of the *Liber* to demonstrate Damian's commentary on I and II Samuel and on the Psalms.

(ca. 1062)[2]

WHO WILL NOT be strengthened and aroused to perfect love? Who, I say, will not be incited not only to practice human compassion but also to return good for evil, when he reads the account of the sorceress who was so deserving of high praise?[3] Following God's example, she did well by Saul who not only was about to lose his royal title, but on the next day would be killed by the swords of the Philistines,[4] and, like the wary serpent in the gospel,[5] showed favor to him from whom she could never hope for a reward. He, moreover, as she stated, had done away with all the soothsayers and magicians in Israel,[6] and had thereby deprived this woman of all profit from her accustomed practice of divination. And yet she prepared a fatted calf that she had even in her consuming poverty and baked unleavened bread by kneading the little meal that she had, and set them before him.[7] When Saul, because of his sorrow and the terror of his approaching death, turned down her request and absolutely refused to eat, she, on the other hand, never stopped insisting, resolutely begging him and plying him with arguments that she should repay him for his request; and, as she had obeyed his command, so should he

---

1. On Desiderius, see Reindel, *Briefe* 2 (1988) 441 n. 1; *infra*, Letter 82 n. 2.
2. The dating of this letter follows Lucchesi, *Vita* no. 160f.
3. Cf. 1 Sam 28.5–6. 4. Cf. 1 Sam 28.7.
5. Cf. Matt 10.16 6. Cf. 1 Sam 28.9.
7. Cf. 1 Sam 28.24–25.

comply with her urgent prayers. "Your servant," she said, "obeyed your command and I risked my life by listening to what you said. Now listen to me: let me set before you a little food to give you strength for your journey."[8]

(2) Who today, after the gospel has been preached, would do what we are told this woman had done under the shadow of the Law, especially since the Old Testament says, "Love your neighbor and hate your enemy,"[9] and since the gospel thunders with a terrifying blast, "For your Father will not forgive your sins unless you each forgive your brother from your hearts"?[10] Now Saul was such an enemy of diviners and sorcerers that he killed almost all of them,[11] and scarcely a single one remained with the exception of this poor woman. And in surviving, she was so hemmed in by the fierceness of the king's persecution that, in not daring to practice divination, she completely lost the income from the art to which she had become accustomed. But in giving what she still had, she gladly offered good for evil and, as the Apostle commanded, provided food for her enemy.[12] This praiseworthy woman did this at a time when she knew that Saul would soon die; thus she could neither hope for reward nor fear his anger. Men will use tricks so that they may refuse lodging to those whom they do not wish to have as guests in their homes, sending them to an inn or to some nearby market town. "After all," they will say, "conditions are here quite primitive, but you will find the other place much more cozy." Or, they will contend that because of bad weather last year the crops failed in this area and the farmers had no yield, but that elsewhere it is reported that the farmers did much better. Again, they will argue that they will have only a short distance to travel, or at other times that it is still early and the sun is high. By this careful choice of words they intend to force late arrivals to find other lodgings. But this frank and prudent

---

8. 1 Sam 28.21–22.
9. Matt 5.43; cf. Lev 19.18, which enjoin the first command. "Hate your enemies," however, is not found in either the Old Testament or the New Testament.
10. Matt 18.35; cf. Matt 6.15.   11. Cf. 1 Sam 28.9.
12. Cf. Rom 12.20; Prov 25.21.

woman spoke like a rhetorician, I might say, and uses all the devices of oratory to entice her enemy to eat after he had declined and refused her offer.

(3) Now the name "Absalom" may be said to mean 'a father's peace.'[13] In him we see the Jewish people who hounded Christ to death. And Isaiah said of this people, "I have sons whom I reared and brought up, but they have rebelled against me."[14] They are properly called the father's peace, because we observe God peacefully residing in a special way among this people by the Law he gave them, through the sacrifices they offered, and lastly in their tabernacle or temple. As David said, "In Judah God is known, his name is great in Israel."[15] And that you might be aware that this people was the father's peace, listen to what follows: "His tent is pitched in peace."[16]

(4) On the other hand, Absalom may represent the traitor Judas, who is also appropriately called the father's peace, as Christ himself referred to him in the psalm, when he said, "Even the man of my peace in whom I trusted, who ate at my table, lifted up his heel against me."[17] And it is not at all incongruous to call Christ father, as the prophet here asserts: "He shall be called mighty God," he says, "Father of the world to come, prince of peace."[18] Christ is therefore called the prince of peace, and Judas, the peace of the Father. Also, at the very beginning of Christ's passion Judas was not denied the kiss of peace.[19] Nor should we wonder that Absalom prefigured the traitor Judas to whom he may be compared, not only in his pursuit of David, but also in the manner of his death. For Absalom was suspended on an oak tree as he wished to pass under it, while Judas, as Scripture reports, hanged himself.[20] While both, like poisonous vipers, were filled with hatred and were unworthy of both heaven and earth, they were suspended between both, and thus would utterly lose the earth and never

---

13. Cf. Jerome, *Nom.hebr.* 48.8 (CC 72.8); *pater pacis*.
14. Isa 1.2; see also Sabatier, 2.515.
15. Ps 75.2.   16. Ps 75.3.
17. Ps 40.10; for variants from the Vulgate, see Sabatier 2.84.
18. Isa 9.6.
19. Cf. Matt 26.49.   20. Cf. Matt 27.5.

aspire to reach heaven. Ahithophel, too, who had also decided to rebel against David, after other efforts, chose the same kind of death.[21] It was he who, in Absalom's rebellion against David, had advised him to have sacrilegious intercourse with his father's concubines whom he left in charge of the palace and, to disgrace his father, he had shameful incestuous relations with his stepmothers.[22]

(5) What is meant by David's ten concubines if not that part of the Jewish people that did not follow the true Christ, namely David fleeing into the wilderness of the gentiles, because they boasted of having the Ten Commandments? Indeed, the number of concubines refers to the number of the Commandments. And these concubines, who did not follow David but stayed behind keeping the palace,[23] are those who persisted in the observance of the Old Law. And so Absalom lay with David's concubines, because the devil who was in Absalom commits fornication together with the likes of him because of his excessive crimes.[24] And it is rightly said that David left them behind in charge of the palace. Indeed, by the provident decision of our redeemer it was God's doing that a remnant of the Jews were left in charge of the palace of the Law, that they might, as it were, be our custodians of the records,[25] and carry with them throughout the world the books of heavenly wisdom in the same language in which they had been written, so that those very people who are opposed to us might remove all ambiguity for us if some obstacle of doubt should arise. To this point the psalmist said, "My God, show me the good things that are in my enemies; do not kill them lest they forget your Law."[26] Clearly, the Hebrew language that spread throughout the world is of great service to the credibility of the Christian faith. For unless that evidence were at hand, what was written by Christians might almost be construed as fiction; but with that

---

21. Cf. 2 Sam 17.23. 22. Cf. 2 Sam 16.21.
23. Cf. 2 Sam 20.3. 24. Cf. 2 Sam 16.20–22.
25. P. Browe, *Die Judenmission im Mittelalter und die Päpste*, Miscellanea historiae pontificiae (1942) 116f., citing Augustine, *Enarrationes in psalmos* 56.9. 699f., where the Jews are referred to as the *librarii*, 'copyists' or 'elementary school masters' of Christians.
26. Ps 58.12; cf. Sabatier 2.117 and *Biblia sacra* 10.145.

proof in existence, all doubt is at once removed. Hence, the psalm rightly continues, "Scatter them by your might,"[27] just as if the Son were to say to the Father, Disperse the survivors of the Jewish people and scatter them throughout the whole world, that from their ancient books they might bear witness to the truth of the new faith.

(6) And when David came to the Midianite camp, Shobi son of Nahash, Machir son of Ammiel, and Barzillai the Gileadite brought him mattresses and blankets and bowls and so forth.[28] What is meant by these Midianites giving King David mattresses and blankets, if not gentiles who have converted to the faith? As they are constant in the practice of good works, they make linen cloths on which the Lord might peacefully rest.[29] These are the tapestries spoken of in the gospel, which the apostles placed on the donkey and had Jesus sit upon.[30] But what follows, that they also brought David bowls, wheat and barley meal, beans and lentils, fried chick peas, honey and curds, sheep and fat cattle[31]—these many kinds of food are the varied ways of acting of holy men. David and his men ate these foods, that is, our redeemer and his saints, like hungry men who are nourished by the upright deeds of the just.

(7) Barzillai the Gileadite, a very old man—he was eighty years old, as the sacred history tells us—came down from Rogelim and brought King David across the Jordan. And the king said to him, "Come and stay in my household in Jerusalem."[32] But he refused to go, offering the excuse of his advanced years, and he left the king and went back to his own home. Now there are some people who follow King David, that is, our savior, and cross over the River Jordan, that is, they either receive the sacrament of baptism or arrive at a second baptism, namely, a spiritual resolve. For since Christ, the author of baptism, was baptized in the Jordan,[33] we may rightly understand that river to mean baptism. But those who change their clothes and not

27. Ps 58.12.
28. Cf. 2 Sam 17.27–28.   29. Cf. Matt 27.59.
30. Cf. Matt 21.7; Mark 11.7; Luke 19.35.
31. Cf. 2 Sam 17.28–29.   32. 2 Sam 19.33.
33. Cf. Matt 21.7; Mark 11.7; Luke 19.35.

their heart, their attire and not their intention, return to their former way of living and resume their worldly mode of action. And since they do not abandon the turbulence of secular affairs, they have no desire to dwell in Jerusalem, that is, with the king in the possession of peace. They are old men, settled in their ways, and therefore find it impossible to lead a new kind of life in exchange for the old. Yet they cross over the Jordan and are eighty years old, that is, they have been baptized and believe in the future resurrection, which is symbolized by the number eighty. But even though they speak humbly and flatteringly to the king, they still desert him and return to the way of life to which they are accustomed. For what does it mean to address the king in flattering terms, but still excuse oneself, as it is said in the gospel, by using artful rather than humble words? "Please accept my apologies,"[34] it says.

(8) And then Barzillai said to the king, "Why should your servant be a burden to my lord, the king? I will attend your majesty for a short way across the Jordan; why should the king reward me so handsomely?"[35] This is how some people act when they appear to speak with all humility to a religious, urging him on to higher things: "We are indeed sinners, father, and are prepared to follow your advice, but we are unable to observe the rule of this strict order. We are weak and frail, and think that it is better for us somehow to live without fame in a less prominent estate, than to perish like heroes under the weight of so great a burden." Moreover, what Barzillai had said above is hardly any different from the interior debility of these men: "Your servant is far too old to go up with your majesty to Jerusalem."[36] And he added, "I cannot distinguish sweet from bitter. I cannot taste what I eat or drink; I cannot hear the voices of men and women singing."[37] Truly, the senses of such men are interiorly blunted because they no longer discern the spiritual refreshment of the soul or the sounds of inner jubilation. They can no longer taste that heavenly food to which

34. Luke 14.18.
35. 2 Sam 19.25–36, a variant of the Vulgate.
36. 2 Sam 19.34.
37. 2 Sam 19.35.

the prophet invites his spiritual guests: "Taste, then, and see," he said, "that the Lord is good."[38] Nor does their taste detect the honeyed drink of which he speaks: "How sweet are your words in my mouth, O Lord, sweeter on my tongue than honey or the honeycomb."[39] They have not yet sat at wisdom's banquet, of which we read in the book of Proverbs: "Wisdom has killed her beasts and spiced her wine, and she has spread her table."[40] And then it continues, "She has sent out her maidens to proclaim from the highest part of the town: 'Come, dine with me and taste the wine that I have spiced.'"[41] These also do not hear the voices of men and women singing, for they are unable to grasp the glorious song of the holy martyrs and saintly virgins offered to their God. For since they live according to the flesh, and do not raise their hearts to a life of contemplation, they are unaware of the sounds of heavenly harmony and the song of the angels that is sweet as honey.

(9) And so, not improperly, Scripture states that the old man Barzillai came from Rogelim,[42] which can be understood to mean 'feet.'[43] Pedestrians go along, indeed, and since they do not know how to depart from the path of their worldliness, they never take the high road where they would appreciate the songs of this heavenly music. They wish only to go on foot, and therefore they are unable to reach the utter joy of inner exaltation. And since earthly affairs in which they are engaged render them hardened and insensitive, they cannot experience the subtleties of spiritual joy.

(10) We might also remark that Barzillai was called a Gileadite, which may be said to mean a 'cairn of evidence.'[44] And since this 'cairn of evidence,' which is called *Gilead*, is known to have been fashioned of stones by Laban and Jacob,[45] men who

38. Ps 33.9.
39. Ps 118.103; see also Sabatier 2.242.
40. Prov 9.1–2.
41. Prov 9.3–5.
42. Cf. 2 Sam 17.27.
43. Cf. Jerome, *Nom.hebr.* 39.23 (CC 72.108), *s.v.* Ragalim.
44. Cf. Jerome, *Nom.hebr.* 7.4 (CC 72.67).
45. Cf. Gen 31.45–48.

are hard as stone are aptly prefigured by this Gileadite. For since their hearts do not grow gentle with the love of the spiritual life, they become as hard as stone in the persistent pursuit of secular affairs. This hardness is also indicated by the name Barzillai, which can be said to mean 'my iron.'[46] For what is harder than iron, and what is more obstinate than an evil heart? "Wisdom will never enter a shifty soul."[47] And aptly does an obstinate and hardened man speak of 'my iron' because, while proposing to retain his own obduracy, he never seeks counsel from another. And since he firmly and inflexibly refuses to mount to the heavenly Jerusalem with King David, using the path on which he began with Barzillai,[48] he is called back to the land of the Midianites, that is, to the very beginning of his former life.

(11) "And when King David came home to Jerusalem, he took the ten concubines whom he had left in charge of the palace, and put them under guard, and did not have intercourse with them, but kept them in confinement to the day of their death, where they lived as widows."[49] The concubines who did not go with David but stayed at home are those who continue the practices of the Old Law. Of these concubines it is rightly said, "David did not have intercourse with them, but they were kept in confinement to the day of their death, where they lived as widows."[50] The Jews are indeed now in confinement and live as widows, because they do not go near their husband, who is the Holy Church. Nor does the heavenly spouse approach them, because he refuses to dwell with them as women made prostitutes by the devil, and gives them a note of dismissal because they were defiled by adultery. And those who do not go with their husband are aptly called concubines and not wives, because since they are utterly unworthy of betrothal and marriage, they do not bear children who will receive the inheri-

46. Cf. Jerome, *Nom.hebr.* 38.6 (CC 72.106).
47. Wis 1.4; cf. Sabatier 2.392.
48. Cf. 2 Sam 19.33–35.
49. 2 Sam 20.3.
50. 2 Sam 20.3.

tance of their father's blessing. But to us, on the other hand, he says, "You have been called that you might receive a blessing for your inheritance."[51] And the apostle Paul here says the same: "Therefore, it is men of faith who share the blessing with faithful Abraham. On the other hand, those who rely on obedience to the Law are under a curse."[52]

51. 1 Pet 3.9.
52. Gal 3.9–10.

INDICES

INDEX OF PROPER NAMES

Aaron, 11, 69, 182, 183
Abigail, 22
Abihu, 11
Abimelech, 98, 101
Abiram, 34
Abishag the Shunammite, 309
Abraham, 248, 262, 378
Abramius, 339
Absalom, 309, 372–73
Acacius, bishop of Caesarea, 183
Acereta, monastery, 16
Achan, 363
Achish, 102
Adalbert, bishop, 118
Adalfredus, bishop of Bologna, 94
Adam, bishop of Fossombrone, 106
Adam, subdeacon, 35
Adler, N., 369
Adonijah, 309
Adoptionism, 215
Africa, 143
Agag, 74
Agapite I, pope, 339, 340
Agnes, empress, 40, 113, 336, 357
Ahab, 13, 73, 75, 154
Ahisamach, 242
Ahithophel, 373
Alaric, 328
Albert, bishop of Velletri or Ostia, 147, 150
Albert, nobleman, 250
Alcuin, 223
Alexander II, pope, 26, 114, 247, 250, 253, 296, 302, 309, 326, 344
Alexandria, 310
Alexius, 144
Alfanus of Salerno, 185, 195–96, 197, 243
Alfred of York, 362

Almericus, archdeacon, 167
Amalekites, 74
Ambrose, archbishop of Milan, 28, 29, 42, 45, 82, 125, 202, 230, 257, 260, 261, 266, 271, 274, 275, 277, 287, 289, 294, 308, 315, 365
Ambrose, deacon, 35
Ambrose, St., church of, 26, 28, 33
Ammiel, 374
Amos, 54, 257
Ananias, 74, 319
Anastasius, 120, 293, 338, 339, 340
Anastsius Bibliothecarius, 27, 37, 315
Anathemas, 221
Anatholius, bishop of Constantinople, 31
Anathoth, 153
Anatolius, subdeacon of Constantinople, 144
Ancient of Days, 55
Andrew, apostle, 118, 139
Angles, 32
Anna, 63
Anne, queen of France, 21
Anselm, bishop of Lucca, 26, 27, 34, 35, 366
Antioch, 97, 137, 310
Antonius, 339
Apocalypse, 98
Apollinaris, 38, 208
Apostolic See, 16, 25, 26, 28, 29, 32, 34, 39, 113, 114, 116, 124, 125, 131, 144, 145, 163, 247, 302–3, 313, 314, 319, 324–25, 333, 334, 335, 337, 341, 342, 356, 364, 366–67, 368
Appio, 120
Apulia, 136

INDEX OF PROPER NAMES

Aquileia, bishop of, 31
Arcadius, 340
Arderatus, 35
Ardericus, 35, 253
Ardoinus, 103–4
Arezzo, church of, 132
Arialdus, deacon, 37
Arians, 308
Arimundus, count, 78
Ariprandus, 35
Aristotle, 190
Arius, 206, 230
Arnulf, bishop of Metz, 134, 135
Arnulfus, 35, 36
Assyrians, 13
Athanasius, 143, 230
Attalus, king, 368
Atticus, bishop, 127, 128
Atto, deacon, 35
Atto, priest, 35
Atto, subdeacon, 35
Atto of Vercelli, 92
Attorney for the Roman Church, 326, 336
Aubert, R., 143
Audollent, A., 143
Augsburg, council, 336
Augustine, 45, 57, 82, 117, 169, 175, 228, 231, 270, 361, 365, 373
Aurea, 137
Avernus, Lake, 18

Baal of Peor, 313
Babylon, 317, 319, 345
Baggio, 26
Baix, F., 309, 336
Balboni, D., 105
Barbatus, 196
Bardy, G., 351
Barroux, M., 21
Barzillai the Gileadite, 374, 375, 376, 377
Bede, 7
Behemoth, 235
Belial, 10
Bella, 244
Benedict, St., 145
Benedict VII, pope, 144
Benedict VIII, pope, 124

Benedict IX, pope, 124–25, 145
Benedict X, antipope, 117
Benhadad, 13, 73
Benjamin, 105
Bentivegna, J., 208
Bethlehem, 102, 310
Beth-Millo, 101
Bezalel, 242
Blanche, countess, 40
Bloch, H., 233
Blum, O.J., 3, 315, 336
Boniface I, pope, 339, 340
Boniface III, pope, 339, 340
Boniface, bishop of Albano, 88, 113, 144
Boniface, marquis, 83
Boniface, St., 146
Bonitus, bishop, 119
Borino, G. B., 16, 36, 131
Botti, F., 110
Boyd, C., 153
Browe, P., 373
Brunhild, queen of the Franks, 114
Bulst-Thiele, M. L., 113
Burchard, 32, 73, 78, 81, 96, 103, 115, 152, 330, 338

Cadalus of Parma, 299, 309, 316, 317, 325, 326, 331, 336, 363, 364, 365, 368, 369
Caesar Augustus, 331
Caesar, Julius, 327, 333
Caiaphas, 34, 318
Cairo, 319
Calabria, 141
Camelot, P., 212
Cana, 41
Candidus, 114
Cantin, A., 105
Capitani, O., 124, 336
Capri, bishop of, 123
Capua, 141
Carloman, 134, 135
Carmi, 363
Cassiodorus, 127, 128, 134, 183, 257
Celestine I, pope, 339, 340
Cerinthus, 350
Cerularius, Michael, patriarch, 202
Charles, emperor, 223

INDEX OF PROPER NAMES

Chasteigner, J. de, 3
Chiazerna, 237
Chiovaro, F., 208
Christ, 10, 12, 27, 28, 30, 31, 33, 34, 40, 43, 44, 45, 46–47, 48, 52, 64, 100, 103, 108, 112, 117, 119, 129, 130, 132, 135, 137, 144, 149, 153, 165, 166, 174, 187, 190, 195, 202, 210, 212–22, 226–32, 236, 237, 242, 249, 256, 261, 266, 268, 281, 284, 289, 291, 298, 307, 323, 325, 345, 348, 350, 351, 352, 353, 354, 359, 360, 363, 372, 373, 374
Cicero, 167, 168, 357
Clement II, pope, 12, 339
Clivus Scaurus, 139, 362
Compostela, 38
Conrad II, emperor, 195
Constantine, emperor, 332, 341
Constantinople, 243, 244, 341
Constantius, emperor, 143, 183, 332
Corbuo, 168
Corinthians, 229
Cornelius, 339
Cotta, Landulf, 102
Cottineau, L., 162, 237, 362
Cowdrey, H., 233, 255
Cozbi, 4, 5
Crescentius II, 334
Crispinus, 339
Cummings, J., 122
Cyril, bishop of Jerusalem, 82, 183
Cyril, St., 221, 230
Cyrus, king, 192, 193

Damascus, 144
Damasus, pope, 114, 339
Dan, 242
Daniel, 55, 140, 318, 336
Daphne, 314
Dathan, 34
David, 6, 17, 22, 63, 74, 92, 170, 186, 191, 305, 308, 309, 310, 311, 329, 330, 372, 373, 374, 377
Davidsohn, R., 17, 86, 310
DeClercq, V. C., 206
Dekkers, E., 210

Demosthenes, 167, 168, 357
Deodatus, archbishop of Trier, 136
Desiderius, abbot, 123, 140, 185, 196, 233, 244, 245, 255, 370
Detschew, D., 90
Diaconus, Paulus, 96, 328, 331, 332, 333
Dibon-gad, 19
Dinah, 322
Diocletian, emperor, 332
Dionysius of Piacenza, 317
Dioscorus, patriarch, 212
Disceptatio synodalis, 326
Doge of Venice, 60
Donatists, 30
Dressler, F., 3, 4, 16, 25, 44, 308
DuCange, C., 145, 160, 238, 333, 355
Duchesne, L., 144
Dvornick, F., 37

Ebion, 351
Egypt, 7, 43, 50, 63, 121, 122, 134, 170, 171, 172, 173, 180, 217, 293, 335
Einhorn, J., 285
Eisenhut, W., 174
Eleazar, 6, 182
Election Decree of 1059, 309, 326
Eli, 7–9, 12, 73, 346
Elijah, 6–9, 13, 304
Elipandus of Toledo, 215
Elisha, 6, 41
Emmanuel, 218, 220, 221, 223–24
Ephesians, 176, 190
Ephesus, 12
Ephraim, 102
Equitius, St., 246
Eribertus, 35
Etherius, bishop of Ravenna, 144
Ethiopians, 141
Euphrates, 262, 345
Eutropius, 96, 327, 328, 331, 332, 368
Eutyches, archimandrite, 212
Eve, 57
Ezekiel, 72–73, 171, 315, 316, 331, 334

Falce, A., 86

Farulfus, bishop of Cisterna, 136
Felix I or II, pope, 339, 340
Felix III, pope, 339, 340
Felix of Urgel, 215
Filas, F., 10
Fischer, B., 365
Florence, 16, 86, 151, 158, 309, 310
Florence, council, 151
Florence of Worcester, 362
Fonte Avellana, 16, 117, 299, 315
Fortunatus, 340
Frederick, archbishop of Ravenna, 146
Frugoni, C., 270
Fuhrmann, H., 25, 27, 152, 311
Fulbert of Chartres, 32, 37
Fuscard, 168

Gad, 7
Gai, 19
Galatians, 228
Galen, 288
Galerius, 332
Galilee, 41
Gams, P. B., 123, 137
Gaudentius, bishop of Ossero, 119
Gaudenzi, A., 202, 230
Gaudiosus, bishop, 143, 144
Gaul, 118, 131, 299, 307
Gebizo, abbott, 15
Gehazi, 149
Gelasius I, pope, 305, 339, 340, 368
Gellhaus, V., 124
Genebald, bishop of Lodi, 118
Gerard, 297, 362, 365, 367
Gerizim, Mount, 97, 98, 99
Germany, 132, 194, 356
Gervase, martyr, 28
Gideon, 98
Gilchrist, J., 25
Gilead, Mount, 235–36
Gill, J., 227
Girbaldus, bishop of Leucha, 136
Glaber, Rodulfus, 335
Godfrey, duke of Tuscany, 70, 71, 79
Gomorrah, 262
Gondebertus, archbishop of Sens, 137
Gordian, 340

Goths, 96–7, 328, 333, 340
Gougaud, L., 44
Grandiavium, 137
Gratian, 27, 145, 340
Greeks, 227, 230
Gregorius of Vercelli, 317
Gregory I, pope, 8, 32, 48, 73, 114, 119, 120, 139–40, 144, 145, 148, 187, 189, 228, 245, 246, 308, 340, 347
Gregory V, pope, 334
Gregory VI, pope, 145
Gregory VII, pope, 157, 315
Gregory, bishop of Nazianzus, 122
Gregory of Tours, 340
Gualberti, John, 194
Guarimpotus, 108
Guido, archbishop of Milan, 26, 33, 35, 36, 37
Guido, count, 16, 17
Guilla, Countess, 83
Guiscard, Robert, 299, 308
Gyndes river, 193

Haggai, 243
Haggith, 309
Haller, J., 362
Hamilton, B., 144
Hamor the Hivite, 322
Hanamel, 153
Hannibal, 331
Hebron, 310, 330
Hefele C. J.-Leclercq, H., 122, 131, 145, 151, 336, 363
Heli, 3
Heliopolis, 269
Henry I of France, 21
Henry III, emperor, 109, 145, 151, 342, 357
Henry IV, king, 114, 336, 344, 347, 356
Herculius, 332
Herod, 217, 265
Herrmann, K. J., 124, 125, 145
Hilary, pope, 339
Hildebrand, archdeacon, 16, 24, 29, 116, 131, 157, 182
Hildulfus, archbishop of Trier, 136
Hippolytus, 137
Hofmeister, A., 245

INDEX OF PROPER NAMES 385

Holy Spirit, 6, 15, 16, 22, 32, 34, 35, 38, 40, 42, 44, 57, 68, 116, 118, 130, 131, 135, 167, 172, 175, 189, 202, 204–8, 212, 215, 219–20, 225–31, 236, 239, 345, 353, 359–60
Honestus, archbishop, 122
Honorius, 340, 342
Honorius II, antipope, 299, 309, 326
Hophni, 9
Horace, 174
Horeb, 74
Hormisdas, pope, 339, 340
Hosea, 258
Hugh, abbot of Cluny, 158
Hugh, duke and marquis of Tuscany, 79, 82–3, 85, 86
Hugh, king, 83
Hugh of Embrun, 131
Hugh of Fleury, 22
Huls, R., 88
Humbert, archbishop, 113, 122, 123, 125
Huns, 97
Hunt, E., 31, 32
Hur, 242

Imperial Counsel, 326, 336
Innocent I, pope, 30, 339
Iordanes, 328
Isaac, 248
Isaiah, 40, 45, 53, 55, 90, 98, 228, 238–39, 243, 256, 258, 263, 268, 281, 291–92, 300–301, 323, 372
Ishbosheth, 74, 92
Isidore of Seville, 18, 57, 125, 141, 160, 170, 176, 199, 260, 261, 263, 264, 265, 266, 268, 271, 273, 274, 275, 276, 277, 282, 284, 285, 286, 287, 288, 314, 365
Israel, 7, 13, 173, 186, 217, 268, 310, 313, 322, 323, 324, 345, 357, 363, 364, 370, 372
Italy, 79, 119, 341

Jacob, 92, 100, 179, 182, 217, 239, 243, 258, 260, 323, 345, 376
Jacob Leuchae, 136

Jadin, L., 196
James the Greater, 304
James the Lesser, 19, 38, 293, 348, 349, 351
Januarius, bishop, 30
Jasper, D., 24, 131, 312, 318
Jeconiah, 47
Jehozadak, priest, 243
Jehu, 41
Jeremiah, 54, 100, 153, 161, 170, 176, 280, 312, 313, 320, 330, 345, 346, 357, 358–59
Jericho, 363
Jerome, 5, 56, 83, 98, 99, 100, 120, 121, 126, 170, 173, 175, 227, 235, 236, 237, 264, 288, 295, 300, 301, 310, 352, 365, 372, 376, 377
Jerusalem, 134, 145, 183, 241, 304, 313, 314, 315, 324, 349, 374, 375, 377
Jerusalem, heavenly, 66–8, 127
Jesus (son of Jehozadak), 243
Jethro, 201
Job, 258
Joel, 230
John the Baptist, 16, 220
John I, pope, 339, 340
John II, pope, 339
John XVI, antipope, 334
John XIX, pope, 124
John, bishop of Comacchio, 105
John the Deacon, 8, 120, 139, 144, 228, 340
John, emperor, 340
John the Evangelist, 48, 52, 67, 86, 100, 180, 187, 218, 228, 229, 260, 272, 281, 304, 311
John of Lodi, 15, 24, 33, 169, 370
John, monk, 237
John, prince, 140–42
Jonadab, 358
Jonah, 186, 269, 326, 346
Jonathan, 354
Jordan, river, 224, 374, 375
Joseph, 10, 39, 86, 182
Joshua, 181
Josiah, king, 345
Jotham, 97–98

INDEX OF PROPER NAMES

Judah, 47, 242, 243, 260, 261, 310, 330, 345, 357, 372
Judaic Law, 348
Judas, 34, 63, 330, 333, 358, 359, 360, 372
Jude, apostle, 52
Judith, 323
Julian, 168
Justin, emperor, 120, 328
Justinian, see of, 144
Justus, bishop of Lyons, 121, 340

Kaufmann, D., 319
Kelly, J., vii
Korahite, 6
Krappe, A. H., 123
Krause, H., 122, 311, 364
Kurtscheid, B., 155
Kuttner, S., 336

Laban, 92, 93, 376
Lambert, bishop of Florence, 137
Landulfus, 35
Lapide, C., 6, 235, 236
Laqua, H. P., 30
Lawrence, bishop of Sabina, 118
Lawrence, St., 244
Leah, 238, 322
Lebanon, Mount, 268
Lebeau, P., 206, 208
Leclercq, J., 243
Leo I, pope, 30, 31, 32, 223, 314, 339
Leo IV, pope, 30, 31
Leo IX, pope, 4, 30, 299, 307
Leo, abbot of Nonantula, 145
Leo, archbishop of Ravenna, 146
Lesne, E., 133
Levi, 322–23
Levites, 8, 74, 102
Linus, 28
Lippold, A., 76
Liprandus, 35
Liutulfus, bishop of Cagli, 138
Lohmer, C., 168
Lokrantz, M., 67, 68, 131, 316, 369
Lombards, 308
Loricatus, Dominic, 40, 64–65, 159
Lots wife, 58, 63

Lucchesi, G., 3, 14, 16, 17, 21, 24, 37, 40, 70, 71, 88, 94, 102, 110, 113, 116, 117, 132, 137, 138, 147, 151, 157, 158, 159, 167, 169, 182, 185, 191, 233, 241, 243, 247, 255, 299, 309, 310, 326, 336, 370
Lucidus, bishop of Ficoclae, 118
Lucifer, 126
Luke, 15, 304, 349–50, 361

Maassen, F., 28
Macarius, bishop of Jerusalem, 183
Maccarrone, M., 12, 24
McGuire, M., 308
Machir, 374
McKenna, S., 215
Magi, 216
Mainardus of Gubbio, 151
Malachi, 53
Manassah, 7
Manicheans, 209
Mantua, 309, 310
Marcellinus, count, 293
Marcian, 340
Marinianus, bishop of Ravenna, 144
Marinus, abbot, 86
Marinus, priest, 111
Mark, 15, 42, 310
Martin, 143
Martirius, bishop of Antioch, 119
Mary, 46, 106, 126, 161, 202, 208, 211, 212, 216, 218, 220, 222, 223, 225, 249
Maurice, emperor, 114, 340
Maximus, bishop of Salona, 114
Maximus, heretic, 231, 340
Melville, G., 25
Memphis, 314
Maphibosheth, 17
Mercurius, pope, 339, 340
Metz, church of, 133, 134, 135
Meyer, H., 278
Micah, 328
Miccoli, G., 302
Michaiah, 75
Michal, 22, 92
Michel, A., 25, 113, 136, 311, 336, 338
Midianites, 374

INDEX OF PROPER NAMES 387

Milan, 24, 25, 26, 28, 33, 39, 40, 103, 159, 162
Milesius, martyr, 134
Mittarelli J. B.-A. Costadoni, 167, 241, 250, 296
Monophysitism, 212
Mosel, 135
Moses, 5, 8, 43, 54, 69, 74, 99, 103, 170, 181, 182, 201, 205, 240, 242, 250, 348, 350, 354
Murphy, F., 204, 212

Nabal, 22
Naboth, 154
Nadab, 11
Nahash, 374
Nahum, 54, 326
Naples, 141
Nazarites, 349
Nazarius, martyr, 28, 254
Necho, pharaoh, 345
Nectarius, 122
Nero, emperor, 328
Nestorians, 230
Nestorius, bishop, 212
Neukirch, F., 3, 70, 102, 185, 202, 250
Nevers, 136
Nicea, council, 227
Nicholas I, pope, 305
Nicholas II, pope, 3, 21, 24, 25, 27, 34, 116, 162, 182, 342, 344, 355, 357, 362, 363, 366
Nicodemus, 86
Nicolaitans, 12, 13, 25, 28, 35, 36, 37
Nicolas, 12
Nicomedes, 368
Nineveh, 326, 346
Noah, 293, 344
Noah's Ark, 317
Nonnus, bishop, 137, 138
Normans, 308
Novations, 30

Obadiah, 329
Obertus, marquis, 83
Odalaericus, 35
Offa, 245
Oholiab, 242

Oldericus, bishop of Fermo, 299
Onam, 236-37
Origen, 19
Orosius, 193, 333
Ostia, 158
Otto I, emperor, 83, 122
Otto II, emperor, 141
Otto III, emperor, 70, 78, 86, 146, 334
Ovid, 333

Palazzini, P., 24, 103, 126, 336
Pambo, 109
Pandulf, prince, 140-41
Papias, 90, 288
Paraclete, 229, 230
Parma, 109, 110, 336, 364, 367
Parthenope, 144
Patarins, 24
Patripassian, 208
Paul, apostle, 15, 28, 47, 62, 74, 75, 99, 148, 162, 234, 291, 305, 310, 322, 342, 347-50, 351, 353-54, 361, 364, 378
Paul the Deacon, 134
Paulinus, bishop, 119
Pavia, 309, 310, 362
Pelagia, 137
Penco, G., 44
Penna, bishop of, 138
Pepin, king, 134, 135
Persia, 134
Peter, apostle, 12, 15, 25, 28, 38, 39, 48, 52, 54, 74, 75, 113, 117, 147, 149, 155, 157, 228, 230, 279, 291, 303, 308, 310, 311, 315, 318, 319, 322, 325, 334, 339, 341, 347-48, 351, 356, 362, 367, 369
Peter, archbishop, 122
Peter, bishop of Ostia, 34
Peter Damian, 3, 14, 16, 21, 24, 40, 50, 62, 67, 70, 71, 78, 79, 81, 86, 88, 92, 94, 102, 113, 116, 147, 151, 157, 159, 167, 168, 169, 182, 185, 202, 230, 233, 241, 247, 250, 255, 299, 303, 309, 316, 325, 326, 370
Peter the Deacon, 141
Peter of Ravenna, 105

INDEX OF PROPER NAMES

Peter, senator, 241
Petronius, 199
Pierucci, C., 154
Pharaoh, 43, 49, 175
Pharisees, 272
Philagathos, John, abbot, 334
Philistines, 7, 49, 329, 370
Phinehas, 3, 4–9, 12, 13
Physiologus, 255
Pilate, 329
Plato, 190
Pliny, 263, 266, 268, 285, 287, 288, 293, 295, 333
Pompey, 333
Prete, S., 299
Priscus, 340
Projectus, 340
Protase, martyr, 28
Prudentius, 123
Pseudo-Ambrosius, 28
Pseudo-Augustine, 210, 211
Pseudo-Isidore, 152
Pseudo-Jerome, 6, 227
Ptolemy, king of Egypt, 327

Quintianus, 339
Quodvultdeus, bishop, 143–44

Rachel, 238
Raguel, 186
Raimundus, count, 78
Ravenna, 114
Rechab, 358
Rechabites, 358
Red Sea, 46, 63
Redle, M., 172
Regensburg, 215
Reindel, K., vii, 3, 15, 16, 17, 18, 21, 25, 28, 33, 35, 37, 38, 59, 66, 69, 70, 78, 81, 83, 86, 90, 102, 108, 114, 118, 119, 121, 123, 131, 145, 237, 260, 278, 315, 317, 327, 334, 335, 342, 356, 362, 366, 370
Remigius, 118
Reuben, 7
Riche, P., 109
Richer, 137
Ries, J., 209
Rimini, see of, 144

Robinson, I., 308
Rodulfus of Gubbio, 14
Rodulfus, count, 78
Rogelim, 374, 376
Romanus, 192
Rome, 3, 4, 38, 109, 111, 114, 124, 130–31, 137, 139, 144, 146, 158, 243–44, 255, 310, 311, 317, 327, 333, 342, 362, 364
Roschini, G., 211
Rudolph, priest, 69
Rufinus, 19
Ryan, J., 8, 13, 25, 27, 28, 30, 31, 32, 37, 73, 81, 96, 151, 152, 153, 155, 221, 227, 230, 305, 307, 311, 312, 315, 318, 319, 330, 336, 337, 338, 340, 342, 344, 347, 352, 356, 363, 365, 366, 368

Sabatier P., 19, 44, 88, 173, 178, 180, 187, 203, 221, 225, 226, 228, 230, 248, 268, 279, 280, 291, 301, 304, 354, 359, 360, 372, 373, 376, 377
Sabellian, 208
Sabellius, 206
Sagunto, 331
Salu, 5
Samaria, 257
Samaritan, 171, 304
Samson, 130, 131
Samuel, 73, 310, 329, 364
San Miniato al Monte, 195
Sapphira, 74
Saracens, 137, 141
Sarah, 186
Satan, 75, 98, 127, 155, 260, 281, 318, 327
Saturn, 333
Saul, 17, 22, 74, 75, 92, 93, 191, 305, 329, 364, 370–71
Scheffer-Boichorst, P., 311
Schmale, F. J., 145
Schmidt, T., 16, 26, 247, 253, 296, 302, 336, 344, 355, 366
Schoeps, H., 351
Schwartz, G., 14, 26, 94, 105, 106, 122, 138, 147, 192, 245, 299, 334

INDEX OF PROPER NAMES

Scots, 139
Scylla, 57, 314, 368
Sergius, bishop, 143, 144
Severus, S., 143
Shallum, 153
Shealtiel, 243
Sheba, queen of, 22
Shechem, 97, 101, 322–23
Shimei, 305
Shobi, 374
Siagrius, bishop of Autun, 114
Siegfried, archbishop of Mainz, 113, 114–15
Siegman, E., 12
Sigibaldus, 340
Silvanus, bishop of Philoppopolis, 127–30
Simeon, 322–23
Simon, 149, 319, 351
Simon the Magician, 33, 34, 369
Simplicianus, St., 162
Simplicius, 339, 340
Sinai, Mount, 169, 170, 171, 180
Sirens, 57
Siricius, pope, 28
Sixtus, 339
Smaragdus, 227, 230, 231
Sodom, 262
Solomon, 22, 48, 70, 78, 80, 188, 189, 192, 238, 241, 242, 250, 298, 301, 327, 359
Somigli, C., 102
Sophia, 58–60
Spain, 38
Spanish heresy, 215
Steindorff, E., 109, 151
Stephen IX, pope, 116, 133, 339, 356, 357
Stephen, Sir, 121
Susanna, 318
Sylvester, St., 126, 339, 341
Symmachus, pope, 339, 340
Syrians, 134

Tamassia, N., 55
Tarshish, 56
Tebaldus, abbot, 15
Tehtgrimus, 16, 17
Tellenbach, G., 124
Tethbaldus, widow of, 66

Teuzo, 192
Teuzolinus, cleric, 110
Theodomar of Monte Cassino, 126
Theodosius, 340
Theodosius, bishop of Senigallia, 14
Theodosius, emperor, 75–77, 122
Theologian, 122
Thessalonians, 229
Thiele, W., 19
Thrace, 127, 130
Tiberius, emperor, 199
Tibertinus, 340
Timothy, 148, 349
Titus, 150, 230
Tobiah the Ammonite, 241
Tobias, 67, 234, 235, 238
Toledo, council, 32
Tostig, earl, 362
Totila, king, 333
Toul, 136
Tours, 38
Troilus, 127

Ubaldus, count, 75
Ugo, bishop of Assisi, 151
Ugo, bishop of Gubbio, 151
Uhlirz, K., 86, 141
Ullmann, W., 24
Ulpius, 138
Urbino, 126, 191
Uzziah, king, 305, 329

V< >, bishop, 151, 185
Valens, emperor, 96–97, 340
Valentinian the Elder, 340
Valentinian the Younger, 340
Valentinian III, 340
Valerius, 340
Valerius, bishop of Hippo, 117, 365
Vandals, 143, 144
Vertumnus, 174
Vesuvius, Mount, 141–42, 327
Vetus-Latina-Institut, Beuron, 19
Victor, bishop, 151
Victor II, pope, 12, 131
Victor III, pope, 233
Victor of Vita, 144
Vincent, St. 104
Vitalis, priest, 69
Vosges, 136

INDEX OF PROPER NAMES

Waimar V, prince, 142
Wemple, S., 92
William, count, 296
Williams, M., 221
Wilmart, A., 102, 105, 110
Woody, K. M., 3, 17, 40, 70, 185, 195, 367

Zafarana, Z., 88
Zechariah, 256, 311
Zedekiah, 130, 345
Zeno, 119
Zerubbabel, 47, 243
Ziba, 17
Zibeon, 236–37
Ziegler, A. K., 305
Zimmermann, G., 160
Zimri, 4, 5
Zion, 98, 281, 324
Zosimus, 339
Zur, 5

INDEX OF SACRED SCRIPTURE

(Books of the Old Testament)

Genesis
1.26: 206
3.1–5: 57
3.5: 302, 319
3.18: 101
4.10: 152
6.3: 344
6.14: 317
7: 257
9.2: 293
18.20–21: 262
19.26: 58, 63
25.5–6: 248
27.27: 258
27.27–29: 179
28: 92
29: 238
30: 92
31.14–15: 92
31.40–41: 92
31.45–48: 376
34.1–3: 322
34.7: 322
35.18: 105
37.23: 182
49.5–7: 323
49.6: 323
49.9: 260
49.10: 345
49.11: 100

Exodus
1.14: 102
1.22: 173
3: 43, 46
3.14: 205
7.17–20: 173
8.16: 174
8.19: 175

8.21: 176
9.6: 176
9.9: 177
9.24: 177
10.13: 178
10.21: 178
11.5: 179
13.17: 50
16.1: 169
16.3: 63
18.18: 201
19–20: 172
19.16: 172
19.18: 172
20.7: 174
20.8: 175
20.12: 176, 250, 254
20.13: 177
20.14: 177, 179
20.15: 178
20.16: 178
20.17: 178, 180
22.18: 81
25: 242
27.8: 242
31.2–6: 242
32.26–27: 8
32.27: 74
32.28–29: 8
32.29: 74
32.31–32: 354
33: 240
33.13: 170
33.22–23: 170

Leviticus
10.1–2: 11
11.9: 257
19.18: 371

20.9: 251

Numbers
3.4: 11
6.5: 349
20.24: 182
20.26: 182
25.4: 5
25.5: 5
25.6–8: 4
25.11: 6
25.12–13: 6
25.14: 5
25.15: 5
30.3: 103
31.15–17: 74

Deuteronomy
1.17: 4
4.24: 16
5.16: 254
5.17: 177
5.18: 177, 179
5.21: 178
5.30–31: 181
6.4: 173
11.29: 99
14.19: 257
21.15–17: 180
25.9: 273
32.42: 54

Joshua
7.13: 363
7.21–26: 363
19.24–25: 181
22.22: 7
22.30–31: 13

Judges
  8.29–31: 98
  9.5: 98
  9.7: 98
  9.7–15: 98
  9.15: 97
  9.20: 101
  16.19: 130
  16.22: 131
  17.1–5: 328
  17.6: 75
  19.1–7: 102
  20.16: 105

1 Samuel
  1.18: 63
  2.22: 7
  2.23–24: 7
  2.27, 29: 8
  2.30: 346
  2.30–31: 9
  2.13–14: 9, 73
  4.17–18: 7
  5.1–12: 329
  13.21: 75
  14.24: 354
  14.45: 354
  15.11: 364
  15.23: 74
  15.26: 364
  16: 310
  16.13: 329
  18.6–10: 191
  18.10: 192
  18.10–11: 191
  18.25: 93
  25: 22
  26.7–12: 305
  28.5–6: 370
  28.7: 370
  28.9: 370, 371
  28.21–22: 371
  28.24–25: 370
  29.6–8: 102

2 Samuel
  1.1–15: 74
  2: 310
  2.1: 330
  3.14: 92
  4.8–12: 74
  5: 310
  6.6–7: 329
  6.20: 22
  6.23: 22
  11.4–5: 308
  13.28–29: 309
  16.20–22: 373
  16.21: 373
  17.23: 373
  17.27: 376
  17.27–28: 374
  17.28–29: 374
  19.18–23: 305
  19.25–36: 375
  19.29: 17
  19.33: 374, 377
  19.34: 375
  19.35: 375
  20.3: 373, 377

1 Kings
  1–2: 309
  10.1–7: 22
  18.40: 13
  20.33: 74
  20.35–36: 13, 73
  20.42: 13, 74
  21.2: 154
  21.3: 154
  22.17: 75

2 Kings
  2.11–12: 6
  4.13: 163
  5.27: 149
  9.11: 41
  22.18–20: 345
  23.29: 345
  25.6–7: 130

1 Chronicles
  9.19–20: 6

2 Chronicles
  1.12: 242
  26.19: 305

2 Ezra
  4.3: 241

Tobit
  2.10–11: 234
  2.11: 238
  3.13: 186
  11.13–15: 235
  13.21–22: 67

Judith
  9.2–3: 323

1 Maccabees
  3.26: 333

Job
  4.2: 367
  5.2: 188
  7.1: 49
  10.22: 61
  16.14: 273
  21.13: 63, 109
  37.2: 229
  40.10: 235
  40.26: 258

Psalms
  1.1: 12, 94, 314, 325
  1.3: 167
  2.7: 217
  6.8: 187
  8.8–9: 258
  10.3: 63, 91
  13.3: 293
  17.11: 269
  17.45: 276
  18.5: 281
  18.9: 187
  21.7: 269
  22.5: 41
  26.12: 273
  31: 65
  31.1: 261
  31.9: 176
  32.6: 229
  33.9: 376
  36.4: 46
  40.10: 372
  44.3: 44, 281
  44.10: 4
  45.11: 175
  51.10: 167

54.7: 42
54.8–9: 42
57.9: 61
58.12: 373, 374
62.10–11: 265
62.12: 18
63.4: 293
64.14: 323
67.19: 268
72.9: 293
72.18: 95, 313
75.2: 372
75.3: 372
84.3: 261
91.4: 181
91.13: 167
101.8: 48
103.15: 41
103.18: 45
103.34: 45
105.3: 78
108.6: 63, 330
108.29: 63, 330
109.3: 217, 221
117.12: 18
117.18: 186
117.22: 232
118.21: 63
118.103: 48, 376
123.7: 86
131.15: 99
134.6: 69
140.5: 91, 234
143.8: 293
143.9: 181

Proverbs
1.10: 91
8.22: 221
8.25: 221
9.1: 222
9.1–2: 376
9.3–5: 376
11.21: 192
11.23: 189
13.8: 154
13.24: 80
14.25: 18
15.1: 188
16.18: 197

16.23–24: 18
18.21: 292
20.21: 179, 248
21.9: 189
22.24–25: 189
23.14: 80
24.12: 367
25.21: 371
25.27: 70
26.11: 261
29.1: 238
29.22: 189
30.30: 260

Ecclesiastes
5.12: 327
7.10: 188
7.17: 80
7.29: 48
9.102: 301
11.10: 198
12.1: 298
12.6–7: 298
28.1: 197
28.2: 198
28.3–4: 198
28.5: 198
28.6–8: 198

Song of Songs (Cant)
1.5: 264
1.12: 46
1.15: 281
2.1: 48
2.9: 294
2.12: 67
2.13–14: 44
2.14: 44, 45
2.15: 265
4.1: 235
4.7: 48
4.11: 18, 46
5.2: 261
5.10: 268
5.10–11, 16: 48
8.6: 47

Wisdom
1.1: 78
1.4: 377

1.6: 226, 360
2.6–9: 171
2.12: 323
6.7–9: 61
12.15: 359
12.18: 188, 253

Sirach
2.16: 234, 270
3.6: 251
3.7: 250
3.8–9: 250
3.9–10: 251
3.11: 251
3.13: 252
3.14–15: 252
3.15–16: 252
3.18: 252
4.10–11: 81
4.36: 165
6.10: 270
7.29–30: 252
8.8: 86
10.1–2: 80
10.3: 80
27.12: 241
28.28: 18
30.1: 80
30.8–10: 80
33.25: 17
33.26: 17
33.27: 17
33.28: 17
37.12: 88
37.12–13: 88

Isaiah
1.2: 273, 372
1.5–6: 256
1.17: 105
1.18: 201
2.11–19: 56
2.13: 56
2.14: 56
2.15: 56
3.18–23: 41
5.1–2: 45
5.6: 257
5.7: 99
7.14: 218

Isaiah (continued)
9.6: 372
9.18: 172
11.4: 228
11.6: 258
13.9–11: 53
14.12: 126
14.14: 364
28.2: 54
28.19: 106
29.6: 54
30.9–11: 239
30.10–11: 90
30.25: 56
30.27–28: 54
30.30: 54
33.15: 89, 165
37.22–24: 324
37.28–29: 324
40.9: 99
41.22–23: 301
43.26: 290
44.3–4: 257
45.23: 207
46.8: 314
49.3: 217
49.6: 217
49.18: 100
52.7: 99
53.4–5: 268
53.9: 268
54.16: 292
54.17: 292
56.3–5: 264
57.16: 291
58.11: 239
58.14: 239
59.21: 228
61.1: 225
61.4: 243
66.2: 175, 189

Jeremiah
2.16: 314
5.3: 185, 273
5.7: 330
5.7–8: 176
5.9: 330
6.7: 129
6.29: 185
8.6: 294
10.21: 322
12.8: 280
12.9: 321
12.10–11: 321
12.12: 54
13.22: 321
13.23: 321
13.25–27: 321
15.10: 312
16.16: 272
17.27: 44
20.14: 312
20.15–17: 312
20.17: 331
22.24: 47
22.29–30: 312
23.1–2: 315
23.9: 313
23.10: 313
23.11: 313
23.12–14: 313
23.15: 314
23.19–20: 318
24.3: 100
26.13: 346
30.18: 243
31.31: 357
32.6–7: 153
32.8–9: 153
32.10–11: 153
34.4–5: 345
35.2: 358
35.5–6: 358
35.19: 359
38.6–13: 161
48.10: 8
50.31–32: 324
51.25–26: 324

Lamentations
3.15: 62

Ezekiel
1.7: 63, 295
7.7–9: 331
7.19–20: 328
7.26: 316
11.9: 129
15.2–3: 64
16.33–34: 315
21.4–5: 54
21.9: 316
21.9–10: 73
21.10: 316
21.10–11: 316
21.11: 316
21.25–26: 317
21.28: 317
21.30–31: 317
22.18: 186
23.20: 125
23.24–25: 334
23.25–30: 335
32.27: 62
34.16: 171

Daniel
2: 238
7.9–10: 55, 336
10.11: 318
13.5: 318
13.41–62: 318

Hosea
1.6: 273
4.1–2: 255
4.3: 258
7.3–4: 256
7.7: 256
13.10: 256
13.11: 256
13.14: 267

Joel
2.28: 230

Amos
3.12: 257
4.7: 257
9.10: 54

Obadiah
3: 329
4: 329

Jonah
2.8: 186
2.10: 186
3–4: 326

INDEX

3.4: 346
4.6–8: 269

Nahum
1.2: 327
3.2–3: 55

Habakkuk
2.4: 203

Zephaniah
1.14–16: 53
2.12: 141

Haggai
1.14: 243
2.7–8: 53
2.8: 318
2.14: 47

Zechariah
2.6,7: 256
3.9: 311
4.2: 311
9.9: 281

Malachi
3.1–2: 53
4.1: 53

Books of the New Testament

Matthew
2.11: 216
2.13–17: 217
3.10: 99
3.16: 215, 219, 225
3.17: 225
4.2: 217
5.8: 235
5.17: 269
5.18: 301
5.19: 304
5.22: 198, 301, 360
5.23–24: 193
5.28: 179, 301
5.39: 360
5.39–41: 303
5.43: 371
6.5: 95
6.9: 248
6.15: 371
6.33: 179
7.2: 76
7.6: 11
7.15: 30
7.19: 367
8.20: 265
9.18–25: 133
10.16: 370
10.20: 229
10.23: 303
11.30: 55
12.36: 292
13.32: 259
13.52: 269
14.24–26: 217
14.30–31: 271

15.4: 254
15.17: 276
16.13: 85
16.15: 85
16.18: 27
16.18–19: 337
16.19: 155
16.23: 75, 155
17.2: 217
17.5: 48
17.24–26: 351
18.21–22: 304
18.35: 371
19.12: 264
19.28: 111
21.5: 281
21.7: 374
21.33: 99
22.13: 61
22.21: 219
23.15: 272
25.35: 152
25.41: 117, 354
26.4: 323
26.7: 237
26.15: 330
26.49: 372
26.50: 358
27.5: 372
27.59: 374

Mark
1.10: 215, 219
3.20–21: 42
4: 367
4.38: 217

11.7: 374
13.19: 57
14.3: 237
14.34: 217
14.66–72: 308
16.15: 259

Luke
2.6–7: 220
2.52: 217
3.21: 215
3.22: 219
6.30: 303
7.41: 170
9.52: 304
9.54: 304
9.55–56: 304
9.58: 265
10.34: 171
11.20: 172, 227
11.52: 306
12.31: 179
13.6: 99
13.32: 265
14.18: 375
14.30: 241
15.15–20: 131
16.6: 170
18.1–8: 79
18.35–43: 130
19.23: 121
19.29: 28
19.35: 374
20.25: 219
22.32: 271
22.45: 217

INDEX

Luke (continued)
  24.25: 360

John
  1.1: 212
  1.3: 212
  1.14: 212, 221
  1.29: 224
  1.32: 215, 219
  1.32–34: 220
  2.2: 41
  2.19: 226
  3.13: 216
  4.32: 281
  6.33–35: 41
  8.37: 273
  8.48–52: 42
  9.39: 172
  10.1: 89
  10.1–2: 320
  10.10: 315
  10.17–18: 226
  10.18: 217, 226, 268
  10.30: 223
  12.3: 237
  12.32: 281
  12.46: 187
  13.1: 272
  13.27: 358
  14.6: 221, 366
  14.10: 227
  14.28: 223
  15.5: 100
  15.12: 187
  15.19: 256
  15.26: 229
  18.9: 272
  18.23: 360
  19.23: 329
  19.40: 87
  20.22: 228
  20.22–23: 230
  43–44: 217

Acts
  1.1: 361
  2.1–4: 172
  2.4: 229
  2.13: 41
  2.33: 230
  4.34–35: 152
  5.1–10: 319
  5.1–11: 74
  8.20: 149, 319, 328
  9.5: 75
  10.13: 291
  15.23–29: 33
  15.41: 349
  16.1: 349
  18.18: 349
  20.35: 165
  21.17–26: 350
  23.3: 361
  23.4–5: 361
  28.22: 3

Romans
  1.17: 24
  1.21: 173
  2.21–22: 306
  2.23: 306
  5.10: 194
  6.13: 62, 200
  8.2: 190
  8.9: 228
  8.11: 226
  8.32: 226, 359
  8.34: 190
  9.1–4: 354
  10.4: 352
  10.15: 99
  12.19: 304
  12.20: 371
  13.3–4: 72
  13.4: 72, 305
  15.4: 159, 160, 306, 353

1 Corinthians
  1.24: 217
  3.11: 232
  4.19–21: 74
  6.15: 10
  6.16: 10
  6.17: 41
  8.1: 15
  9.9: 289
  9.20: 348
  9.27: 305
  10.4: 44, 289
  10.12: 58
  11.3: 48
  15.54: 67
  15.55: 267
  16.13: 234

2 Corinthians
  1.18–19: 204
  1.21: 229
  2.14–16: 281
  4.2: 260
  4.7: 22
  6.14–15: 10
  11.14: 266
  11.20: 266
  13.4: 209

Galatians
  2.11: 348
  2.12: 348
  2.14: 348
  2.20: 226, 261, 359
  3.9–10: 378
  3.13: 226, 354, 360
  4.4: 212, 219, 225, 306
  4.6: 228
  5.2: 350, 353
  5.6: 187
  5.15: 178
  5.19–21: 265
  6.14: 47
  6.17: 47

Ephesians
  2.4: 306
  2.14: 367
  2.19: 99
  4.8: 268
  4.26: 189, 191
  4.28: 178
  4.31: 190
  5.5: 12, 152
  5.27: 96
  6.1–3: 176
  6.17: 305

Philippians
  2.6–7: 225
  2.9: 226

3.7–8: 350
4.11–13: 148
4.18: 148

Colossians
3.2: 284
3.8: 190

1 Thessalonians
4.8: 229
5.17: 175

2 Thessalonians
2.4: 365
2.8: 228

1 Timothy
2.5: 209
3.7: 148
4.16: 175
5.22: 96
6.16: 239

2 Timothy
2.16–17: 291
3.8: 279

Titus
2.7–8: 150
3.5–6: 230

Hebrews
1.1–2: 215
4.12–13: 283

4.16: 239
9.7: 319
10.27: 12
10.31: 197
10.34: 161
10.38: 24, 203
11.6: 203
11.36–37: 162
12.1: 162
12.4: 161
12.29: 16
13.7: 162

James
1.2: 161
1.20: 188
3.5–8: 293
3.7–8: 293

1 Peter
1.10–11: 229
1.12: 48
2.9: 248
2.12: 148
2.13–14: 82
2.22: 268
2.22–24: 161
3.9: 99, 378
3.16: 148
3.22: 268
4.8: 355
5.8: 13, 279
5.13: 310

2 Peter
2.22: 261, 271
3.7: 54
3.10: 52
3.11–12: 52

1 John
1.1: 218
2.11: 187
3.2: 67
4.7–8: 233
4.8: 207
4.13: 229
4.18: 355

Jude
14.15: 52

Revelation
1.5: 48, 100, 180
1.7: 53, 170
1.13: 311
1.16: 228
2.5: 311
2.6: 12
2.9: 98
2.24: 260
3.16: 279
4.10: 143
5.8: 143
14.9: 272
18.7: 61
20.2–3: 281
21.8: 142
21.21: 67
21.23: 67

www.ingramcontent.com/pod-product-compliance
Lightning Source LLC
Chambersburg PA
CBHW032023290426
44110CB00012B/644